CONTENTS

ISBN 0 85147 785 2

First Edition 1972
Second Edition, fully revised 1972
Third Edition, fully revised 1973
Fourth Edition, fully revised 1973
Fifth Edition, fully revised 1974
Reprinted 1974
Sixth Edition, fully revised 1975
Seventh Edition, fully revised 1976
Reprinted 1977
Eighth Edition, fully revised 1978

753

Printed in Brighton England for Autobooks Ltd by G. Beard and Son Ltd
Bound in Hove England for Autobooks Ltd by Jilks Ltd G

Dennis Faulkner, Company Secretary, Autobooks Ltd, with his Datsun 120Y at 10,500 miles

Datsun 1000, 1200, 120Y 1968-78 Autobook

By Kenneth Ball

Associate Member, Guild of Motoring Writers
and the Autobooks Team of Technical Writers

Datsun 1000 Series B10 1968-69
Datsun 1200 Series B110 1970-73
Datsun 120Y Series B210 1973-78
Datsun 1200 Pick-up 1973-75

Autobooks

Autobooks Ltd. Golden Lane Brighton BN1 2QJ England

The AUTOBOOK series of Workshop Manuals is the largest in the world and covers the majority of British and Continental motor cars, as well as the majority of Japanese and Australian models.

ACKNOWLEDGEMENT

My thanks are due to Datsun for their unstinted co-operation and also for supplying data and illustrations.

Considerable assistance has also been given by owners, who have discussed their cars in detail, and I would like to express my gratitude for this invaluable advice and help.

Kenneth Ball
Associate Member, Guild of Motoring Writers
Ditchling Sussex England.

INTRODUCTION

This do-it-yourself Workshop Manual has been specially written for the owner who wishes to maintain his vehicle in first class condition and to carry out the bulk of his own servicing and repairs. Considerable savings on garage charges can be made, and one can drive in safety and confidence knowing the work has been done properly.

Comprehensive step-by-step instructions and illustrations are given on most dismantling, overhauling and assembling operations. Certain assemblies require the use of expensive special tools, the purchase of which would be unjustified. In these cases information is included but the reader is recommended to hand the unit to the agent for attention.

Throughout the Manual hints and tips are included which will be found invaluable, and there is an easy to follow fault diagnosis at the end of each chapter.

Whilst every care has been taken to ensure correctness of information it is obviously not possible to guarantee complete freedom from errors or omissions or to accept liability arising from such errors or omissions.

Instructions may refer to the righthand or lefthand sides of the vehicle or the components. These are the same as the righthand or lefthand of an observer standing behind the vehicle and looking forward.

CHAPTER 1

THE ENGINE

1 :1 Description

There are four engine sizes used in the range of cars covered in this manual. Apart from the fact that the smallest engines have a three main bearing crankshaft, against five for the larger engines, the engines may be regarded as completely similar for servicing purposes. Where differences occur, they will be mentioned if necessary, but all important details of specification will be found in **Technical Data** in the **Appendix**.

The four engine sizes are as follows:

Capacity	*Bore*	*Stroke*
988 cc (60.3 cu. inch)	73 (2.87)	59 (2.32)
1171 cc (71.5 cu. inch)	73 (2.87)	70 (2.76)
1288 cc (78.59 cu. inch)	73 (2.87)	77 (3.03)
1397 cc (85.2 cu. inch)	76 (2.99)	77 (3.03)

The cylinder block is of special cast iron and is integral with the crankcase. The cylinder head is light alloy with shrunk in valve seat inserts. Two sectional views of the engine are given in **FIG 1 :1**.

The counterbalanced crankshaft is a treated alloy steel forging and has plain shell bearings, axial thrust being taken at the centre main bearing. The forged steel connecting rods have plain shell big-end bearings and bushed small-end bearings. A single belt drives both the generator and the water pump from a pulley mounted at the front of the crankshaft.

The concave head pistons are of cast aluminium and incorporate slipper skirt design and invar-strut construction. Gudgeon pins are of special hollow steel type, fully floating in the piston bores and press fitted into the connecting rods.

The eccentric vane type oil pump, which is driven from a gear on the crankshaft, is located at the lower front of the crankcase, oil being drawn through a pipe and strainer assembly in the engine sump. Pressure oil is filtered before being passed to the lubrication points in the engine. The external filter is of the fullflow type and incorporates a relief valve which regulates oil pressure.

The inlet and exhaust manifolds are mounted together on the left side of the cylinder head, the exhaust manifold incorporating flanged connections for exhaust pipe attachment.

1 :2 Removing the engine

The normal operations of decarbonizing and servicing the cylinder head can be carried out without removing the engine, as described in **Sections 1 :3** and **1 :4**. A major overhaul, however, can only be carried out with the engine removed from the car. If the operator is not a skilled automobile engineer it is suggested that he will find much useful information in **Hints on Maintenance and Overhaul** at the end of this manual, and that he read it before starting the work.

The engine and gearbox should be removed as a unit by lifting from the car, using a suitable gantry and lifting

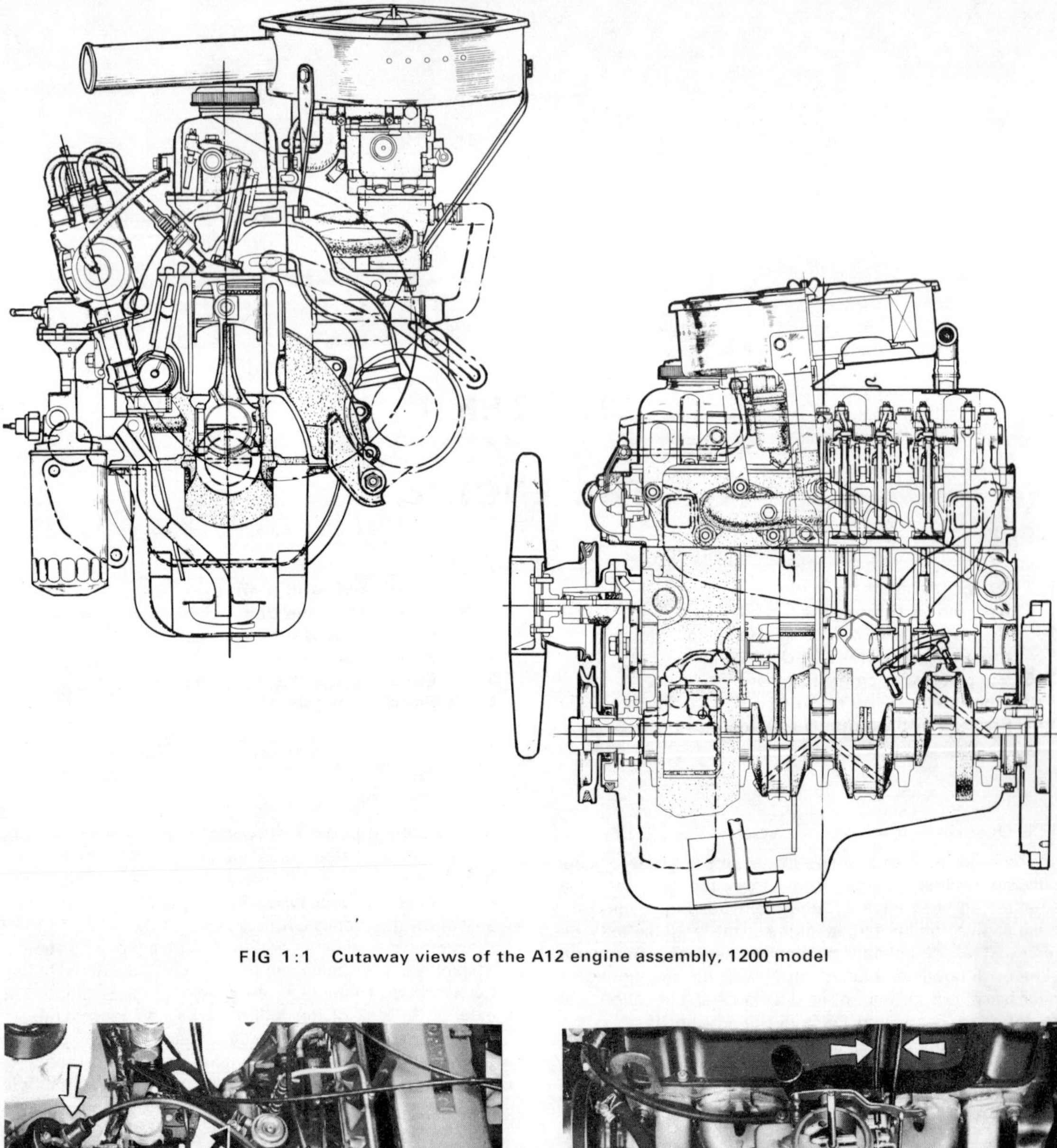

FIG 1:1 Cutaway views of the A12 engine assembly, 1200 model

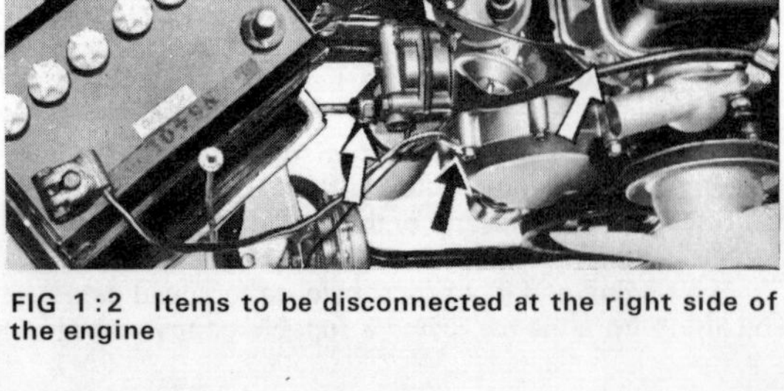

FIG 1:2 Items to be disconnected at the right side of the engine

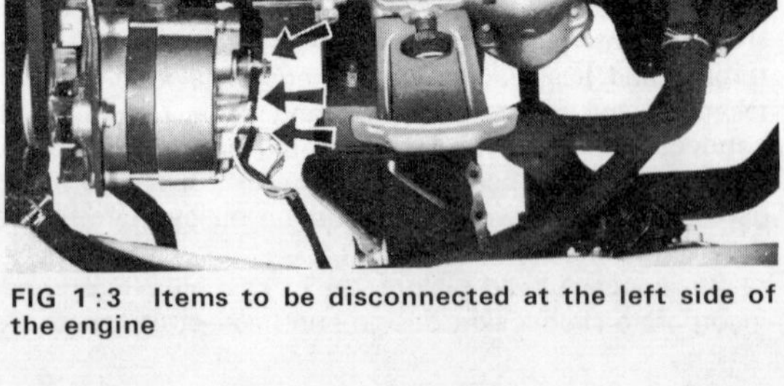

FIG 1:3 Items to be disconnected at the left side of the engine

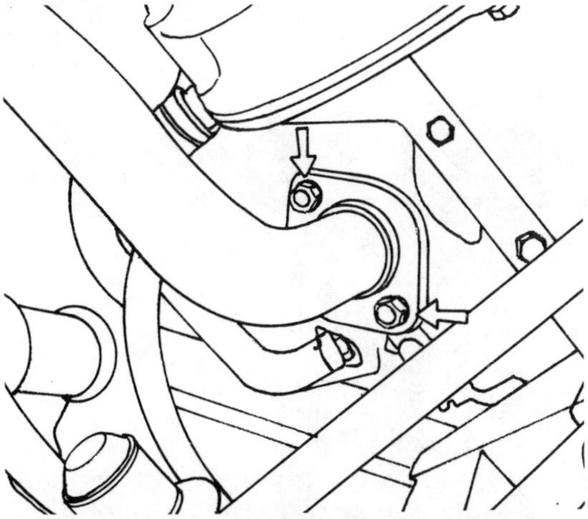

FIG 1:4 Removing the front exhaust pipe

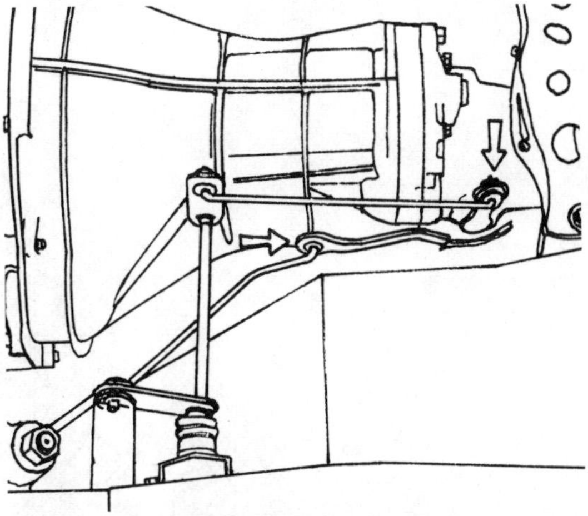

FIG 1:5 Removing the remote control rod

tackle. Assistance will be necessary to tilt and guide the assembly upwards and forwards as it is raised. It must be stressed that all lifting equipment must be sound and the gantry firmly based and not likely to collapse under the weight of the engine and gearbox assembly.

The following description will include many items of equipment which will not be fitted to all models, these will be obvious as the work proceeds.

Removal:

1 Disconnect and remove the battery. Mark the bonnet hinge location, remove the securing bolts and have an assistant to help lift it from the car. Remove the under cover. Remove the radiator as described in **Chapter 4**.

2 Remove the carburetter air cleaner and then the carburetter control cables and pipes.

3 Disconnect the following cables and hoses as applicable:
High tension and starter cables. Leads to distributor, thermal transmitter, oil pressure switch and alternator. Wiring harness connectors. Air pump hoses and hoses to carbon canister and other emission control components. Heater hoses and servo vacuum hose. Many of these items are shown in the typical under-bonnet views in **FIGS 1:2** and **1:3**.

4 According to the type of clutch control fitted, disconnect the cable at the withdrawal lever or remove the slave cylinder from the clutch housing, it is not necessary to detach the fluid hose but it must be supported out of the way.

5 If a steering column gear change is fitted, disconnect the remote control rod at the outer lever and remove (see **FIG 1:5**). With a floor mounted gear change, remove the gear lever boot, withdraw the lockpin or bolt and remove the gear lever.
On automatic transmission, either disconnect the gearbox selector lever or remove the pins at each end of the cross shaft and remove the shift rod. Disconnect the inhibitor switch, and the downshift solenoid.

6 Disconnect the front exhaust pipe from the manifold, as shown typically in **FIG 1:4**. On California models remove the catalytic converter attachments. Refer to **Chapter 8** and remove the propeller shaft.

7 Place a jack under the transmission and attach suitable engine lifting gear to take the weight. Remove the front engine mounting nuts (see **FIGS 1:6** and **1:7**). Remove the rear mounting bolts and detach the rear mounting.

8 Make sure that all connections between the engine/transmission assembly and the body have been detached, then remove the complete power unit from the car, raising the front of the engine at an angle of about 45 deg.

Refitting:

Refitting the engine and transmission unit to the car is the reverse of the removal procedure. New hoses must be obtained to replace any which show signs of deterioration and the required quantities of engine and transmission oil obtained. Observe the torque tightening figures for the various components given in the text, noting that these apply to clean and lightly lubricated threads.

When installation is complete, rock the engine on its mountings to settle them, then tighten the mountings securely. Do this before refitting the ancilliary components to avoid stresses, particularly in the exhaust system. Check the valve clearances as described in **Section 1:5** and the ignition timing as described in **Chapter 3**. The instructions given in **Section 1:3** must be carried out when refitting the cylinder head to ensure that the head bolts are correctly tightened. If necessary, adjust the carburetter as described in **Chapter 2**.

1:3 Removing and refitting the cylinder head

1 If the engine has not been removed from the car, disconnect the battery and drain the cooling system. Disconnect the sparking plug leads and the several hoses and cables mentioned in the engine removal procedure.

2 Remove the carburetter and the EGR valve if applicable. Detach the exhaust pipe and remove the inlet and

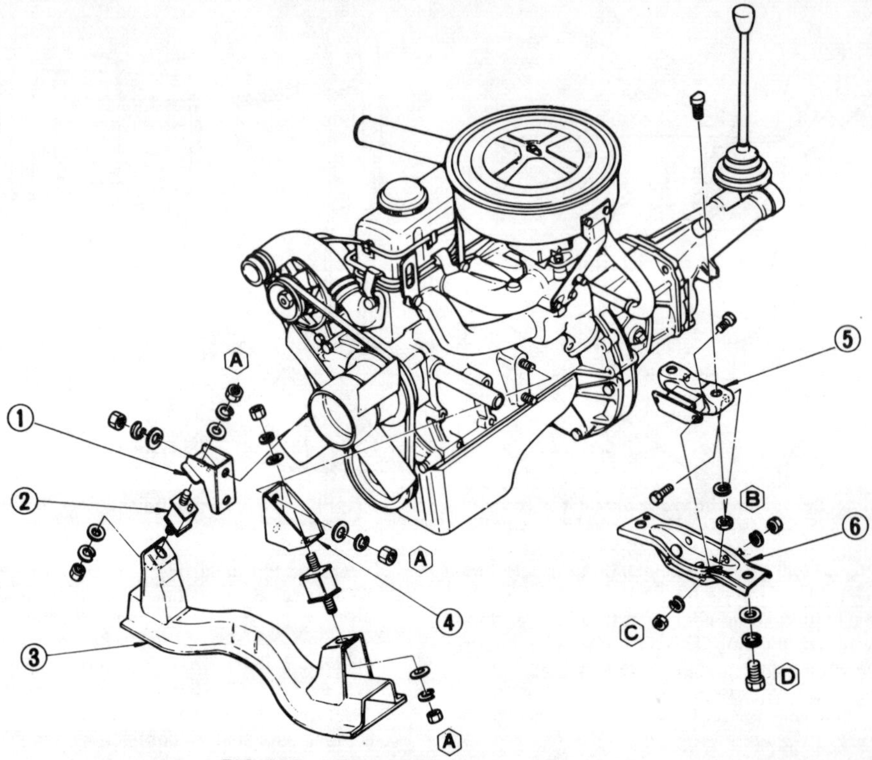

FIG 1 : 6 Engine mountings for 120Y model

Key to Fig 1 : 6 1 Front mounting bracket, righthand 2 Front insulator 3 Front crossmember 4 Front mounting bracket, lefthand 5 Rear insulator 6 Rear crossmember A Torque load to 6.5 to 8.7 lb ft B Manual 14 to 19 lb ft, Automatic 23 to 29 lb ft C 4.3 to 5.8 lb ft D 23 to 29 lb ft

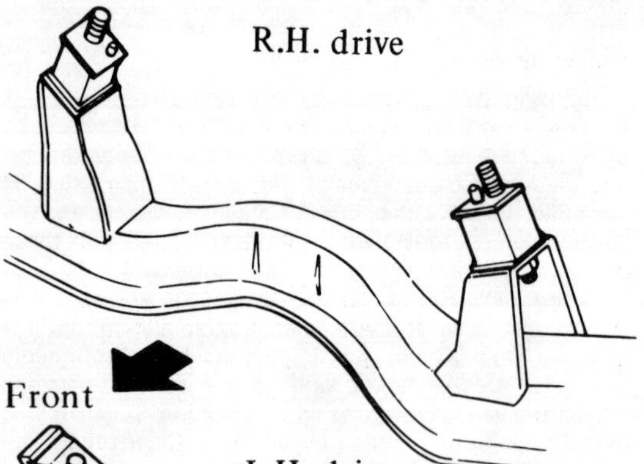

FIG 1 : 7 Front insulator types

exhaust manifolds as shown in **FIG 1 : 8**. Remove the rocker gear cover.

3 Loosen the five bolts securing the rocker shaft to the head progressively and lift off the rocker shaft assembly. Withdraw the pushrods and keep them in order, so that they may be refitted in their original positions.

4 Loosen the cylinder head bolts a little at a time in the order shown in **FIG 1 : 9**. Remove the head, handling it carefully to avoid damaging the relatively soft alloy.

Refitting:

Remove and discard the old cylinder head gasket, cleaning all traces of gasket material and sealing compound from the cylinder head and block joint faces. Take care not to damage the face on the head, using blunt tools only. Two types of cylinder head gasket are obtainable, as shown in **FIG 1 :10**. If the first type shown is used, apply suitable sealing agent to the areas marked in the figure. Fit the new gasket into position and place the cylinder head on top. Fit the cylinder head bolts, noting that the bolt used in the centre righthand position is different from the remaining bolts, this bolt being either smaller and having a hollow head or marked with a T stamped onto the bolt head. Turn the bolts down finger-tight, then tighten them a part of a turn at a time to a final

FIG 1:8 Removing the inlet and exhaust manifolds

FIG 1:9 Cylinder head bolt loosening sequence

torque of 40 to 43 lb ft for the two smaller engines or 51 to 54 lb ft for the two larger sizes, following the tightening sequence shown in **FIG 1:11**.

Install the pushrods in the correct order, making sure they seat properly. Fit the rocker shaft to the cylinder head, guiding the pushrods into the cupped seats on the rocker arms. Tighten the rocker shaft fixing bolts as shown in **FIG 1:12**, to a final torque of 15 to 18 lb ft. Tighten the bolts gradually in several stages, working from the centre bolt outwards. Refit the remaining parts in the reverse order of removal, tightening the manifold attaching bolts to between 7 and 10 lb ft. Use new gaskets throughout. On completion, adjust the valve clearances as described in **Section 1:5**.

1:4 Servicing the head and valves

Remove the head as described in the previous sections. If decarbonizing is intended, plug all the water and oil-ways in the cylinder block with pieces of rag to prevent the entry of dirt or carbon. Scrape the carbon from the combustion chambers before removing the valves to avoid damage to the valve seats, and avoid the use of sharp tools which could damage the light alloy cylinder head.

Use a spring compressor tool to remove the valves from the cylinder head. With the spring compressed, remove the split taper collets, then release the spring and remove the valve cap and spring. Remove the valve and mark it for correct refitting in its original position.

	I	II
Cylinder block side (Steel sheet)	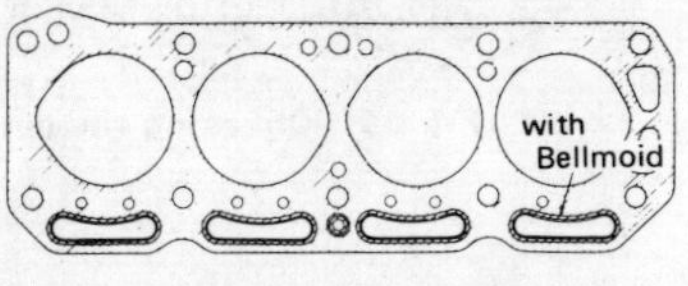 Apply sealing agent on overall surface	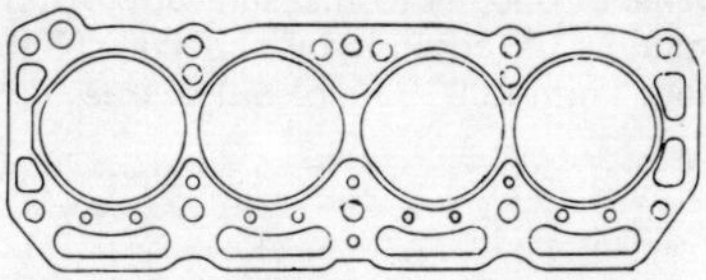 Sealing agent; not required
Cylinder head side (Joint sheet)	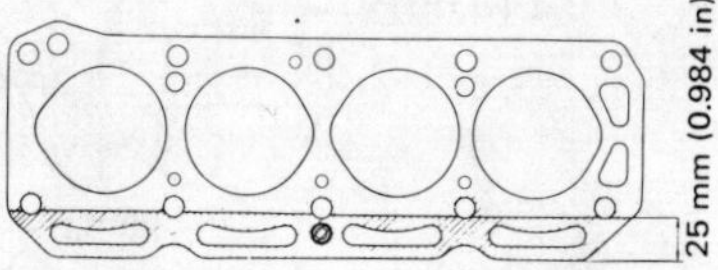 Apply sealing agent to oblique lined portion	 Sealing agent; not required
Remarks	Install immediately after applying sealing agent. Be sure to apply sealing agent to the push rod side sufficiently.	Install without applying sealing agent. Be careful not to damage the push rod side because this side has previously been provided with sealing agent.

FIG 1:10 Alternative types of cylinder head gaskets

FIG 1:11 Cylinder head bolt tightening sequence

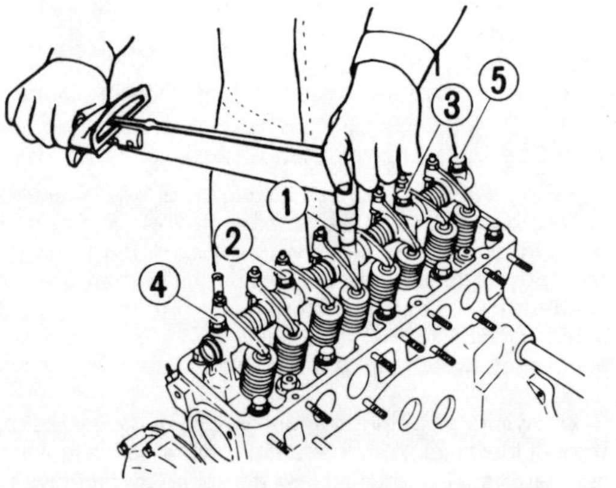

FIG 1:12 Tightening the rocker shaft mounting bolts

Cylinder head:

Check the cylinder head for flatness by placing a long straightedge across the joint face as shown in **FIG 1:13** and using feeler gauges to measure any distortion. The head face should be reground by a specialist if the surface is more than .1 mm (.0039 inch) out of true.

Valves:

When the valves have been cleaned of carbon deposits they must be inspected for serviceability. Valves with bent stems or badly burned heads must be renewed. Valves that are too pitted to clean up on grinding to their seats may be refaced at a garage, but the amount of metal that can be removed in this operation is limited and new valves will be required if refacing cannot be successfully carried out. Check the valve stem for wear or scoring. Check for worn, damaged or deformed valve caps and cotters, renewing parts as necessary.

Valve springs:

Test the valve springs by comparison with the figures given in **Technical Data**, or compare their efficiency with that of a new spring. To compare with a new spring, insert the old and the new end to end with a metal plate between them into the jaws of a vice or under a press. If the old spring is weakened it will close up first when pressure is applied. Take care to avoid the springs from flying out when they are compressed during this test. If any spring is shorter or weaker than standard it must be renewed.

Valve guides:

Valve guides that are worn or scored must be renewed. Old guides must be pressed out, new guides pressed in with the head heated to 200°C, then the guide reamed to the correct finished size. Due to the need for special equipment, this work should be carried out by a service station. A simple method to test for wear on guides and valve stems is to push the valve into the guide and move the valve stem from side to side in the guide. Do this in a direction parallel to the rocker arm, as this is where the greatest wear occurs. If the valve wobbles in the guide to a measured deflection of .2 mm (.0079 inch) or more at the tip of the stem, then the clearance between the valve and guide is more than the wear limit of .1 mm (.0039 inch). If this is so, the valve, guide or both must be renewed as necessary. See **FIG 1:14**.

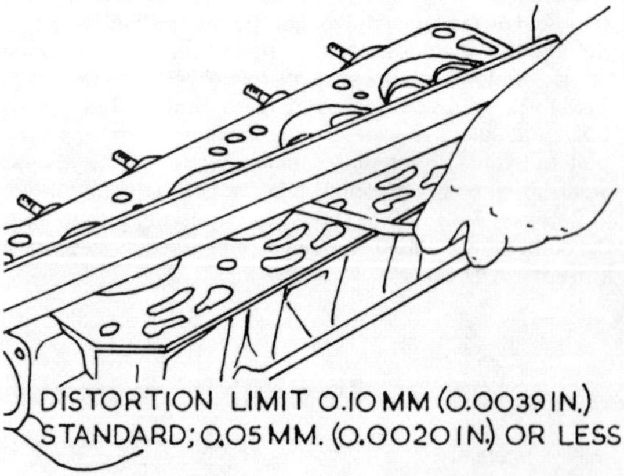

FIG 1:13 Checking the cylinder head joint face

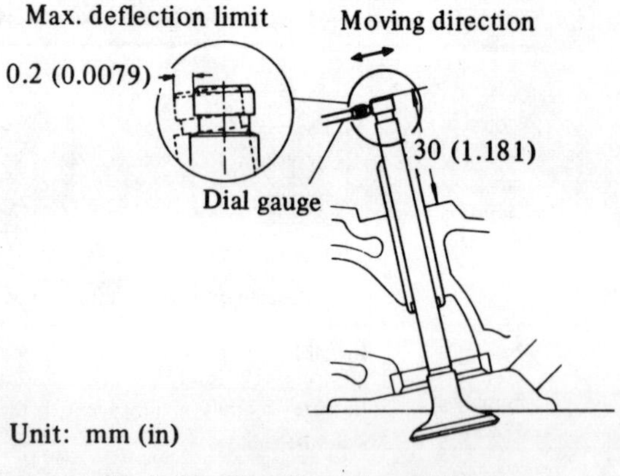

FIG 1:14 Checking valve guide wear

Valve seat inserts:

Valve seat inserts that are too pitted to clean up on grinding to the valves may be refaced at a garage. If the inserts are too far gone to be refaced in this manner they must be renewed. Worn inserts must be bored out until they collapse and can be removed. New inserts must be press-fitted with the head heated to 200°C, then recut to ensure concentricity. Due to the need for special equipment, this work must be carried out by a service station.

Rocker shaft and arms:

FIG 1:15 shows these components. Check the rocker shaft and arms for wear or seizing at the bearing surfaces and renew parts as necessary. Rocker to shaft clearance should be .02 to .05 mm (.0008 to .0020 inch). When the part of the rocker tip that contact the valve stem is excessively or unevenly worn, have the rocker tips reground at a service station, or renew the rocker if wear is too great. The grinding allowance for rocker tips is .5 mm (.0197 inch) or less.

Decarbonizing and valve grinding:

Avoid the use of sharp tools which could damage the light alloy cylinder head surfaces. Remove all traces of carbon deposits from the combustion chambers, inlet and exhaust ports and joint faces. Make sure that all waterways and oil holes in the cylinder block are plugged with rag, then clean the carbon from the piston crowns.

Grind the valves to their seats, starting with coarse grade carborundum paste and finishing with fine grade, unless the seats are in very good condition when fine grade paste can be used at once. Use a suction type valve grinding tool and work with a semi-rotary movement, lifting the valve clear of the seat occasionally and turning the valve to a different position before continuing. When the seats of both valve and insert show a smooth, matt grey finish on their matching surfaces grinding is complete. When the work is finished, clean away every trace of grinding paste from the cylinder head, valves and guides.

Reassembly:

This is a reversal of the dismantling procedure. Use engine oil to lubricate the valve stems and guides when they are being refitted.

1:5 Valve clearance adjustment

The correct adjustment of valve clearances is important as they affect engine timing and performance considerably. Excessive clearance will reduce valve lift and opening duration and reduce engine performance, causing excessive wear on the valve gear components and noisy operation. Insufficient or zero clearance will again affect engine timing and, in some circumstances, can cause the valve to be held clear of its seat. This will result in much reduced performance and the possibility of burned valves and seats. Valve clearances should be checked and adjusted every 6000 miles as routine maintenance and, additionally, whenever the cylinder head has been refitted or its mounting bolts tightened. Proceed as follows:

If the engine has been reassembled after dismantling and it is necessary to set the clearances cold so that the engine will run, set the clearances to .010 inch (.25 mm) for inlet and exhaust valves. Always make final adjustments in the following manner, with the engine hot.

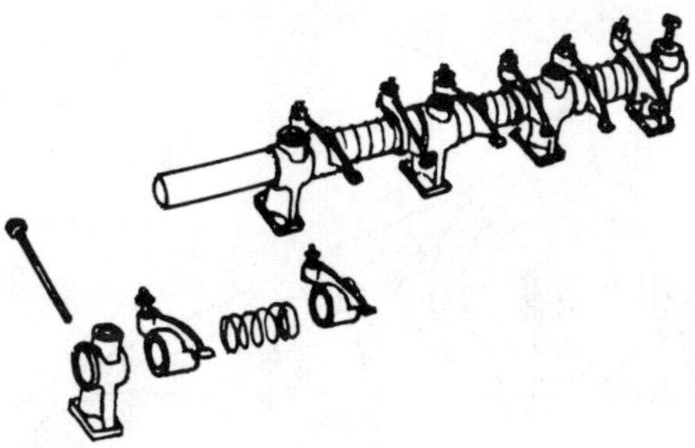

FIG 1:15 The rocker shaft and rocker arms

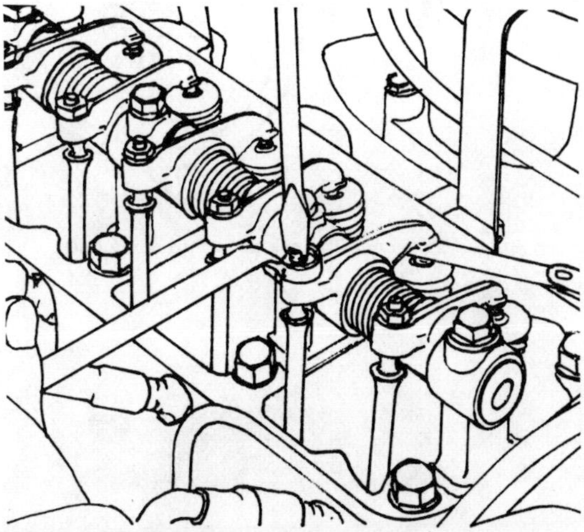

FIG 1:16 Checking and adjusting valve clearances

Start the engine and allow it to run until normal operating temperature is achieved, then stop the engine and remove the rocker cover from the cylinder head. The engine will be easier to turn over if the sparking plugs are removed, but this is not essential. To turn the engine, make sure that the car is on a flat surface so that it will not move when the brake is released, then select top gear and release the handbrake. The car can then be pushed backwards or forwards to turn the engine. On cars fitted with automatic transmission, the engine must be turned by hand pressure on the fan belt and crankshaft pulley, removing the sparking plugs so that engine compression will not resist the turning effort.

The clearances of the inlet and exhaust valves in No. 1 cylinder must be adjusted when No. 1 is at TDC on the compression stroke, with both valves fully closed. At the same time the two valves on No. 4 cylinder will be on the overlap i.e. one just opening and one just closing. Now check the clearance between the valves and rocker tips at No. 1 cylinder, using feeler gauges as shown in **FIG 1:16**. The clearance must be .014 inch (.35 mm), this figure being for both inlet and exhaust valves.

To adjust the clearance, loosen the locknut and use a screwdriver as shown to turn the adjuster until the correct

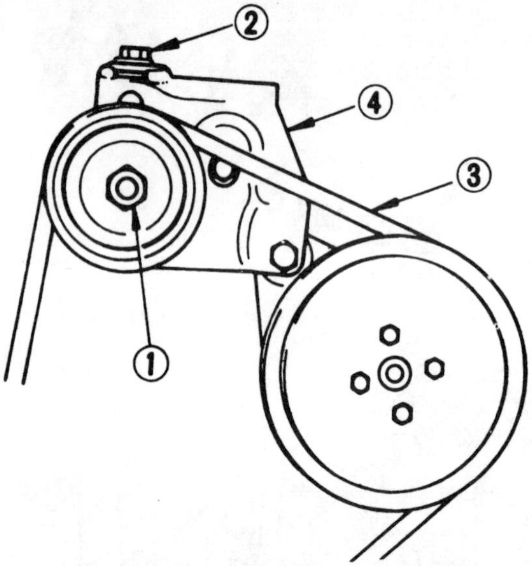

FIG 1:17 Removing the air pump drive belt

Key to Fig 1:17 1 Idler pulley nut 2 Adjusting bolt 3 Belt 4 Pulley bracket

FIG 1:18 The sump removed, showing the oil strainer assembly

gap is obtained. The feeler gauge should move in the gap between the rocker tip and valve stem with a slight drag, being neither tight nor loose. When this is so, tighten the locknut without moving the adjuster and recheck the clearance with the gauge. When both clearances are correct at No. 1 cylinder, proceed to the next cylinder. Check the clearances at No. 3 cylinder with the valves at No. 2 cylinder on the overlap as described, No. 4 with No. 1 on the overlap and No. 2 with No. 3 on the overlap. On completion, refit the rocker cover and the sparking plugs if removed. Run the engine and check for oil leaks at the rocker cover.

1:6 Dismantling the engine

In order to cover adequately the later and more comprehensively equipped engines, this section will again refer to certain components which are not fitted to earlier engines or those intended for markets where anti-pollution regulations are less stringent.

1 Remove the engine as described in **Section 1:2** and clean as much as possible of the dirt and oil from the engine exterior before proceeding, to prevent contamination of the internal components during dismantling. The use of an engine stand is recommended, if available.

2 Refer to **Chapter 5** and remove the clutch. Remove the alternator and fan belt, remove also the alternator bracket and adjusting bar.

3 Refer to **FIG 1:17** and remove the idler pulley, air pump belt 3 and the pulley bracket 4, loosening first the idler pulley nut 1 and then the belt adjusting bolt 2. Remove the fan, spacer and pulley. Unclip the distributor cap and remove the distributor. Remove the fuel pump. Remove the thermostat housing and thermostat.

4 Remove the righthand engine bracket, also the oil pump and sparking plugs. The engine attachment ST05200000 may now be installed on the vacant studs and mounted on the stand ST0501S000 if available. Remove the lefthand engine bracket.

5 Disconnect all attachments to the air cleaner and remove it with its bracket. Remove the vacuum control valve and then the carburetter. Remove the cylinder head as described earlier in **Section 1:3**.

6 Invert the engine to remove the sump and oil strainer (see **FIG 1:18**). Remove the water pump and then the crankshaft pulley and the timing chain cover and tensioner assembly as shown in **FIG 1:19**. On later engines the tensioner is mounted inside the chain.

7 Unbolt the camshaft sprocket and remove both sprockets and the timing chain. Rotate the engine as necessary and remove the connecting rod cap from each assembly in turn pushing the piston out through the top of its bore and making sure that each is fully identified for later assembly.

FIG 1:19 Removing the timing chain cover

8 Remove the flywheel and rear plate. Progressively unscrew the main bearing cap bolts, remove the caps seeing that they are correctly marked and also the rear oil seal. Lift out the crankshaft.

9 Remove the baffle plate and net assembly, as shown in **FIG 1:20**.
Remove the camshaft retaining plate and very carefully withdraw the camshaft to the front. Remove the valve lifters, or tappets, and keep them in order.

1:7 Pistons and connecting rods

Pistons are removed from the connecting rods by pressing out the gudgeon pins under an arbor press, using the special tool as shown in **FIG 1:22**. Piston rings are removed by easing them out of the grooves and over the top of the piston with the fingers. **FIG 1:23** shows the connecting rod, piston and rings.

Clean carbon deposits from the piston crown and ring grooves and inspect for score marks or any signs of seizure, which would dictate renewal. Fit the piston rings one at a time into the bore from which they were removed, pushing them down with the crown of the piston to ensure squareness. Measure the piston ring fitted gap with feeler gauges as shown in **FIG 1:24** and compare with the values given in **Technical Data**. If the measurements are at or near the wear limits, new rings must be fitted. Measure the side clearance of the rings in their correct grooves in the piston as shown in **FIG 1:25** and compare with the figures given. If the wear limit for any ring is reached, the rings and, possibly, the piston must be renewed. Excessive ring side clearance can be responsible for high oil consumption and poor performance. Piston rings are available in standard and six oversizes.

Check the cylinder bores for score marks and remove glaze and carbon deposits. Badly scored or worn surfaces will necessitate a rebore. Pistons are supplied in standard and six oversizes to fit rebored cylinders and, additionally, three undersizes of cylinder liner are available to cater for conditions where further reboring is impossible. All such work must be carried out by a specialist motor engineer.

Gudgeon pins:

Gudgeon pins and their bores in the pistons can be measured and the working clearance gauged and compared with the figures in **Technical Data**. The pin should be a smooth sliding fit in the piston bores at room temperature, checked by pressing into the piston by hand as shown in **FIG 1:26**. The pin should be a tight machine-press fit in the connecting rods. Fit new piston and gudgeon pin assemblies to replace faulty components.

Connecting rods:

If there has been a big-end bearing failure, the crankpin must be examined for damage and for transfer of metal to its surface. The oilway in the crankshaft must be checked to ensure there is no obstruction. Big-end bearing clearance can be checked by the use of Plastigage as described in **Hints on Maintenance and Overhaul** at the end of this manual. The working clearance should be .0008 to .0020 inch (.020 to .050 mm). If the bearing clearance exceeds .0039 inch (.1 mm) the crankpin should be reground to accept undersize bearing shells, which are available in six undersizes. Fit the shells, connecting rod

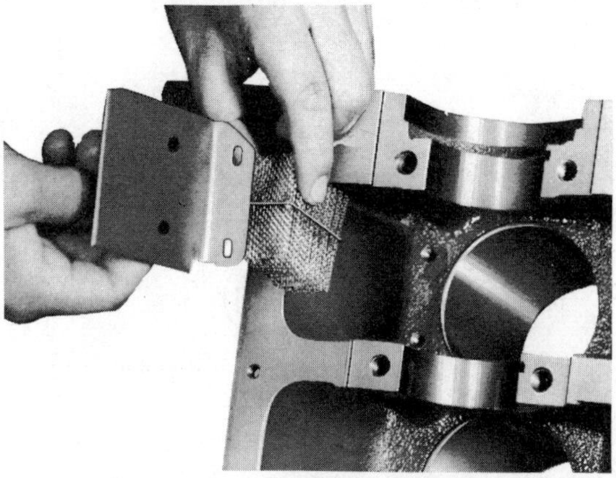

FIG 1:20 Removing the baffle plate and cylinder block net

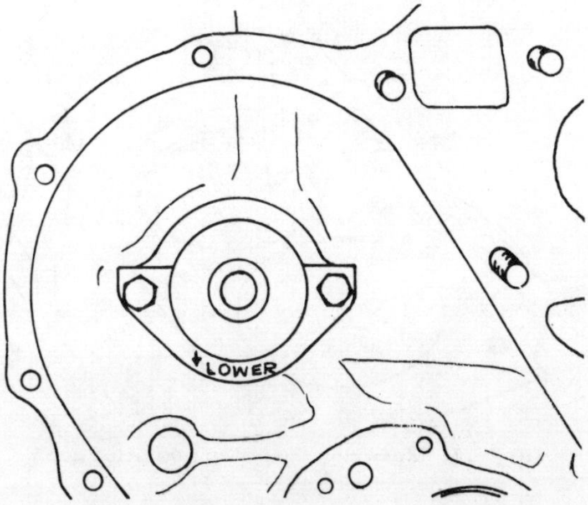

FIG 1:21 The camshaft retaining plate

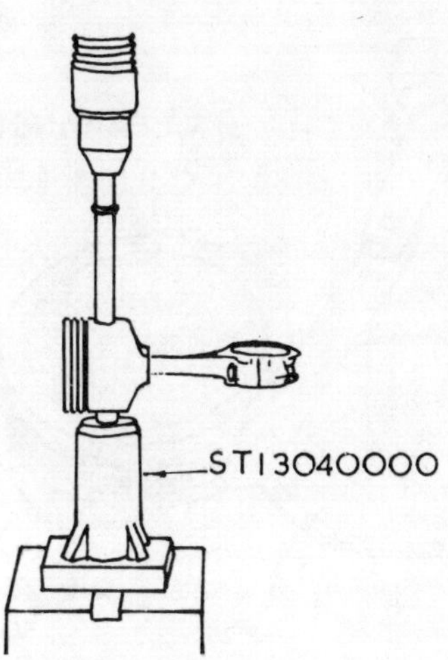

FIG 1:22 Gudgeon pin removal

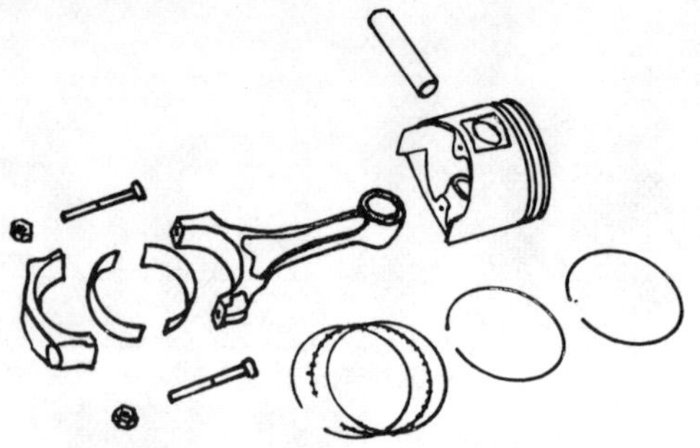

FIG 1:23 The connecting rod, piston and rings

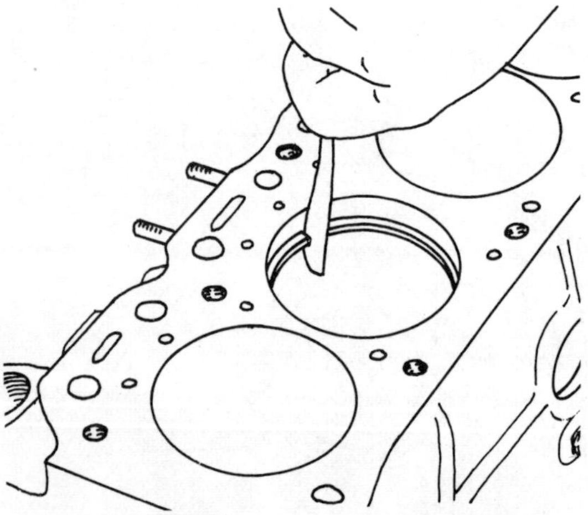

FIG 1:24 Measuring the piston ring fitted gap

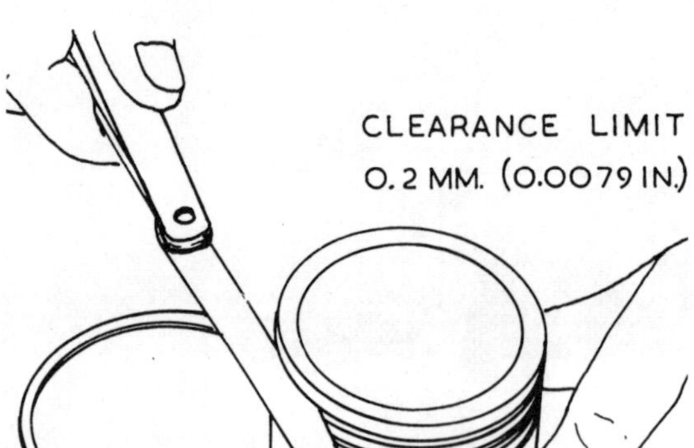

FIG 1:25 Measuring the piston ring side clearance

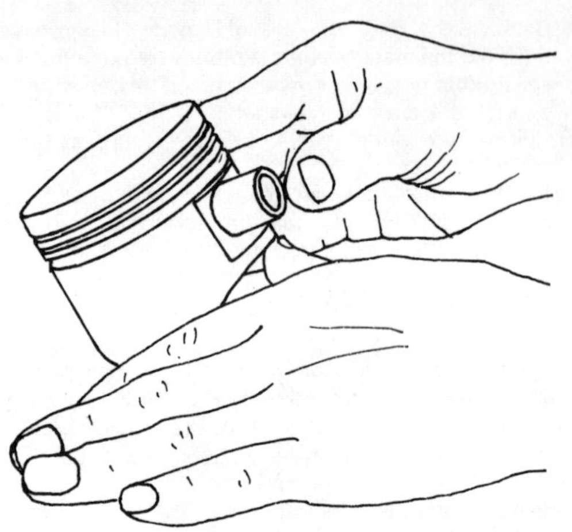

FIG 1:26 Checking the gudgeon pin fit in the piston

and cap together and tighten the cap bolts to a torque of 25 to 26 lb ft, then loosen one cap bolt. Measure the gap between the rod and cap with feeler gauges as shown in **FIG 1:27**. The gap should be between .0012 and .0032 inch (.030 and .080 mm). If the gap is outside these limits, new bearing shells must be fitted. On no account must the bearing caps, connecting rods or bearing shells be filed to take up wear.

Fit the connecting rod and bearing assembly to the correct crankpin and tighten the cap bolts to the specified torque. Use feeler gauges to check for a side clearance of .0079 to .0118 inch (.2 to .3 mm) as shown in **FIG 1:28**. If the figure is .0157 inch (.4 mm) or more, a new connecting rod will be required.

Always check the crankshaft and main bearings whenever wear or damage is found at any big-end bearing position.

1:8 Crankshaft and main bearings

Remove the crankshaft from the engine as described in **Section 1:6** and remove the main bearing shells from the caps and crankcase, keeping them in the correct order. If there has been a main bearing failure, the crankshaft must be checked for damage and for transfer of metal to its surface. The oilway must be checked to ensure there is no obstruction. Main bearing clearance can be checked by the use of Plastigage as described in **Hints on Maintenance and Overhaul** at the end of this manual. Working clearance should be .0008 to .0024 inch (.02 to .062 m). If the bearing clearance exceeds .0039 inch (.1 mm) the journals should be reground to accept undersize bearing shells which are obtainable in four undersizes. Fit the shells and main bearing cap together and tighten the cap bolts to 37 to 38 lb ft, then loosen one cap bolt. Measure the gap between the cap and upper shell housing with feeler gauges as shown in **FIG 1:27**. The gap should be between zero and .0024 inch (zero and .06 mm). If the gap exceeds the maximum stated, or if the cap is tight, new bearing shells must be fitted. On no account must the bearing caps, bearing housing or bearing shells be filed to take up wear.

Fit the crankshaft and main bearing assemblies into position and tighten the cap bolts to the specified torque.

Use feeler gauges to check the crankshaft end play at the centre main bearing position as shown in **FIG 1:29**. If the wear limit shown is exceeded, new thrust shims must be fitted.

Check the clutch shaft pilot bearing at the rear of the crankshaft for wear or damage, renewing the bearing if any defects are detected. Check the crankshaft for bending by measuring the runout at the centre main bearing with a dial gauge, supporting at the front and rear journals. Runout will be half the total gauge reading when taken as shown in **FIG 1:30** and must not exceed the bending limit stated. If the crankshaft is bent beyond the limit stated, it may be possible for straightening to be carried out by a specialist engineer, otherwise the unit must be renewed. Check the flywheel ring gear for chipped or broken teeth and, if necessary, have a new ring gear press-fitted at a service station.

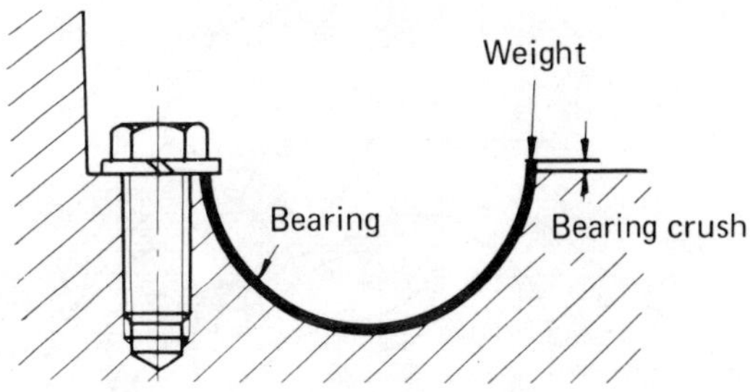

FIG 1:27 Checking main or big-end bearing crush

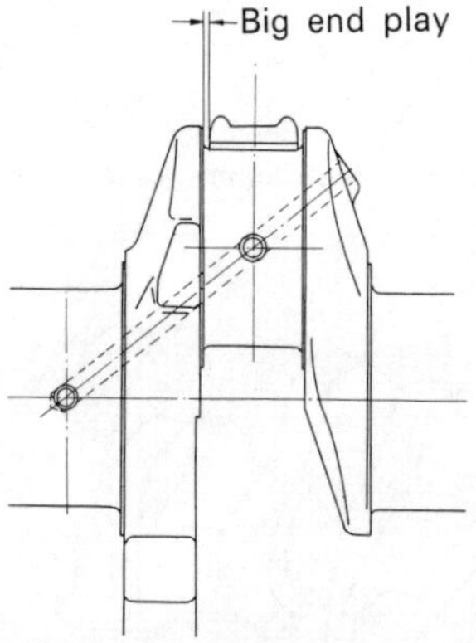

FIG 1:28 Measuring big-end bearing side play

1:9 Camshaft drive gear

Camshaft:

Check the camshaft for worn or damaged journals. Check camshaft runout in the manner described for crankshaft units, noting that a runout limit of .0020 inch (.05 mm). Check the camshaft bearing clearances, which should be between .0012 and .0027 inch (.03 to .07 mm) with a limit of .0059 inch (.15 mm). If the clearance limit is exceeded, consult the Datsun agent with regard to rectification. On early engines a new crankcase is necessary, but on later versions it may be possible for new bearings to be pressed in. Check the camshaft end float by fitting the retaining plate and using feeler gauges as shown in **FIG 1:31**. If not within the figures stated, renew the camshaft retaining plate.

Chain and sprockets:

Check the sprockets for worn, hooked or damaged teeth, renewing any sprocket found defective. Check the camshaft sprocket for runout as shown in **FIG 1:32**. A new sprocket must be fitted if runout exceeds the limit stated.

Check the timing chain for damage, wear and stretching. If the chain links and rollers show play when the chain is pushed and pulled along its length, the chain should be renewed. Make this test at several points along the chain, with the chain stretched across a flat surface. Excessive wear in the timing chain or sprockets will cause faulty valve timing, apart from noisy operation.

Check the chain tensioner and guides for wear and deep scoring, renewing parts as necessary.

1:10 Oil pump and oil filter

Removal:

The oil pump assembly is in unit with the external oil filter and is attached by three bolts to the lower crankcase. If the engine has been removed from the car, removal is as shown in **FIG 1:33** after removing the three mounting bolts. If the engine is installed, drain the engine oil and remove the front stabiliser bar and splash shield before removing the pump as stated. On later cars such dismantling may not be necessary, but will facilitate the operation.

Servicing:

Unscrew the retaining bolt and separate the cover from the pump body. Take out drive and inner parts. **FIG 1:34** shows the oil pump assembly. Clean the parts in petrol and examine them for wear or damage. Check the following clearances. Side clearance between outer and inner rotors, .0020 to .0047 inch (.05 to .12 mm); clearance between outer rotor and body, .0059 to .0083 (.15 to .21 mm) and a tip clearance of .05 inch (.12 mm). Renew parts as necessary if any clearance figure is exceeded or any part worn or damaged. Close tolerances are essential to correct pump operation and full oil pressure delivery.

Refitting:

This is a reversal of the removal procedure, using new gaskets.

Oil filter:

The oil filter is a cartridge type, mounted on the oil pump assembly. **FIG 1:35** shows a section through the filter assembly. The oil filter must be renewed at 6000 mile intervals. Unscrew and discard the old element, using a clamp tool for removal if the unit is stiff to turn. Check the seals on the new unit then screw it carefully into position, by hand pressure only, until the seal and the contact faces are in touch and then a further two-thirds of a turn only. **Do not overtighten.** An excessively tight filter can leak oil. Check for oil leaks around the new element after running the engine for a while.

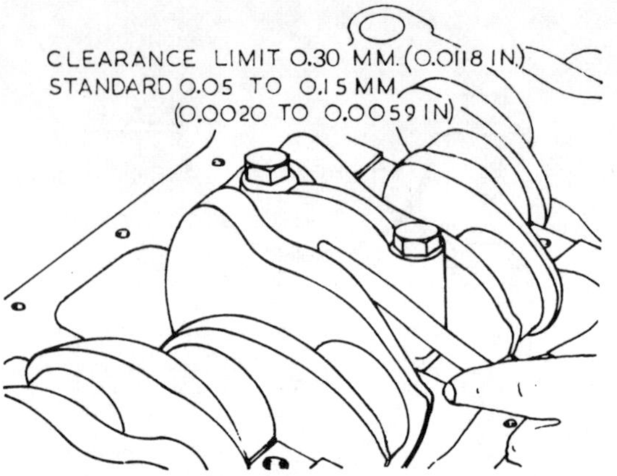

FIG 1:29 Checking crankshaft end float

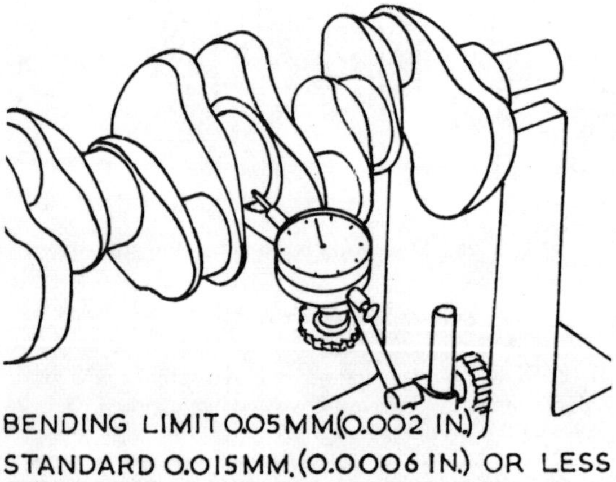

FIG 1:30 Checking the crankshaft for runout

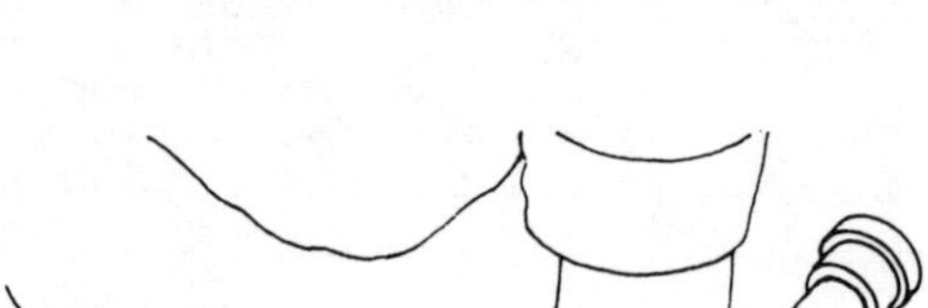

FIG 1:31 Checking camshaft end float

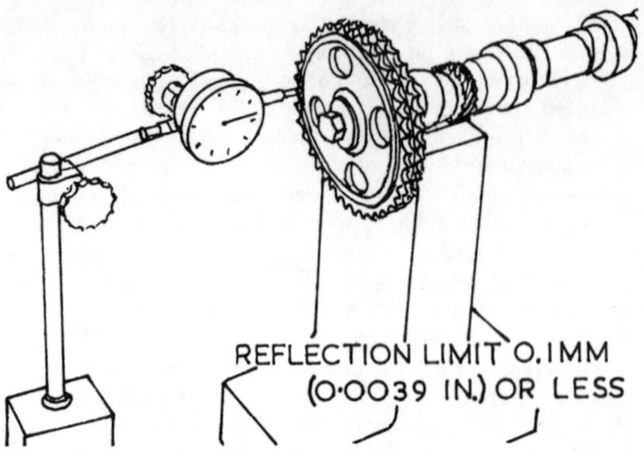

FIG 1:32 Checking camshaft sprocket runout

FIG 1:33 Removing the oil pump

Pressure relief valve:

The valve is not adjustable. **FIG 1:36** shows the valve components. The parts should be cleaned and checked for good condition, any defective parts being renewed. Check the free length of the spring, which should be 1.71 inches (43.5 mm). Renew the spring if it is shorter than standard, or deformed or damaged.

1:11 Engine reassembly

Make sure that all parts are thoroughly clean and keep them clean during reassembly, as even small particles of dirt or grit can clog small oilways or cause wear and scoring of the working parts. Lubricate all moving parts with engine oil during reassembly, especially highly-loaded bearings such as the big-end and main bearing shells. Use new gaskets throughout and renew all oil seals unless the originals are in perfect condition. Observe the torque tightening figures given in the text and in **Technical Data** in the **Appendix**, noting that these figures apply to clean and lightly lubricated threads.

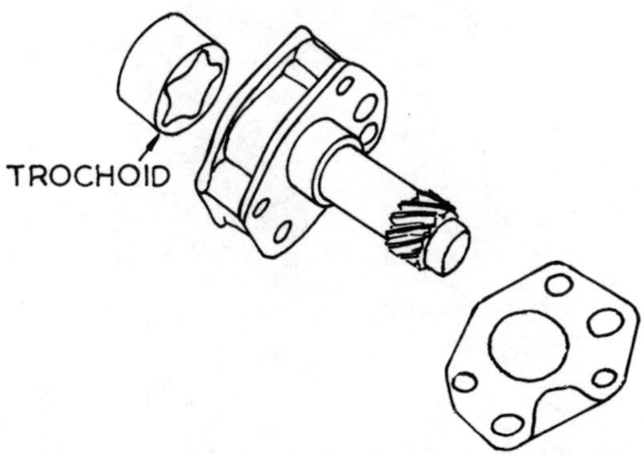

FIG 1:34 Oil pump components

1 Refit any pistons that where removed, oiling the gudgeon pins before pressing them into position. Make sure that all top and second piston rings are fitted with the marks facing upwards. Make sure that the backs of all bearing shells as well as the components to which they fit are totally clean. Any dirt behind shell bearings will deform them when they are tightened and may cause bearing failure in use.

2 Invert the engine and fit the valve lifters. Carefully slide the camshaft into position and fit the retaining plate, noting that the 'Lower' mark on the plate must be towards the lower side of the engine, as shown in **FIG 1:21**. Tighten the retaining plate bolts to 2.9 to 3.6 lb ft.

3 Fit the shell bearings to the crankcase and main bearing caps, fit the crankshaft into position, then fit the caps in their correct positions. The arrow marks on the caps must face towards the front of the engine. Tighten the bolts a little at a time, working from the centre bearing outwards, to a final torque of 37 to 38 lb ft. Check that the crankshaft rotates smoothly and check the end play as described in **Section 1:8**. Fit the rear main bearing oil seal. Install the flywheel using new lockwashers, then tighten the retaining bolts to 47 to 54 lb ft.

4 Fit the piston and connecting rod assemblies to the cylinder from which they were removed, using a ring clamp to enter the rings into the cylinders. Make sure that the ring gaps are spaced 180 deg. apart around the piston circumference. Arrange the pistons so that the F mark on the crowns face the front of the engine as shown in **FIG 1:37**. Arrange the connecting rods and caps so that the cylinder numbers are facing the same direction. Tighten the connecting rod cap bolts to 24 to 28 lb ft and check the side clearance as described in **Section 1:7**.

5 Fit the crankshaft and camshaft sprockets temporarily, then check the height of each sprocket as shown in **FIG 1:38**. The difference in height between the sprockets must not exceed .0197 inch (.5mm). If the difference is greater than this, it must be brought to within limits by fitting adjusting washers as shown, these being .006 inch (.15mm) in thickness. Fit any necessary washers, then install the timing chain and sprockets as shown in **FIG 1:39**, lining up the engine timing marks correctly. Tighten the camshaft sprocket fixing to 33 to 36 lb ft. Fit the chain tensioner into

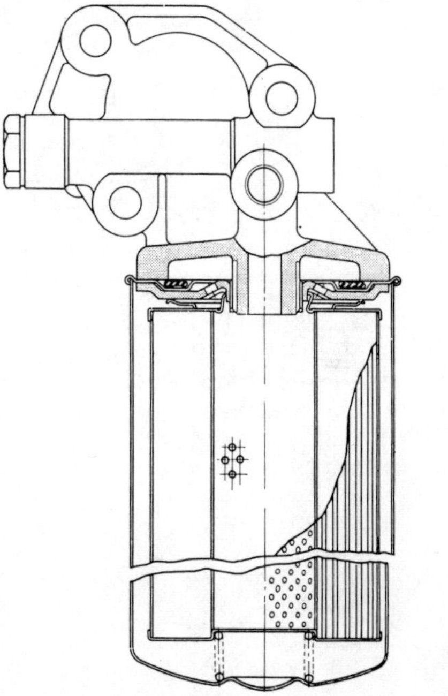

FIG 1:35 Section through the oil filter assembly

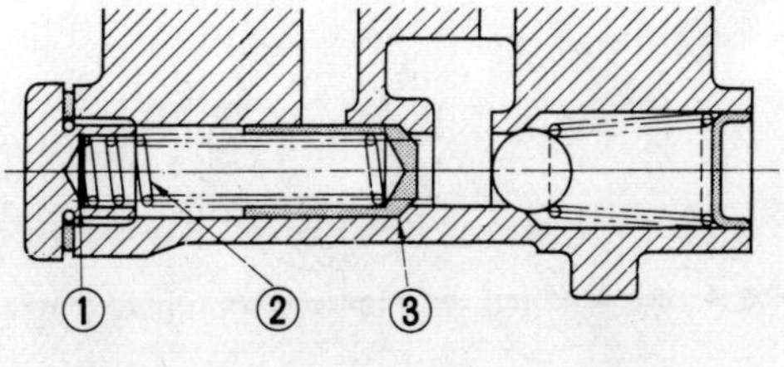

FIG 1:36 The oil pressure relief valve

Key to Fig 1:36 1 Adjusting shim 2 Valve spring 3 Regulator valve

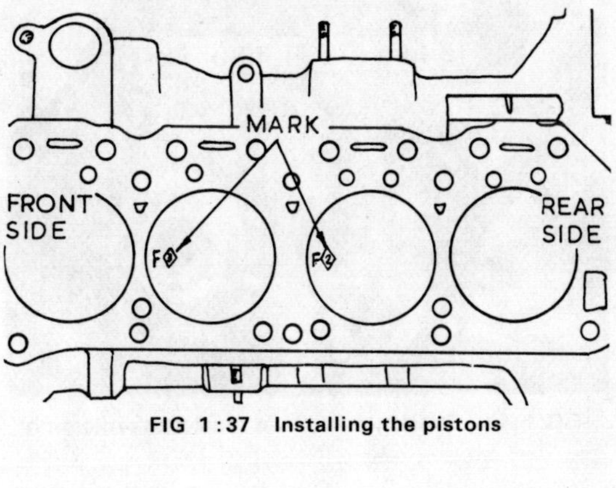

FIG 1:37 Installing the pistons

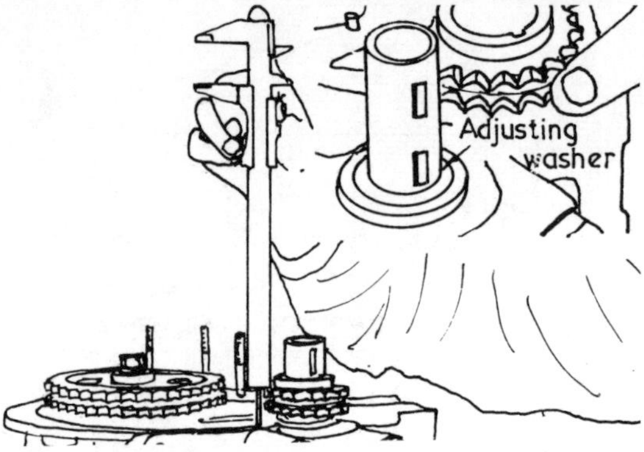

FIG 1:38 Checking the height of the timing chain sprockets

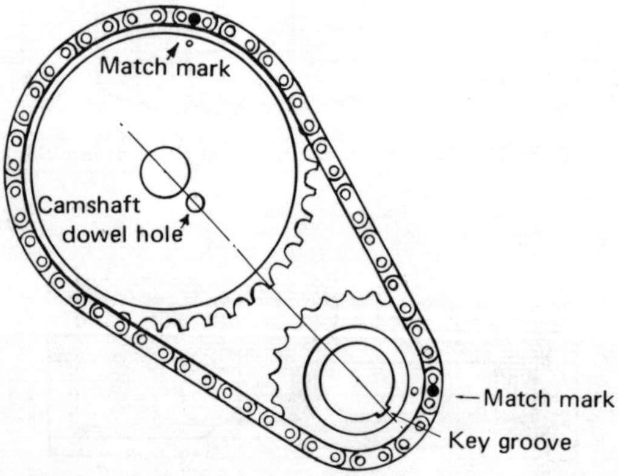

FIG 1:39 Aligning the engine valve timing marks

FIG 1:40 Checking the chain tensioner projection

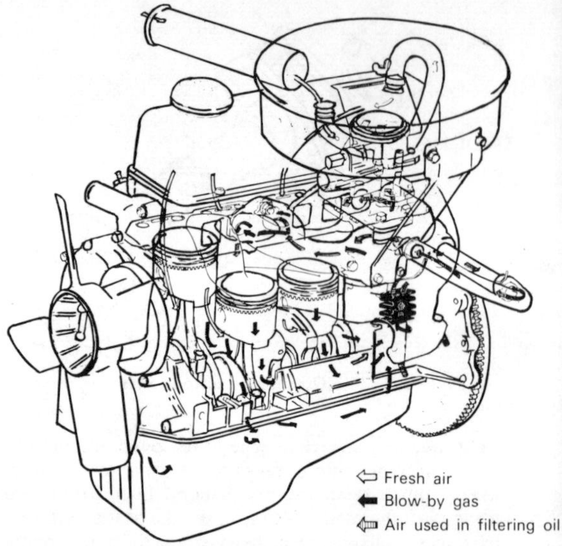

FIG 1:41 Closed crankcase vent system operating at normal speeds

position and check the spindle projection as shown in **FIG 1:40**. If the measurement stated is exceeded, a new tensioner must be fitted. Fit the oil thrower to the crankshaft. Fit a new oil seal into the timing cover, then install the cover on the front of the engine, using a new gasket and applying sealing compound to both sides of the gasket. Tighten the cover bolts to 3.6 to 4.3 lb ft.

6 Make sure that the oil strainer assembly is thoroughly clean, then fit it in position. Apply sealing agent to both sides of the oil sump gasket, then fit the gasket and sump to the crankcase, tightening the retaining bolts to 2.9 to 4.3 lb ft.

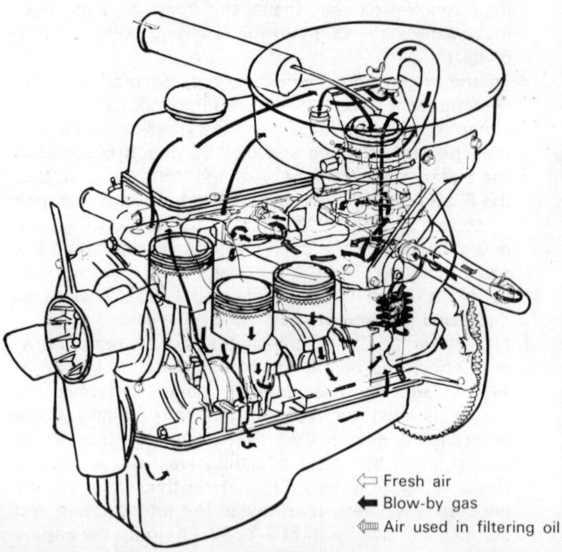

FIG 1:42 Closed crankcase vent system operating at high speed

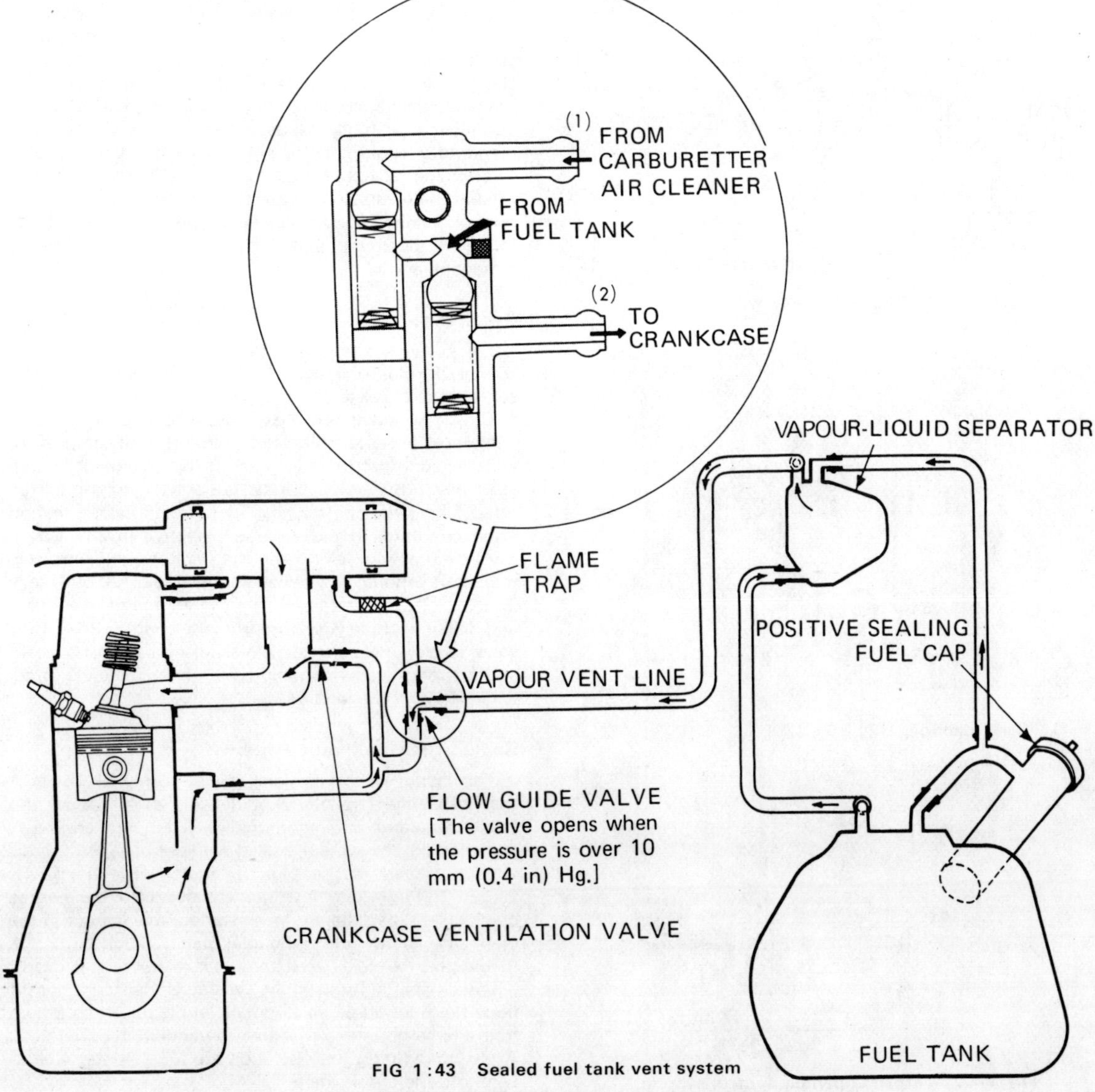

FIG 1:43 Sealed fuel tank vent system

7 Refit the cylinder head assembly as described in **Section 1:3**. Fit the oil pump as described in **Section 1:10**. Install the alternator, water pump, fan and fan belt. Refit the distributor, referring to **Chapter 3, Section 3:5** to obtain correct ignition timing. Install the sparking plugs and connect the distributor high-tension leads. Remember to set the valve clearances to the correct settings after the engine has been refitted and run up to operating temperature. Make sure that the engine and gearbox oil levels are correct and that the cooling system is filled. Adjust the carburetter, ignition timing and clutch free play according to the instructions in the appropriate Chapters.

1:12 Emission control systems

Emission control systems are fitted to cars exported to the USA in order to reduce the exhaust, crankcase and fuel system gas emissions to the levels required by law. The control of polluting emissions from these vehicles is achieved in several different ways and a number of different systems have been fitted, depending on the area in which the vehicle is to be operated and the degree of reduction demanded. Some early, or less sophisticated, installations are described in this chapter, others are discussed in **Chapter 2** with the **Fuel System** with which they are more closely concerned. It must, however, be stressed that the testing of these devices cannot

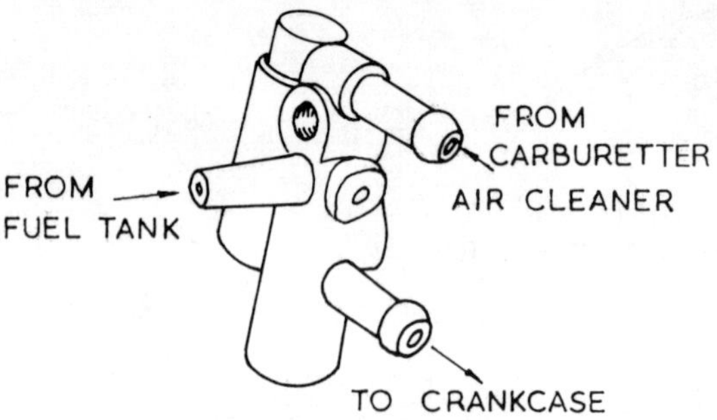

FIG 1:44 The flow guide valve

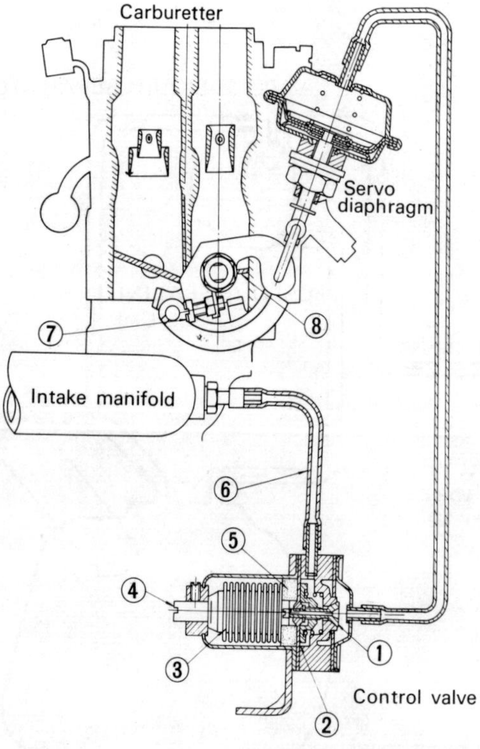

FIG 1:45 Throttle opening control system

Key to Fig 1:45 1 Valve 2 Diaphragm 3 Altitude corrector 4 Vacuum adjusting screw 5 Filter 6 Manifold vacuum tube 7 Adjusting screw 8 Primary throttle valve

satisfactorily be undertaken by the home operator, and in many cases rectification of a fault must be by renewal of the component. For this reason, and if legal requirements are to be observed, a fault in an emission control system or its regular testing should be referred to a qualified service station.

Closed crankcase ventilation system:

The operation of this system is shown under normal speed operation in **FIG 1:41** and under high-speed operation in **FIG 1:42**. The system returns blow-by gas to both the inlet manifold and the carburetter air cleaner. The vent control valve conducts gas to the inlet manifold. At normal speeds, with the throttle partly open, the gas is sucked through the valve and burnt in the engine combustion chambers. The ventilating air is then drawn from the air cleaner and enters the crankcase by way of a tube connection. At high speeds, with the throttle fully open, manifold vacuum is sufficient to draw the engine gases through the valve, so the gas flows through the connecting tube in the reverse direction. This system ensures that all internal engine vapours are kept in the crankcase or burnt in the combustion chambers, none being vented into the atmosphere.

Servicing:

Once a year or every 12,000 miles, whichever occurs sooner, the closed crankcase ventilating system should be serviced as follows:

Check all hoses and hose connectors for leaks. Disconnect all hoses and blow them through with compressed air to ensure that they are clear. If this treatment fails to clear any hose which is blocked, a new hose must be fitted. Check the control valve for correct functioning and good condition. If the valve is defective in any way it must be renewed, as no servicing is possible. Normally, the valve should be renewed at about 30,000 mile intervals. To test the valve, run the engine at idle speed and disconnect the vent hose from the control valve. If the valve is working correctly a hissing noise will be heard and a strong vacuum should be felt immediately a finger is placed over the inlet valve.

Sealed fuel tank vent system:

The layout of this system is shown in **FIG 1:43**. A sealed fuel filler cap, a flow guide valve and a vapour and liquid separator are incorporated. When the engine is switched off, the system is filled with petrol vapour. If this vapour exceeds a pressure of .4 inch Hg, the gas is vented through the flow guide valve into the engine crankcase. When the engine is started, this vapour in the crankcase is drawn into the inlet manifold and burned in the engine. As fuel is used and the level in the tank drops, a partial vacuum forms in the system. Under these conditions the flow guide valve opens and supplies air drawn from the carburetter air cleaner to ventilate the fuel tank. At no time during the operation are fuel vapours free to vent into the atmosphere.

Servicing:

Apart from routine checks for leaks at the hose connections and the fuel filler cap, no maintenance should be required. If faulty operation is suspected, or if fuel starvation has been traced to insufficient tank ventilation, the flow guide valve should be checked for correct operation and the fuel and vent lines checked for obstructions.

Flow guide valve:

This assembly is shown in **FIG 1:44**. The valve is mounted inside the engine compartment and can be removed after disconnecting the pipelines. The valve is marked A, F and C to indicate the vapour vent line connections. If low-pressure air is fed into the fuel tank connection on the valve, this air should pass through the valve

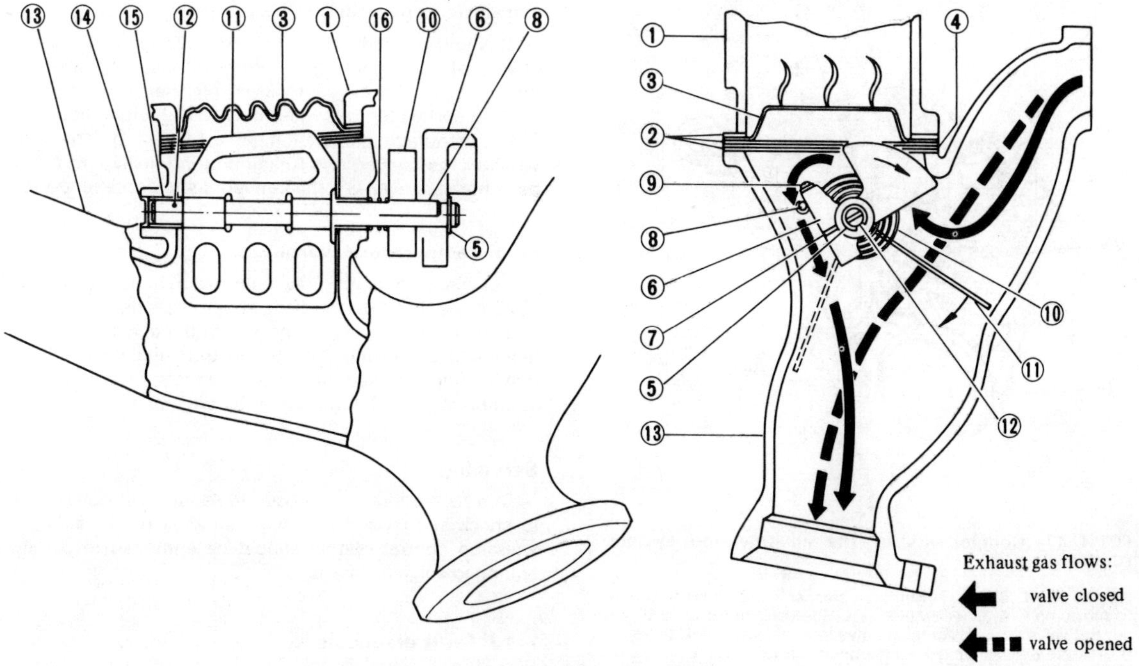

FIG 1:46 Details of the controlled hot spot device

Key to Fig 1:46 1 Inlet manifold 2 Gaskets 3 Manifold stove 4 Heat shield 5 Circlip 6 Counterweight 7 Key 8 Stop pin 9 Screw 10 Thermostat spring 11 Heat control valve 12 Shaft 13 Exhaust manifold 14 Cap 15 Bush 16 Coil spring

and come out through the crankcase connection. When air is fed to the crankcase connection, it must not come out through either of the other connections. If the valve does not function as described, it is faulty and a new valve must be fitted, no repairs being possible. If the valve is satisfactory and fuel starvation problems persist, check the vent and fuel supply hoses for blockages and repair or renew any faulty sections.

Throttle opening control system:

The layout of this system is shown in **FIG 1:45**. Carburetter and distributor modifications plus a throttle opening device are incorporated. The throttle opener operates to open the carburetter throttle valve slightly when the car is coasting. During deceleration, manifold vacuum rises and, as the small intake charge is not enough to allow normal combustion, a large amount of unburnt gas is emitted. The throttle opening device prevents this happening by ensuring that a sufficient charge is delivered to the cylinders under these conditions, allowing normal combustion to continue. This reduces the exhaust emissions to a minimum.

Immediately the manifold vacuum decreases, as when decelerating, the control valve opens to transfer manifold vacuum to the servo diaphragm chamber and the carburetter throttle valve opens slightly. As the car speed decreases, the manifold vacuum decreases and the control valve closes gradually to maintain a constant effect. As a result, emission control is effected while engine braking action is unaltered.

Controlled hot spot:

This device is shown in the two sectional diagrams of **FIG 1:46** and operates to ensure that the fuel/air mixture in the inlet manifold is heated by the exhaust gases when the engine is cold.

When starting from cold, the counterweight 6 and thermostat spring 10 combine to hold the valve plate 11 in the closed position, this diverts the exhaust flow as shown by the solid arrows and results in the manifold stove 3 being heated and so warm up the fuel mixture.

As the temperature around the coil spring rises so the spring uncoils and moves the weighted valve plate to the open position. The exhaust now passes directly down the exhaust pipe as shown by the broken arrow lines and no heating is applied.

No servicing to the device is possible and it must be renewed if faulty.

Air injection systems:

These are systems whereby air is injected into each exhaust port in order to reduce carbon monoxide and hydrocarbons in the exhaust through a recombustion process. The most sophisticated system is fitted to California models and is shown in **FIG 1:47**; other models are similar but do not include the air valve control 6 and the emergency air relief valve 10.

The only items suitable for home servicing are the air cleaner, in which the viscous paper element requires periodic replacement, and the air pump driving belt. The tension of the belt is correct when thumb pressure in the

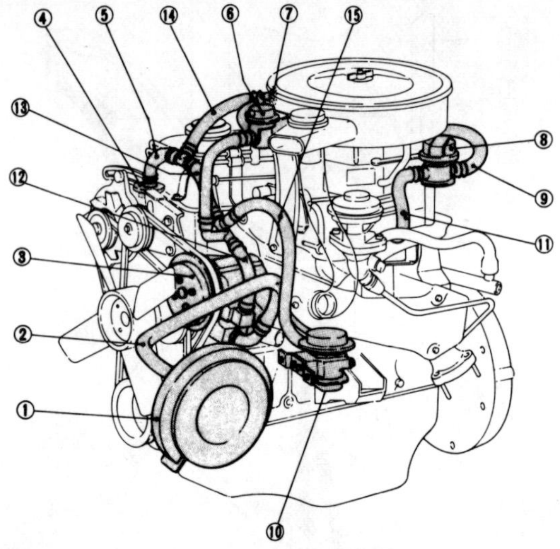

FIG 1:47 Components of the air injection system (California type)

Key to Fig 1:47 1 Pump air cleaner 2 Hose to pump 3 Air pump 4 Check valve 5 Hose to connector 6 Air control valve 7 Air relief valve 8 Anti-backfire valve 9 Hose to air cleaner 10 Emergency air relief valve 11 Air hose to inlet manifold 12 Hose, pump to connector 13 Hose 14 Hose to air relief valve 15 Hose

centre of the top run produces a deflection of $\frac{1}{3}$ to $\frac{1}{2}$ inch. Adjustment is by means of an adjusting bolt above the idler pulley wheel.

Exhaust gas recirculation system:

In this system a metered amount of exhaust gas is returned to the engine combustion chambers, via the inlet manifold, in order to reduce combustion temperatures and so the quantity of nitrogen oxide in the exhaust gases.

On all cars, except those for California and Canada, a warning system is also included whereby a counter, mounted at the front of the engine compartment, registers every $\frac{1}{4}$ mile and at 50,000 units (12,500 miles or 20,000 km) illuminates a warning lamp on the instrument panel. This indicates that the system should be inspected. Note that this warning lamp also comes on when the ignition switch is turned to START, but goes out if the specified distance has not been covered.

If it is not convenient to take the car to a service station the EGR control valve can be cleaned as follows:

Remove the vacuum hose between the EGR valve and the thermal vacuum valve by flattening the clip and pulling the hose off its union and then unscrew the two valve mounting nuts.

Use a wire brush to clean deposits from the seating surface and around the valve and port.

The valve can be tested by applying suction to the port and observing the valve. It should move over its full range and remain open for 30 seconds at least after the suction has ceased.

After inspection and refitting of any part of the system removed the counter unit must be reset to zero.

Catalytic converter:

This unit is fitted in the front exhaust pipe and has the effect of changing the hydrocarbons and carbon monoxide in the exhaust gases into non-toxic carbon dioxide and water. It is fitted only to California models.

The manufacturers recommend a CO test to determine whether the converter is functioning normally and if the percentage is over .3% the converter should be renewed.

Floor temperature warning:

A switch, operating at temperatures above 135°C (275°F), is fitted on the floor above the exhaust pipe to give warning of excessive heat from the exhaust pipe by illuminating a lamp on the instrument panel. Such overheating is likely to be caused by severe driving conditions or a malfunction in the engine.

Servicing:

Due to the need for special tools and test equipment to check and repair the system, all work on the exhaust emission control system should be entrusted to a fully equipped service station.

1:13 Fault diagnosis

(a) Engine will not start

1 Defective coil
2 Faulty distributor capacitor
3 Dirty, pitted or incorrectly set contact points
4 Ignition wires loose or insulation faulty
5 Water on sparking plug leads
6 Battery discharged, corrosion of terminals
7 Faulty or jammed starter
8 Sparking plug leads wrongly connected
9 Vapour lock in fuel pipes
10 Defective fuel pump
11 Overchoking or underchoking
12 Blocked fuel filter or carburetter jets
13 Leaking valves
14 Sticking valves
15 Valve timing incorrect
16 Ignition timing incorrect

(b) Engine stalls

1 Check 1, 2, 3, 4, 5, 10, 11, 12, 13 and 14 in (a)
2 Sparking plugs defective or gaps incorrect
3 Retarded ignition
4 Mixture too weak
5 Water in fuel system
6 Petrol tank vent blocked
7 Incorrect valve clearances

(c) Engine idles badly

1 Check 2 and 7 in (b)
2 Air leak at manifold joints
3 Carburetter adjustment wrong
4 Air leak in carburetter
5 Overrich mixture
6 Worn piston rings
7 Worn valve stems or guides
8 Weak exhaust valve springs

(d) Engine misfires

1 Check 1, 2, 3, 4, 5, 8, 10, 12, 13, 14, 15 and 16 in (a)
2 Weak or broken valve springs

(e) Engine overheats (see Chapter 4)

(f) Compression low

1 Check 13 and 14 in (a); 6 and 7 in (b) and 2 in (d)
2 Worn piston ring grooves
3 Scored or worn cylinder bores

(g) Engine lacks power

1 Check 3, 10, 11, 12, 13, 14, 15 and 16 in (a); 2, 3, 4 and 7 in (b); 6 and 7 in (c) and 2 in (d). Also check (e) and (f)
2 Leaking joint washers
3 Fouled sparking plugs
4 Automatic advance not working

(h) Burnt valves or seats

1 Check 13 and 14 in (a); 7 in (b) and 2 in (d). Also check (e)
2 Excessive carbon around valve seats and head

(j) Sticking valves

1 Check 2 in (d)
2 Bent valve stem
3 Scored valve stem or guide
4 Incorrect valve clearances

(k) Excessive cylinder wear

1 Check 11 in (a)
2 Lack of oil
3 Dirty oil
4 Piston rings gummed up or broken
5 Badly fitting piston rings
6 Connecting rod bent

(l) Excessive oil consumption

1 Check 6 and 7 in (c) and check (k)
2 Ring gaps too wide
3 Oil return holes in pistons choked with carbon
4 Scored cylinders
5 Oil level too high
6 External oil leaks

(m) Crankshaft and connecting rod bearing failure

1 Check 2 in (k)
2 Restricted oilways
3 Worn journals or crankpins
4 Loose bearing caps
5 Extremely low oil pressure
6 Bent connecting rod

(n) Internal water leakage (see Chapter 4)

(o) Poor water circulation (see Chapter 4)

(p) Corrosion (see Chapter 4)

(q) High fuel consumption (see Chapter 2)

(r) Engine vibration

1 Loose alternator bolts
2 Engine mountings loose or defective
3 Misfiring due to mixture, ignition or mechanical faults

NOTES

CHAPTER 2

THE FUEL SYSTEM

2:1 Description

A mechanical fuel pump is fitted, operated by a rocker arm which bears on an eccentric on the camshaft, from which the drive is taken. A renewable cartridge type fuel filter is housed in a transparent container for ease of inspection

A Hitachi dual-barrel carburetter is fitted, this being a single unit incorporating two separate intake systems. The primary system is used for normal running and the secondary system is used additionally for full load running, giving a small intake bore for economy at low and cruising speeds and a large intake bore for high power outputs when needed. Both primary and secondary throttle valves are operated from the accelerator linkage, as is the accelerator pump which operates to richen the mixture during sudden acceleration. A single float chamber assembly supplies fuel to both primary and secondary systems. In addition, a vacuum operated power valve mechanism is employed, to improve high-speed performance on the larger engines only.

In order that the operation of these vehicles shall comply with increasingly stringent legislation in certain areas, a number of additions or modifications to the standard production have been incorporated. Some of these are described in the second part of this chapter, even though no home servicing may be possible or recommended.

2:2 Air cleaner

A viscous paper cartridge type air cleaner is fitted, housed in a pressed steel container mounted on the carburetter intake. Filter elements must be renewed at 24,000 mile intervals, no cleaning or servicing being required between these intervals. Never attempt to clean the filter element by brushing or air-blasting.

The element is removed for replacement by taking off the air cleaner cover and lifting out the element, as shown in **FIG 2:1**. Locate the new element in position after wiping the inside of the housing clean, then refit the cover. Check the cover seal for good condition.

2:3 Fuel filter

The cartridge type fuel filter is mounted in the engine compartment as shown in **FIG 2:2**. The filtering element may be either a fibre mat or a paper screen and in either case the condition of the filter can be observed through the casing.

The filter should be removed and a new unit fitted at intervals of 12,000 miles (20,000 km) or earlier, if inspection shows excessive deposits inside the filter housing.

Taking suitable steps to deal with fuel running out, pull off the two supply hoses from their unions (see **FIG 2:3**) and remove the complete filter unit.

Fit a new unit in the reverse order.

FIG 2:1 Removing the air cleaner filter element

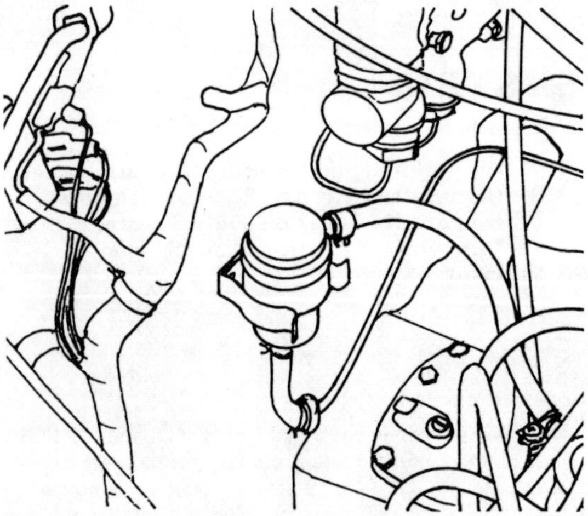

FIG 2:2 The fuel filter assembly

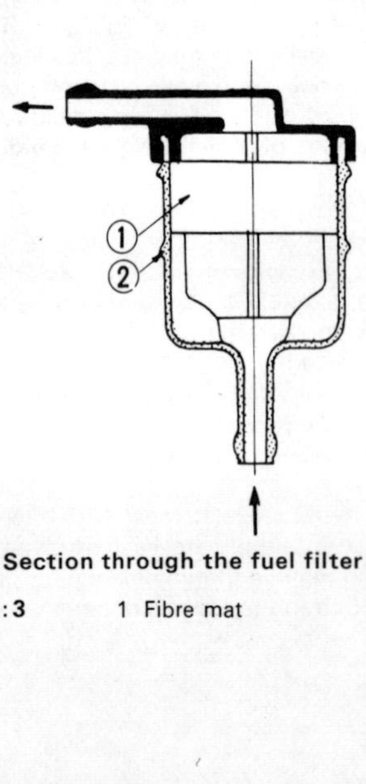

FIG 2:3 Section through the fuel filter assembly

Key to Fig 2:3 1 Fibre mat 2 Nylon case

2:4 Fuel pump

Testing:

Before testing the pump ensure that the fuel tank vent system is not blocked. If it is suspected that fuel is not reaching the carburetter, disconnect the carburetter fuel feed pipe and hold a suitable container under the end of the pipe. Turn the engine over a few times with the starter and watch for fuel squirting from the pipe, which indicates that the pump is working. If so, check that the float needle valve in the carburetter is not sticking, as this would prevent fuel from entering the carburetter float chamber. If a good supply of fuel is available from the pump and the carburetter needle valve is working properly, suspect blocked carburetter jets or passages as the cause of fuel starvation. Refer to **Section 2:7** for details of carburetter dismantling and cleaning.

Reduced fuel flow from the pump can be caused by blocked fuel pipes or a clogged filter. Check the filter element which can be seen through the transparent bowl and, if it appears clogged, renew it as described in **Section 2:3**. If an obstructed pipeline is suspected, it may be cleared with compressed air. Disconnect the pipeline at the pump and carburetter. **Do not pass compressed air through the pump or the valves will be damaged.** If there is an obstruction between the pump and the tank, remove the tank filler cap before blowing through from the pump end of the pipe. On cars fitted with emission control equipment, disconnect the pipes from the flow guide valve, referring to **Chapter 1, Section 1:12.**

If the pump delivers insufficient fuel, suspect an air leak between the pump and the fuel tank, dirt under the pump valves or faulty valve seatings. If no fuel is delivered, suspect a faulty pump diaphragm. **FIG 2:4** shows the flow through the pump.

Removal:

Unscrew the two mounting nuts and withdraw the pump from the engine block, collecting the gasket. Refitting is carried out in the reverse order, making sure that the mating flanges are clean and using a new flange gasket.

Dismantling:

FIG 2:5 shows the components of the fuel pump. Remove the screw and lift off the cap and gasket. Take out the setscrews and separate the pump upper and lower parts. Unscrew the elbow and the connector.

Remove the two screws and take off the valve retainer, after which the valve assemblies can be removed. Note the locations of the parts for correct refitting. To remove the diaphragm, spring and lower body seal and washer, refer to **FIG 2:6** and press the diaphragm down against the spring and tilt it to unhook from the rocker arm link. Support the pump body to prevent damage, then drive out the rocker arm pivot pin with a hammer and drift, then take out the rocker arm.

Servicing:

Wash all parts in clean fuel. Check the upper and lower halves of the pump body for cracks and other damage. Check the diaphragm for small holes, tears or stretching. Renew the diaphragm if its condition is at all suspect.

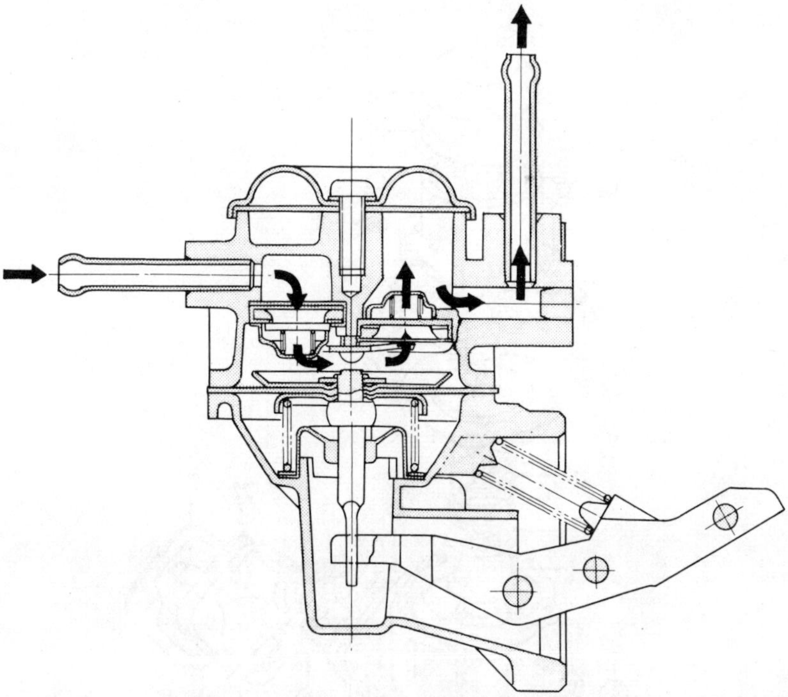

FIG 2:4 Fuel flow through the fuel pump valves

Examine the rocker arm for wear at the point where it contacts the cam. Check the rocker arm pin for wear, as a loose fitting pin can be the cause of oil leaks around the pump unit.

Make sure that the valves are in good condition and that their seats are smooth and free from dirt, then refit the valve assemblies to the pump upper part. Test valve operation by blowing and sucking at the inlet and outlet points. It should be possible to blow air in through the pump inlet but not to suck air out, and it should be possible to suck air out of the pump outlet but not to blow air in. If the valves do not work properly according to this test, fit new valve components, or, if the seats in the pump body are defective, fit a new pump upper part complete.

Renew any pump component which is found defective when examined.

Reassembly:

This is carried out in the reverse order of dismantling, noting the following points. Always use new gaskets throughout. Lubricate the rocker arm link, rocker arm pin and the lever pin before refitting these parts. Operate the rocker arm a few times before finally tightening the screws which hold the upper and lower body parts together, to settle the diaphragm.

The pump can be tested after reassembly by attaching a suitable length of tubing to the inlet and holding the pump about 1 metre (3.3 feet) above a container of fuel. Immerse the free end of the tubing into the fuel and operate the rocker arm by hand. If the pump will, under these conditions, draw fuel up the tube and deliver it from the outlet hole, the operation of the pump is satisfactory.

2:5 The carburetter

The carburetter on each engine is a dual barrel instrument with differential opening of the two throttles. The types fitted to the different engines are very similar apart from jet sizes and the fitting to the larger capacity units of a power valve. This latter is an extra fuel jet, brought into operation only at wide throttle openings by the depression in the inlet duct below the throttles, which passes an additional supply of fuel to the main nozzle in the venturi at times of full load or acceleration. Emission control additions are described in **Section 2:8**.

Removal:

Take off the air cleaner cover, lift out the filter element and remove the air cleaner assembly from the carburetter. Disconnect the fuel line, vacuum line and choke control wire from the carburetter. Remove the throttle lever. Undo the four nuts and washers retaining the carburetter and lift it from the inlet manifold. Remove and discard the carburetter flange gasket.

Refitting:

This is the reverse of the removal procedure, using a new flange gasket.

2:6 Carburetter adjustments

The slow-running adjustments described in this Section should be carried out after any carburetter, ignition system or valve clearance adjustments or servicing have been made, or at any time if engine idling is rough or at too

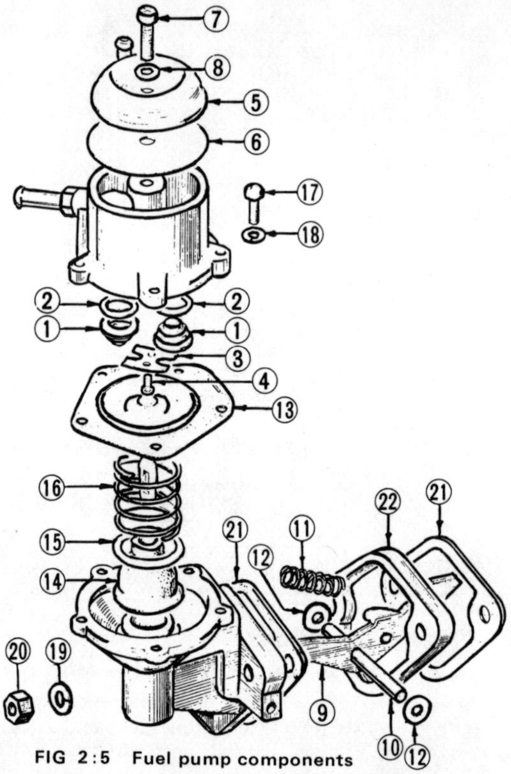

FIG 2:5 Fuel pump components

Key to Fig 2:5 1 Valve assembly 2 Packing 3 Retainer 4 Screw 5 Cap 6 Gasket 7 Screw 8 Washer 9 Rocker arm 10 Rocker pin 11 Rocker arm spring 12 Spacer 13 Diaphragm assembly 14 Oil seal 15 Retainer 16 Diaphragm spring 17 Screw 18 Washer 19 Washer 20 Nut 21 Packing 22 Spacer

high a speed. It must be pointed out, however, that these adjustments will only be effective if the sparking plugs and ignition system are in good order, and that the engine must be at normal operating temperature when they are carried out.

The remaining instructions for checks and adjustments are not routine maintenance, but should be carried out if poor performance has been traced to the carburetter and after any major carburetter servicing has been carried out.

Idle speed setting:

Idle speed settings are made by turning the adjustment screws shown in **FIG 2:7** while the engine is running. Make sure that the engine has been run sufficiently to attain normal running temperature, then tighten the throttle adjustment screw to obtain a fast-idle. When this is achieved, adjust the idle adjustment screw to obtain the fastest possible idle without further adjustment to the throttle screw. Now loosen the throttle adjustment screw

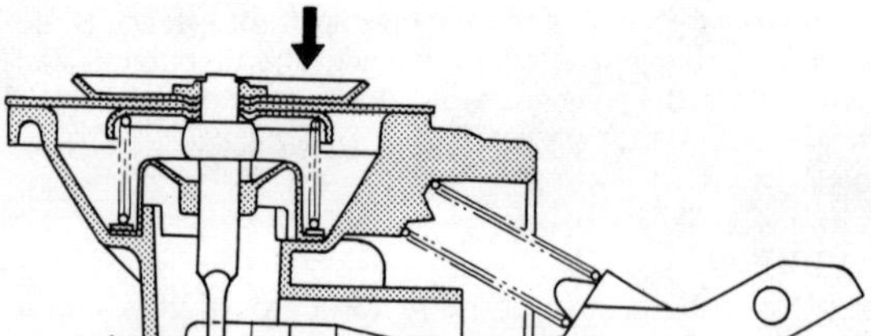

FIG 2:6 Removing the pump diaphragm

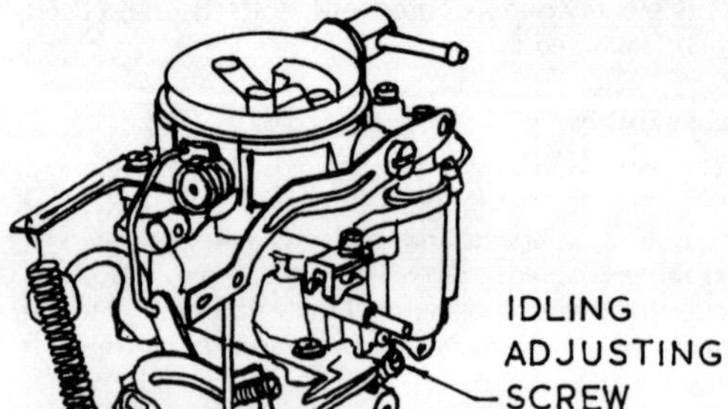

FIG 2:7 The carburetter adjustment screws

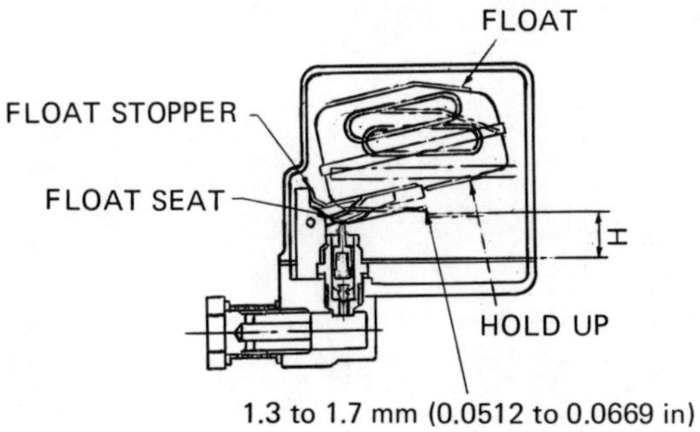

FIG 2:8 Adjusting the float level

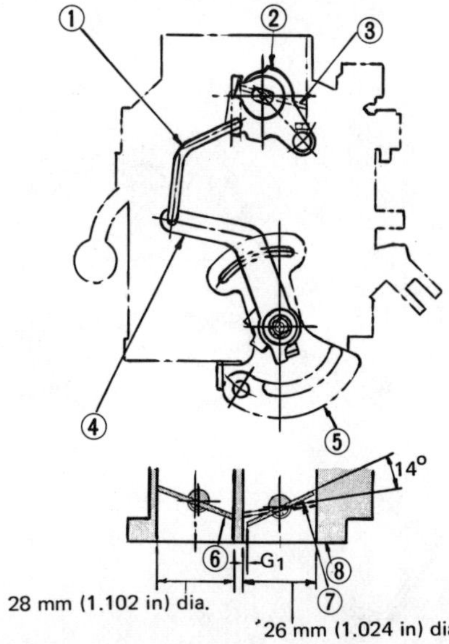

FIG 2:9 Measuring starting interlock valve opening

Key to Fig 2:9 1 Secondary connecting lever 2 Choke lever 3 Choke valve 4 Choke connecting lever 5 Throttle lever 6 Secondary throttle valve 7 Primary throttle valve 8 Throttle chamber

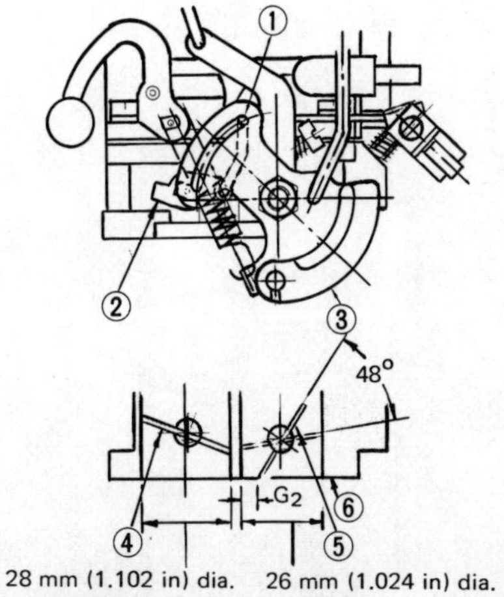

FIG 2:10 Adjusting the throttle valve interlock opening

Key to Fig 2:10 1 Connecting rod 2 Secondary connecting lever 3 Throttle lever 4 Secondary throttle valve 5 Primary throttle valve 6 Throttle chamber

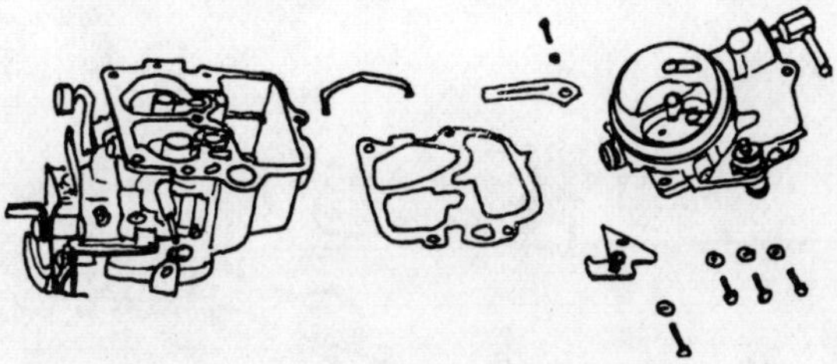

FIG 2:11 Removing the choke chamber

to drop the engine speed to about 600 rev/min. Repeat the operation as necessary to obtain a smooth, slow idle. **Never fully tighten the idle adjustment screw.** If this is done, the fine tapered needle at the end of the screw may be damaged and precise adjustment becomes impossible.

Fuel level adjustment:

Refer to **FIG 2:8**. Invert the float chamber assembly and check the measurement **H** as shown, with the float resting on the needle valve under its own weight. This measurement should be 12 mm (.472 inch) on 1200 models or 10·5 mm (.413 inch) on 1000 models. To correct the measurement if necessary, carefully bend the float seat. This operation will correctly set the float upper position, which governs the fuel level in the float chamber. If the level is too high, flooding may occur, accompanied by excessive fuel consumption. If the level is too low, a weak mixture may occur, giving poor idling and acceleration.

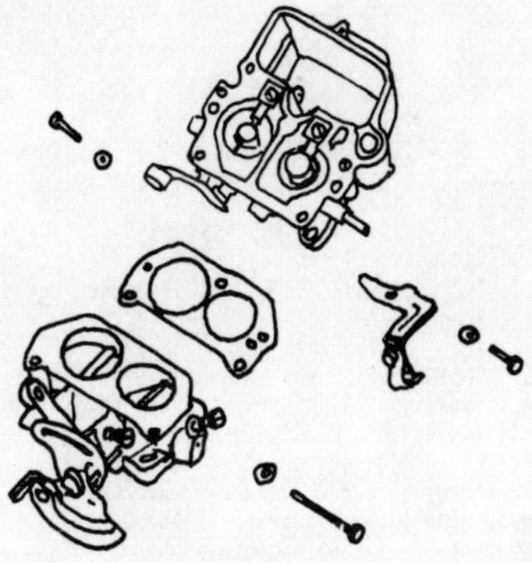

FIG 2:12 Removing the throttle chamber

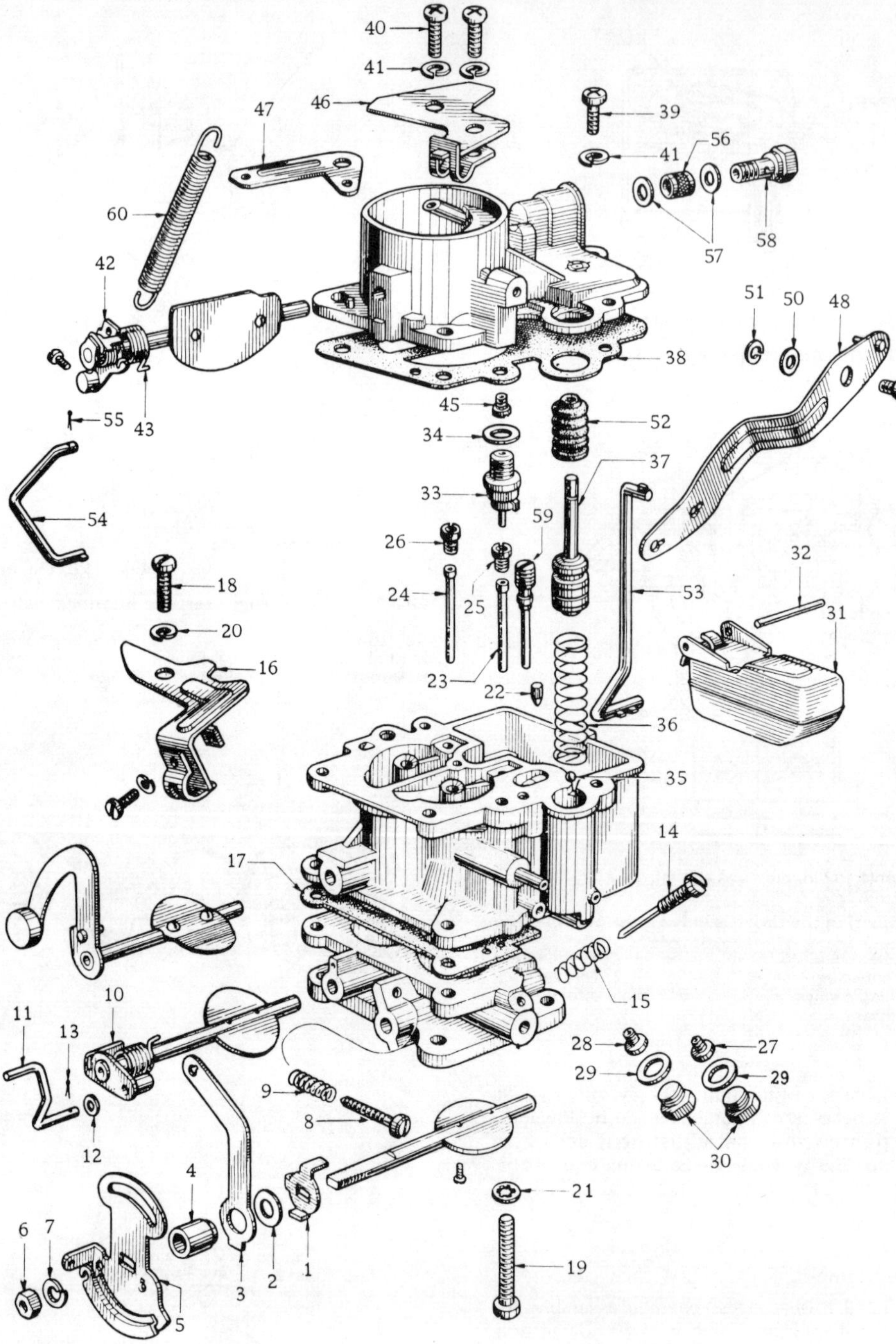

FIG 2:13 Components of the carburetter. Type DCG286 for 988 cc engines

Key to Fig 2:13 1 Throttle adjusting plate 2 Washer 3 Starting lever 4 Sleeve 5 Throttle lever 6 Nut 7 Spring washer 8 Throttle adjusting screw 9 Spring 10 Throttle return spring 11 Connecting rod 12 Washer 13 Splitpin 14 Idle mixture screw 15 Spring 16 Clamp plate 17 Gasket 18 Screw 19 Screw 20 Spring washer 21 Washer 22 Check valve weight 23 Emulsion tube (P) 24 Emulsion tube (S) 25 Slow air bleed (P) 26 Slow air bleed (S) 27 Main jet (P) 28 Main jet (S) 29 Washer 30 Drain plug 31 Float 32 Float pivot 33 Needle valve 34 Washer 35 Ball 36 Spring 37 Piston 38 Gasket 39 Screw 40 Screw 41 Spring washer 42 Choke lever 43 Choke return spring 45 Idle air bleed 46 Clamp plate 47 Return spring bracket 48 Pump lever 49 Pivot 50 Washer 51 Spring washer 52 Pump cover 53 Pump rod 54 Choke connecting rod 55 Splitpin 56 Filter 57 Spacers 58 Union bolt 59 Idle jet 60 Throttle return spring

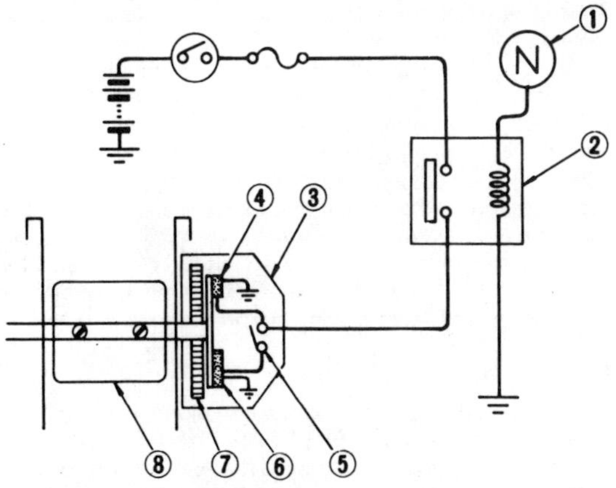

FIG 2:14 Schematic diagram showing the operation of the electric automatic choke

Key to Fig 2:14 1 Alternator 2 Automatic choke relay 3 Cover 4 Heater 5 Bi-metal switch 6 Heater 7 Bi-metal spring 8 Choke plate

When the float upper position is correct as described, adjust the float lower position. To do this, hold up the float as shown and check that the distance between the float seat and the needle valve is within the stated measurements. If not, correct by carefully bending the float stopper.

Starting interlock valve setting:

Refer to **FIG 2:9**. Fully close the choke valve and measure the clearance between the primary side throttle valve and the interior of the throttle chamber. The clearance **G1** should be 1.22 mm (.0480 inch), which will give a correct angle of 14 deg. at the valve. If adjustment is required, carefully bend the choke connecting rod until the clearance is as stated.

Throttle valve interlock adjustment:

Refer to **FIG 2:10**. Open the primary throttle valve 48 deg. from the fully closed position. Make sure that the linkage is positioned as shown, then measure the clearance **G2** between the primary side throttle valve and the interior of the throttle chamber. The clearance should be 5.83 mm (.2295 inch). If adjustment is required, carefully bend the connecting rod until the setting is as stated.

2:7 Dismantling and servicing the carburetter

Dismantling:

As parts are removed from the carburetter, note their respective positions to ensure correct refitting. In particular, care must be taken not to mix the parts of the primary and secondary barrels. Jet sizes and carburetter settings are given in **Technical Data** in the **Appendix.** Clean the outside of the carburetter thoroughly before dismantling to prevent external dirt from entering the jets and passages.

Remove the main jets and needle valves from both primary and secondary barrels, then remove the primary and secondary emulsion tubes by removing the main air bleeds on the respective sides. All of these components are accessible from the carburetter exterior. To check the

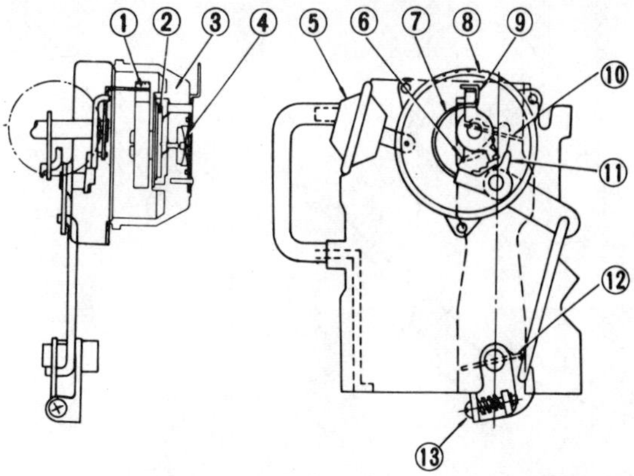

FIG 2:15 Sectional diagrams showing the construction of the automatic choke

Key to Fig 2:15 1 Bi-metal spring 2 Heater 3 Cover 4 Bi-metal switch 5 Vacuum diaphragm 6 Fast-idle cam 7 Bi-metal spring 8 Index mark 9 Choke shaft lever 10 Choke plate 11 Unloader tag 12 Throttle plate 13 Fast-idle screw

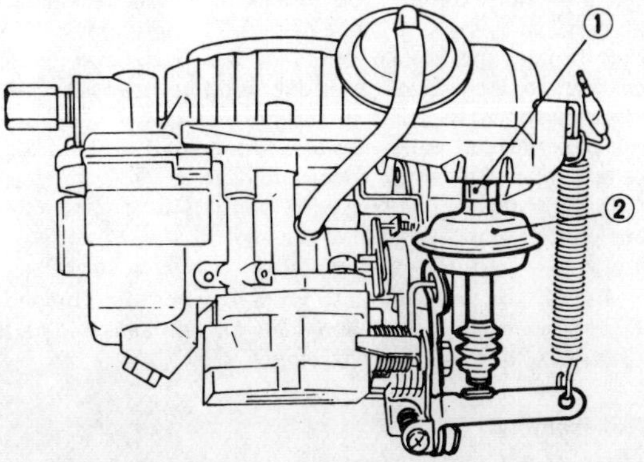

FIG 2:16 Adjusting the throttle dash pot

Key to Fig 2:16 1 Locknut 2 Dash pot body

accelerator pump, remove the cover and remove the spring and inlet valve ball and the piston assembly.

Take out the fixing screws and remove the choke connecting rod, and pump lever, then detach the choke chamber from the carburetter body as shown in **FIG 2:11**. Remove the gasket. Remove the three setscrews and detach the throttle chamber from the carburetter body as shown in **FIG 2:12**. Do not disturb the throttle valves or shafts unless it is necessary to renew faulty components. If these parts are dismantled, make certain that the secondary throttle is installed gap-free when refitted to the body, otherwise engine idle and low-speed performance will be poor.

Remove the remaining internal parts from the carburetter, shown in **FIG 2:13**.

Servicing:

Wash all parts of the carburetter in clean petrol. Clean out all sediment from the float chamber, jets and passages using compressed air, clean petrol and a small, stiff brush. **Do not use cloth or a wire probe.**

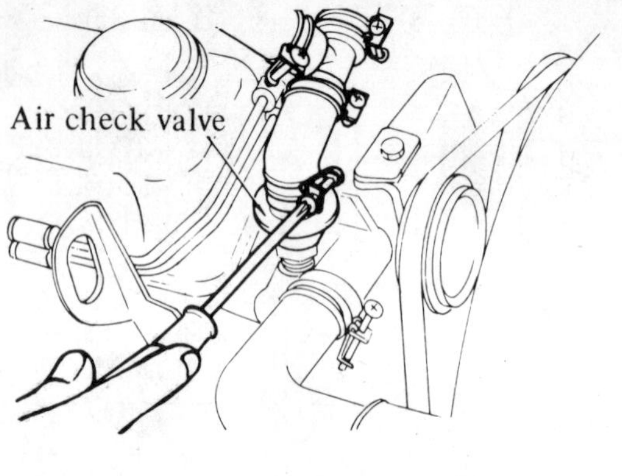

FIG 2:17 Showing the location of the aircheck valve and disconnecting the hose

Check the float needle valve assembly. If there is a noticeable ridge on the tapered seat of the needle, or if the needle has any tendency to stick in the housing, the assembly must be renewed. Check the float for leaks or damage and renew it if not in perfect condition. Check the throttle and choke bores in the body and cover castings for wear or out of round conditions. Inspect the idle adjustment needles for burrs or ridges. Check that the filter is clean, renewing if it is damaged or distorted, or if it will not clean up successfully.

Fill the float chamber with petrol and operate the acclerator pump by hand. Make sure that a strong jet of fuel is delivered from the pump nozzle at each stroke.

Renew any parts found to be defective during inspection. Discard all gaskets and seals and obtain new parts to replace them during reassembly.

Reassembly:

This is the reverse of the dismantling procedure, using new gaskets throughout. Make sure that all operating linkages are correctly fitted and that they operate smoothly, with no tendency to stick or bind. Carry out the carburetter adjustments described in **Section 2:6**. After the carburetter has been refitted, carry out the idle speed adjustments, opening the idle adjusting screw about three turns from the fully closed position to get a basic setting to allow the engine to run.

2:8 Carburetter fitted to EC equipped cars

The carburetter fitted to vehicles operating in strictly controlled areas is of a similar basic type to that already described, but has a number of additional devices and a different procedure is required for setting the idle speed and mixture.

The throttle opener system described in **Chapter 1** is included, and also a dash pot system. This is designed to prevent the engine from stalling when the accelerator pedal is suddenly released by reducing the speed at which the throttle closes.

An addition to the system shown in **FIG 1:45** is a speed controlled valve. This opens the servo diaphragm to atmosphere when the road speed drops below 10 mile/hr and permits the throttle to close normally. These conditions also apply when an automatic transmission is in N or P position.

An 'anti-dieseling' solenoid valve prevents the engine from 'running-on' after the ignition is switched off. This is achieved by shutting off the fuel completely in the carburetter idling system.

An electric choke is employed by means of which the fuel supply is automatically enriched according to the engine and ambient temperatures.

On vehicles for California an altitude compensator may be fitted, whereby the air/fuel mixture ratio is adjusted according to barometric pressure.

Electric choke:

The operation of the automatic choke can be described with reference to **FIG 2:14**.

Before starting the engine, full depression of the accelerator pedal will ensure that the choke plate closes properly.

If the ambient temperature is low, an electric current flows through the relay 2, located on a front wheel arch under the bonnet, to the heater 4. This warms up the bi-metal spring 7 slowly and gradually causes the choke plate 8 to open.

If the temperature is high, the bi-metal switch 5 will be ON and both heaters 4 and 6 will be energised and the choke will open quickly.

The construction of the electric choke assembly is shown in **FIG 2:15**.

In addition to the opening of the choke plate in accordance with the under-bonnet temperature, a fast-idle cam 6 determines the opening of the throttle plate 12 so that the correct amount of mixture is delivered to the engine corresponding to the choking effect applied.

An unloader 11 causes the choke to open if the engine is accelerated while cold and prevents strangulation at this time.

The vacuum diaphragm 5 is fitted in order to open the choke to the pre-determined extent once the engine has been started.

No maintenance or adjustment is required for this system and it is suggested that the home operator should

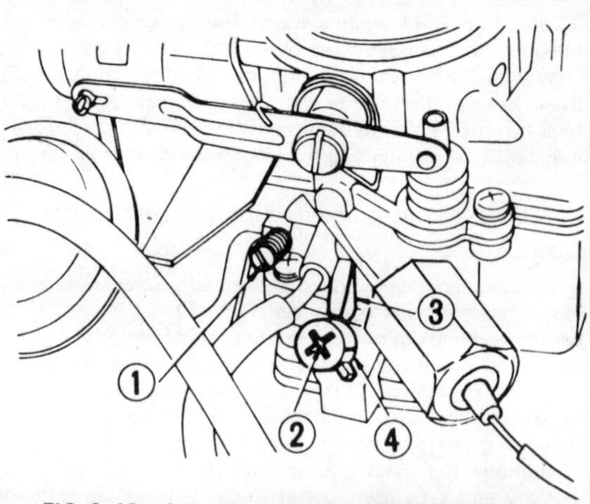

FIG 2:18 Adjusting the idle speed and mixture

Key to Fig 2:18 1 Throttle (speed) adjusting screw 2 Idle mixture screw 3 Stop 4 Idle limiter cap

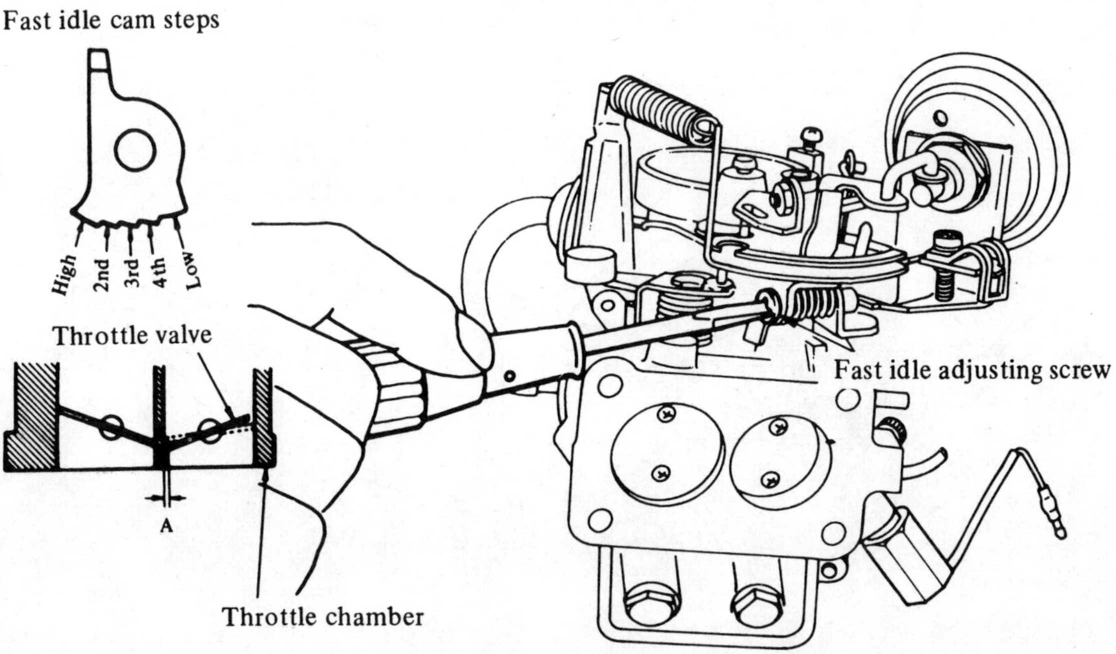

FIG 2:19 Adjusting the fast-idle speed. See text for dimension A

confine himself to ensuring that the moving parts are clean and free to move as required. The index mark on the bi-metal cover 3 must be in the centre of the choke housing index marks.

Dash pot:

It is important to ensure that this device is brought into operation at the correct engine speed and adjustment for this is as follows:

Ensure that the idle speed and mixture are correctly set and that the engine is fully warmed up. Refer to **FIG 2:16**.

Open the throttle and note the engine speed when on closing the throttle the dash pot spindle just touches the lever arm. Compare this with the speed given below.

If adjustment is required, loosen the locknut and rotate the dash pot as necessary.

Automatic transmission ..	1900 to 2000 rev/min
Manual transmission	2300 to 2400 rev/min
Manual transmission (California)	1900 to 2000 rev/min

Altitude compensator:

This component, which may be fitted to California models, is mounted inside the carburetter air cleaner. It is in effect an aneroid controlled air bleed to the carburetter, designed to admit more air when operating at higher altitudes when the lower density of air causes an excessively rich mixture. It is designed to come into operation above approximately 2000 ft (600 m).

No adjustments are possible, but the following information may be of assistance to check for correct operation.

Low altitudes:

If mouth suction or blowing at the inlet and outlet hoses allows free passage of air, the unit is faulty and must be renewed.

Possible symptoms are:

Hesitation or slow response to throttle movements. Surging in the middle speed range.

High altitudes:

Sucking or blowing through the inlet or outlet hoses should now allow free air passage.

Possible symptoms are:

Hesitation and surging. Incorrect engine response to increasing throttle opening. Poor acceleration. Smooth engine running varies according to altitude.

Float level:

The instructions for setting the float level are the same as those given in **Section 2:6**, but the dimension H is 15 mm (.59 inch) for the two larger engines in the range covered in this manual.

Adjusting the idle:

Before commencing this operation, warm the engine thoroughly and connect a reliable tachometer and CO meter according to the makers' instructions.

On automatic transmission models the selector must be in D position and the road wheels securely chocked.

Check the ignition timing. 10 deg. BTDC at 700 rev/min for manual transmissions, 10 deg. BTDC at 650 rev/

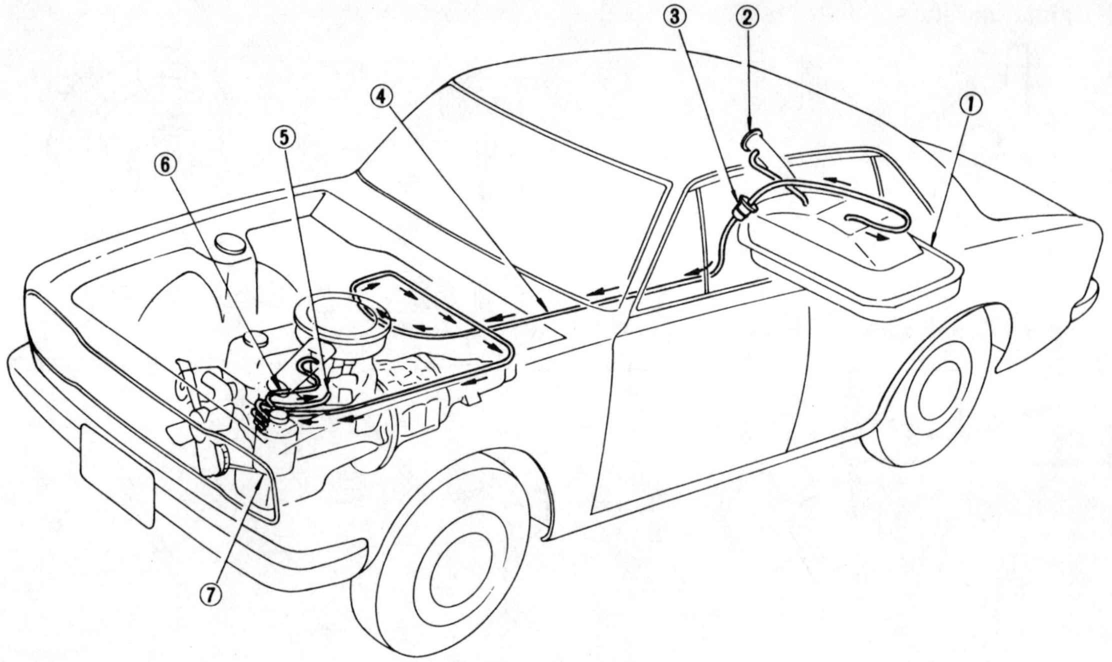

FIG 2:20 Layout of later type evaporative emission control system

Key to Fig 2:20 1 Fuel tank 2 Filler cap with vacuum relief valve 3 Fuel check valve 4 Vapour vent line 5 Canister purge line 6 Vacuum signal line 7 Charcoal canister

min for automatics (8 deg. BTDC in California).

Refer to **FIG 2:17** and disconnect the air hose from the air check valve and fit a cap on the valve port.

Refer to **FIG 2:18** and use the throttle adjusting screw 1 to obtain the idle speed specified above. Now adjust the idle mixture screw to obtain the specified CO content of 2 ± 1%.

Race the engine a few times and recheck the CO meter reading, making any further adjustments as necessary.

If a CO meter is not available, an acceptable result should be obtainable by using the following method:

Prepare and proceed as before, setting the idle speed to the specified figures of 765 rev/min for manual or 670 rev/min for automatic transmissions. Use the idle mixture screw 2 to obtain the fastest engine speed possible.

Speed up the engine a few times, let it idle and repeat the last procedures until the maximum engine speed obtained is 765 or 670 rev/min as appropriate.

Now carefully turn the idle mixture screw clockwise until the speed drops off by 60 to 70 rev/min for manual or 15 to 25 rev/min for automatic transmissions. If the idle limiter cap interferes with proper adjustment, it may be removed but must be replaced, preferably while checking the CO percentage with a meter. Its installed position should leave it with $\frac{1}{8}$ turn available in 'CO-rich' (anticlockwise) direction.

Remove the cap on the air check valve and if the engine speed increases, reduce it to the specified rate with the throttle adjusting screw 1.

Fast-idle adjustment:

Remove the cover over the bi-metal spring mechanism and move the fast-idle arm on the second step of the fast-idle cam (see **FIG 2:19**).

Adjust the fast-idle screw as shown so that the gap A between the throttle plate and its bore is according to the table below.

	Gap A in inches (mm)	*Engine speed (rev/min)*
Automatic transmission	.042 to .046 (1.07 to 1.17)	2800 ± 100
Manual transmission	.031 to .035 (.80 to .88)	2550 ± 100

2:9 Evaporative emission control system

In certain territories the sealed fuel tank system described in **Chapter 1** is further modified as shown in **FIG 2:20**. A fuel check valve 3 may be fitted in place of the liquid/vapour separator tank and a canister filled with charcoal is included in the pipe between the fuel tank and the carburetter.

Fuel vapours from the sealed tank are led to the canister where they are adsorbed by the charcoal. When the engine is started, the vacuum in the inlet manifold opens a valve in the canister and the adsorbed vapours are sucked into the engine for combustion.

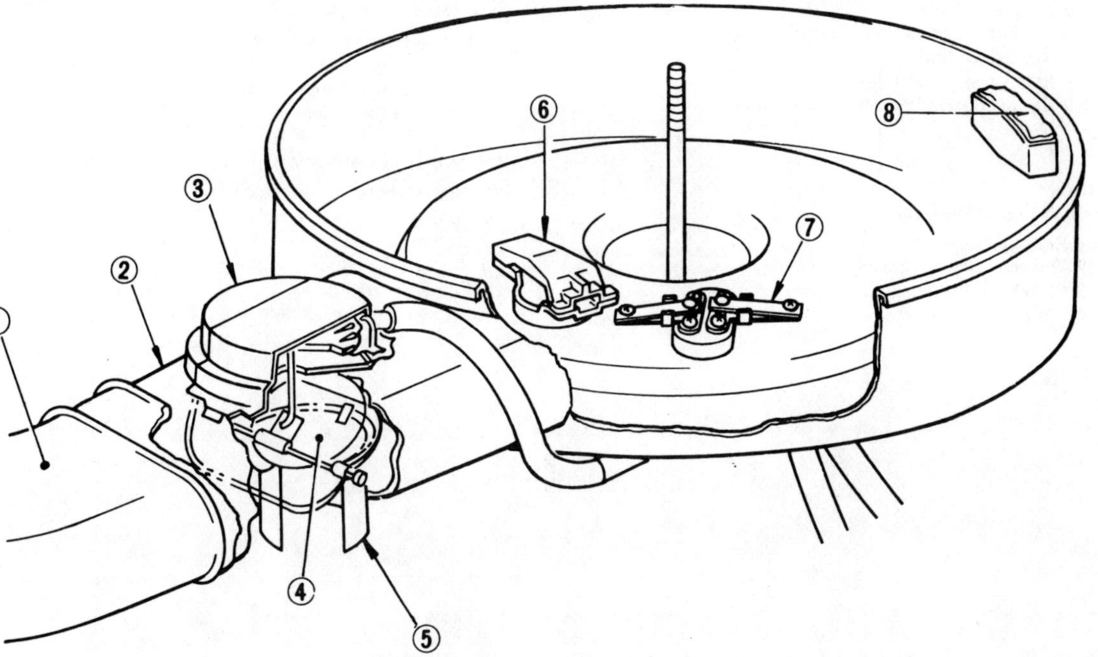

FIG 2:21 Cut-away view of the temperature controlled air cleaner

Key to Fig 2:21 1 Fresh air duct 2 Air inlet 3 Vacuum motor 4 Air control valve 5 Hot air inlet 6 Temperature sensor 7 Idle compensator 8 Blow-by gas filter

The charcoal filter element should be renewed at intervals as stated in the owner's guide. It may be easily removed from the bottom of the canister without removal from the car.

2:10 Temperature controlled air cleaner

This device is shown in **FIG 2:21** and operates as follows:

When the engine is cold the vacuum in the inlet manifold is applied by the hose shown to the vacuum motor 3 which actuates the valve 4 opening the hot air inlet 5. If, however, increased power is wanted from the engine under these conditions, the inlet vacuum is low and insufficient to open the hot air inlet and cold air is admitted to ensure maximum engine output.

When the under-bonnet temperature is high the temperature sensor 6 closes the vacuum passage to the vacuum motor and the diaphragm spring causes the valve to close the hot air pipe and to open the cold inlet 1.

Thus by selectively opening and closing the two air inlets the temperature sensor maintains an optimum temperature for the air supplied to the carburetter.

Apart from the periodic replacement of the filter element no servicing or adjustments are required, and if any of the internal units are faulty, they must be renewed. Faulty operation of the cleaner assembly is not likely to be noticed in hot weather but in cold weather the symptoms of weak mixture may be observed.

The idle compensator:

This device, shown as item 7, is in effect a thermostatic valve, designed to pass air from the air cleaner directly to the inlet manifold in order to compensate for excessively rich idling mixtures when high temperatures are experienced.

Two separate valves are included in the unit; one having an opening temperature of 60° to 70°C, the other between 70° and 80°C. No adjustments to the device are possible, but the operation of the thermostatic valves can be checked by heating them in water similarly to the thermostat in the cooling system.

2:11 Fault diagnosis

(a) Leakage or insufficient fuel delivered

1 Air vent to tank restricted
2 Fuel pipes blocked
3 Air leaks at pipe connections
4 Fuel filter blocked
5 Pump gaskets faulty
6 Pump diaphragm defective
7 Pump valve sticking or seating badly

(b) Excessive fuel consumption

1 Carburetter requires adjustment
2 Fuel leakage
3 Sticking choke control
4 Float level too high

5 Dirty air cleaner
6 Excessive engine temperature
7 Brakes binding
8 Idling speed too high
9 Car overloaded or tyres under-inflated

(c) Idling speed too high

1 Rich fuel mixture
2 Throttle control sticking
3 Choke control sticking
4 Worn throttle valves

(d) Noisy fuel pump

1 Loose pump mountings
2 Air leaks on suction side of diaphragm
3 Obstruction in fuel pipeline
4 Clogged fuel filter

(e) No fuel delivery

1 Float needle valve stuck
2 Tank vent system blocked
3 Defective pump diaphragm
4 Pump valve stuck
5 Pipeline obstructed
6 Bad air leak on suction side of pump

CHAPTER 3

THE IGNITION SYSTEM

3:1 Description

The ignition system employed on these cars is of the coil and distributor type and the standard equipment includes a conventional contact breaker type distributor. Later models, however, for California have a transistor ignition unit and distributor, thus dispensing with the wear and consequent servicing needed for the contact breaker and giving more accurate and consistent timing of the spark. The standard installation will be described first in this chapter and the main points of difference in the electronic type later (**Section 3:7**).

The conventional distributor has automatic timing control by means of centrifugal mechanism and a vacuum controlled unit. As engine speed increases, the centrifugal action of rotating weights pivoting against the tension of small springs moves the contact breaker cam relative to the distributor drive shaft and progressively advances the ignition. The vacuum unit is connected by small bore pipe to a fitting on the carburetter. At high degrees of vacuum the unit advances the ignition, but under load, at reduced vacuum, the unit progressively retards the ignition. By these means near optimum settings for different speeds and loads are achieved.

The ignition coil is of Hitachi manufacture. It is a high output type and has a series resistor incorporated. When the starter is switched on, the series resistor is disconnected and full battery voltage is fed to the coil to obtain the best possible spark at cranking speeds, but when the starter is switched off the resistor automatically functions to reduce the voltage supplied to the coil. The ignition coil and series resistor are located in the engine compartment.

3:2 Routine maintenance

Pull off the two spring clips and remove the distributor cap. Pull the rotor from the top of the distributor shaft. Apply a tiny drop of oil to the moving contact point pivot and a light smear of grease to the four-lobed cam. Avoid allowing grease or oil to contaminate the contact breaker points, lubricating sparingly for this reason.

Adjusting the contact points:

Turn the engine until one of the cams has opened the points to the fullest extent, then check the gap between the points with a clean feeler gauge as shown in **FIG 3:1**. The correct gap is .018 to .020 inch. To adjust the gap, use a screwdriver at the point shown to loosen the adjusting screw. Move the fixed contact until the gap is correct, then tighten the adjusting screw and recheck the gap.

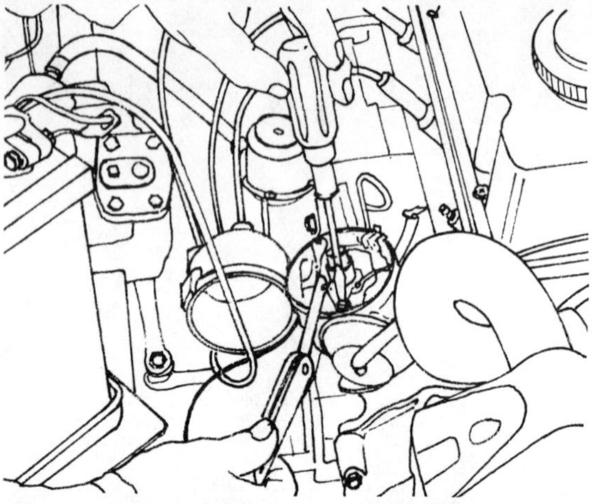

FIG 3:1 Checking the contact points gap

Cleaning the contact points:

Use a fine carborundum stone, fine emerycloth or a contact point file to polish the points if they are dirty or pitted, taking care to keep the faces flat and square. On completion, wipe away all dust with a cloth moistened in petrol. The contact points may be dismantled to assist cleaning, in the following manner, referring to **FIG 3:2**.

Unscrew the two setscrews by 1 to $1\frac{1}{2}$ turns, then remove the primary lead terminals and remove the contact points set from the distributor. Refit in the reverse order, lubricating the upper distributor parts as described previously.

If the points are badly pitted or burned and would require excessive removal of material to clean up, a new contact set should be obtained and fitted.

3:3 Ignition faults

If the engine runs unevenly, set it to idle at about 1000 rev/min and, taking care not to touch any metal part of the sparking plug leads, remove and replace each lead from its plug in turn. Doing this to a plug which is firing properly will accentuate the uneven running, but will make no difference if the plug is not firing. To avoid shocks during this test it is advisable to wear a thick glove, or to use a pair of insulated pliers to pull off the leads. **Note:** The high tension cables should not be removed from the sparking plugs while the engine is running if the distributor is the electronic type as fitted to California models.

Having located the faulty cylinder, stop the engine and remove the plug lead. Remove the plug connector from the lead so that the metal end of the lead is exposed. Start the engine and hold the lead carefully to avoid shocks so that the end of the lead is about $\frac{1}{8}$ inch away from the cylinder head. A strong, regular spark confirms that the fault lies with the sparking plug, which should be cleaned as described in **Section 3:6** or renewed if defective.

If the spark is weak and irregular, check the condition of the lead and, if it is perished or cracked, renew it and repeat the test. If no improvement results, check that the inside of the distributor cap is clean and dry and that there is no sign of 'tracking', which can be seen as a thin black line between the electrodes or to some metal part in contact with the cap. 'Tracking' can only be rectified by fitting a new cap. Check that the carbon brush in the centre of the cap is clean and that it moves freely against its spring and makes good contact on the rotor arm.

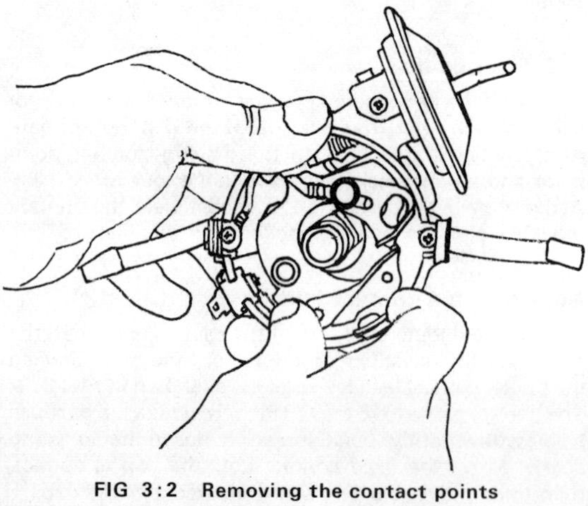

FIG 3:2 Removing the contact points

Testing the low-tension circuit:

The low-tension circuit connects the battery, ignition switch, coil primary winding and contact breaker assembly, and provides timed pulses of current to the coil primary windings as the contact points open and close. These pulses control the secondary coil winding which provides current at high voltage to the distributor, where the distributor rotor arm directs it through the high-tension leads to the sparking plugs. **FIG 3:3** shows the ignition wiring circuit.

Check that the contact breaker points are clean and correctly set. Disconnect the thin wire from the coil that connects to the distributor. Connect a 12-volt test lamp between these terminals, switch on the ignition and turn the engine slowly. If the lamp lights and goes out as the points close and open, the circuit is in order. If the lamp fails to light, there is a fault in the low-tension circuit. Remove the lamp and reconnect the wire to the coil and distributor.

If the fault lies in the low-tension circuit, use the test lamp to carry out the following tests with the ignition switched on.

Remove the wire from the ignition switch side of the coil and connect the lamp between the end of this wire and earth. If the lamp fails to light it indicates a fault in the wiring connections between the battery and the coil, or in the ignition switch. Reconnect the wire if the lamp lights.

Disconnect the wire from the coil that leads to the distributor. Connect the lamp between the coil terminal and earth. If the lamp fails to light it indicates a fault in the primary winding and a new coil must be fitted. Reconnect the wire if the lamp lights and disconnect its other end from the distributor. If the lamp does not light when connected between the end of this wire and earth it indicates a fault in that section of wire.

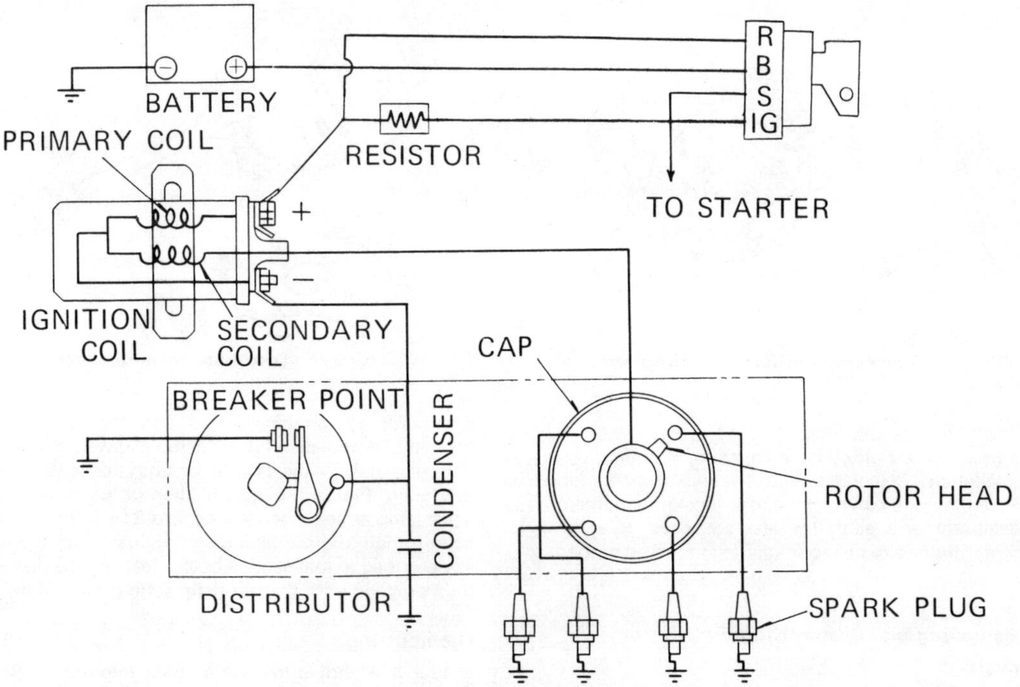

FIG 3:3 Ignition system circuit diagram

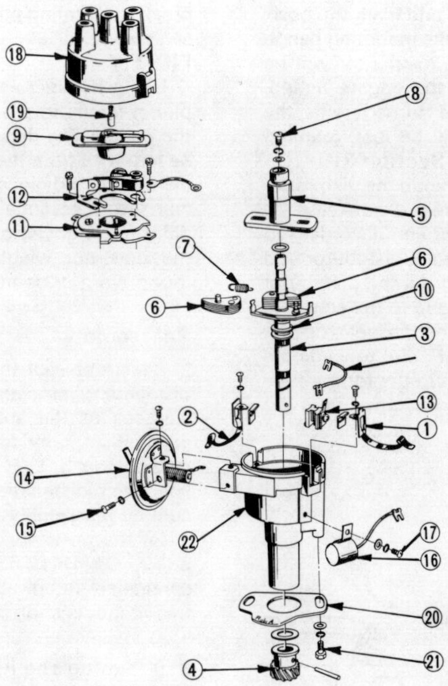

FIG 3:4 Distributor components (typical)

Key to Fig 3:4 1 Cap clip 2 Cap clip 3 Shaft 4 Pinion 5 Cam 6 Weight governor 7 Spring governor 8 Screw 9 Rotor head 10 Thrust washer 11 Breaker plate 12 Contact set 13 Terminal 14 Vacuum control 15 Screw 16 Condenser 17 Screw 18 Distributor cap 19 Carbon point 20 Fixing plate 21 Bolt 22 Housing

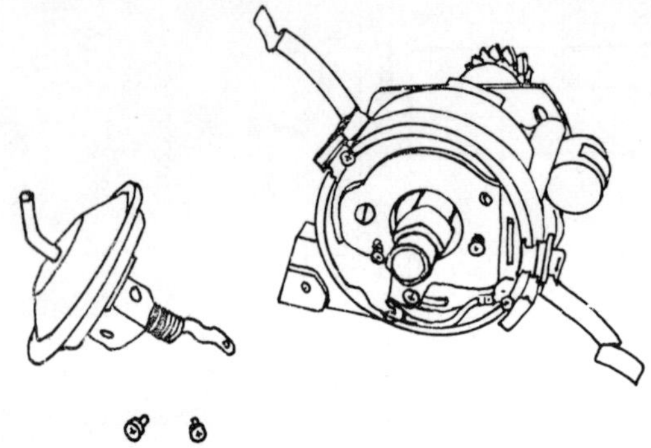

FIG 3:5 Removing the vacuum control unit

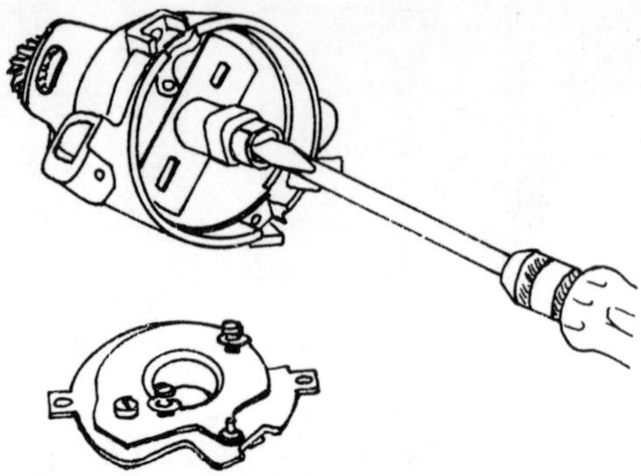

FIG 3:7 Distributor cam removal

Capacitor:

The best method of testing a capacitor (condenser) is by substitution. Disconnect the original capacitor and connect a new one between the low-tension terminal on the distributor and earth for test purposes. If a new capacitor is proved to be required, it can then be properly fitted.

3:4 Removing and dismantling distributor

Removal:

Remove the distributor cap and disconnect the low-tension wire from the side of the distributor. Pull off the vacuum hose. Mark the position to which the rotor arm points on the distributor upper casing and mark the position of the distributor body relative to the mounting flange on the engine. This ensures that the distributor will be refitted correctly without disturbing the engine timing. Note that the engine must not be turned with the distributor removed or the timing will be lost, retiming then being necessary as described in **Section 3:5**.

With the marks made as described, undo the distributor mounting clamp and pull the unit from the crankcase.

Align the distributor body and rotor arm according to the marks made during removal. Offer the distributor into position, then carefully press it down. As the distributor seats, the rotor arm will turn slightly, due to the action of the bevelled teeth as they mesh with the gear on the camshaft. When seated the rotor must point towards the mark made. Remove the distributor, turn the rotor a little and refit if this is not so. Repeat this operation until the distributor is correctly seated and the rotor correctly aligned. Fit the distributor clamp, leaving it just loose enough to allow the distributor body to be turned in its mounting. Precise timing can then be carried out, using a test lamp as described in **Section 3:5**. If the engine has been turned and the timing setting lost, align the engine as described in that section before refitting the distributor, then proceed with the test lamp setting as before.

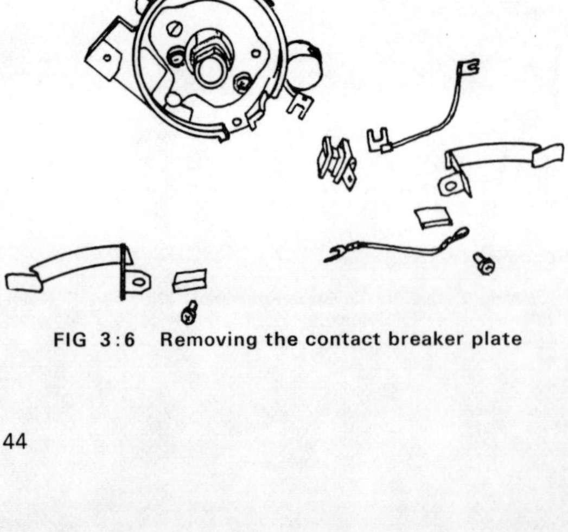

FIG 3:6 Removing the contact breaker plate

Dismantling:

FIG 3:4 shows the distributor components. Remove the contact breaker points as described previously. Remove the vacuum control unit as shown in **FIG 3:5**. Take out the securing screws and remove the contact breaker mounting plate as shown in **FIG 3:6**. Remove the setscrew and take off the distributor cam as shown in **FIG 3:7**.

Use a hammer and pin punch to carefully tap out the pinion retaining pin as shown in **FIG 3:8**, then remove the pinion. The distributor shaft and rotary unit can then be removed from the housing, as shown in **FIG 3:9**. The centrifugal advance mechanism should only be dismantled if essential. If so, take care not to stretch or deform the governor springs when removing them from the governor weights. Clean all parts and renew any found worn or damaged.

Reassembly:

Reassembly of the distributor unit is a reversal of the dismantling procedure, applying grease to the bearing surfaces of the shaft and to the centrifugal advance mechanism. Lubricate the upper distributor as described in **Section 3:2**. If the centrifugal advance mechanism has been dismantled, note the following points concerning reassembly.

Fit the governor springs and cams as shown in **FIG 3:10**. On D412.63 model distributors, two governor springs are fitted. Spring **A** can easily be identified as its free length is shorter than that of spring **B**.

3:5 Timing the ignition

If the engine has been turned with the distributor removed and the timing lost, or if the engine has been dismantled, correct alignment must be achieved as follows before the distributor is fitted. This procedure is not necessary, however, if the distributor has been removed and refitted as described in **Section 3:4**, it only being necessary to check the timing with a test lamp.

Remove the rocker cover from the cylinder head so that the valve gear can be seen. Turn the engine until the piston in No. 1 (front) cylinder is at the top of the cylinder on the compression stroke. This will be when both valves for No. 1 cylinder are closed, the rocker tips being just clear of the valve stems. Now turn the engine a little more as necessary until the TOP mark shown in **FIG 3:11** aligns with the pointer mark on the timing cover at the front of the engine. With the crankshaft pulley and pointer mark correctly aligned, offer the distributor unit into position and press it into position. When the distributor seats, the rotor must be in the position shown in **FIG 3:12**, the rotor being aligned squarely with the mark or spring clip mounting on the side of the distributor. As the rotor will turn slightly when the distributor is fitted, due to the action of the bevel gears meshing, the rotor must be positioned a little away from the final position before seating the distributor so that it aligns correctly when seated. Remove and refit the distributor, turning the rotor a little each time, until the final correct alignment is achieved. Fit the distributor clamp, leaving it just loose enough to allow the distributor body to be turned in its mounting by hand, then set the ignition timing exactly, using a test lamp as described next.

Electrical setting:

Turn the engine until it is approaching the TDC position for No. 1 cylinder described above and it reaches the static timing point for the engine, this is 8 deg. for the 988 cc or 7 deg. for the 1171 cc. These engines, when fitted with emission control equipment, and the two larger engines in the group must later be timed with a stroboscopic lamp and so the setting at this point in the operation is not critical provided it permits the engine to be run. 8 deg. to 10 deg. BTDC will be satisfactory.

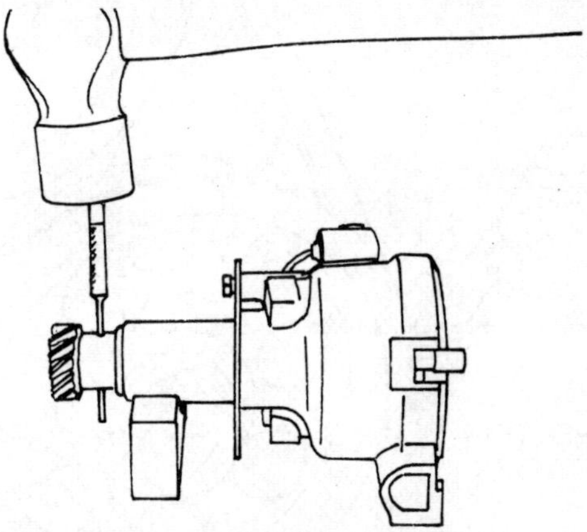

FIG 3:8 Driving out the pinion retaining pin

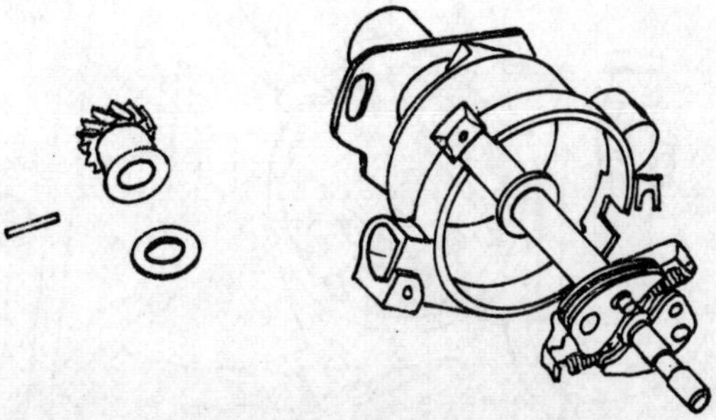

FIG 3:9 Removing the distributor shaft

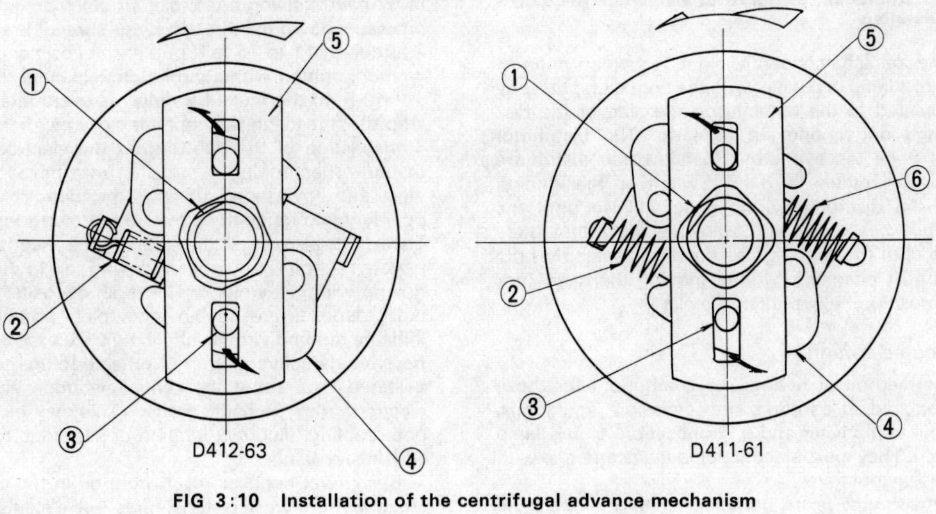

FIG 3:10 Installation of the centrifugal advance mechanism

Key to Fig 3:10 1 Rotor positioning tip 2 Governor spring (A) 3 Weight pin 4 Governor weight 5 Cam 6 Governor spring (B)

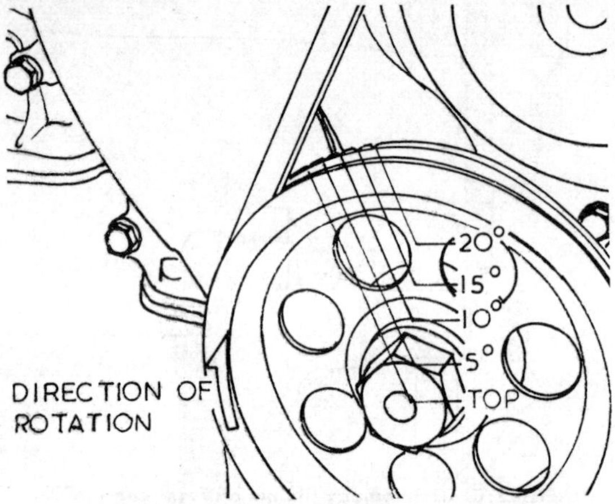

FIG 3:11 The engine timing marks

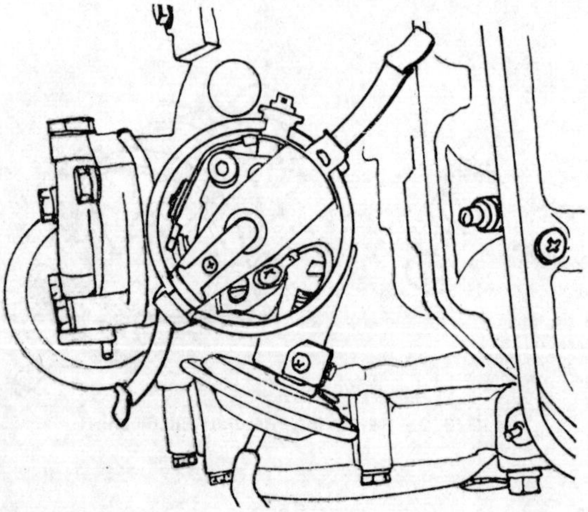

FIG 3:12 Alignment of the rotor arm when the distributor is installed

With the crankshaft correctly aligned as stated, connect a 12-volt test lamp in parallel with the contact points, one lead connected to the terminal on the side of the distributor and one connected to earth. The distributor clamp must be loose enough to allow the distributor housing to be rotated by hand. Switch on the ignition and turn the distributor body anticlockwise until the contacts are closed. Slowly rotate the distributor body clockwise until the lamp lights, which indicates that the points are just opening. Without moving the distributor from this position, fully tighten the clamp.

Stroboscopic timing:

For this method of timing, most important for those models required to conform with emission regulations, an accurate tachometer and a stroboscopic timing lamp are required. They must be connected in accordance with the makers' instructions.

Bring the engine up to normal operating temperature and apply a spot of white paint to the appropriate timing marks to render them more visible.

On standard cars disconnect the vacuum pipe from the capsule on the distributor and plug the open end. On emission controlled engines, if applicable, disconnect the hose from the air check valve and fit a cap on the valve port.

Start up the engine and let it run at the idling speed specified in the table below. Shine the timing lamp on the timing marks and if the mark on the rim of the pulley does not appear against the pointer on the front engine cover, slacken the distributor clamp bolts and turn the distributor body as required to obtain alignment. Secure the clamp bolt when satisfactory.

Engine	*Degrees BTDC at engine speed*	
988 cc	8	700 rev/min
1171 cc	7	600 rev/min
988 and 1171 cc (EC) . .	5	600 rev/min
1288 cc (Manual) . .	5	800 rev/min
(Automatic in D) . .	5	650 rev/min
1397 cc (Manual) . .	10	700 rev/min
(Automatic in D) . .	10	650 rev/min

3:6 Sparking plugs

Inspect, clean and adjust sparking plugs regularly. New sparking plugs of the correct grade should be fitted at about 12,000 mile intervals.

When removing sparking plugs, ensure that their recesses in the head are clean and dry so that nothing can fall into the cylinders. Plug gaskets can be re-used provided that they are not less than half their original thickness. Have sparking plugs cleaned on an abrasive-blasting machine and tested under pressure with the electrode gaps correctly set at .031 to .035 inch (.8 to .9 mm). The electrodes should be filed until they are bright and parallel. The gaps must always be set by adjusting the earth electrode. **Do not try to bend the centre electrode.**

Before refitting the plugs, clean the threads in the cylinder head with a tap if the plugs cannot be screwed in by hand. Failing a tap, use an old sparking plug with crosscuts down the threads. Plugs should be tightened to a torque of 11 to 15 lb ft but, in the absence of a torque wrench, tighten with a normal box spanner through half a turn. Refit the plugs carefully, as overtightening could strip the threads in the light alloy cylinder head.

Inspection of the deposits on the electrodes can be helpful when tuning. Normally, from mixed periods of high and low-speed driving, the deposit should be powdery and range in colour from brown to greyish-tan. There will also be slight wear of the electrodes. Long periods of constant speed driving or low-speed city driving will give white or yellowish deposits. Dry, black, fluffy deposits are due to incomplete combustion and indicate running with a rich mixture, excessive idling and, possibly, defective ignition. Overheated plugs have a white, blistered look about the centre electrode and the side electrode may be badly eroded. This may be caused by poor cooling, incorrect ignition or sustained high speeds with heavy loads.

Black, wet deposits result from oil in the combustion chamber from worn pistons, rings, valve stems or guides. Sparking plugs which run hotter may alleviate the problem, but the cure is an engine overhaul.

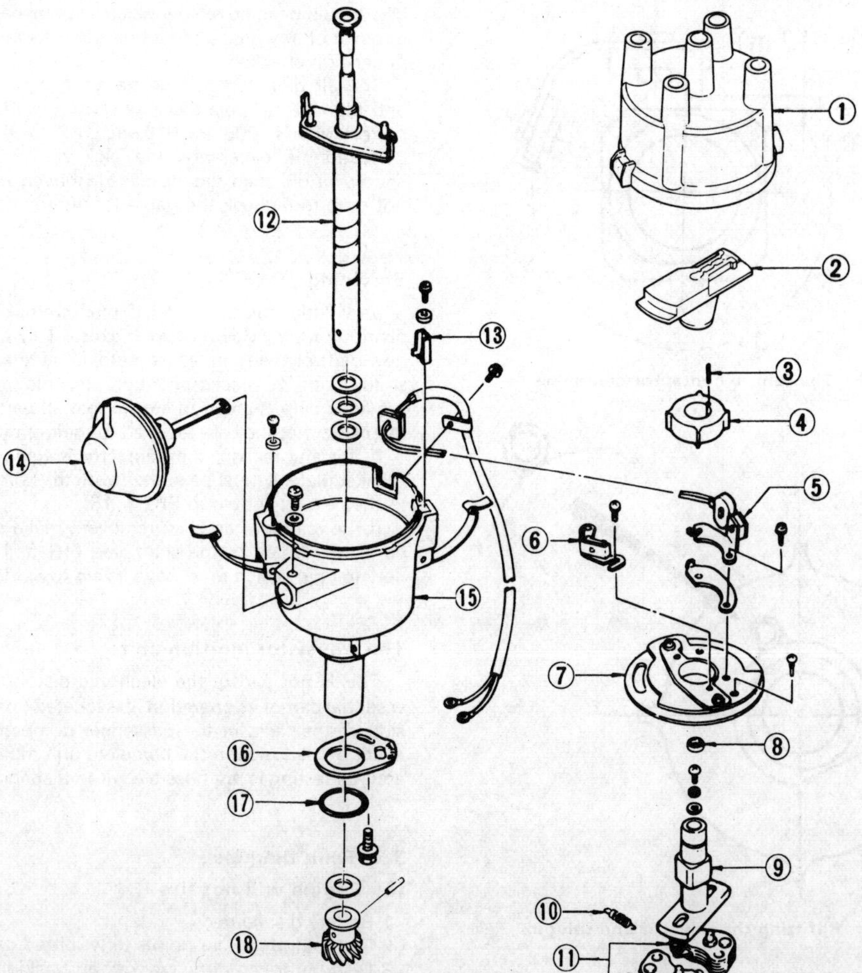

FIG 3:13 The components of an electronic distributor

Key to Fig 3:13 1 Cap 2 Rotor 3 Roll pin 4 Reluctor 5 Pick-up coil 6 Contactor 7 Breaker plate 8 Packing 9 Cam and rotor shaft 10 Governor spring 11 Weights 12 Shaft 13 Cap setter 14 Vacuum capsule 15 Body 16 Mounting plate 17 'O' ring 18 Pinion

Sparking plug leads:

Renew high-tension leads if they are defective in any way. Inspect for broken, swollen or deteriorated insulation which can be the cause of 'tracking,' especially in wet weather conditions. Check the condition of the rubber covers on the terminals and renew them if perished or damaged.

3:7 The electronic distributor

With the introduction of the 1397 cc engine in 1975 this contactless distributor was also introduced for California model cars. Externally it is similar to a conventional unit, as is the remainder of the ignition system.

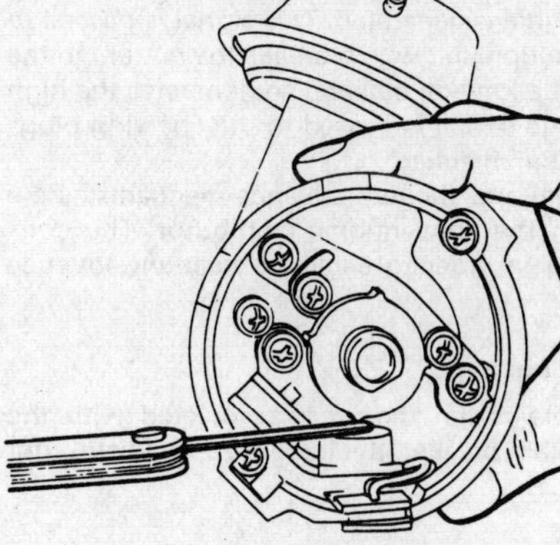

FIG 3:14 Measuring the air gap

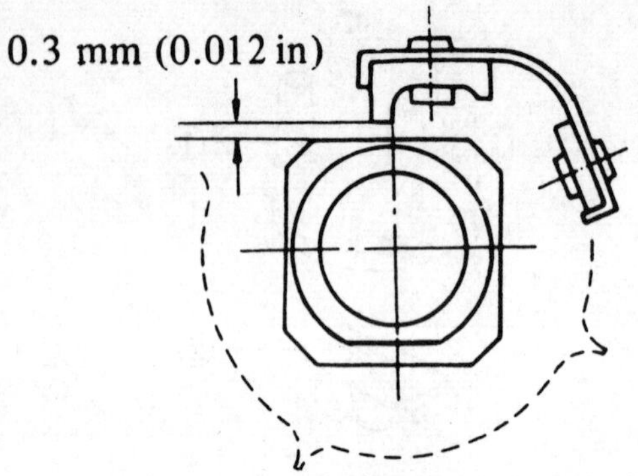

FIG 3:15 The cam to contactor clearance

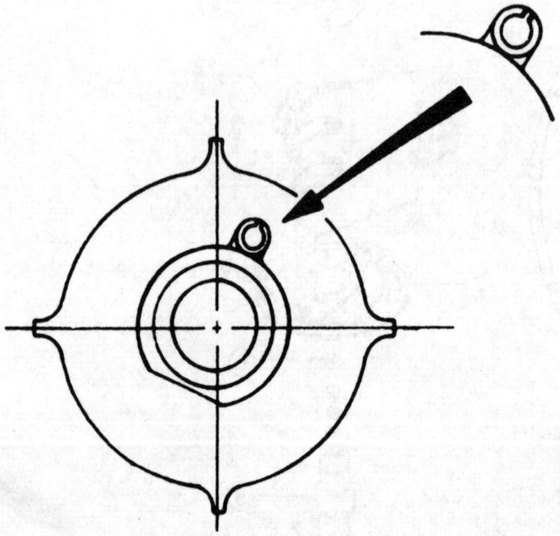

FIG 3:16 Refitting the reluctor and roll pin

An exploded view showing the components of the electric distributor is given in **FIG 3:13** and its method of operation is briefly as follows:

Instead of the firing current to the sparking plug being initiated by the cam and contact breaker arm, their function is carried out by the reluctor 4 on the shaft 12, and the pick-up coil 5. As one of the protrusions on the reluctor comes opposite the pole piece in the pick-up and electrical signal is generated. This signal is passed to the transistor ignition unit which breaks the current in the primary coil of the ignition coil and so generates the high secondary voltage which is passed to the sparking plugs in the conventional manner.

The centrifugal and vacuum advance mechanisms are the same as on the conventional distributor. The contactor 6 is fitted in order to eliminate vacuum advance hysteresis.

Adjusting the air gap:

Although there is not the wear associated with the mechanical contact breaker, the interior of the distributor cap should be removed periodically for inspection and the removal of any dust and carbon deposits and the air gap dimension checked.

The air gap is measured between a rotor protrusion and the pick-up pole piece as shown in **FIG 3:14**. The correct gap is .008 to .016 inch (.2 to .4 mm) and if correction is necessary, the pick-up securing screws should be loosened and the pick-up moved as required. Do not omit to recheck the gap after tightening the screws.

Servicing:

Very little can be done if the internal parts of the distributor breakdown or wear excessively beyond fitting new parts or even a new distributor complete. Dismantling should not be necessary, but presents no difficulties provided care is taken to ensure that all parts are marked to ensure that they are restored to their original positions.

If, for any reason, the contactor is removed from the breaker plate, it must be refitted with the correct clearance to the cam as shown in **FIG 3:15**.

If the reluctor has been removed, make sure that it is correctly refitted to the shaft, see **FIG 3:16**, and use a new roll pin which must have its slit towards the outside.

The transistor ignition unit:

This is not part of the electronic distributor, but is an essential part of its operation. It is located on the righthand side of the facia in the passenger compartment. In the event of malfunction the complete unit must be replaced and full testing is not possible without special equipment.

3:8 Fault diagnosis

(a) Engine will not fire

1 Battery discharged
2 Distributor contact points dirty, pitted or maladjusted
3 Distributor cap dirty, cracked or 'tracking'
4 Distributor cap contact brush not touching rotor
5 Faulty cable or connection in low tension circuit
6 Cracked or damaged rotor
7 Faulty coil
8 Broken contact breaker spring
9 Contact points stuck open
10 Air gap too wide
11 Pick-up coil defective
12 Faulty transistor unit

(b) Engine misfires

1 Check 2, 3, 5, 7, 10, 11 and 12 in (a)
2 Weak contact breaker spring
3 High tension plug and coil leads cracked or perished
4 Sparking plug(s) loose
5 Sparking plug gap incorrectly set
6 Ignition timing too far advanced
7 Dirt on pick-up
8 Worn breaker plate or shaft

CHAPTER 4

THE COOLING SYSTEM

4:1 Description

The cooling system is pressurized and thermostatically controlled, using a corrugated fin type radiator. Water circulation is assisted by a centrifugal pump which is mounted at the front of the cylinder block and the cooling fan, which is fitted to the same shaft as the pump, draws air through the radiator. The pump, fan and the alternator are driven from a pulley on the crankshaft by a common belt, the tension of this belt being adjustable at the alternator mounting.

The pump takes coolant from the bottom of the radiator and delivers it to the cylinder block from which it rises to the cylinder head. At normal operating temperatures the thermostat is open and the coolant returns from the head to the top of the radiator. At lower temperatures the thermostat is closed and the coolant bypasses the radiator and returns to the pump inlet. This provides a rapid warm-up.

4:2 Maintenance

The cooling system should periodically be drained, flushed to remove sediment and refilled. If antifreeze is in use, the coolant may be collected for re-use but should be discarded after two winters or 24,000 miles, whichever occurs first. Check that the clips are tight on all hoses and that the radiator pressure cap is in good condition and that it seals effectively.

Draining:

Remove the radiator pressure cap and open the two cooling system drain plugs, one plug being fitted at the bottom of the radiator, the other on the side of the engine block. Collect the coolant in a clean container if it is to be re-used.

Flushing:

Use a hose to run clean water in through the radiator filler until it runs clean at the drain plugs. Close the drain plugs, fill the system with water and run the engine for long enough to open the thermostat for complete circulation. Stop the engine and drain the system again before sediment has time to settle. Repeat the flushing operation, close the drain plugs and refill the system. It is recommended that Nissan long life coolant be used in preference to plain water in the cooling system. Apart from acting as a corrosion inhibitor and water pump lubricant, this coolant is an antifreeze solution and will protect the system in winter conditions.

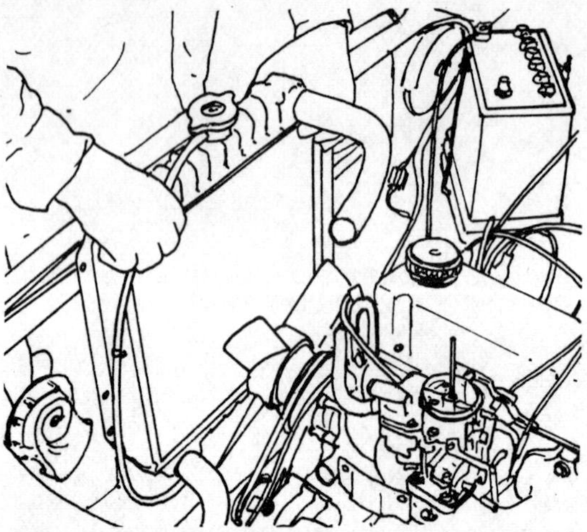

FIG 4:1 Removing the radiator

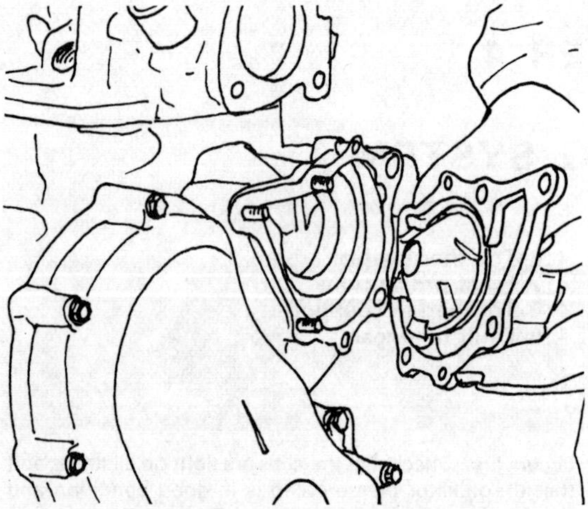

FIG 4:2 Removing the water pump

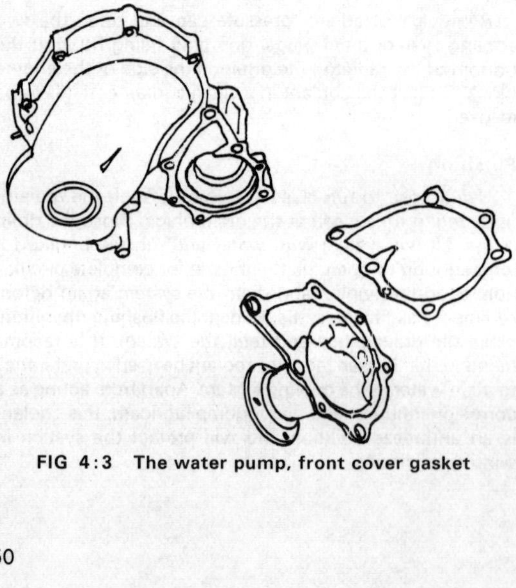

FIG 4:3 The water pump, front cover gasket

4:3 Removing the radiator

Drain the cooling system as described in **Section 4:2** and disconnect the top and bottom radiator hoses. Disconnect the hose to the reservoir tank. Remove the six radiator fixing bolts and lift the radiator from the car, as shown in **FIG 4:1**. Note that, on cars equipped with automatic transmission, the transmission oil cooler is in unit with the radiator and must be disconnected.

Refitting is a reversal of the removal procedure. On completion, refill the cooling system as described in **Section 4:2**.

4:4 Adjusting the fan belt

The fan belt tension is correct when it can be pressed down about half an inch with firm hand pressure applied in the centre of the top belt run. To adjust the belt tension, loosen the alternator mounting bolts and swing the alternator in the required direction before tightening the bolts and rechecking. The belt can be removed by slackening the bolts and pushing the alternator inwards until the belt can be taken over the fan and pulleys.

A tight fan belt will cause undue wear on the pulleys and the pump and alternator bearings, a slack belt will cause slip and, possibly, overheating and reduced alternator output.

4:5 The water pump

Removal:

Drain the cooling system and remove the fan belt as described previously. Remove the fan and pulley assembly, then remove the water pump from the front of the cylinder block as shown in **FIG 4:2**.

Dismantling:

Use a screwdriver to remove the wire which locks the bearing shaft unit. Fit the water pump assembly on a suitable support, then use a press to remove the shaft from the vane. Note that the shaft cannot be withdrawn from the hub side. Take care not to damage the seal, and completely separate the shaft from the body. The seat is fitted to the vane and can be removed by hand. Use a press to remove the seal.

Clean and inspect all parts, renewing any found worn or damaged. Always renew the shaft and hub together. **FIG 4:3** shows the water pump and front cover.

Note that on USA models the aluminium pump has its outer bearing race press fitted and it cannot be dismantled. If the inner parts are rusted, corroded or badly worn the complete pump must be renewed.

Reassembly:

Thoroughly clean the seal and seat surfaces with a piece of dry cloth. Carefully fit the seat to the vane so that it is parallel. Apply suitable sealing compound to the seal, then fit it to the body. Fit the pump shaft. Fit the vane, then adjust its position in accordance with the information in **FIG 4:4**. Lightly tap with a hammer and fit the lock wire.

Refitting:

This is the reverse of the removal procedure, using a new gasket.

4:6 The thermostat

The thermostat is located in a housing in the water outlet passage in the cylinder head.

Removal:

Drain sufficient coolant to bring the level below that of the thermostat housing. Disconnect the upper hose from the housing, then remove the housing 2 and lift out the thermostat 1, as shown in **FIG 4:5**.

Testing:

Clean the thermostat and immerse it in a container of cold water together with a zero to 100°C thermometer. Heat the water, keeping it stirred and check that the valve opens at about 82°C and is fully open at 95°C. If the thermostat operates satisfactorily it may be refitted, if not, a new unit must be obtained. When refitting, use a new gasket coated on both sides with sealing compound. Top up the cooling system to the correct level, on completion.

4:7 Frost precautions

If antifreeze is to be used, the system should first be drained and flushed as described in **Section 4:2**. Ethylene-glycol type antifreeze or, preferably, Nissan long life coolant should be added in the proportions recommended by the manufacturer, to give protection from freezing in the lowest temperatures at which the car is to be operated. After the second winter or 24,000 miles, whichever is the sooner, drain and flush the system and refill with fresh solution.

4:8 Torque fan coupling

This unit, fitted to some later cars, is filled with a silicone oil to act as a fluid coupling in order to reduce fan speed at higher engine speeds. This reduces power loss and fan noise.

The coupling cannot be serviced, and if an oil leak is observed, the unit must be renewed.

To remove, loosen the fan belt and remove the blade assembly from the coupling. Unscrew the securing nuts and remove the coupling from the pulley and water pump hub.

4:9 Fault diagnosis

(a) Internal water leakage

1 Cracked cylinder wall
2 Loose cylinder head bolts
3 Cracked cylinder head
4 Faulty head gasket

(b) Poor circulation

1 Radiator blocked
2 Engine water passages restricted
3 Low coolant level

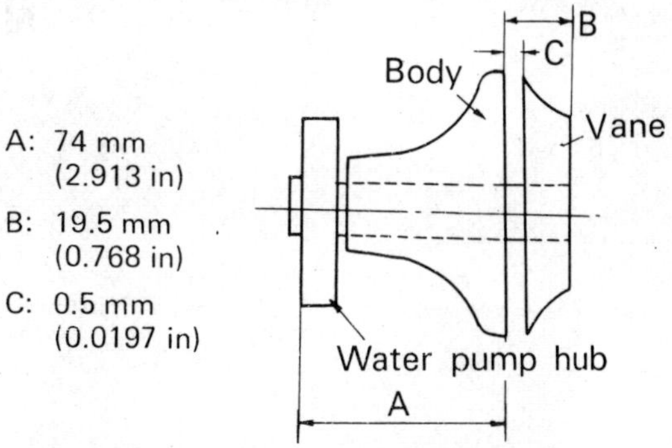

FIG 4:4 Fitting the water pump vane

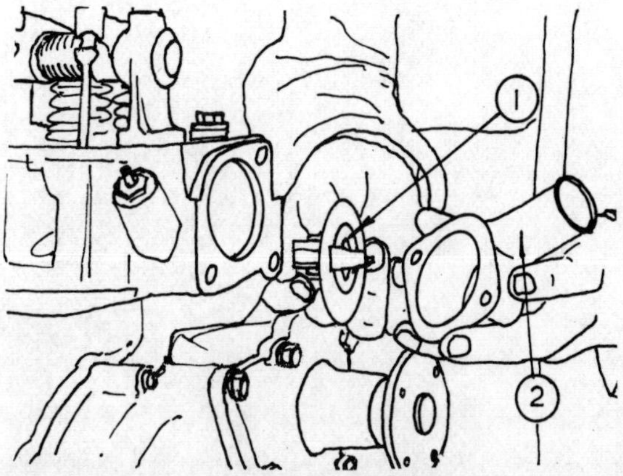

FIG 4:5 Removing the thermostat

4 Slack fan belt
5 Defective thermostat
6 Perished or collapsed radiator hose

(c) Corrosion

1 Impurities in the coolant
2 Infrequent draining and flushing

(d) Overheating

1 Check (b)
2 Sludge in crankcase
3 Faulty ignition timing
4 Low oil level in engine sump
5 Tight engine
6 Choked exhaust system
7 Binding brakes
8 Slipping clutch
9 Incorrect valve timing
10 Retarded ignition
11 Mixture too weak

NOTES

CHAPTER 5

THE CLUTCH

5:1 Description

The clutch is a single dry plate unit of diaphragm spring type. The main components are the driven plate, pressure plate assembly and release bearing.

The driven plate consists of a resilient steel disc attached to a hub which slides on the splined clutch shaft. The friction linings are riveted to both sides of the disc.

The pressure plate assembly consists of the pressure plate, diaphragm spring and housing. The release bearing is a ballbearing of special construction with an elongated outer ring that presses directly against the diaphragm spring when the clutch pedal is operated. The bearing is mounted on a guide sleeve in the gearbox bellhousing.

Lefthand drive vehicles are fitted with hydraulically operated clutch mechanisms, righthand drive vehicles with cable operated clutch mechanisms.

On hydraulic installations, the clutch pedal actuates a master cylinder where pressure on the fluid is generated, this pressure being transmitted through a hose to a slave cylinder mounted on the gearbox case. Slave cylinder action is transmitted to the release bearing by a clutch lever pivoted on the transmission case.

On cable installations, clutch pedal movement is transmitted to the release bearing by a sheathed steel cable attached to a clutch lever pivoted on the transmission case.

There are a few slight differences in the clutch release mechanism as installed on the cars covered in this manual, but the essential details are similar and it is not considered necessary to go fully into these minor details. The following instructions should enable the owner to carry out all normal servicing operations on either type without difficulty.

5:2 Removing and dismantling clutch

Refer to **Chapter 6** and remove the gearbox. Loosen the bolts holding the clutch assembly to the engine flywheel alternatively and evenly to avoid distortion, then lift off the clutch assembly. Slide the driven plate from the splined shaft, taking care not to get grease or oil on the friction linings. **FIG 5:1** shows the clutch pressure plate 1 and the driven plate 2.

Refer to **FIG 5:2**. Remove the dust cover from the bellhousing, remove the return spring 2 from the bearing

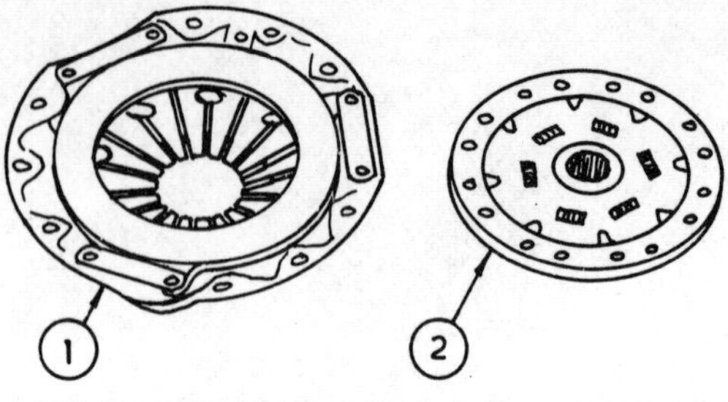

FIG 5:1 The clutch pressure and driven plates

sleeve, then separate the withdrawal lever 1 from the bearing sleeve. Remove the release bearing 3 and sleeve and take the withdrawal lever from the lever ballpin. Use a suitable puller to remove the release bearing from the sleeve. Operations for lefthand drive are similar.

Servicing:

Thoroughly clean all parts in a suitable solvent, with the exception of the driven plate friction linings and the release bearing. The release bearing must not be cleaned with solvent as this would wash the internal lubricant from the bearing.

The clutch cover, spring and pressure plate assembly is an integral unit and must not be dismantled. If any part is defective the assembly must be renewed complete.

Inspect the surface of the flywheel where the driven plate makes contact. Small cracks on the surface are unimportant, but if there are any deep scratches the flywheel should be machined smooth or renewed. Check the pressure plate for scoring or damage and that the operating surface is flat and true. Check the diaphragm springs for cracks and other damage and the release bearing for roughness when it is pressed and turned by hand. Any parts which are worn or damaged must be renewed.

Check the driven plate for loose rivets and broken or very loose torsional springs. The friction linings should be well proud of the rivets and have a light colour, with a polished glaze through which the grain of the material is clearly visible. A dark, glazed deposit indicates oil on the facings and, as this condition cannot be rectified, a new

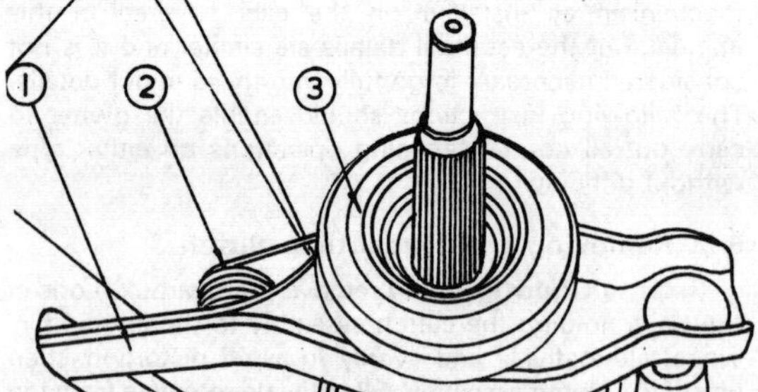

FIG 5:2 Dismantling the clutch release bearing, righthand drive

or relined plate will be required. Any sign of oil in the clutch will call for examination of the crankshaft main bearing oil seal as described in **Chapter 1**. Check the disc for runout at the outer circumference, preferably using a dial gauge. Maximum permissible runout is .02 inch, any figure in excess of this being liable to cause clutch judder or snatch in operation, plus rapid wear of the components. A slightly twisted driven plate can usually be corrected by mounting it on the gearbox splined shaft and using hand pressure to straighten it.

It is not recommended that owners attempt to reline the clutch driven plate themselves, as the linings must be riveted and trued on the disc and the whole checked under a press. For this reason, the driven plate should be relined at a service station or an exchange unit obtained and fitted. Check the driven plate hub for a smooth sliding fit on the clutch shaft, removing any burrs on the shaft or in the hub.

5:3 Assembling and refitting the clutch

Tightly fit the release bearing on the bearing sleeve as shown in **FIG 5:3**. When it is pressed fully home, turn the bearing with the fingers to check for smooth operation. Apply multi-purpose grease to the groove in the sleeve as shown in **FIG 5:4** and to the withdrawal lever 2 and ballpin 1 (see **FIG 5:5**). Install the release mechanism, fit the return spring and press in the dust cover.

The clutch assembly must be aligned with special tool ST.20610000 when it is fitted to the flywheel. Fit the special tool through the pressure plate and driven plate, then offer the assembly up to the flywheel locate on dowels and enter the tool into the pilot bush in the flywheel, as shown in **FIG 5:6**. Fit the mounting bolts and tighten them alternately and evenly to a final torque of 11 to 15 lb ft. Refit the gearbox as described in **Chapter 6**, then adjust the clutch as described in the next section.

5:4 Adjusting the clutch

The pedal height should be correctly set according to the following instructions, particularly after any dismantling operation has been carried out on the clutch or operating mechanism. Correct adjustment of the release bearing clearance is essential. Insufficient clearance will cause the release bearing to press on the diaphragm when the clutch is engaged, causing clutch slip and excessive bearing and driven plate wear. Excessive clearance will prevent proper disengagement of the clutch, resulting in clutch drag and consequent difficult gearchanging.

Hydraulic clutch:

Pedal clearance:

Refer to **FIG 5:7**. Adjust the pedal pad height on 1000, and 1200 to 5.65 inch (143.5 mm), with the pedal stop 3 loosened off, by inserting shims between the master cylinder mounting flange and the body panel as shown. Loosen the master cylinder mounting bolts and add or subtract shims as necessary, making sure that the upper and lower shim thicknesses are the same. Now screw in the pedal stop until the pedal height is reduced to 5.57 inch (141.5 mm) and secure the stop with the locknut. Make sure that the points marked are properly lubricated with multi-purpose grease. On 120Y and B210 models,

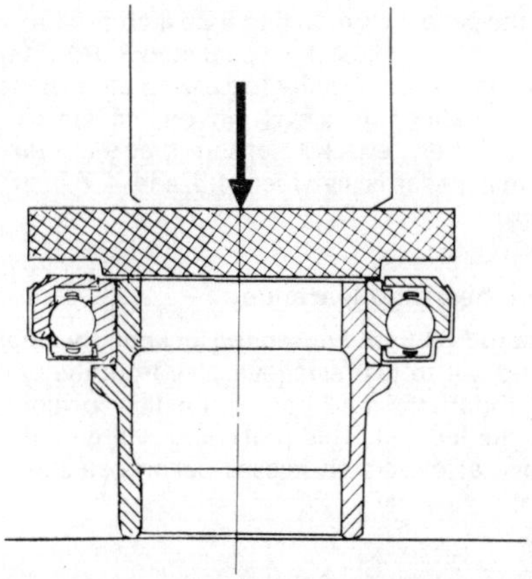

FIG 5:3 Fitting the release bearing to the sleeve

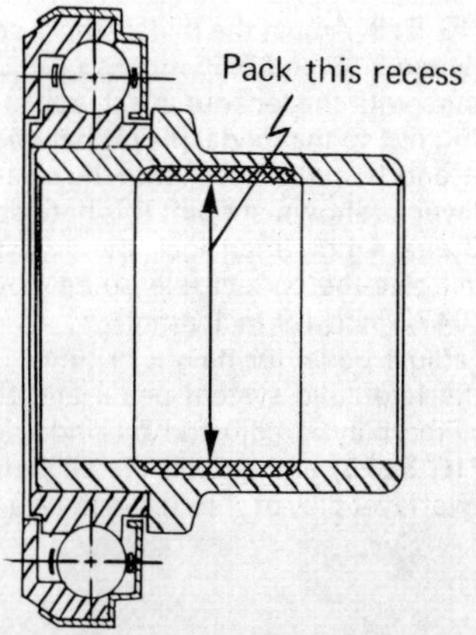

FIG 5:4 Lubricating the release bearing sleeve

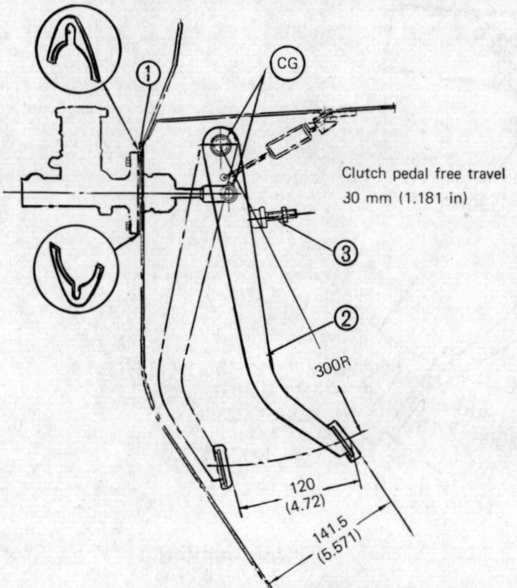

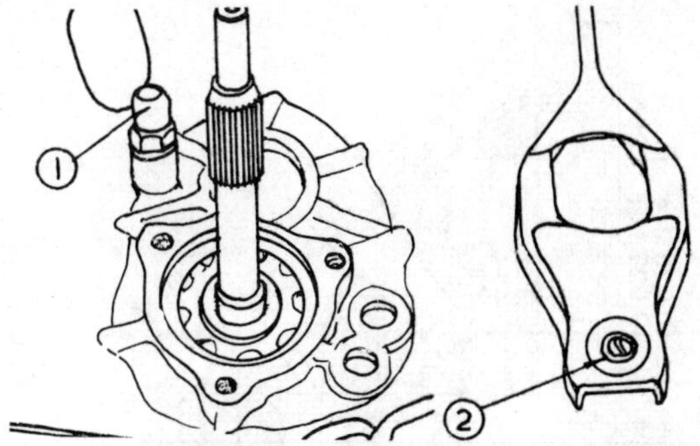

FIG 5:5 Lubricating the ballpin and withdrawal lever

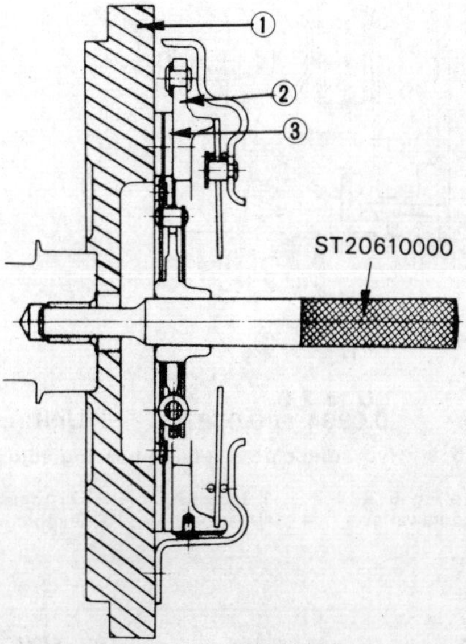

FIG 5:6 Aligning the clutch assembly with the special tool

Key to Fig 5:6 1 Flywheel 2 Pressure plate 3 Driven plate

Adjusting shim

Part number	Thickness mm (in)
30611 27260	1.6 (0.0630)
30612 27260	0.8 (0.0315)
30613 27260	0.5 (0.0197)

Unit: mm(in)

FIG 5:7 Hydraulic clutch pedal adjustment, 1000, 1200 models

Key to Fig 5:7 1 Adjusting shim 2 Pedal lever 3 Pedal stopper adjust the pedal height to 6 to 6.26 inch (153 to 159 mm) by means of the adjustable pedal stop 3. Adjust the pedal free play to .04 to .12 inch (1 to 3 mm) at the pedal pad by suitably rotating the clevis pin on the master cylinder pushrod. Finally, check to ensure that the total travel of the clutch pedal is between 4.5 and 4.7 inch (114 to 120 mm).

Release bearing clearance:

Refer to **FIG 5:8**. Loosen the locknut, then tighten the adjusting nut to just eliminate play from the withdrawal lever 3. Return the nut $1\frac{1}{4}$ turns from this position and lock it with the locknut. This procedure will give the correct clearance at the clutch release bearing as shown in the diagram.

Mechanical clutch:

Pedal and release bearing clearance:

Refer to **FIG 5:9**. Adjust the pedal stop 3 so that pedal height is between 5.49 and 5.65 inches (139.5 and 143.5 mm) and secure with the locknut. Next, adjust the control cable adjusting nut so that pedal play is between .433 and .591 inch (11 and 15 mm). Check that the clearance at the withdrawal lever as shown at point **P** is between .118 and .158 inch (3 and 4 mm) then lock the adjustment. This procedure will give the correct release bearing clearance of .0354 to .0472 inch (.9 to 1.2 mm).

On 120Y adjust pedal for height or travel in the same manner as the hydraulic system pedal and to the same dimensions. Free play is adjusted by undoing the locknut 2 (see **FIG 5:13**) and setting the adjusting nut 1 to give withdrawal lever play of .1 to .14 inch (2.5 to 3.5 mm).

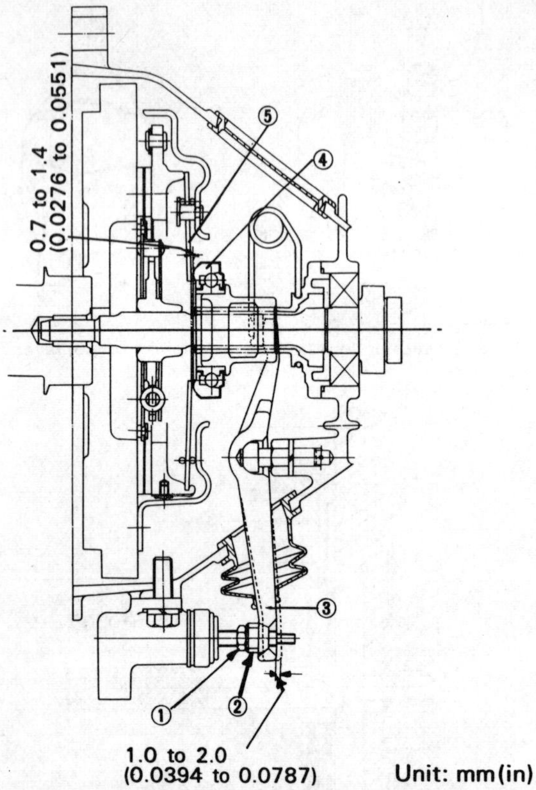

FIG 5:8 Hydraulic clutch release bearing adjustment

Key to Fig 5:8 1 Locknut 2 Adjusting nut 3 Withdrawal lever 4 Release bearing 5 Diaphragm spring

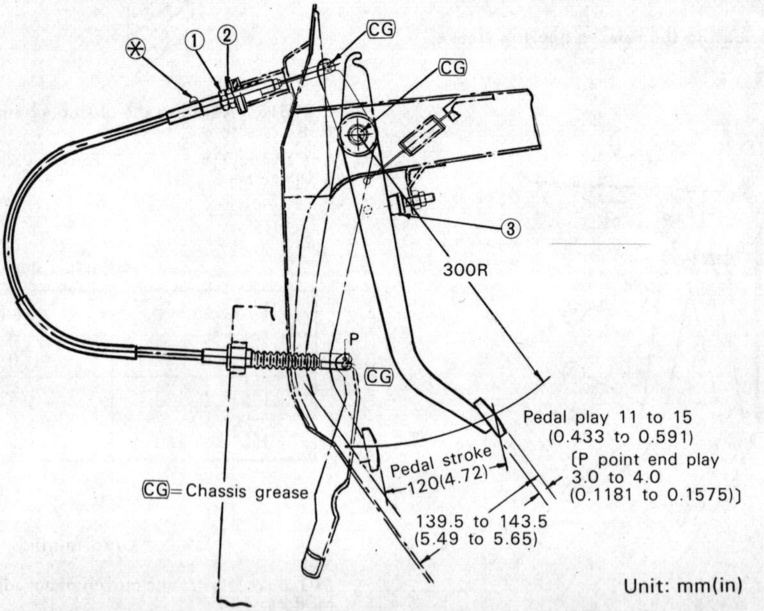

FIG 5:9 Mechanical clutch pedal and release bearing adjustment, 1200 model

Key to Fig 5:9 1 Locknut 2 Adjusting nut 3 Pedal stopper

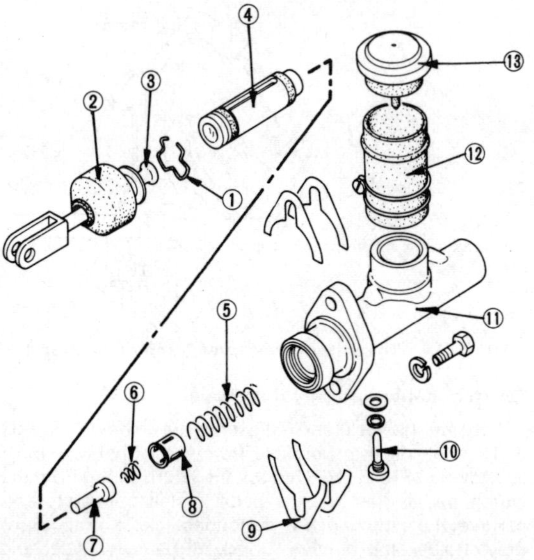

FIG 5:10 Clutch master cylinder components, 1000, 1200 models

Key to Fig 5:10 1 Snap ring 2 Dust cover 3 Pushrod 4 Clutch piston 5 Piston spring 6 Inlet valve spring 7 Inlet valve 8 Spring retainer 9 Shim 10 Inlet valve release pin 11 Body 12 Oil reservoir 13 Oil reservoir cap

5:5 Servicing hydraulic clutch system

An occasional check should be made on the level of fluid in the master cylinder supply tank. Wipe dirt from around the cap before removing it. Top up the fluid if necessary to bring the level to the mark on the side of the tank. Use only the correct grade of fluid as recommended by the agent.

Removal:

Disconnect the pushrod from the clevis. Disconnect the fluid line from the master cylinder and, holding a container beneath the threaded hole, drain the fluid from the supply tank by having an assistant pump the clutch pedal. Take out the securing bolts and lift the master cylinder from the car, collecting the shims and noting their positions.

On the 120Y and USA models the shims 9 are not used; the pushrod 3 is adjustable for length.

Refitting:

Refit the master cylinder in the reverse order of removal. On completion, adjust the clutch as described in **Section 5:4** and bleed the system as described later.

Servicing:

FIG 5:10 shows the 1000 and 1200 master cylinder components. Remove the filler cap and drain any remaining fluid. Pull back the dust cover and remove the snap ring. Remove the retaining washer, pushrod, piston assembly, valve assembly and return spring from the cylinder. The 120Y and B210 are similar with a modified recuperation valve assembly.

Thoroughly clean all parts in brake fluid. Check the piston and cylinder for wear or scoring. Clearance between the piston and cylinder must not exceed .0059 inch (.15 mm). Check the dust cover, fluid supply tank, filler cap and the fluid pipe for damage and distortion. Renew any part found defective. Always fit a new rubber piston seal.

Reassemble the master cylinder in the reverse order of dismantling, observing absolute cleanliness to ensure that dirt does not enter and score the highly polished bores or prevent the rubber seals from working properly. Dip all parts in the correct grade of fluid and assemble them wet with the fluid. Ensure that the lip of the piston seal faces inwards.

Slave cylinder:

Removal:

Remove the return spring if fitted and disconnect the fluid hose from the slave cylinder. Disconnect the pushrod from the withdrawal lever, release the two mounting bolts and remove the slave cylinder from the bellhousing.

Refitting:

Refit the slave cylinder in the reverse order of removal. On completion, bleed air from the system as described later and adjust the clutch as described in **Section 5:4**.

Servicing:

Refer to **FIG 5:11**. Remove the dust cover, release the snap ring and withdraw the internal components. Wash all parts in brake fluid and examine for wear, scoring or

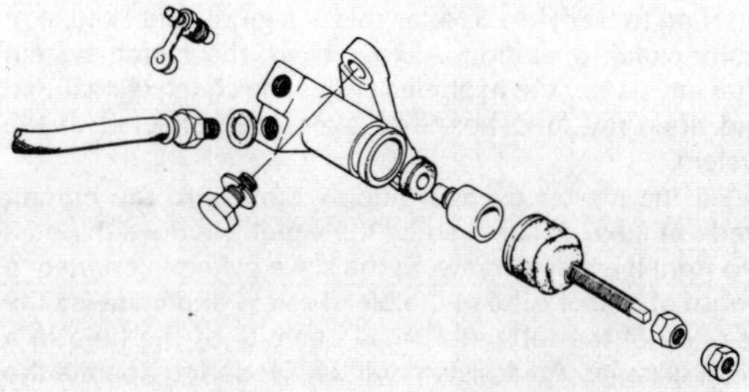

FIG 5:11 Clutch slave cylinder components

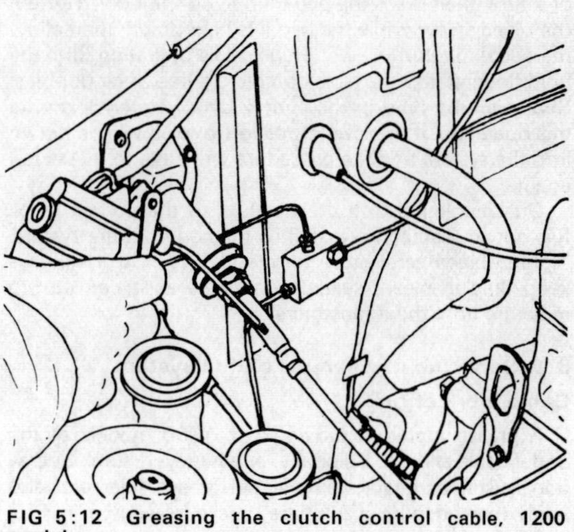

FIG 5:12 Greasing the clutch control cable, 1200 model

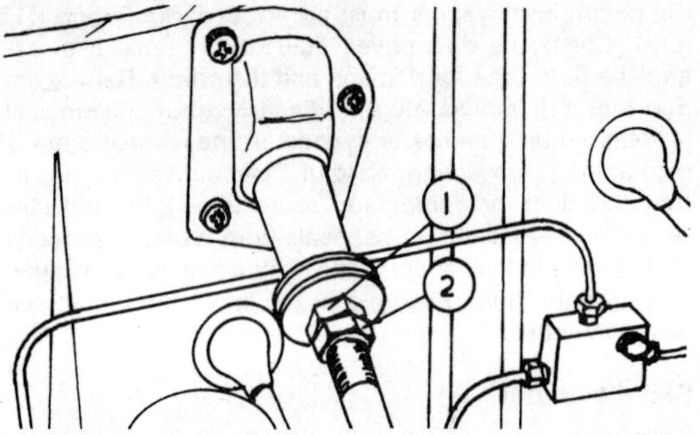

FIG 5:13 The cable adjusting 1 and locknut 2

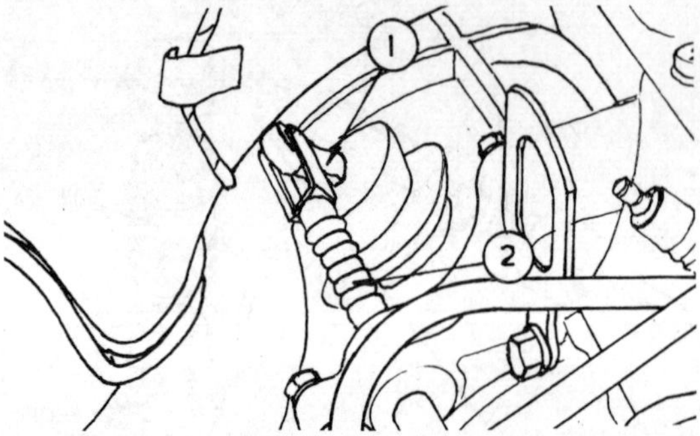

FIG 5:14 The withdrawal lever 1 and connector 2

damage, renewing any part found defective. Always fit a new rubber piston seal with lip facing inwards.

Observing absolute cleanliness, dip all parts in the correct grade of fluid and assemble them in the reverse order of dismantling.

Bleeding the clutch system:

This operation is necessary to remove any air which may have entered the system due to the removal of components, or if the fluid level in the supply tank has been allowed to drop too low and air has entered through the fluid supply passage. The need for bleeding will be indicated by a failure of the clutch to release properly, even though the pedal is pressed right to the floor. Check, however, that the cause is not improper clutch adjustment, referring to **Section 5:4**, as this is a more usual cause of faulty clutch operation. Always bleed the clutch system after any part of the hydraulic system has been dismantled and after any fluid hose has been disconnected in the system.

Fill the master cylinder supply tank with the correct grade of fluid, as supplied by the agent. Remove the dust cap from the bleed screw on the slave cylinder, connect a length of rubber tube to the bleed screw and immerse the free end of the tube in a small quantity,of the fluid in a clean glass jar. An assistant will be needed to operate the clutch pedal. Open the bleed screw about three-quarters of a turn, then press the pedal firmly to the floor. Tighten the bleed screw while the pedal is held down, then allow the pedal to return slowly. Repeat this operation until the fluid flowing into the jar is completely free of air bubbles. Replenish the fluid in the supply tank frequently during this operation. If the level drops too low, air will be drawn into the system and the procedure will have to be started again.

On completion, top up the fluid to the correct level. It is not advisable to re-use fluid drained from the system. Tighten bleed screw to a torque of 5 to 6 lb ft. Always keep fluid in clean, sealed containers as it can absorb moisture from the atmosphere.

5:6 Servicing mechanical clutch system

Cable lubrication:

A grease nipple is provided on 1200 models at the upper cable end. Occasionally, or whenever clutch operation is stiff or heavy, remove the grease filler cap and apply molybdenum disulphide grease as shown in **FIG 5:12**. On 120Y models, renew cable.

Control cable and pedal removal:

Loosen the lock and adjusting nuts shown in **FIG 5:13**, then release the cable from the withdrawal lever as shown in **FIG 5:14**. Unhook the return spring from the clutch pedal. Remove the pedal installation bolts and remove the clutch pedal disconnect cable from withdrawal lever and remove. Check all parts for wear and renew any found defective.

Refit in the reverse order of removal, adjusting the clutch as described in **Section 5:4**.

5:7 Fault diagnosis

(a) Drag or spin

1 Oil or grease on driven plate linings
2 Leaking master cylinder, slave cylinder or hose
3 Control cable binding
4 Distorted driven plate
5 Warped or damaged pressure plate
6 Broken driven plate linings
7 Air in hydraulic system
8 Excessive clutch operating clearance

(b) Fierceness or snatch

1 Check 1, 2, 3, 4 and 5 in (a)
2 Worn driven plate linings

(c) Slip

1 Check 1 in (a) and 2 in (b)
2 Weak diaphragm spring
3 Seized slave cylinder piston
4 Seized control cable
5 Insufficient clutch operating clearance

(d) Judder

1 Check 1, 4 and 5 in (a)
2 Contact area of friction linings unevenly worn
3 Bent or worn clutch shaft
4 Badly worn splines in driven plate hub
5 Faulty engine or gearbox mountings

(e) Tick or knock

1 Badly worn driven plate hub splines
2 Worn release bearing
3 Bent or worn clutch shaft
4 Loose flywheel

CHAPTER 6

THE GEARBOX

6:1 Description

Four types of gearbox are used in these cars. A three-speed (R3W 56A) or a four-speed (F4W 56A) was fitted to all models up to 1975. From then on, a new type of four-speed unit (F4W 60) or a five-speed (FS5W 63A) was used on USA models. Gear ratios and other specifications will be found in **Technical Data** at the end of this manual. Both four-speed units are similar in design and construction and any differences will be noted in the text. Automatic transmission units are covered in **Chapter 7**.

All gearboxes are equipped with synchromesh on all forward speeds which are selected by a steering column mounted lever (three-speed) or a floor mounted shift lever (four- and five-speed).

Maintenance and servicing instructions given in this chapter concern the four-speed gearboxes. Three-speed and five-speed units are similar and can be removed and refitted in the same manner, as described in **Section 6:2**. Any servicing procedures which differ for the three-speed unit will be detailed in **Section 6:6**, while **Section 6:7** describes the differences for the five-speed unit. **FIG 6:1** is a sectional view of a typical four-speed gearbox.

The gearbox assembly is constructed in three main parts, the transmission case which houses the gear assemblies, the rear extension housing containing the gear selector linkage and gearbox output shaft and the front bellhousing which encloses the clutch unit.

Gearbox oil level should be maintained at the level of the plug in the side of the transmission case and should be checked and, if necessary, topped up to the correct level at 3000 mile intervals. Every 30,000 miles the gearbox should be drained while the oil is hot, then refilled with API.GL-4 oil (SAE 80W).

6:2 Removing and refitting the gearbox

Removal:

Jack up the car and safely support it on four floor stands, to provide the necessary access beneath the car. Refer to **FIG 6:2**. Disconnect the front exhaust pipe 1 from the exhaust manifold, then remove the propeller shaft 2 as described in **Chapter 8**. Disconnect the speedometer cable 3 and the reversing light cable from the extension housing.

On cars fitted with steering column gearchange linkages, disconnect the rods from the levers on the gearchange linkage by removing the cotterpins, then remove the cross-shaft 4. On cars fitted with floor gearchange, remove the gearlever boot, withdraw the lockpin and remove the gearlever, this operation being carried out from the inside of the car.

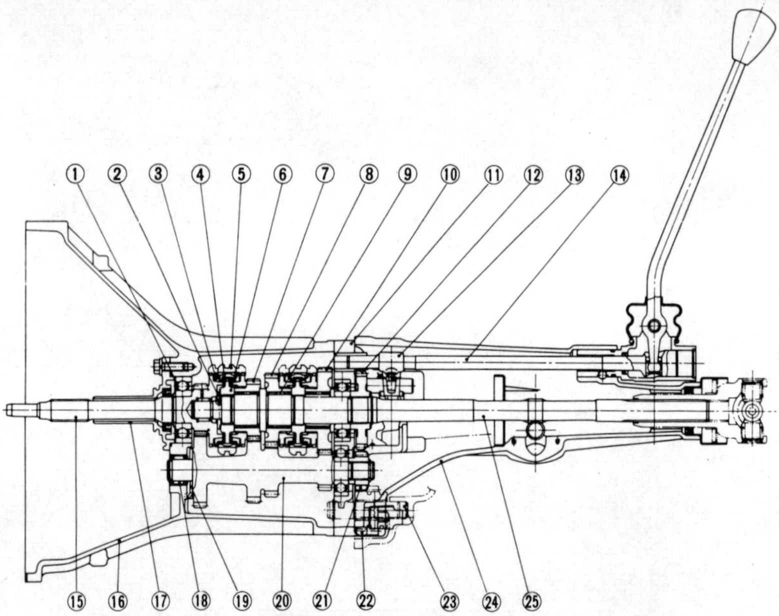

FIG 6:1 Sectional diagram of a typical four-speed gearbox

Key to Fig 6:1 1 Front cover adjusting shim 2 Synchro-hub thrust washer 3 Baulk ring 4 Shifting insert 5 Coupling sleeve 6 Synchroniser hub 7 Third gear, mainshaft 8 Second gear, mainshaft 9 Needle bearing 10 First gear, mainshaft 11 Adaptor plate 12 Reverse gear, mainshaft 13 Striking lever 14 Striking rod 15 Main drive gear 16 Transmission case 17 Front cover 18 Countershaft needle bearing 19 Counter gear thrust washer 20 Counter gear 21 Reverse counter gear 22 Reverse idler gear 23 Reverse idler shaft 24 Rear extension 25 Mainshaft

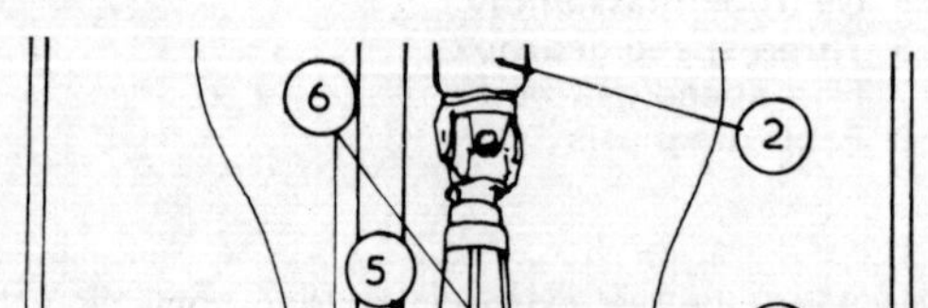

FIG 6:2 Items to be disconnected before gearbox removal

On certain models it will be necessary to remove the centre console to gain access to the floor cover plate and boot.

Refer to **Chapter 5** and, depending on the type of clutch control fitted, disconnect the cable at the withdrawal lever or remove the slave cylinder and support it clear of the work. The slave cylinder need not be disconnected from the fluid pipe.

Support the engine with a jack placed beneath the oil sump, noting that the jack must not bear on the drain plug. Use a block of wood between the jack and the sump to prevent damage. Place a jack under the gearbox to support it, then remove the two nuts 1 (see **FIG 6:3**) attaching the gearbox to the crossmember and the two bolts 2 attaching the crossmember to the car body. Raise the jack supporting the engine to tilt the engine rearwards, which will provide sufficient space for gearbox removal. Remove the starter motor and the bolts securing the bellhousing to the engine block. Keeping the gearbox supported by the jack, carefully slide it downwards and rearwards to release the splined shaft from the clutch unit, then lower and remove the gearbox from beneath the car. **Never allow the weight of the gearbox to hang on the splined shaft, or the clutch driven plate will be seriously damaged.**

Refitting:

This is a reversal of the removal procedure, again taking great care to prevent clutch damage by ensuring that the splined shaft slides smoothly into position while the gearbox weight is supported by the jack. On completion, check that all systems operate correctly and top up the gearbox oil as necessary.

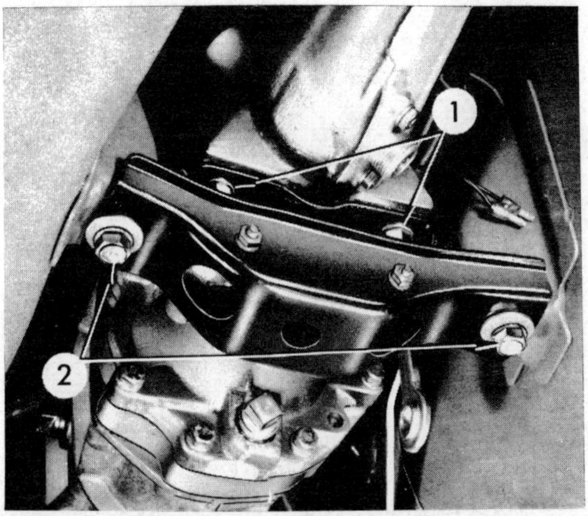

FIG 6:3 Removing the rear crossmember

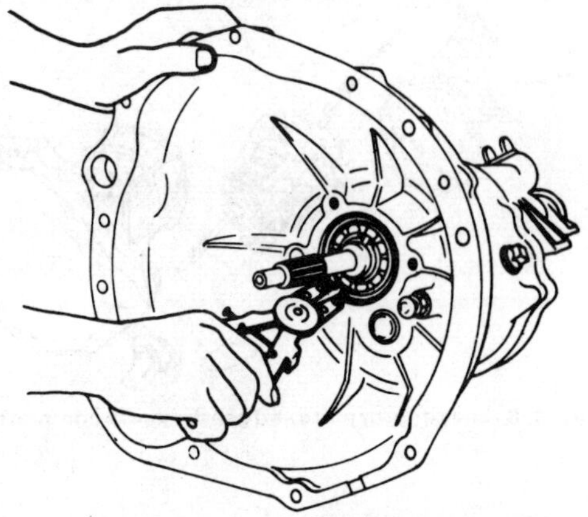

FIG 6:5 Removing snap ring from input shaft

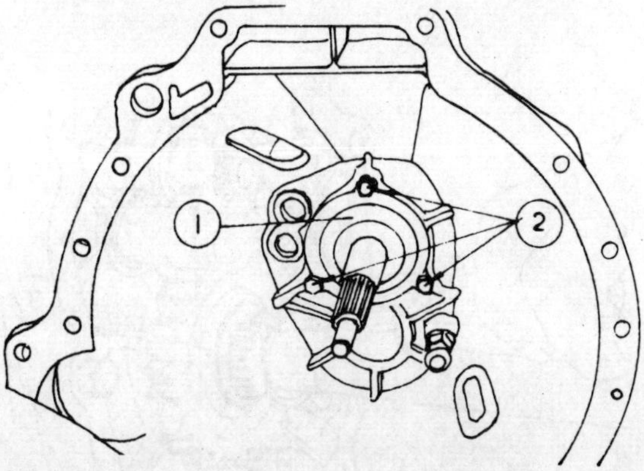

FIG 6:4 Removing the front cover

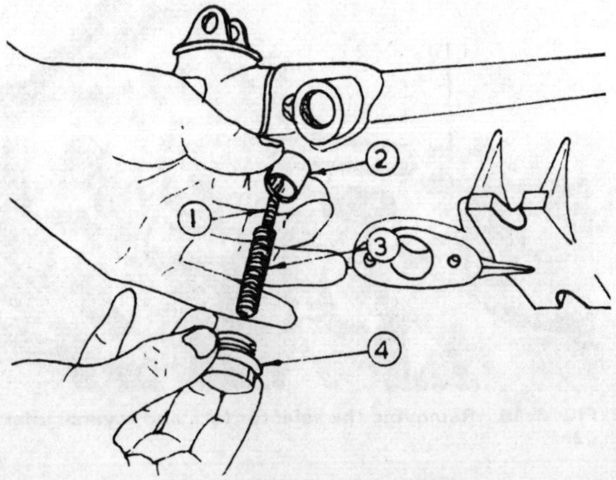

FIG 6:6 Removing the return spring

6:3 Dismantling the gearbox

1 Thoroughly clean the outside of the gearbox and front and rear housing assemblies to remove road dirt and grit. Drain the oil from the gearbox. Remove the clutch release lever and release bearing assembly as described in **Chapter 5**. Handle the gearbox casing parts with care to avoid damage to the light alloy castings, particularly the joint faces.

2 Remove the front cover 1 after taking out the three bolts 2 shown in **FIG 6:4**, noting, if applicable, the 'O' ring and cover adjusting shim. Refer to **FIG 6:5** and use circlip pliers to remove the input shaft snap ring. Remove the speedometer drive pinion assembly from the rear extension housing. Remove the return spring plug 4 and remove the return spring 3, plunger 1 and bush 2 from the housing as shown in **FIG 6:6**. Remove the striking rod pin as shown in **FIG 6:7** and separate the striking rod from the control lever bracket.

3 Remove the eight bolts which secure the extension housing to the transmission case, then remove the extension housing by lightly tapping with a wooden mallet. Separate the adaptor plate which supports the

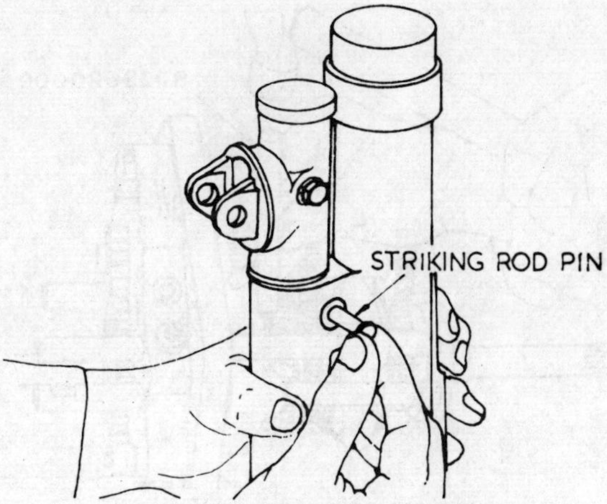

FIG 6:7 Removing the striking rod

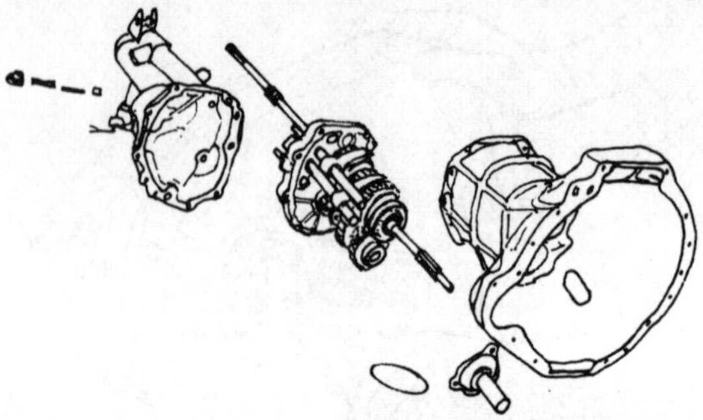

FIG 6:8 The adaptor plate and gearbox case components

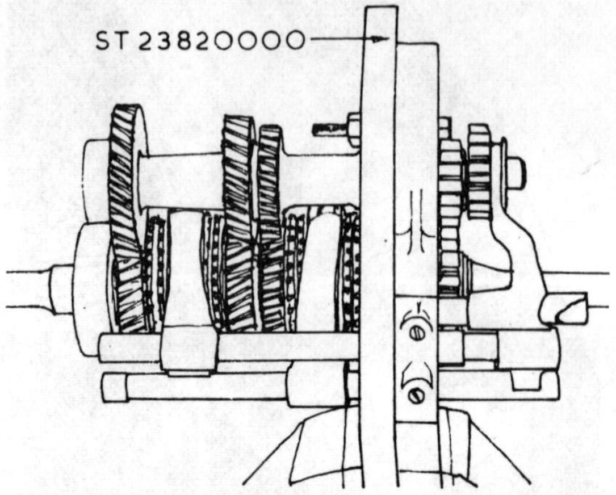

FIG 6:9 Mounting the gear units on the special plate

FIG 6:10 Removing the selector fork and reverse idler gear

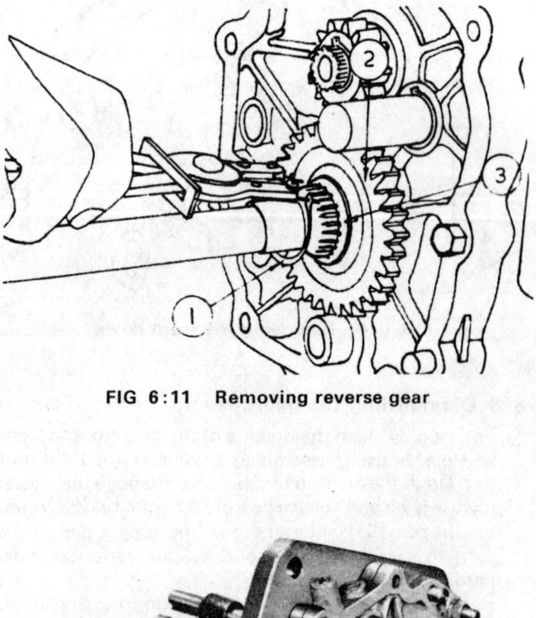

FIG 6:11 Removing reverse gear

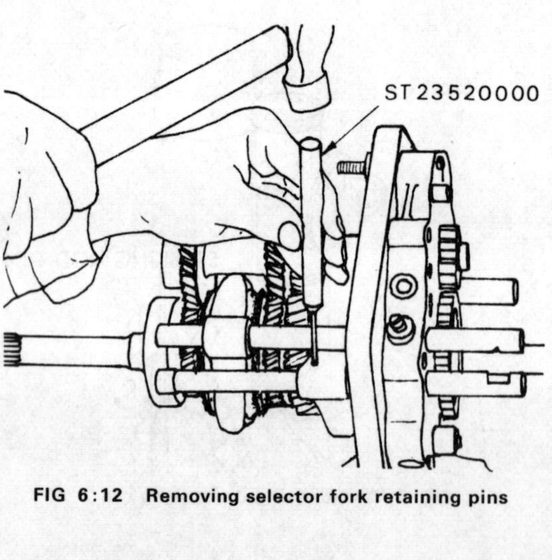

FIG 6:12 Removing selector fork retaining pins

FIG 6:13 Check ball removal

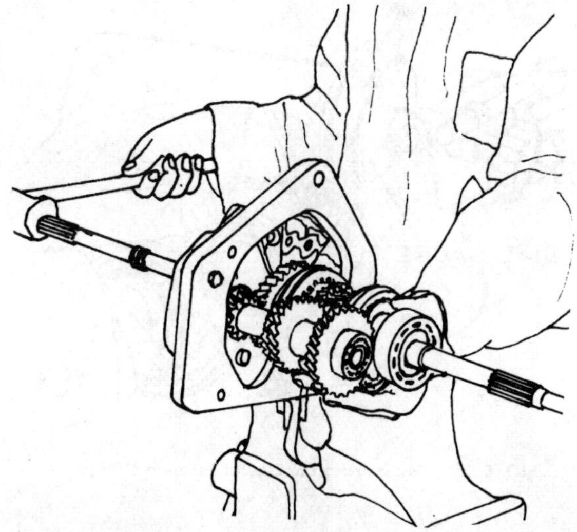

FIG 6:14 Separating the gear assemblies from the adaptor plate

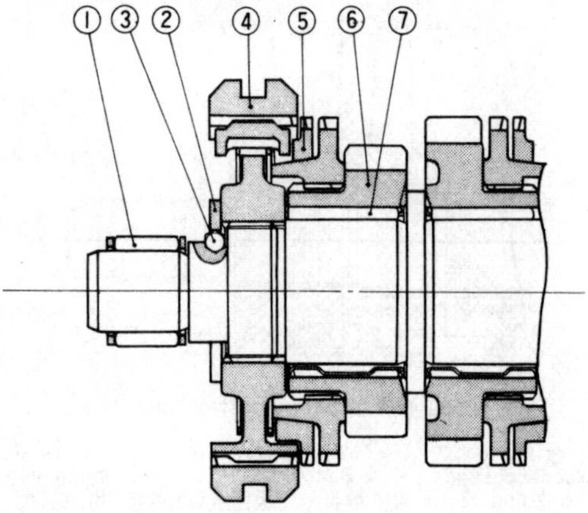

FIG 6:15 Mainshaft details

Key to Fig 6:15 1 Needle bearing 2 Thrust washer 3 Steel ball 4 Coupling sleeve 5 Baulk ring 6 3rd gear 7 Needle bearing

mainshaft and countershaft from the gearbox case, taking care not to lose the bearing washer installed on the front end of the countershaft when doing so. **FIG 6:8** shows the adaptor plate removed.

4 The use of special tool ST.23820000 attached to the adaptor plate and secured in a vice as shown in **FIG 6:9** will greatly facilitate the dismantling of the gear units. Remove the retaining pin with a suitable punch and withdraw the reverse selector fork 1 and reverse idler gear 2, as shown in **FIG 6:10**. Remove the snap ring 1 and withdraw the washer 3 and reverse gear 2, as shown in **FIG 6:11**.

5 Remove the retaining pin from each selector fork, using a punch as shown in **FIG 6:12**. Remove the check ball plugs for all selector rods as shown in **FIG 6:13**, taking care not to lose the check balls and springs as the plugs are released. Remove all of the selector rods from the adaptor plate. If fitted, remove the mainshaft rear bearing retainer. This is secured by four screws which are very tight, requiring an impact screwdriver to loosen. Detach the retainer and then use circlip pliers to remove the mainshaft rear bearing snap ring. Lightly tap the mainshaft with a wooden mallet and separate the mainshaft and countershaft assemblies from the adaptor plate, as shown in **FIG 6:14**. Take care not to drop the gear assemblies during removal as they are easily damaged.

6 Refer to **FIG 6:15**. Remove the needle bearing, thrust washer, steel ball, third and fourth gear synchronizer mechanism, baulk ring, third gear and mainshaft needle bearing. These parts are removed towards the front of the shaft in the order given. To remove the main drive bearing from the mainshaft, use tool ST. 22730000 and a press as shown in **FIG 6:16**. Refer to **FIG 6:17** and remove the thrust washer, first gear, needle bearing, baulk ring, first and second gear synchronizer mechanism, baulk ring, second gear and needle bearing from the mainshaft. Remove the bearing from the countergear. Remove the snap ring from the main drive gear and remove the bearing.

6:4 Servicing gearbox components

Thoroughly clean all parts in petrol or paraffin and dry them. Examine the gearbox case, extension housing and bellhousing castings for cracks or defects which may cause oil leakage. Clean all bearings and dry them and remove dust with compressed air, taking care not to spin the bearings as the air jet is applied.

Turn the ballbearings between the fingers to test for roughness or slackness. Inspect needle bearings for wear,

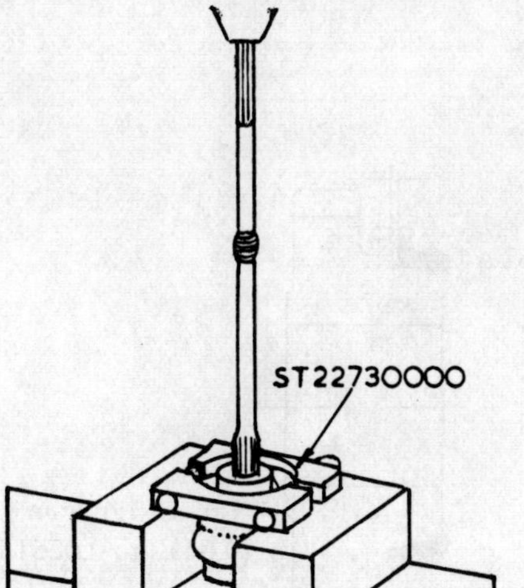

FIG 6:16 Removing the mainshaft bearing

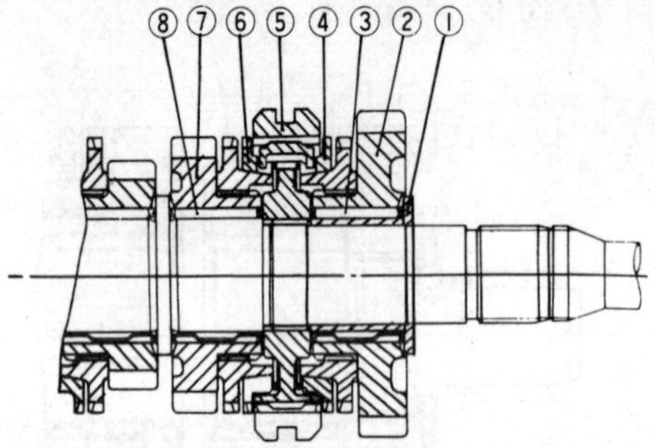

FIG 6:17 Mainshaft details

Key to Fig 6:17 1 Thrust washer 2 1st gear 3 Needle bearing 4 Baulk ring 5 Coupling sleeve 6 Baulk ring 7 2nd gear 8 Needle bearing

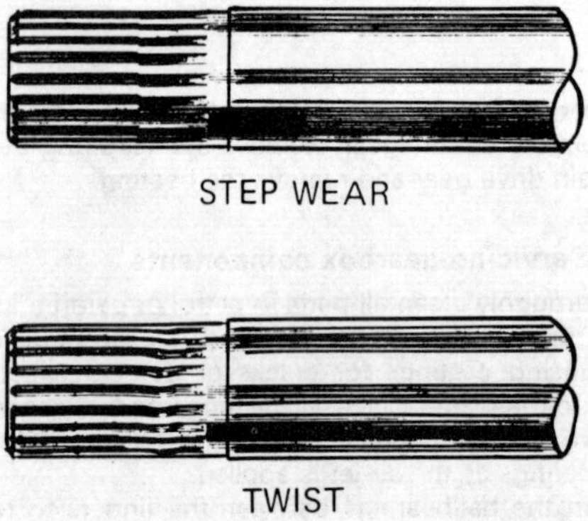

FIG 6:18 Two possible types of wear on gearbox shaft splines

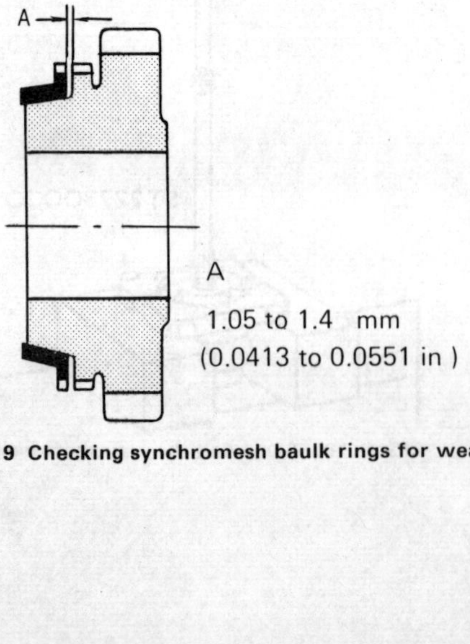

FIG 6:19 Checking synchromesh baulk rings for wear

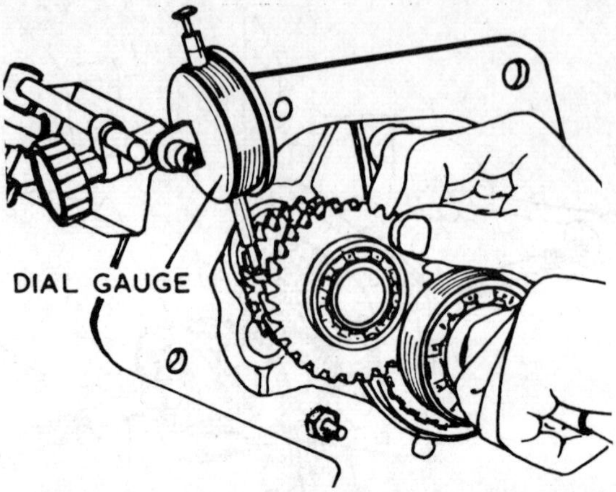

FIG 6:20 Measuring backlash between the gears

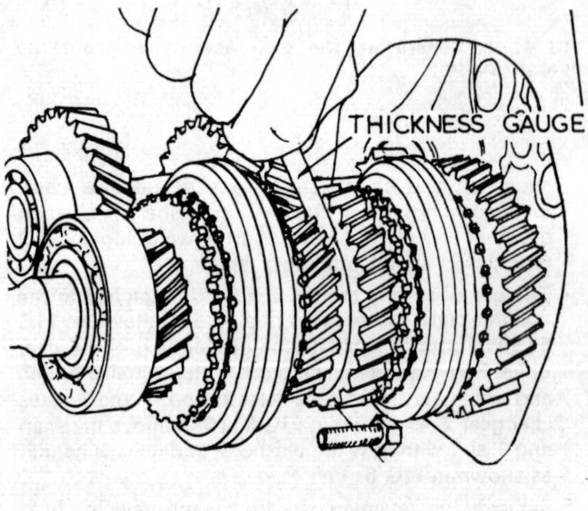

FIG 6:21 Checking gear end play

damage or roughness in operation. The rear extension housing bush should be checked, and renewed if not in good condition.

Check the splines on the gearbox main drive shaft which mate with those on the clutch driven plate hub. They should be smooth, square and without burrs or distortion. Two possible wear patterns are shown in **FIG 6:18**. If the splines are worn or damaged, renew the shaft. Any gearbox shaft which is bent, cracked or worn should be renewed.

Check the gears and synchromesh assemblies for wear or damage and inspect for chipped or broken teeth. Measure the synchromesh baulk ring wear as shown in **FIG 6:19**. Press the baulk ring onto the cone of the gear and measure the gap between the front face of the teeth and the end face of the baulk ring. The gap should be between .041 and .055 inch (1.05 and 1.4 mm). If it is less than .020 inch (.5 mm) the baulk ring is worn and should be renewed.

When the gears are reassembled, measure the backlash between the gears as shown in **FIG 6:20**, using a dial gauge. Hold one gear firmly and measure the movement

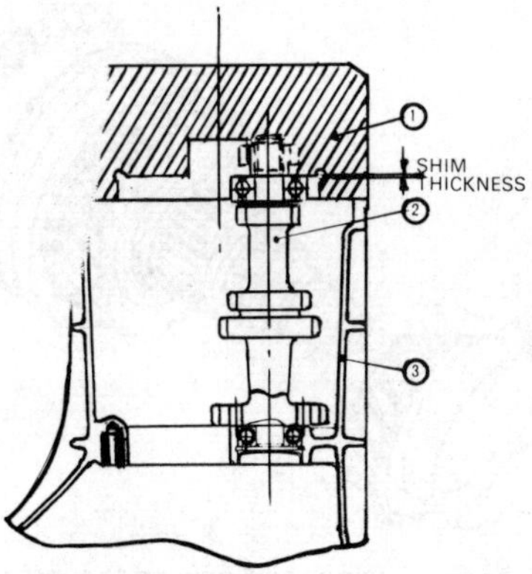

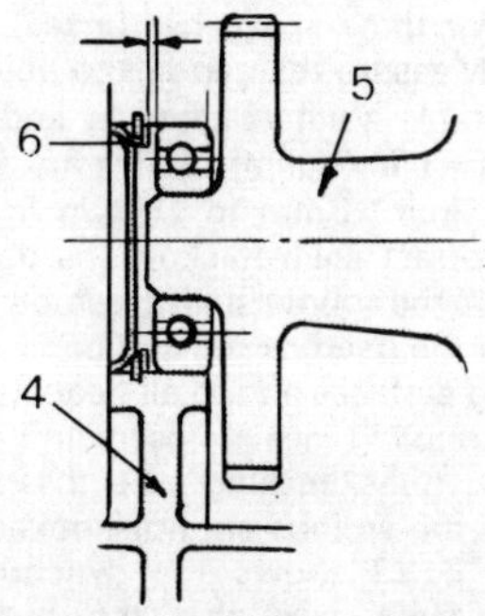

FIG 6:22 Selecting countershaft front bearing shim

Key to Fig 6:22 1 ST.23040000 (3-speed) ST.23050000 (4-speed) 2 Countershaft 3 Transmission case 4 Transmission case 5 Countershaft 6 Adjusting shim

of the meshing gear. Backlash should be between .003 and .006 inch (.08 and .15 mm). If backlash exceeds the figures stated, it is recommended that a complete new set of gears be obtained and fitted, rather than replacing single components.

End play of the gears on the shaft should be checked with feeler gauges as shown in **FIG 6:21**. First and second gear end play should be between .006 and .010 inch (.15 and .25 mm), third and fourth gear end play should be between .006 and .014 inch (.15 and .35 mm). If the play is beyond the limits stated, select a suitable snap ring from the oversizes available to correct the play.

Renew the oil seal if not in perfect condition. Check for worn, deformed or cracked seal lips and for loose springs. Always discard all old gaskets and obtain new ones to replace them.

6:5 Gearbox reassembly

1 Press the bearings onto the front and rear of the countershaft, making sure that they are fully home on the shaft. Fit the countershaft assembly into the gearbox case and install special tool ST.23050000 (ST.

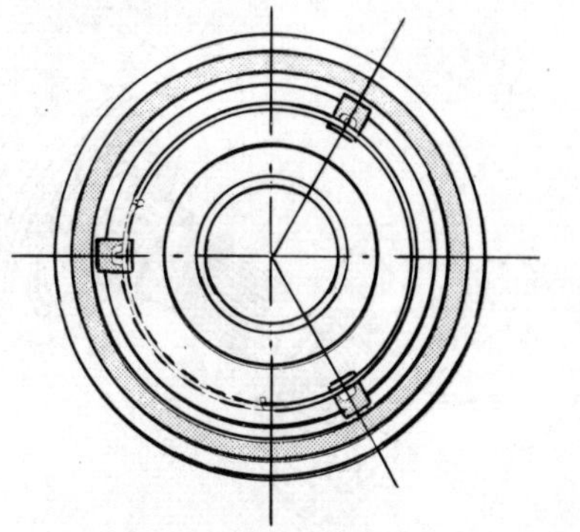

FIG 6:23 Synchromesh spring installation

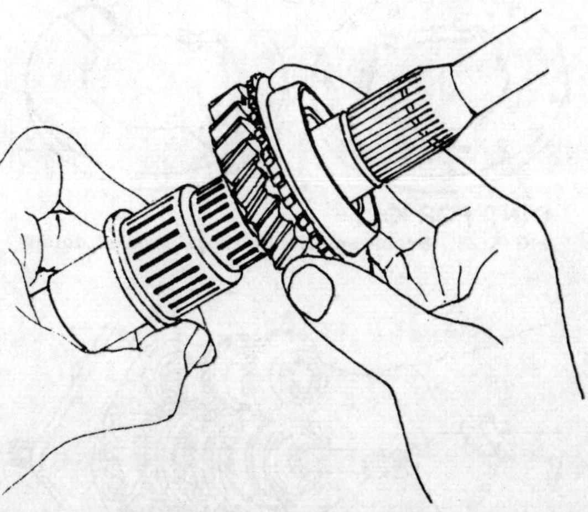

FIG 6:24 Installing second gear

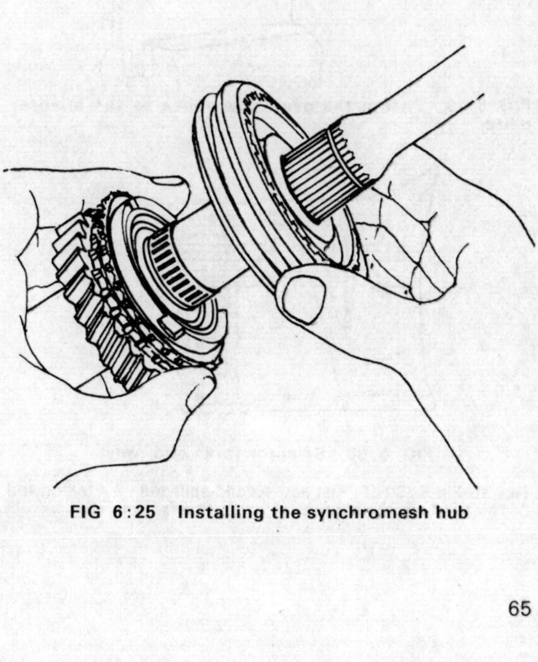

FIG 6:25 Installing the synchromesh hub

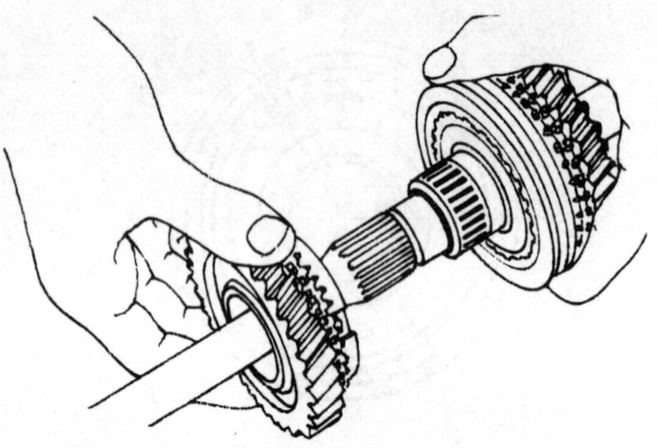

FIG 6:26 Fitting first gear to the mainshaft

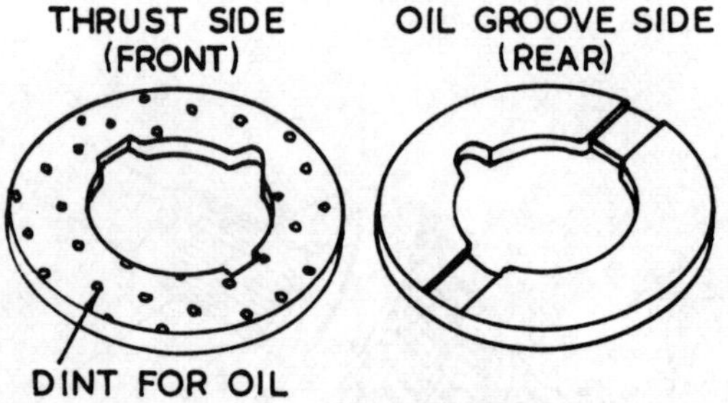

FIG 6:28 Synchromesh hub thrust washer details

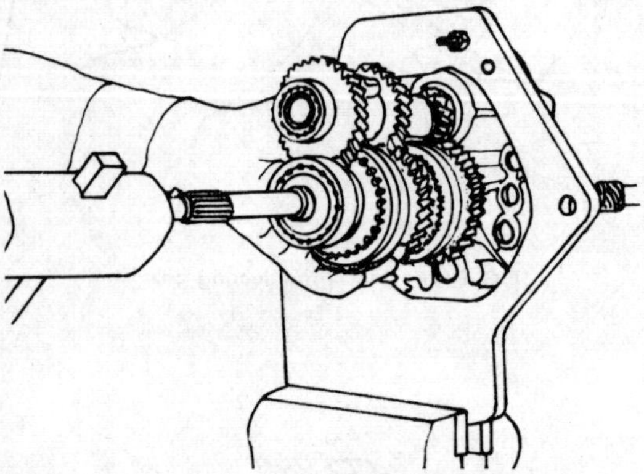

FIG 6:29 Fitting the gear assemblies to the adaptor plate

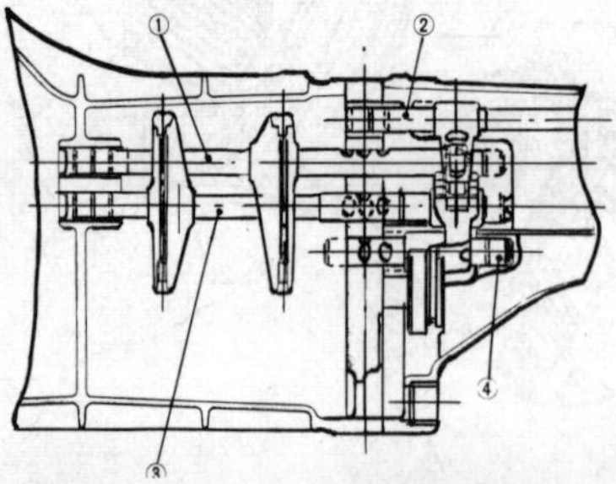

FIG 6:30 Selector forks and rods

Key to Fig 6:30 1 First and second shift rod 2 Striking rod 3 Third and fourth shift rod 4 Reverse shift rod

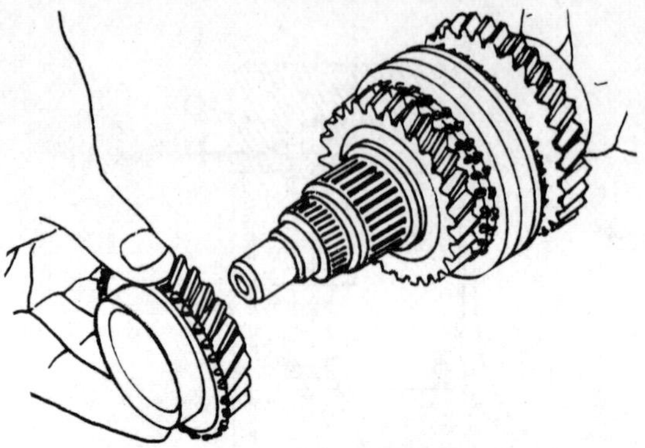

FIG 6:27 Fitting third gear to the mainshaft

23040000 for three-speed gearboxes), as shown in **FIG 6:22**. Measure the gap at the point shown and select a suitable shim to give an end play of .004 to .008 inch (.1 to .2 mm). Shims are available in six thicknesses, from .8 mm to 1.3 mm in .1 mm steps. When the correct shim thickness is determined and noted, remove the countershaft assembly from the case.

2 When fitting the gearbox moving parts, apply gear oil to the sliding surfaces and to all bearings and bushes. Install the coupling sleeve, insert and spring on the synchromesh hubs, making sure that the front and rear ends of the springs are not hooked to the same insert. **FIG 6:23** shows the synchromesh spring installation. Make sure that the hub and sleeve operates smoothly and correctly by hand.

3 Install the needle bearing from the rear end of the mainshaft, then fit the second gear as shown in **FIG 6:24**. Install the baulk ring. Fit the synchromesh hub assembly, lining up the insert to the groove on the baulk ring, as shown in **FIG 6:25**. Install the first gear side needle bearing, baulk ring and first gear as shown in **FIG 6:26**, fitting the parts in the order stated. Install the mainshaft thrust washer and fit the mainshaft rear bearing, using a suitable length of steel tubing or tool ST.22350000 as a drift.

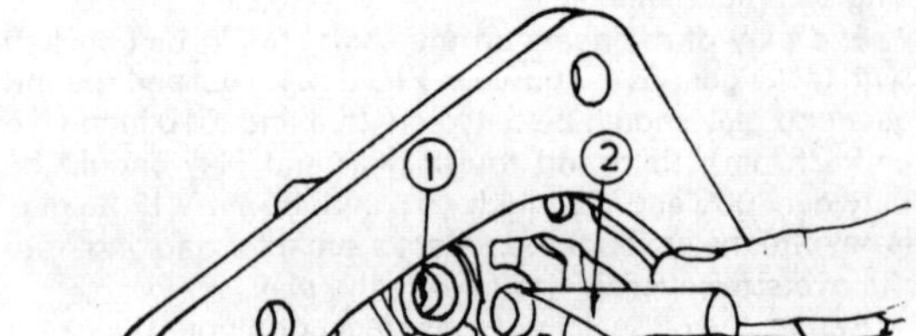

FIG 6:31 Installing selector check ball 1 with the special tool 2

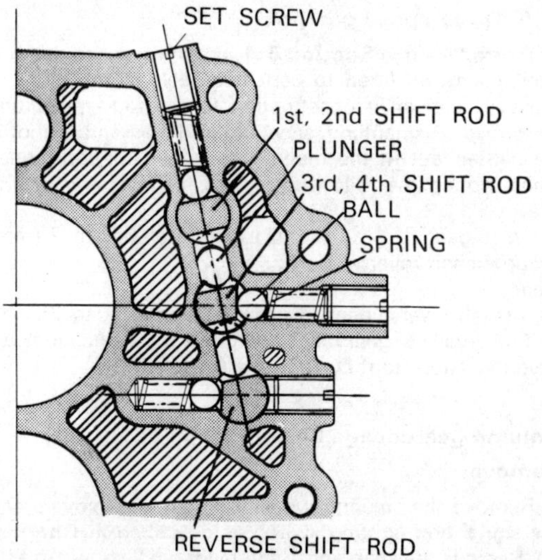

FIG 6:32 Check ball assemblies

4 Install the needle bearing, third gear, baulk ring and synchromesh hub assembly from the front end of the mainshaft, **FIG 6:27** showing the installation of the third gear. Install the steel ball, synchromesh hub thrust washer and mainshaft pilot bearing. When fitting, grease the sliding surface of the steel ball and thrust washer, and make sure that the thrust washer is located correctly according to the details in **FIG 6:28**.

5 Using a suitable length of steel tubing or tool ST. 22350000 as a drift, install the front bearing to the main drive gear and fit the main bearing washer and snap ring. Make sure that the web portion of the washer faces the bearing and that the snap ring is securely fitted in the groove.

6 Install the baulk ring on the main drive gear and complete the gear unit assembly. Mate the mainshaft and countershaft assemblies and fit them to the adapter plate. Start the front mainshaft bearing into position, then line up the countershaft bearing and lightly tap the shaft with a wooden mallet to install the units, as shown in **FIG 6:29**.

7 Install the selector forks on the rods, making sure that there is no gap between the forks and rods. **FIG 6:30** shows the layout of these components. Install each rod together with the check ball, spring, interlock plunger and plug, using the fork rod guide ST.23620000 to install the check balls as shown in **FIG 6:31**. Fit each rod so that the groove coincides with the check ball. Apply thread locking agents to the plugs and install them so that they are flush with the upper surface of the adaptor. **FIG 6:32** shows the layout of the check ball assemblies. Drive in the selector fork retaining pins.

8 Install reverse gear, reverse gear thrust washer with the web part towards the gear, then fit the snap ring to secure these parts. Install the reverse idler gear together with the reverse selector fork. Drive in the fork retaining pin. Install the third and fourth gear selector fork and fit the retaining pin.

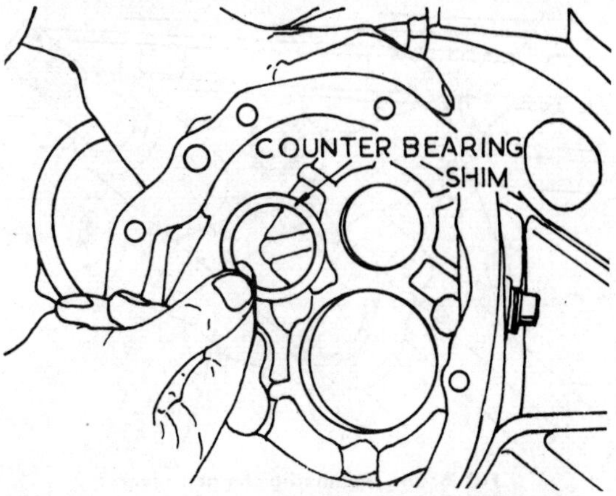

FIG 6:33 Fitting the counter bearing shim

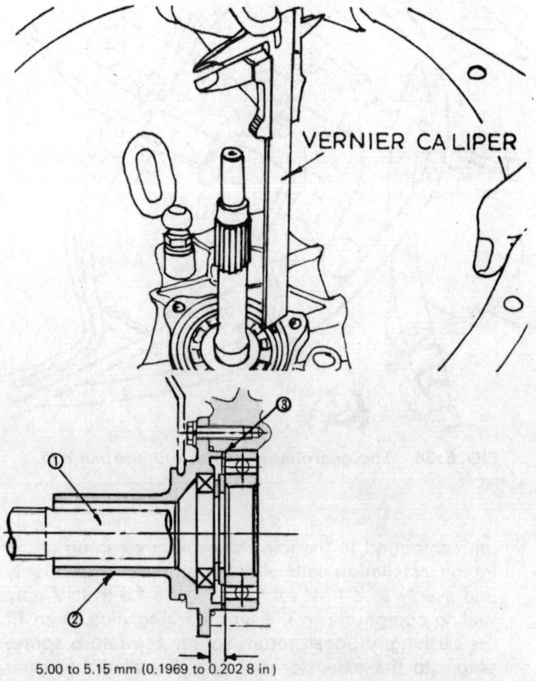

FIG 6:34 Measuring the mainshaft bearing depth to determine the necessary shim thickness

Key to Fig 6:34 1 Main drive gear 2 Front cover 3 Front cover adjusting shim

9 Remove the adaptor plate from the mounting attachment, if such has been used. Install the counter bearing shim previously selected, as shown in **FIG 6:33**. Clean oil and grease from the adaptor plate and gearbox case mating surfaces, then apply sealing compound to the joint faces and fit the plate to the case. Tap into position with a wooden mallet, being sure to line up the pin hole.

10 Line up the striking lever correctly and install the rear extension housing to the gearbox case, applying seal-

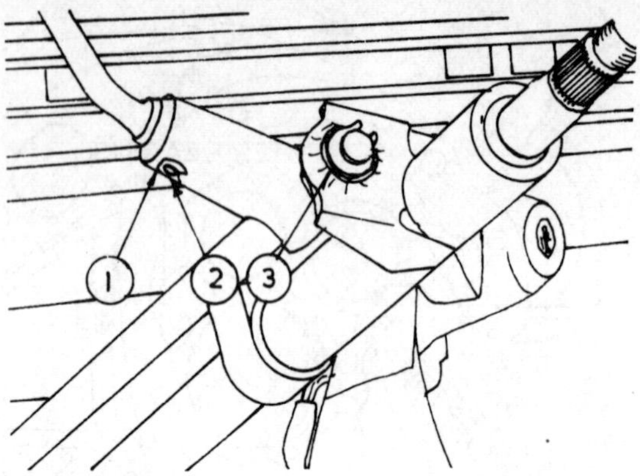

FIG 6 : 35 Removing the gearlever

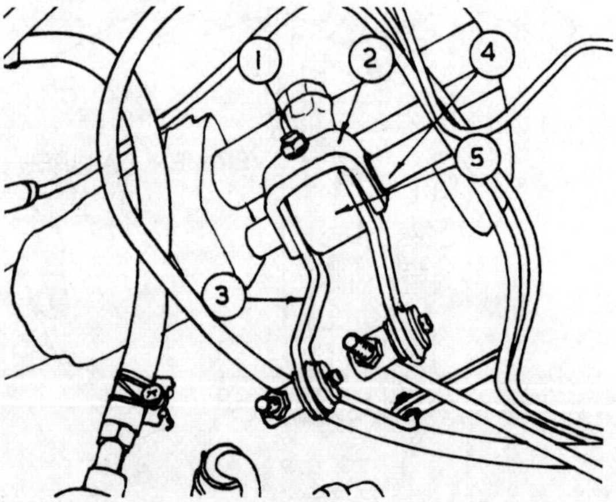

FIG 6 : 36 The gearchange lever and control rod

ing compound to the joint faces after cleaning them. Fit the installation bolts and tighten them alternatively and evenly to a final torque of 11 to 15 lb ft. Apply sealing compound to the return spring plug, then fit the bushing, plunger, return spring and return spring plug into the extension housing. Install the stopper pin and E-ring. Install the speedometer drive pinion.

11 Measure the depth from the front cover fitting surface to the end face of the main bearing outer race, using a vernier caliper as shown in **FIG 6 : 34**. Noting this measurement, select shims to give a measurement of .197 ±.006 inch (5.0 ±.15 mm). Shims are available in .197, .008 and .004 inch (.5, .2 and .1 mm) thicknesses and can be used singly or combined to give the correct depth. Grease the lip of the oil seal, then install it on the front cover. Fit the front cover together with the shim(s) just selected and the O-ring. Tighten the cover bolts to 8 to 11 lb ft.

12 Fit the clutch release bearing, return spring and withdrawal lever as described in **Chapter 5**. Check that all gears can be selected easily, then refit the gearbox as described previously and fill with the correct grade of oil.

6 : 6 Three-speed gearbox

As explained in **Section 6 : 1**, the three-speed gearbox which may be fitted to certain models in the range is basically similar in construction to the four-speed unit described. Dismantling, servicing and reassembly should be carried out in the manner described for four-speed units, noting the following figures for reverse gear end play.

Reverse gear	.002 to .008 inch (.05 to .20 mm)
Countershaft reverse gear	.002 to .006 inch (.05 to .15 mm)
Mainshaft reverse gear	.004 to .010 inch (.10 to .25 mm)

Full details of gear ratios and general specifications are given in **Technical Data** in the **Appendix**.

Column gearchange linkage:

Removal:

Remove the steering wheel, column shell covers and the signal and lighting switch as described in **Chapter 10**. Remove the snap ring 1 and pivot pin 2 shown in **FIG**

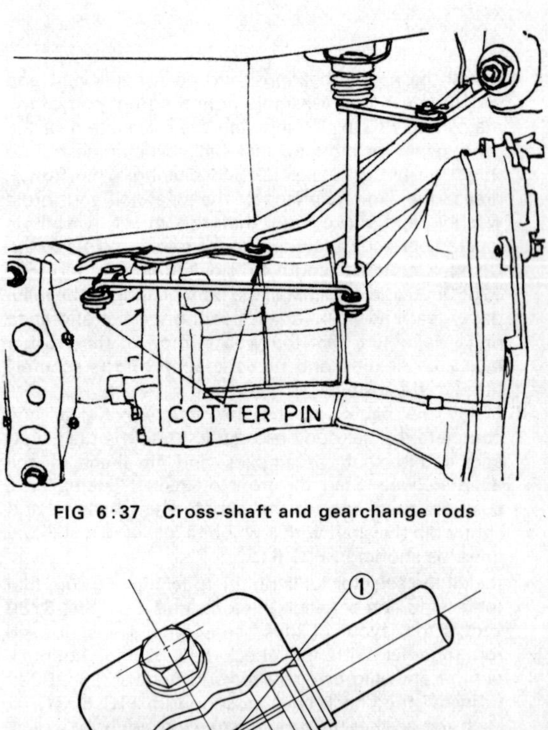

FIG 6 : 37 Cross-shaft and gearchange rods

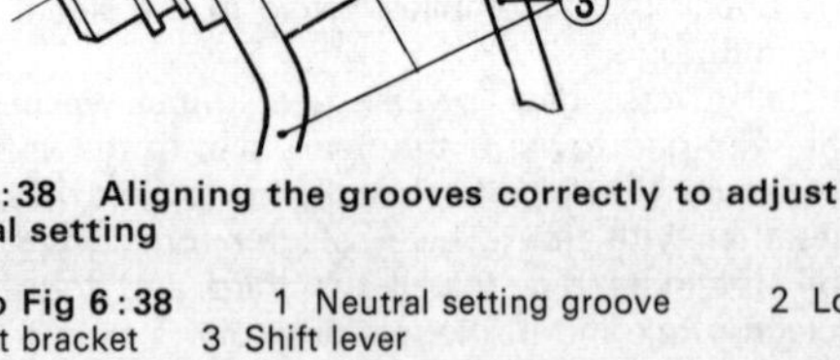

FIG 6 : 38 Aligning the grooves correctly to adjust the neutral setting

Key to Fig 6 : 38 1 Neutral setting groove 2 Lower support bracket 3 Shift lever

6 : 35, then remove the gearlever. Remove the C washer 3.

Refer to **FIG 6 : 36**. Remove the retainer bolt 1 and the retainer 2. Remove the second and top gearchange lever and bush 3 from the control rod 4. Lower the control rod so that the control lever pin comes out of the lower bracket 5, then withdraw the control lever pin. Withdraw the control rod from the passenger compartment.

Remove the cotterpins shown in **FIG 6 : 37** and disconnect the gearchange rods. Remove the cross-shaft from the sidemember and withdraw the cross-shaft assembly.

Inspection:

Check all sliding parts for wear and scoring and all other parts for bending or damage. If any slackness in the axial direction has been noted in the control rod operation, the control rod should be renewed. If the control rod is of the collapsible type, as fitted to models with telescopic steering columns, take care not to apply loads or shocks to the end of the rod as it may be damaged.

Refitting:

This is a reversal of the removal procedure. Apply multi-purpose grease to the sliding parts. Take care not to damage collapsible type control rod assemblies during refitting.

Adjustment:

Set the transmission gearlever to the neutral position. Temporarily connect the trunnion on the lower support bracket head to each rod. Set the rod on the lever with the grooves on the upper surface of the lower support bracket and on each lever aligned, as shown in **FIG 6 : 38**.

When the adjustment is correct as described, operate the gearlever to check that movement is smooth and positive between all gears. Readjust finely, if necessary, to correct any dragging or slackness noticed.

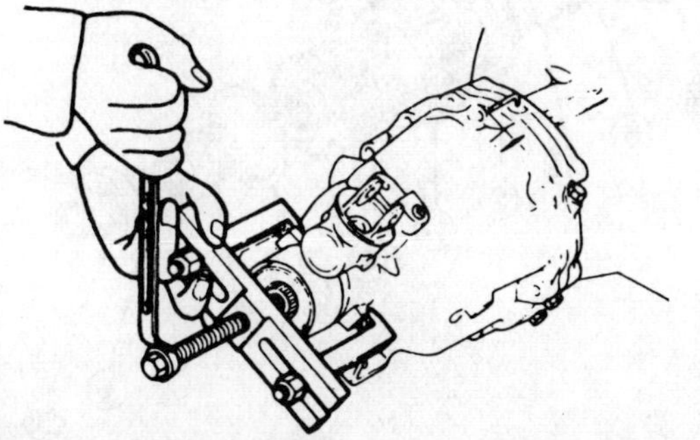

FIG 6 : 39 Removing the five-speed rear extension housing

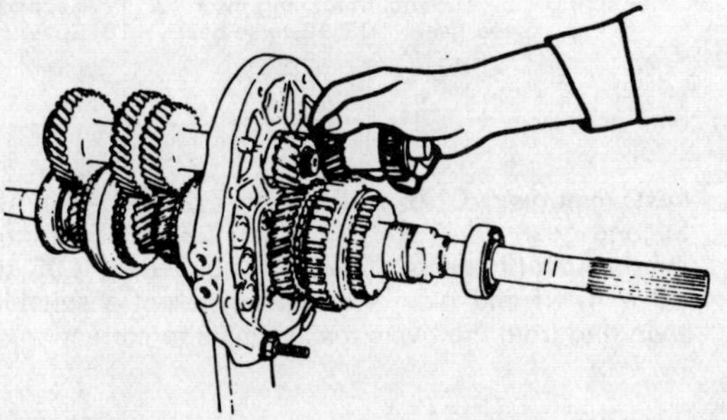

FIG 6 : 40 Removing reverse idler gear and shaft (five-speed gearbox)

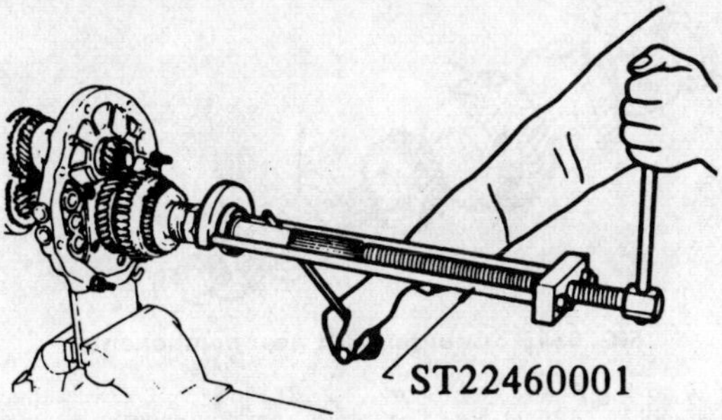

FIG 6 : 41 Removing mainshaft rear bearing

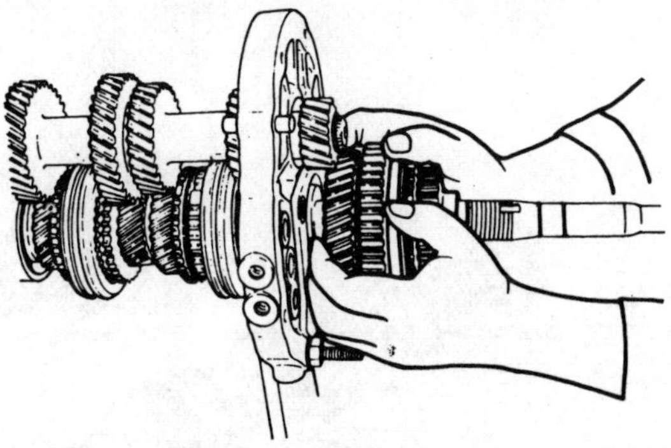

FIG 6 : 42 Removing reverse and first gears (five-speed)

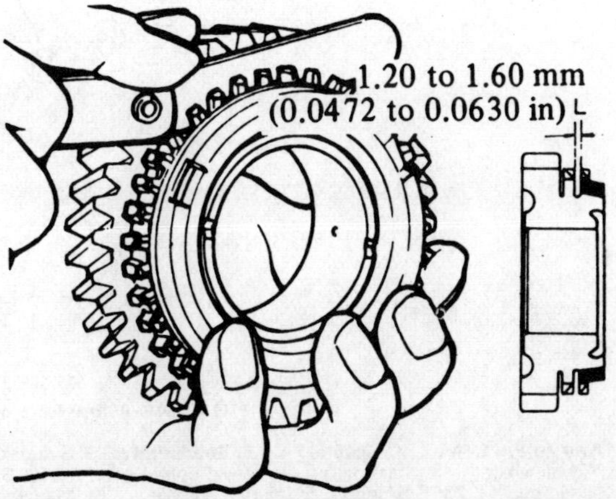

FIG 6 : 43 Measuring baulk ring to gear clearance

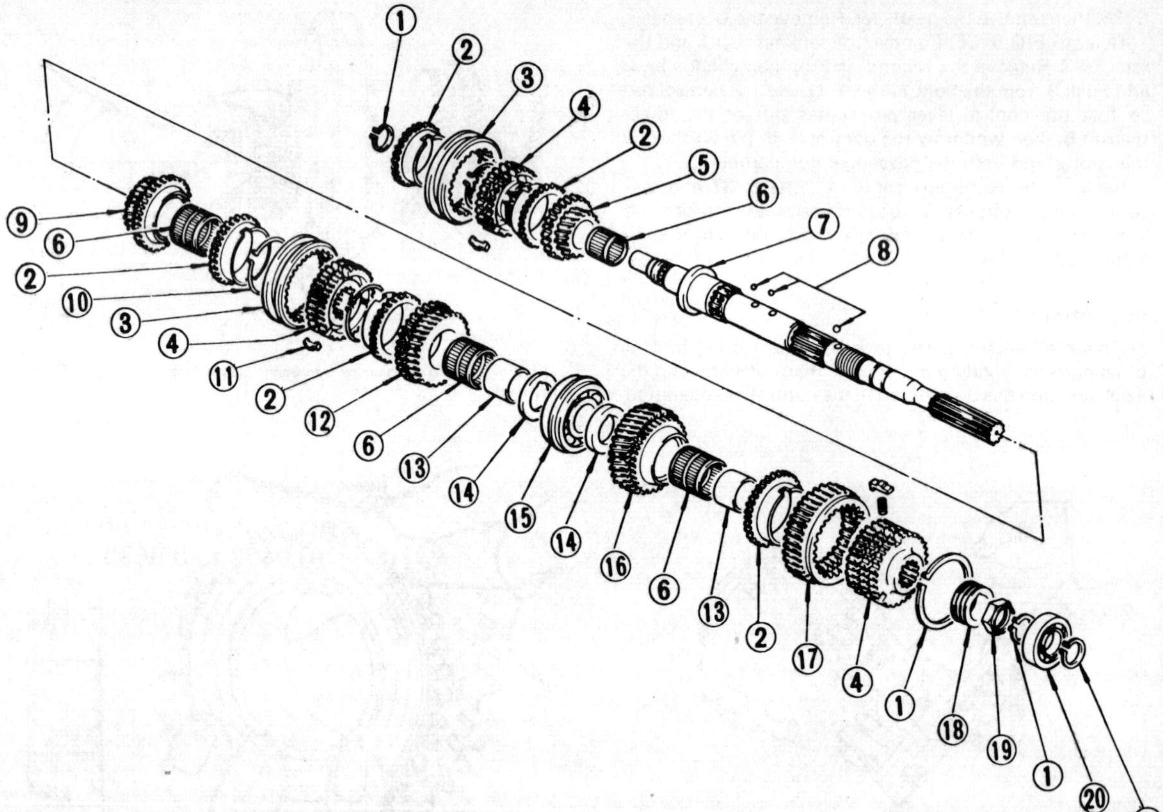

FIG 6:44 **Mainshaft gear components (five-speed)**

Key to Fig 6:44 1 Snap ring 2 Baulk ring 3 Synchro sleeve 4 Synchro hub 5 Fifth-speed gear 6 Needle bearing 7 Mainshaft 8 Steel balls 9 Third-speed gear 10 Synchro spreader spring 11 Synchro locking insert 12 Second-speed gear 13 Bushing 14 Thrust washer 15 Mainshaft bearing 16 First-speed gear 17 Reverse gear 18 Speedometer drive pinion 19 Mainshaft nut 20 Mainshaft rear bearing

6:7 Five-speed gearbox

The method of removal, refitting and servicing the four-speed unit, detailed in **Section 6:2** onwards, apply to this gearbox with the following exceptions:

1 Use a standard puller as shown in **FIG 6:39** to remove the rear extension housing.
2 The reverse idler gear is removed as shown in **FIG 6:40**, complete with its shaft.
3 The mainshaft rear bearing should only be removed using a long puller such as the tool shown in **FIG 6:41**.
4 Reverse and first gears are mounted at the rear of the unit and can be removed (after undoing the mainshaft nut) as shown in **FIG 6:42**, taking care not to lose the steel ball which retains the speedometer drive gear. Take care also not to lose the thrust washer fitted behind the first gear.

Tolerances:

1 Gear end play can be measured in the same way shown in **FIG 6:21**, using the specifications detailed next: First gear, .0126 to .0165 inch (.32 to .42 mm). Second gear, .0087 to .0126 inch (.22 to .32 mm). Third and fifth gears, .0020 to .0059 inch (.05 to .15 mm). If end play is excessive, select a suitable snap ring from the oversizes available to correct.

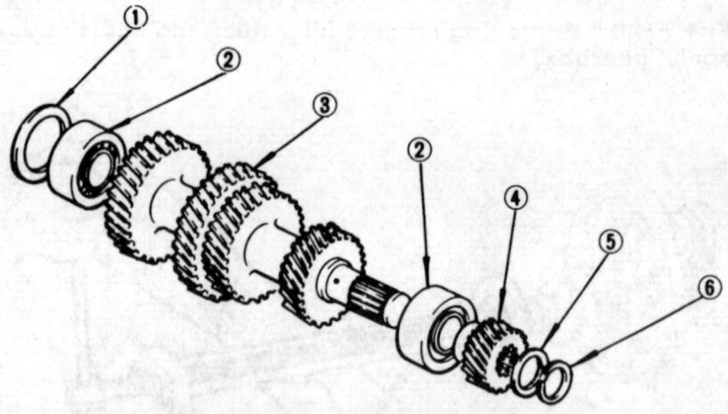

FIG 6:45 Countershaft gear components

Key to Fig 6:45 1 Shim 2 Bearing 3 Countergear assembly 4 First-speed countergear 5 Spacer 6 Snap ring

2 Baulk ring to gear clearance should be measured as shown in **FIG 6:43**. If the clearance exceeds .047 to .063 inch (1.20 to 1.60 mm), the relevant baulk ring must be replaced by a new one.

Reassembly:

This is mostly as detailed in **Section 6:5**, using the variations detailed at the beginning of this section. The gear components are shown in **FIGS 6:44** and **6:45**.

6:8 Fault diagnosis

(a) Jumping out of gear

1 Broken spring behind selector rod locating ball
2 Excessively worn groove in selector shaft
3 Worn synchromesh units
4 Fork loose on selector shaft
5 Column gearchange linkage incorrectly adjusted

(b) Noisy transmission

1 Insufficient oil
2 Worn or damaged bearings
3 Worn or damaged gearwheels

(c) Difficulty in engaging gear

1 Incorrect clutch adjustment
2 Worn synchromesh assemblies
3 Worn or loose selector forks
4 Gearchange linkage faulty

(d) Oil leaks

1 Worn or damaged oil seals
2 Damaged faces on gearbox case components
3 Faulty gaskets

NOTES

CHAPTER 7

AUTOMATIC TRANSMISSION

7:1 Description

Automatic transmission is fitted to some models as an optional alternative to the clutch and manual change gearbox.

The automatic transmission unit is composed of two main sub-assemblies, a torque converter and a hydraulically controlled epicyclic gearbox providing three forward speeds and reverse. The internal arrangement of the parts can be seen in **FIG 7:1**.

The torque converter is on the left, the epicyclic gear train in the centre and the channels and valves of the hydraulic control system in the section beneath. The rear extension housing to the right contains a hydraulic governor with the output shaft beyond. Gearbox and torque converter share the same special oil which acts both as lubricant and hydraulic fluid.

The torque converter is made up of three main elements; the impeller, coupled to the engine crankshaft, the stator, mounted on a one-way clutch so that it can spin in one direction but not in the other, and the turbine, attached to the gearshaft. The blades of the turning impeller set up a spiral flow of fluid which passes through the stator and drives the turbine (see **FIG 7:2**). When impeller speed is higher than turbine speed, the stator is stationary, and a torque multiplication effect like that of a reduction gear train is created. As the turbine speed rises, the torque multiplication decreases until the unit is acting simply as a fluid coupling with input and output speeds only slightly different and the stator spinning with the other elements. This combined torque multiplication and fluid coupling effect replaces the conventional clutch and smooths out the transitions between the gears so that three ratios are sufficient to cover the full range of performance.

The planetary gear set consists of an inner driven sun gear, an outer reaction gear and, intermeshed between them, the planet gears and carriers. By holding one member and applying power to another, the various gear ratios are achieved and smooth gearchanges obtained.

Gear changing is carried out by plate clutches within the gearset and band brakes around the outside. These clutches and brakes are operated by hydraulic servos. The hydraulic control system activates the servos in the right combinations according to road speed (monitored by the governor), selector lever position, engine speed (monitored by a pump incorporated in the front of the torque converter), throttle pedal position through the

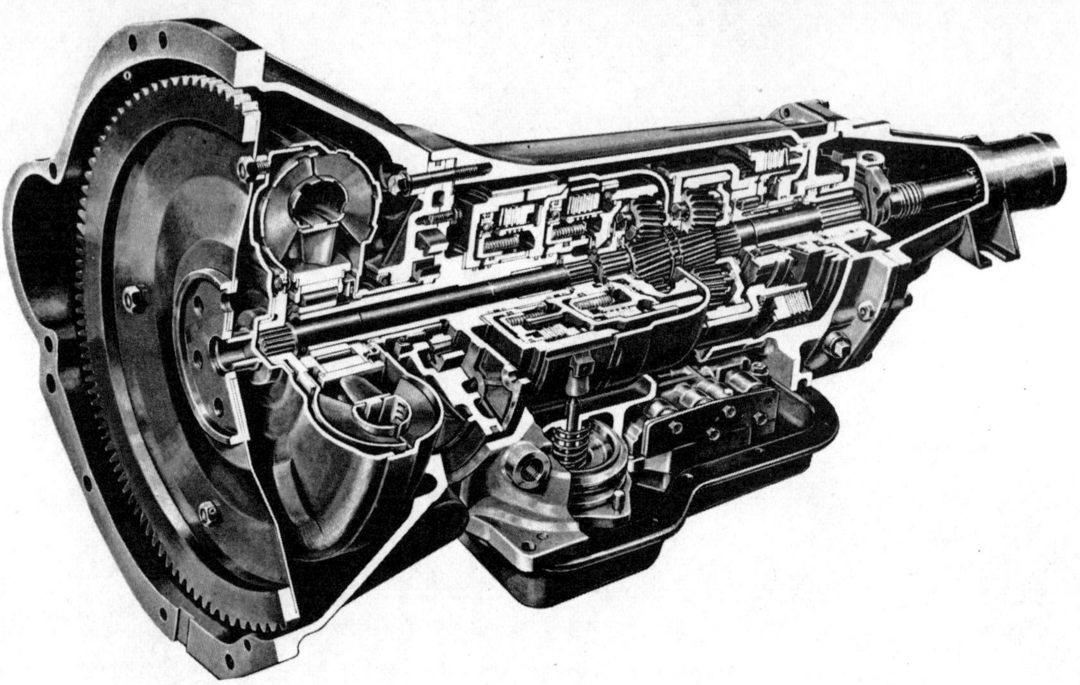

FIG 7:1 Cutaway view of the automatic transmission unit

kick-down solenoid and engine inlet manifold depression sensed by a vacuum capsule.

Though the underlying principles of the transmission are relatively simple, their translation into an effective and smooth running, reliable mechanism is the result of much development and experiment with valve dimensions, spring pressures and channel proportions all of which are permanently set in the dimensions of the component parts. The sole faults that are likely to occur in the valve and hydraulic system are those due either to the use of wrong hydraulic fluid, allowing the fluid level to fall too low or the admission of dirt or grit into the hydraulic system.

Routine maintenance and adjustments are described in this chapter. The rectification of major faults or the overhaul of a worn unit requires specialised knowledge and equipment and is, unfortunately, beyond the scope of the amateur. Many garages, too, would pass the work on to a specialist.

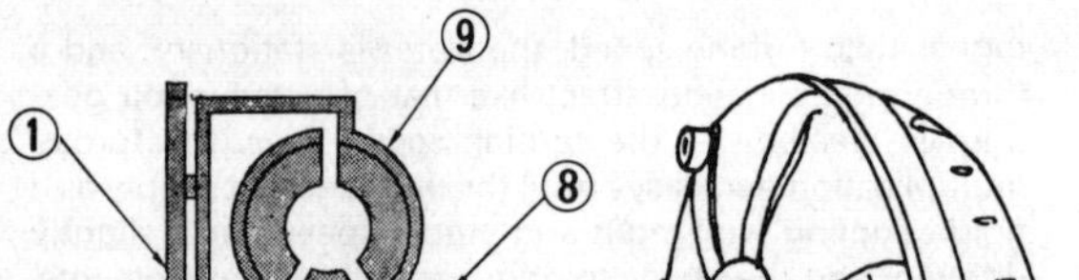

FIG 7:2 The torque converter assembly

Key to Fig 7:2 1 Drive plate 2 Crankshaft 3 Turbine 4 Impeller 5 Stator 6 One-way clutch 7 Input shaft 8 Oil pump 9 Torque converter casing

7:2 Testing

Parking lock:

With the car stationary on a gradient, select **P** and release the handbrake. The parking lock should prevent the car from moving.

'Rocking':

With the car stationary and the engine running, release the handbrake and apply light throttle. Select **D** and **R** alternately. As the gearchanges occur the car should 'rock' backwards and forwards.

Stall tests:

These tests are carried out to check the transmission performance by measuring the engine rev/min while the car is stationary and full throttle applied. Components which are tested by this means are the brake bands, torque converter and clutch units. An accurate tachometer will be needed to measure engine rev/min.

Run the engine until it reaches its normal operating temperature. Mount the tachometer in a position where it can easily be seen from the driving position. In all of the

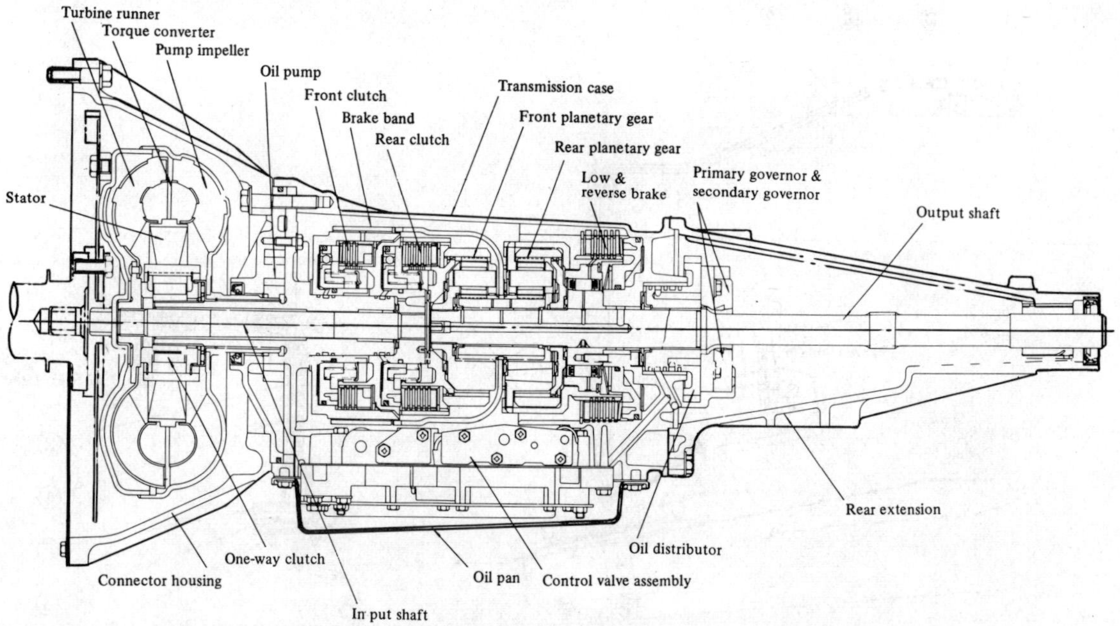

FIG 7:3 Section through the transmission, showing the layout of the components

following tests, the rev/min figure achieved should be between 1750 and 2000 for 1000 and 1200 models or 2000 to 2200 rev/min for the B210 series cars.

With the engine running, chock the front and rear wheels, apply the handbrake firmly and depress the brake pedal firmly with the left foot. These precautions are necessary to prevent the car from suddenly accelerating forwards, possibly with dangerous results. Place the lever in the **D** position. Now press the accelerator pedal slowly to the floor. With the accelerator pedal fully depressed and the engine turning steadily, read and record the engine rev/min figure. Act quickly to carry out the whole test operation within five seconds, otherwise heat which builds up rapidly in the torque converter will give a false reading.

Place the selector lever in the **N** position and run the engine at 1200 rev/min for about two minutes. Do this between all tests to cool the torque converter assembly. Repeat the test as before with the selector lever in **2**, **1** and **R** ranges.

If, when the transmission is in the stall condition, the engine revolutions exceed the figure quoted, it indicates that one or more of the clutches is slipping. If the rev/min figures were high in all ranges, low fluid pressure may be the cause. High rev/min in all ranges will indicate a slipping rear clutch, high rev/min in **D** and **2** only will indicate a slipping one-way clutch. High rev/min in **R** only indicates either a slipping front clutch or reverse brake band. Any faults in the transmission which are found as a result of these tests should be referred to a fully equipped service station for rectification.

7:3 Maintenance and adjustments

Maintenance:

Every 3000 miles, or sooner if transmission operation is faulty, the level of the fluid in the automatic transmission should be checked and, if necessary, topped up to the correct level. Low fluid level will cause many common transmission faults. The transmission must never be overfilled, however, as this may cause frothing of the fluid and result in faulty operation.

To check the fluid, the engine and transmission must be at normal operating temperature and the engine idling in neutral. With the car standing on a level surface with the engine idling, apply the handbrake and move the selector lever to each position in turn, then leave it in the **N** position. Pull out the transmission dipstick which is located on the right side of the transmission, wipe the dipstick clean with a piece of clean lint-free cloth, then replace it in position. Push the dipstick down firmly, then remove it quickly, so that oil splash will not give a false

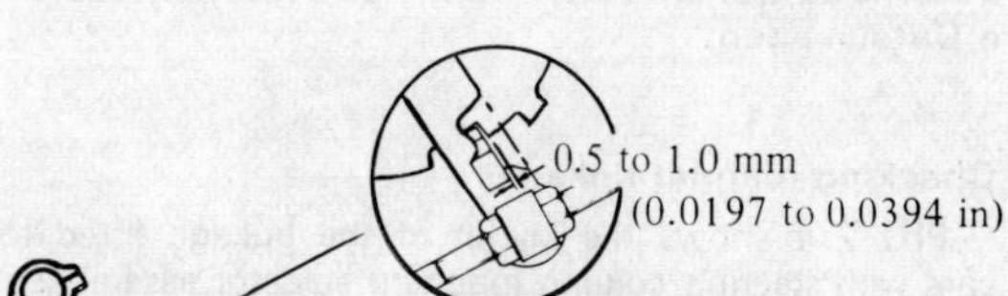

FIG 7:4 The steering column mounted gearchange linkage

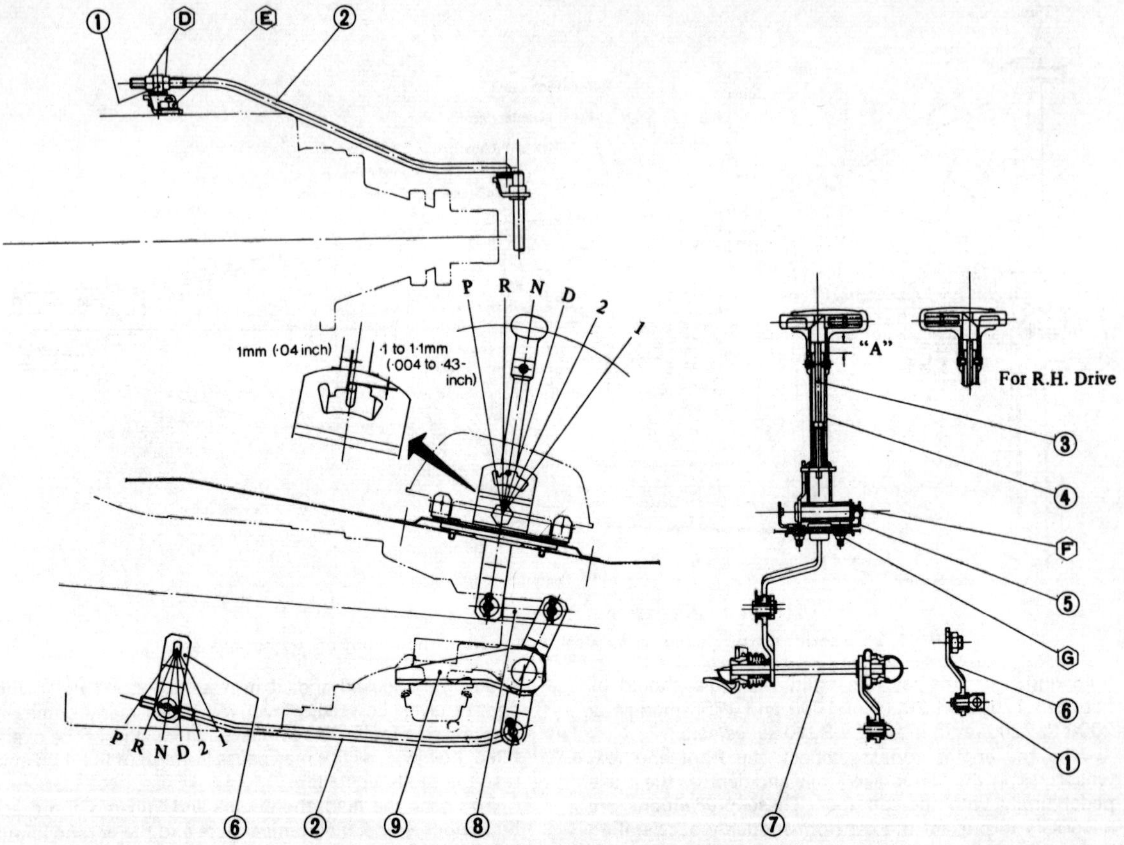

FIG 7:5 Floor mounted gear selector mechanism

Key to Fig 7:5 1 Trunnion 2 Lower shift rod 3 Pushrod 4 Selector 5 Bracket 6 Lever 7 Cross-shaft 8 Link 9 Support
Torque tightening values: D 14 to 21 lb ft E 22 to 29 lb ft F 12 to 16 lb ft G 2.5 to 3.3 lb ft

reading. Top up the level to the **F** mark on the dipstick if necessary, adding fluid a little at a time and checking each addition with the dipstick. **Use only 'Dexron' type automatic transmission fluid, as recommended by a Datsun agent.**

Checking manual linkages:

FIG 7:4 shows the layout of the linkage fitted to cars with steering column mounted selector assemblies, **FIG 7:5** the layout for cars fitted with floor mounted selector assemblies. The linkage must be adjusted at the nuts on the control rod until the lever is correctly positioned in **N** when the selector is in **N**. Move the lever on the transmission until it is in the **N** position, feeling for a click as the detent operates. Now adjust the nuts so that the selector lever is positioned in **N**. The adjuster nuts are on the control rod at the selector lever on column change models, on the control rod beneath the car on floor change models. Referring to **FIG 7:5**, first set the dimension A to .43 to .47 inch (11 to 12 mm) before fitting the selector lever knob. Next rotate the pushrod 3 as necessary to obtain the dimension (arrowed) of .004 to .43 inch (.1 to 1.1 mm).

Loosen the adjusting nuts D and see that both the hand selector lever 4 and the transmission lever 6 are in the **N** position. Set the dimension .04 inch (1 mm) by suitably adjusting the nuts D on the trunnion 1 at the lever 6.

On completion, move the control lever through all positions to check for smooth gear changing, without sticking, binding or squeaking, then recheck the adjustment in the **N** position.

The inhibitor switch:

This is coupled to the selector shaft on the transmission as shown in **FIG 7:6** and if faulty operation is experienced, check and adjust the switch as follows:

Disconnect the selector rod and turn the transmission selector lever to **N** position, the slot in the shaft will be vertical.

Using a test lamp, check for circuit continuity between the two black/yellow wires in the **N** position and then in **P**. Check also the two red/black wires in **R** position. The switch should complete a circuit in the positions specified and about 3 deg. on either side.

If necessary, unscrew the lever securing nut 6 and the two switch mounting screws and remove the screw under the switch body. Set the selector lever in **N** position.

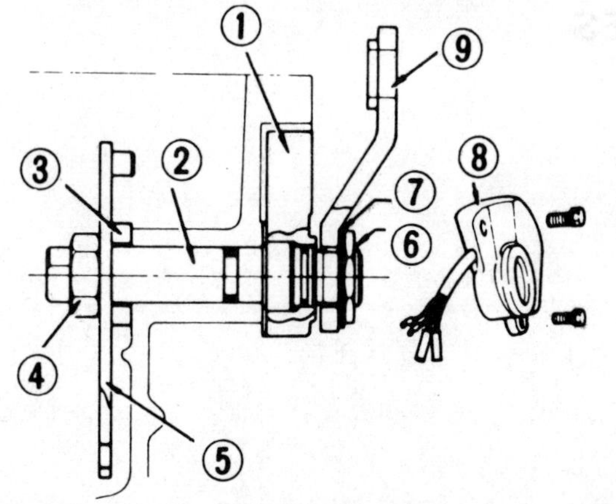

FIG 7:6 Sectional diagram of inhibitor switch mounting

Key to Fig 7:6 1 Inhibitor switch 2 Selector shaft 3 Washer 4 Nut 5 Plate 6 Nut 7 Washer 8 Inhibitor switch assembly 9 Transmission selector lever

Move the switch just sufficiently to align the screw hole with the pin hole in the internal rotor on the selector shaft and check by inserting a 1.5 mm diameter pin into the holes. Tighten the switch mounting screws, withdraw the pin and refit the screw in the hole.

Recheck the circuits and renew the switch if the operation is still not correct.

7:4 Removing and refitting transmission

Removal:

Jack up the car and support it safely on floor stands, to provide the necessary access to the underside. Disconnect the battery terminals. Disconnect the accelerator control from the carburetter linkage. Remove the front exhaust pipe.

Disconnect the wiring connections from the inhibitor switch and 'kick-down' solenoid at the transmission case. Disconnect the vacuum tube from the vacuum diaphragm unit. If oil cooler pipes are fitted, disconnect both inlet and outlet pipes from the transmission. Remove the connecting pin from the control lever and disconnect the speedometer cable from the housing.

Remove the propeller shaft as described in **Chapter 8**, plugging or covering the rear of the transmission to prevent fluid leakage. Support the engine by placing a jack beneath the oil sump, using a piece of wood between the jack and the sump to prevent damage.

Remove the bellhousing cover and scribe mark the torque converter and drive plate to ensure correct refitting in their original positions. Remove the bolts attaching the torque converter to the drive plate, as shown in **FIG 7:7**. Undo the two securing bolts and remove the starter motor. Place a jack beneath the transmission to support it, then remove the rear supporting crossmember from the transmission and the car body. Lower the transmission a little to provide access, then remove the bolts securing the bellhousing to the engine. Lower the transmission and remove it rearwards from the car. The torque converter can then be removed.

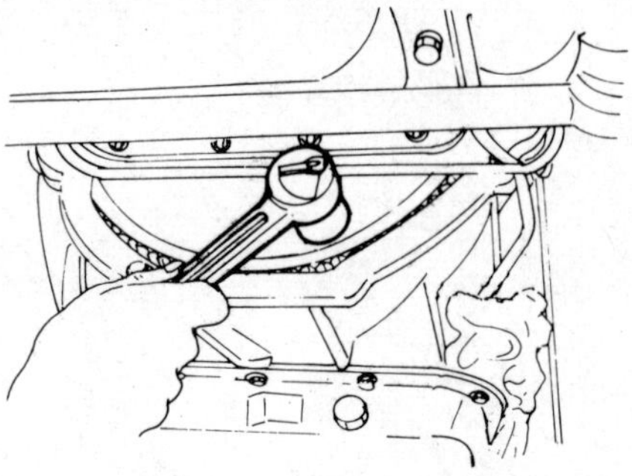

FIG 7:7 Removing the torque converter attaching bolts

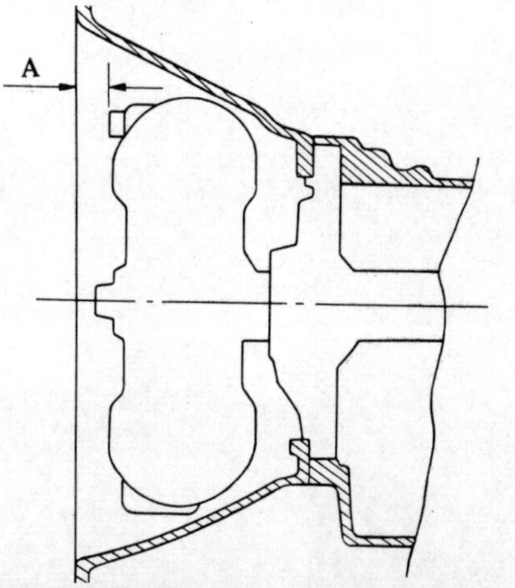

FIG 7:8 Torque converter installation

Refitting:

This is a reversal of the removal procedure, noting the following points. Check the drive plate for runout, using a dial gauge. Runout should not exceed .012 inch (.3 mm). If runout is .020 inch (.5 mm) or more, a new drive plate should be fitted.

When refitting the torque converter, line up the notch with the notch in the oil pump, and take great care not to cause any undue stresses during installation. Check the dimension (**A** in **FIG 7:8**) to ensure that the torque converter has been correctly fitted, this dimension being correct at .65 inch (16.5 mm). Tighten the torque converter to drive plate bolts to 5.5 to 7.5 lb ft, and the bellhousing to engine bolts to 30 to 36 lb ft torque. On completion, check the level of the transmission fluid and the manual linkage adjustment as described in **Section 7:3**.

NOTES

CHAPTER 8

THE PROPELLER SHAFT, REAR AXLE AND REAR SUSPENSION

8:1 Description

A tubular steel propeller shaft is used, fitted with a flanged universal joint at the rear axle connection and a splined sleeve mounted universal joint to connect to the transmission output shaft. A live rear axle assembly is fitted, mounted on semi-elliptical leaf springs and controlled by hydraulic telescopic dampers. The hypoid bevel type differential assembly is housed in the centre of the rear axle unit.

8:2 Maintenance

After the first 600 miles from new and thereafter at intervals of 30,000 miles, the oil should be drained from the differential unit when it is warm and fresh oil used to refill the unit. Every 3000 miles, the oil level should be checked and, if necessary, topped up to the correct level. Oil level in the differential unit should be maintained at the level of the combined filler and level plug situated at the rear of the casing. The drain plug is located beneath the unit. Use only the correct hypoid gear oil as specified by a Datsun agent.

8:3 The propeller shaft

Removal:

The propeller shaft is finely balanced as an assembly, therefore must be refitted in the same position relative to the flanges that it occupied before removal. Check for alignment marks at the splines and flanges and, if none are visible, use paint or make punch marks to ensure correct realignment when refitting.

Disconnect the rear propeller shaft flange from the pinion flange by removing the bolts shown in **FIG 8:1**. Lower the rear of the propeller shaft and slide it rearwards to disengage the splined front sleeve from the transmission output shaft. Use a suitable plug or cover at the rear of the transmission to prevent oil loss when the propeller shaft is removed. **FIG 8:2** shows the propeller shaft components.

Refitting:

Carefully enter the splined front sleeve into the transmission extension housing, ensuring that the splines are clean. Index the alignment marks made during removal and mate the rear flange to the pinion flange. Tighten the flange bolts to 20 lb ft torque.

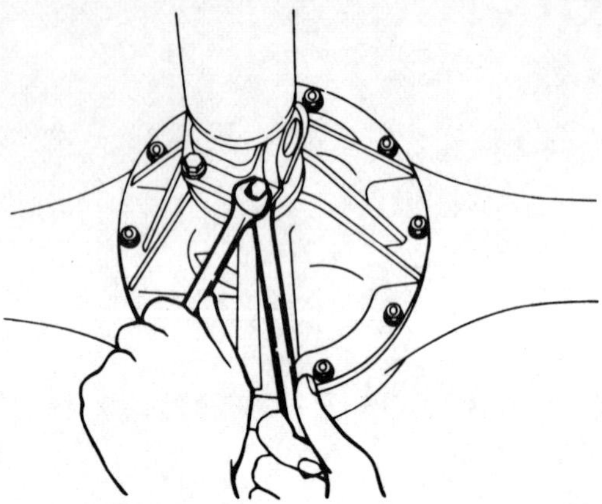

FIG 8:1 Removing the propeller shaft

Universal joints:

To prevent the balance of the propeller shaft from being disturbed, the universal joint assemblies on 1000, 1200 models should only be dismantled when it is necessary to renew them, due to wear of their component parts. **FIG 8:3** shows the parts of a universal joint. Universal joints on the 120Y and B210 cannot be dismantled, and if defective must be replaced by a new propeller shaft.

Remove the snap rings which secure the journal bearings in the flanges, using suitable pliers. If the snap rings are difficult to remove, tap the journal lightly with a wooden mallet to relieve the pressure on the snap ring. Tap the side of the yokes with a wooden mallet to remove the bearing races, after which the centre spider can be removed. If the bearing races are difficult to remove, tap one race with a flat-faced brass drift to push the opposite race out of the yoke, then remove the second race in a similar manner. Clean all parts in petrol and examine for wear or damage, renewing any defective components. A new universal joint assembly should be used.

Reassemble the universal joint assembly, packing the bearings with multi-purpose grease. Tap the bearings into position with a brass drift, until they line up with the snap ring grooves. Fit the snap rings into position and check that the whole joint assembly is tight. If there is any slackness, oversize snap rings should be selected and fitted, using matched pairs for each yoke so that the joint maintains a central position. Oversize snap rings are available in three thicknesses, colour-coded as follows: White, .0575 inch (1.46 mm); Yellow, .0583 inch (1.48 mm) and Red, .0591 inch (1.50 mm).

8:4 Axle shafts and wheel bearings

Removal:

Chock the front wheels and release the handbrake, then raise the rear of the car and safely support on floor stands. Remove the road wheel and the brake drum, slackening the brake adjuster as described in **Chapter 11** if the brake shoes bind and prevent easy drum removal. Refer to **FIG 8:4** and disconnect the brake pipe 1, fitting a suitable plug in the pipe to prevent fluid loss. Straighten and remove the cotterpin 2. Remove the clevis pin and disconnect the handbrake cable from the lever. Remove the handbrake return spring 3.

Remove the four bolts which secure the brake backplate to the axle housing. Withdraw the axle shaft and

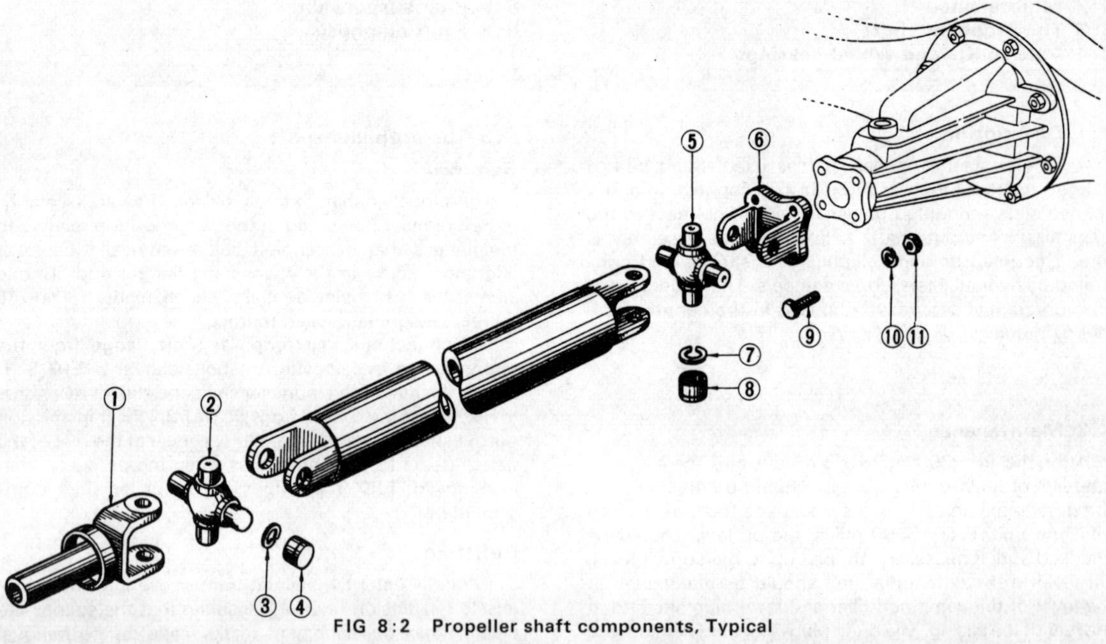

FIG 8:2 Propeller shaft components, Typical

Key to Fig 8:2 1 Yoke sleeve 2 Spider journal 3 Snap ring 4 Bearing race 5 Spider journal 6 Yoke flange 7 Snap ring 8 Bearing race 9 Bolt 10 Lockwasher 11 Nut

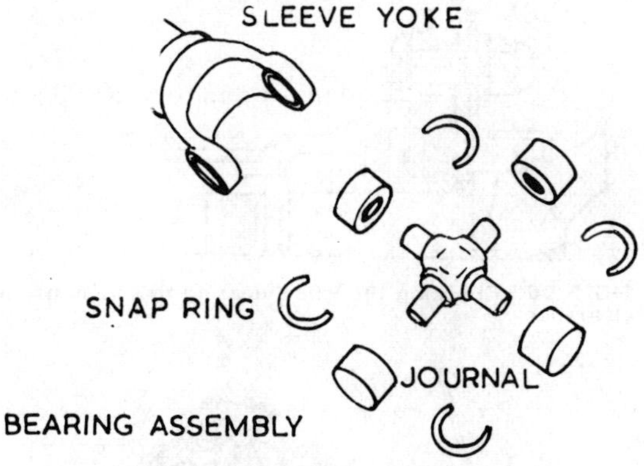

FIG 8:3 Universal joint components

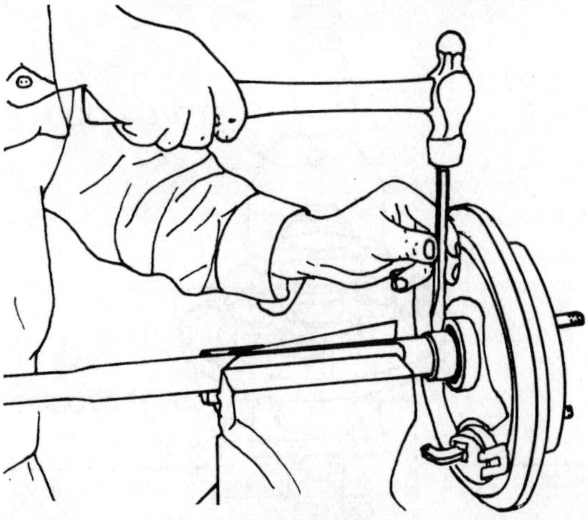

FIG 8:6 Removing the rear wheel bearing collar

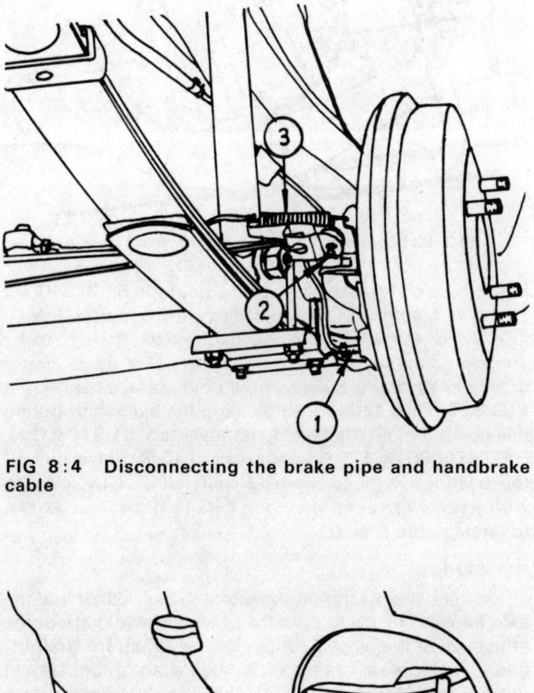

FIG 8:4 Disconnecting the brake pipe and handbrake cable

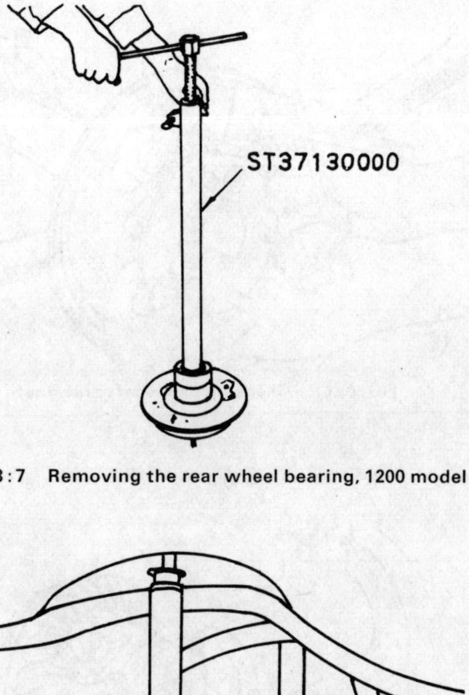

FIG 8:7 Removing the rear wheel bearing, 1200 model

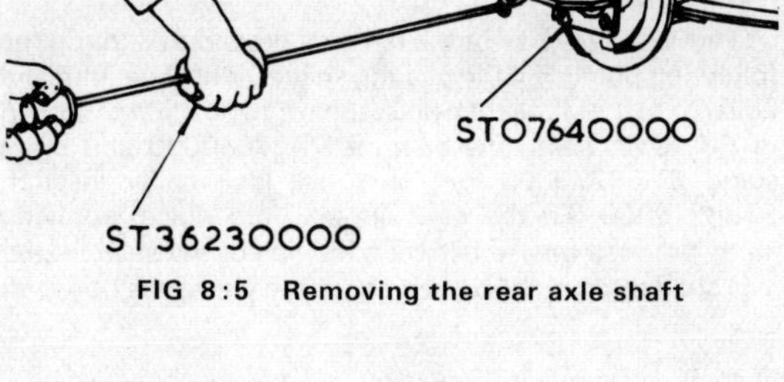

FIG 8:5 Removing the rear axle shaft

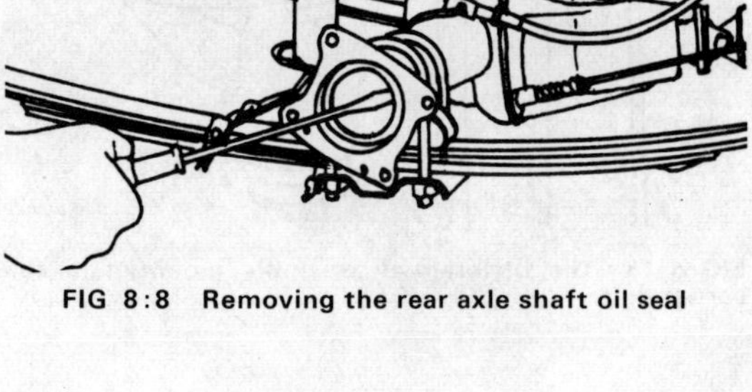

FIG 8:8 Removing the rear axle shaft oil seal

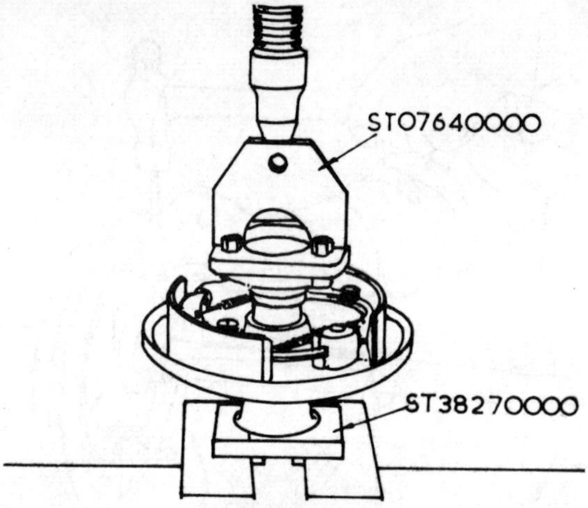

FIG 8:9 Installing the rear wheel bearing

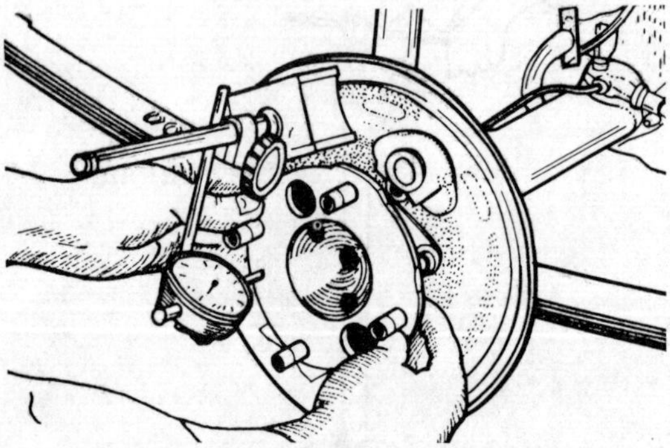

FIG 8:11 Checking axle shaft end float

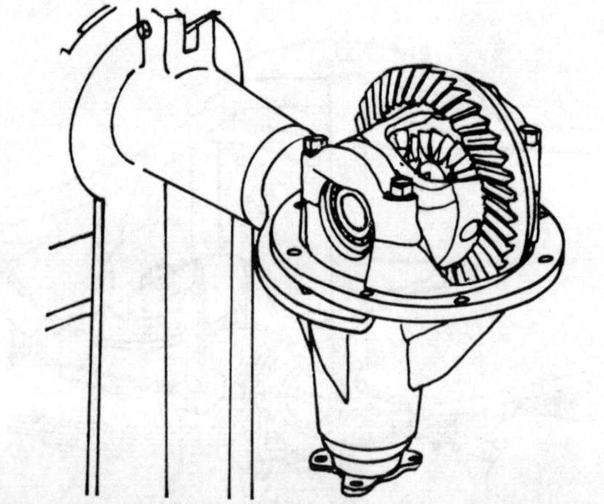

FIG 8:13 The differential assembly mounted in the carrier unit

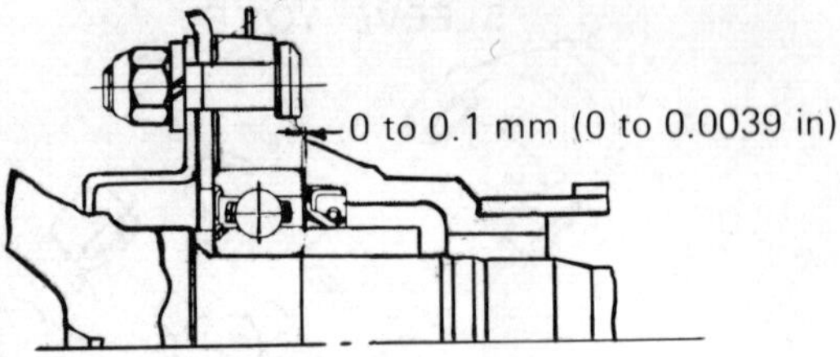

FIG 8:10 Checking the wheel bearing to axle housing clearance

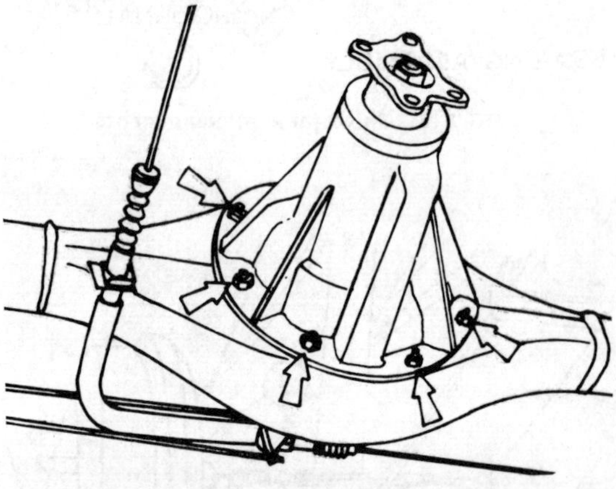

FIG 8:12 Removing the differential carrier

brake backplate assembly, using adaptor ST.07640000 and slide hammer ST.36230000 as shown in **FIG 8:5**.

If either the wheel bearing or the axle shaft is to be renewed, remove the bearing locking collar by nicking it deeply in several places, using a cold chisel as shown in **FIG 8:6**. Take care not to damage the axle shaft during this operation. Fit the bearing remover tool ST.37130000, HT72480000 on 120Y, as shown in **FIG 8:7** and pull off the bearing. Remove the axle shaft oil seal by levering with a screwdriver as shown in **FIG 8:8**, taking care not to damage the casing.

Servicing:

Examine the machined surface of the axle shaft and the axle housing for wear or damage which would affect the efficiency of the oil seal. Check the axle shaft for straightness, cracks, wear or distortion. Axle shaft runout should not exceed .118 inch (.3 mm). If the shaft is bent, it may be possible to have it straightened under a press at a specialist service station. If not, or if the shaft is otherwise defective, it must be renewed.

Refitting:

This is the reverse of the removal procedure, noting the following points. Fit the bearing spacer, wheel bearing and collar onto the shaft, then press them into position as shown in **FIG 8:9**, using the adaptor ST.07640000 and press stand ST.38270000, on 120Y use lock collar inserter, ST38210000. Fit the new oil seal into place, applying multi-purpose grease between the lips of the seal. Fit the axle shaft into position, then check the clearance between

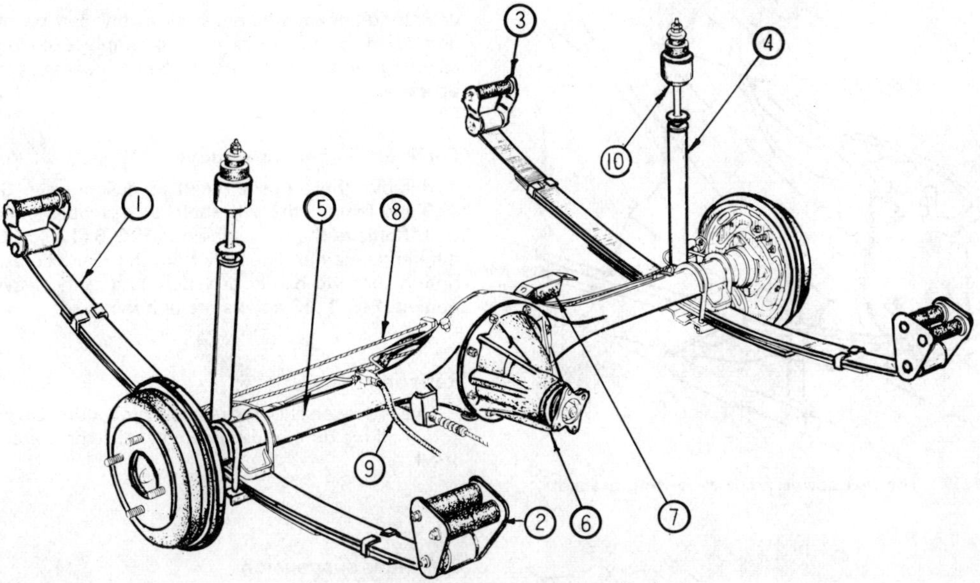

FIG 8:14 The rear suspension, Typical

Key to Fig 8:14 1 Leaf spring 2 Front mounting 3 Shackle 4 Damper 5 Axle housing 6 Differential carrier 7 Rubber buffer 8 Handbrake cable 9 Brake hose 10 Rubber buffer

the wheel bearing and the housing face, as shown in **FIG 8:10**. If the clearance exceeds the limit stated, adjust to within specifications by selecting and fitting a suitable shim.

Tighten the backplate to housing flange bolts to between 11 and 14 lb ft. Check that the end float of the fitted axle shaft does not exceed .004 inch (.1 mm), .0177 inch (.45 mm) on 120Y, using a dial gauge as shown in **FIG 8:11**. On completion, bleed the brakes as described in **Chapter 11**.

8:5 Differential assembly

The hypoid bevel gear crownwheel and pinion assembly is fitted to a cast aluminium carrier unit housed in the rear axle casing. Instructions are given in this section for the removal and refitting of the differential carrier unit, but it must be pointed out that, due to the need for specialized knowledge and many special tools to measure and set component preload, dismantling and internal component renewal should only be carried out by a fully equipped service station. It should be noted, however, that a new

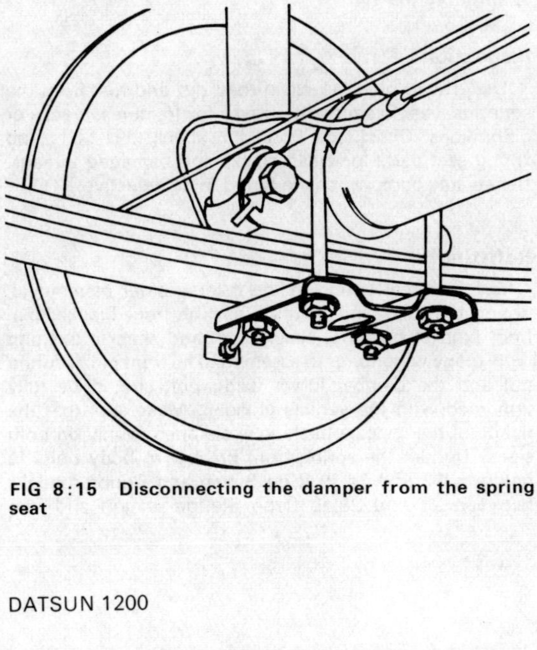

FIG 8:15 Disconnecting the damper from the spring seat

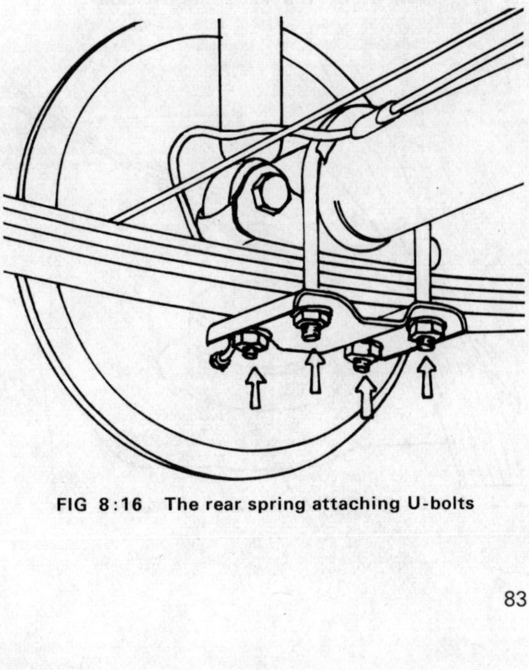

FIG 8:16 The rear spring attaching U-bolts

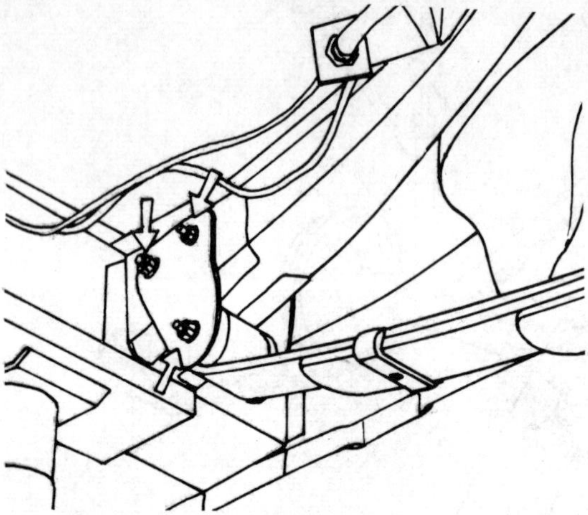

FIG 8:17 The rear spring front mounting bracket

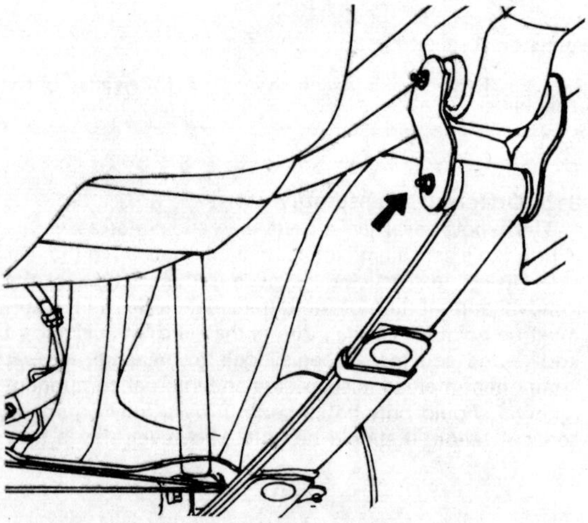

FIG 8:18 The rear spring shackle

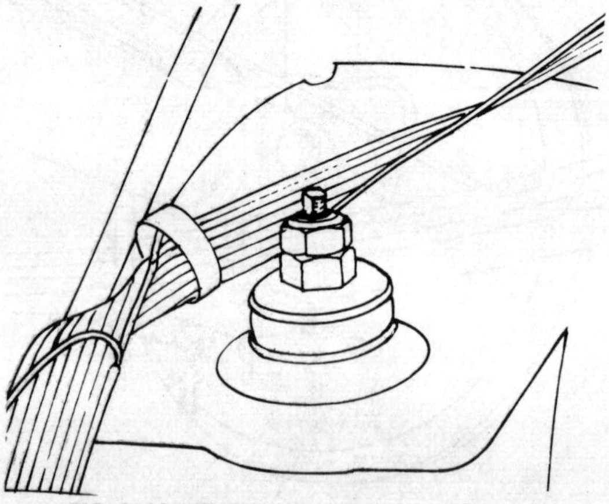

FIG 8:19 The damper upper mounting nuts

or reconditioned differential assembly can be obtained and fitted, as the units can be simply exchanged, no resetting of the components being necessary for this operation.

Differential carrier removal:

Remove the propeller shaft as described in **Section 8:3** and remove the axle shafts as described in **Section 8:4**. Remove the nuts shown in **FIG 8:12** and take the differential carrier assembly from the rear axle assembly, noting that the carrier assembly is a fairly heavy component. **FIG 8:13** shows the unit removed.

Refitting:

This is a reversal of the removal procedure. On completion, refill the differential assembly with the correct grade of oil.

8:6 Rear suspension

FIG 8:14 shows the layout of the rear suspension, which comprises the rear axle unit, semi-elliptic leaf springs, hydraulic dampers and rubber buffers.

Rear spring removal:

Chock the front wheels, raise the rear of the car and support it safely on floor stands placed beneath the rear side body members. Disconnect the damper from the spring seat by removing the bolt arrowed in **FIG 8:15**. Support the rear axle housing with a jack. Remove the locknuts arrowed in **FIG 8:16** and remove the U-bolts, spring seat location plates and seat pads. Loosen the three fixing nuts shown in **FIG 8:17** which secure the front spring bracket to the body, then remove the bracket from the body and the spring front eye and lower the spring. Remove the upper and lower nuts shown in **FIG 8:18** which retain the spring rear shackle and remove the spring from the car.

Inspection:

Use a wire brush to clean road dirt and rust from the spring leaves. Examine the leaves for fractures, cracks or deformities. Check the front pin, shackle, U-bolts and spring seat parts for wear, cracks and damaged threads. Renew any parts which are found to be defective.

Refitting:

Refit the rear spring in the reverse order of removal, noting the following points. Coat the front bracket pin, front bracket bushing, shackle pin and shackle bushing with soapy water prior to assembly. The front pin securing nut and the damper lower fixing bolt should be fully tightened with the vehicle unladen. Make sure that the flange of the shackle bushing is clamped evenly on both sides. Tighten the spring front bracket to body bolts to between 12 and 14 lb ft on Sedan and Coupé models, between 23 and 28 lb ft on Station wagon and Van models. Shackle pin nuts should be tightened to between 11 and 14 lb ft in all cases, and spring U-bolts to between 23 and 28 lb ft. On 120Y spring U-bolts to 29 to 36 lb ft (Sedan, Coupé) 33 to 40 lb ft (Van).

Rear dampers:

The telescopic hydraulic dampers are of the sealed type and require no maintenance. If a damper becomes defective, a replacement must be fitted.

Removal:

Chock the front wheels and jack up the rear of the car, supporting it on floor stands placed under the rear axle housing. Remove the lower end of the damper as shown in **FIG 8:15**. Remove the damper upper fixing nuts shown in **FIG 8:19**, these being located under the rear seat backrest.

Inspection:

Check the damper unit for leakage, cracks and other damage. Check that the damper shaft is straight and that the rubber bushings are not damaged or perished. Renew any faulty components.

Refitting:

Refit the damper to the car in the reverse order of removal. Tighten both upper and lower damper fixings to between 26 and 32 lb ft on Sedan, Station wagon and Van models, to between 7 and 8 lb ft on Coupé models. On 120Y Sedan the upper end nut is tightened to 14 to 17 lb ft, and Coupé to 6.5 to 8.7 lb ft.

8:7 Fault diagnosis

(a) Noisy axle

1 Insufficient or incorrect lubricant
2 Worn bearings
3 Worn gears

(b) Excessive backlash

1 Worn gears or bearings
2 Worn axle shaft splines
3 Worn propeller shaft joints

(c) Oil leakage

1 Defective seals in differential unit
2 Defective axle shaft seals
3 Damaged gaskets or joint faces

(d) Vibration

1 Propeller shaft out of balance
2 Worn universal joint bearings

(e) Rattles

1 Worn universal joints
2 Worn spring bushes or shackles
3 Worn or damaged rubber bushes
4 Damper fixing loose

(f) 'Settling'

1 Weak or broken spring leaves

NOTES

CHAPTER 9

FRONT SUSPENSION AND HUBS

9:1 Description

Two completely different layouts are used for the front suspension on these cars. On 1200, 120Y and B210 models a McPherson strut system is employed, while on the 1000 a transverse leaf spring was used together with double control arms and telescopic dampers. The strut type layout will be described first as this is the current version and the essential features of the earlier type will be covered in the later part of this chapter.

FIG 9:1 shows the pressed steel crossmember and suspension units which are bolted to the car frame on 1200 models, 120Y and B210 models are similar, but have disc brakes. Transverse links pivoting at bushed joints in the crossmember and at ball joints at the wheel swivels, accommodate vertical movement of the suspension and wheels. Tension rods attached to the transverse links and anchored at points on the car body resist forward and backward movement of the links. The suspension is controlled by combined coil spring and hydraulic damper struts, vertically mounted between the car body and the transverse link outer ends. Body roll on cornering is resisted by a transverse stabilizer bar attached to the car body and the transverse links by rubber-bushed pivots.

9:2 Maintenance

Apart from an occasional check on the general condition of the suspension units and rubber bushes, routine maintenance is confined to lubrication of the ball joint assemblies every 30,000 miles or every two years, whichever is the sooner.

Ball joint lubrication:

A plug is fitted to the lower part of the ball joint as shown in **FIG 9:2**. This plug must be removed and a grease nipple installed in its place, in order to lubricate the joint. Use a grease gun to inject fresh multi-purpose grease into the ball joint, allowing grease to bleed through the outlet in the upper cover of the joint until the old grease is removed and the joint filled with new grease. If pressure greasing equipment is used, care must be taken to keep the pressure low, to prevent the grease from being forced out under the ball joint clamp part. On completion, remove the grease nipple and refit the plug.

9:3 Wheel hubs

Removal:

Apply the handbrake, jack up the front of the car under the point shown in **FIG 9:3**, then remove the road wheel. Loosen the brake tube connecting nut as shown in **FIG 9:4**, remove the brake hose locking spring, withdraw the plate, then remove the brake hose from the strut assembly. Plug the end of the brake line to prevent fluid loss. Take care not to allow dust or dirt to enter the brake hoses.

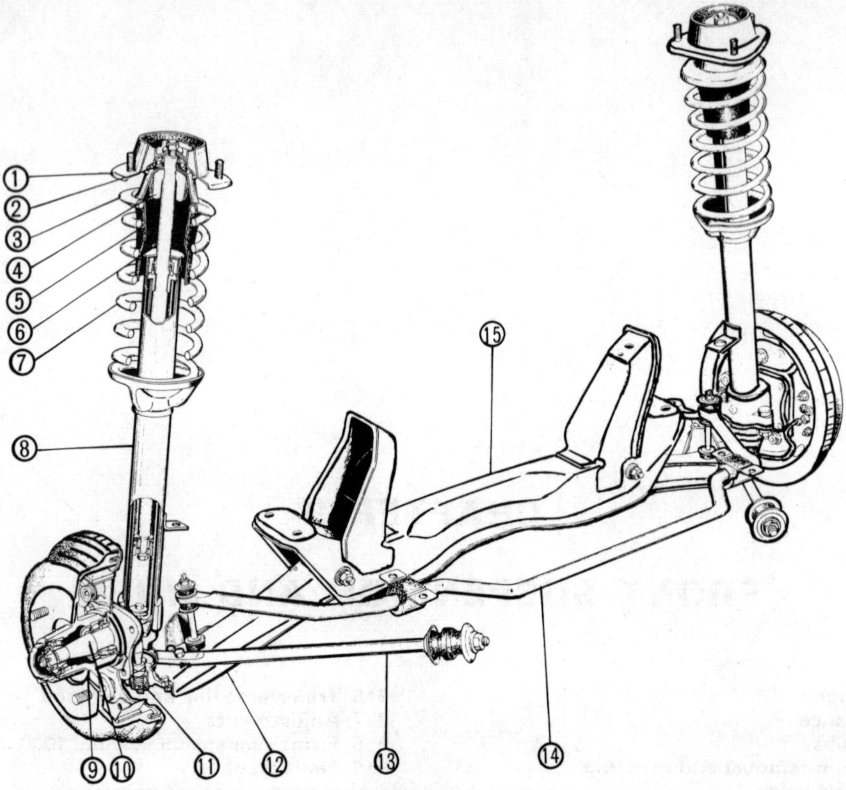

FIG 9:1 Front axle and suspension assembly, 1200 models

Key to Fig 9:1 1 Strut mounting insulator 2 Strut mounting bearing 3 Upper spring seat 4 Bumper rubber 5 Dust cover 6 Piston rod 7 Front spring 8 Strut assembly 9 Hub assembly 10 Spindle 11 Ball joint 12 Transverse link 13 Tension rod 14 Stabilizer 15 Suspension member

Refer to **Chapter 11** and remove the caliper from the disc on cars with disc front brakes, or the brake drum assembly on cars fitted with drum front brakes. Remove the hub grease cap by placing the flat blade of a screwdriver at the joint and tapping the screwdriver lightly.

Take out the cotterpin from the wheel bearing locknut and remove the nut. With the wheel bearing and washer remaining on the hub, remove the hub assembly from the spindle as shown in **FIG 9:5**, noting that, on cars fitted with disc brakes, the hub and disc are removed as a unit. The wheel bearing assemblies can then be removed. To remove the bearing outer race from the hub, use a drift as shown in **FIG 9:6**, utilizing the two grooves in the hub to guide the drift.

If necessary, the brake shoes and backplate can be removed from drum brake assemblies, taking out the bolts arrowed in **FIG 9:7**; or the brake disc shield removed from disc brake assemblies, taking out the screws arrowed in **FIG 9:8**.

Servicing:

Wash all hub and bearing parts in petrol and dry them. **FIG 9:9** shows a section through the bearing assembly and indicates the inspection points. Inspect for broken, cracked or pitted rollers and inner and outer races. Assemble the races and rotate them by hand to check for wear, play or roughness. Renew faulty components. Examine the grease seal and renew it if not in perfect condition.

Refitting:

Refit the brake backing plate or disc brake shield if removed. Refit the wheel bearings in the reverse order of removal. If the bearing outer race was removed, refit by driving into position with a suitable drift such as tool ST.35310000. Fill the wheel hub and hub grease cap with multi-purpose grease, up to the lines shown in **FIG 9:10**. Fill the spaces between the bearing roller and the pocket in the grease seal with similar grease. Apply grease thinly to the spindle shaft and threaded parts, wheel bearing washer and locknut surfaces. Refit the wheel bearing and seal and install the parts on the wheel spindle, taking care not to allow dirt or grit to stick to the greased surfaces. Adjust the wheel bearings as follows and, on completion, bleed the brakes as described in **Chapter 11**.

Wheel bearing adjustment:

With the front of the car raised and the road wheel removed, take off the hub grease cap and remove the cotterpin from the wheel bearing locknut. Tighten the

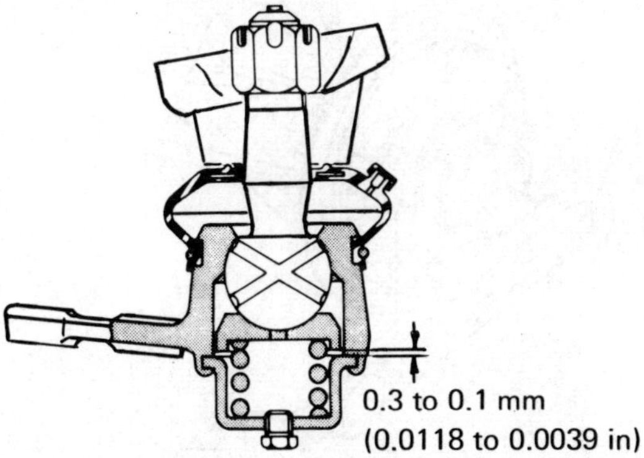

FIG 9:2 Section through a suspension ball joint

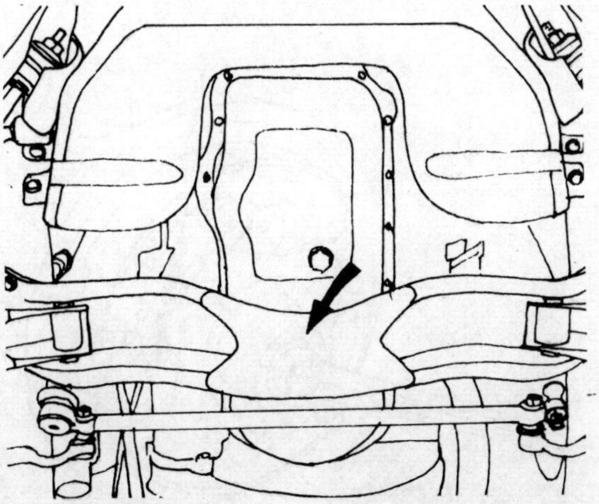

FIG 9:3 Front crossmember jacking point

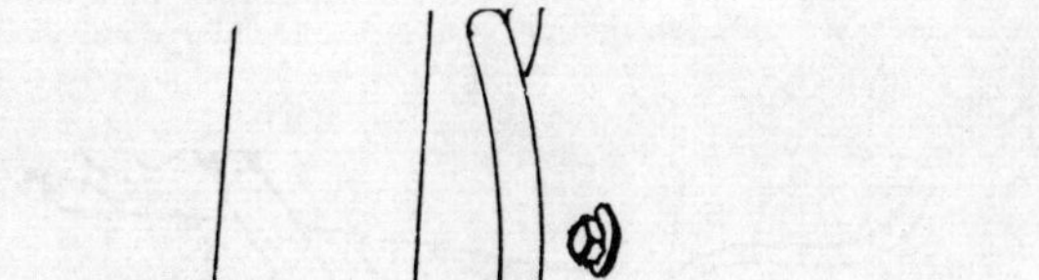

FIG 9:4 Detaching a front brake hose

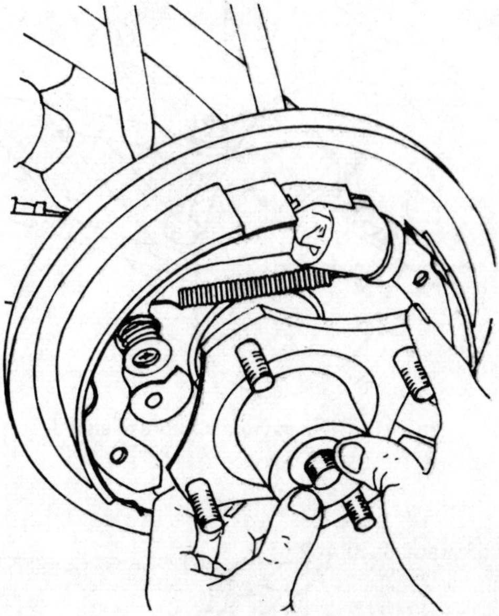

FIG 9:5 Removing the wheel hub

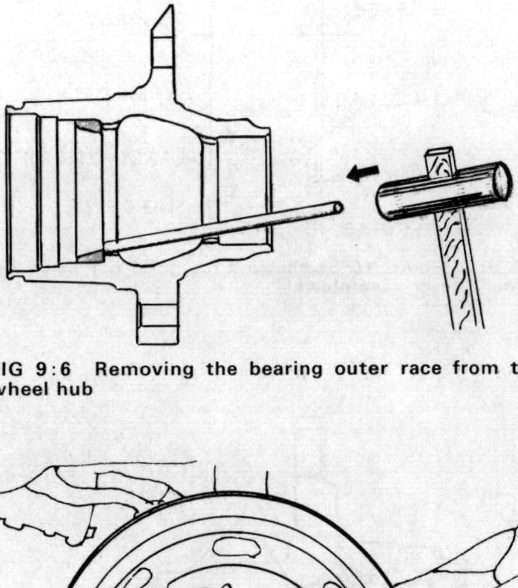

FIG 9:6 Removing the bearing outer race from the wheel hub

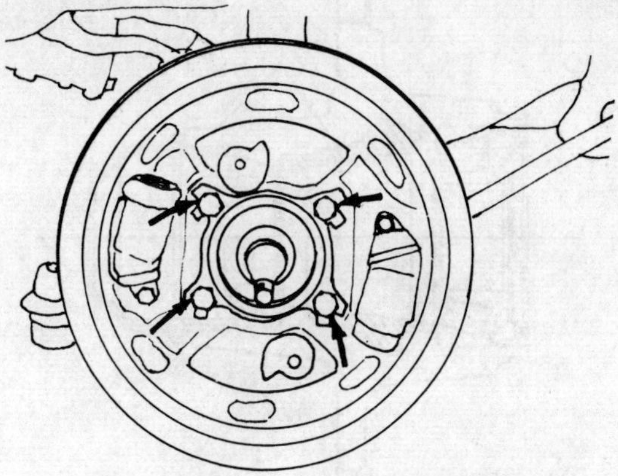

FIG 9:7 Removing a drum brake backplate

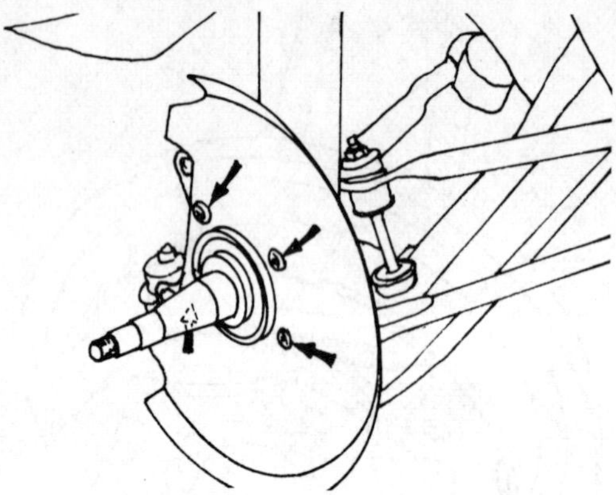

FIG 9:8 Removing a disc brake shield

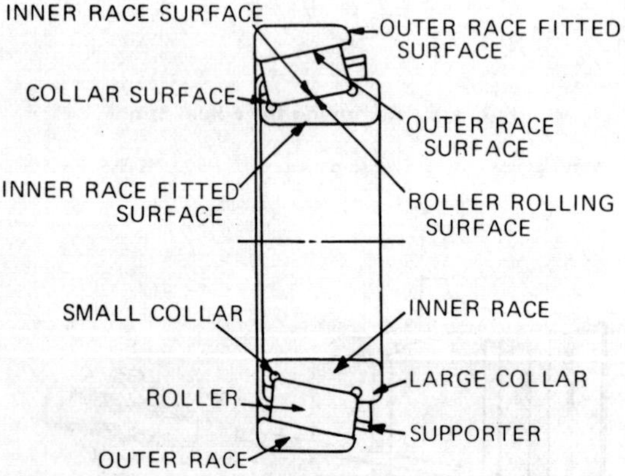

FIG 9:9 Points to be checked for good condition on wheel bearing assemblies

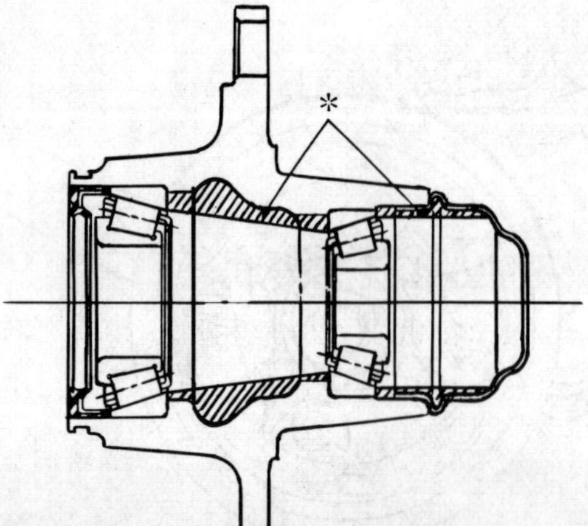

FIG 9:10 Greasing the wheel hub and hub cap

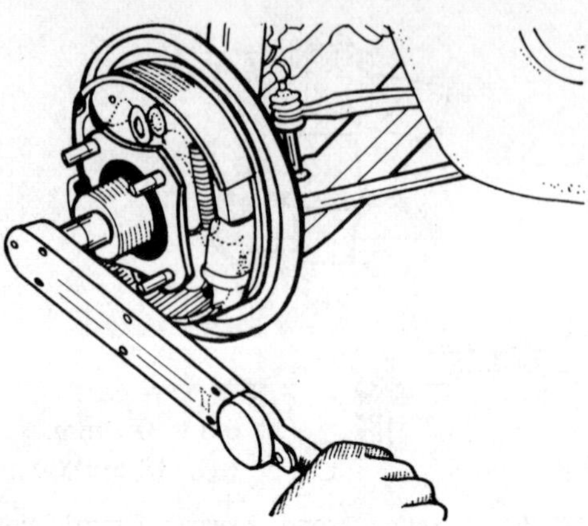

FIG 9:11 Tightening the wheel bearing locknut

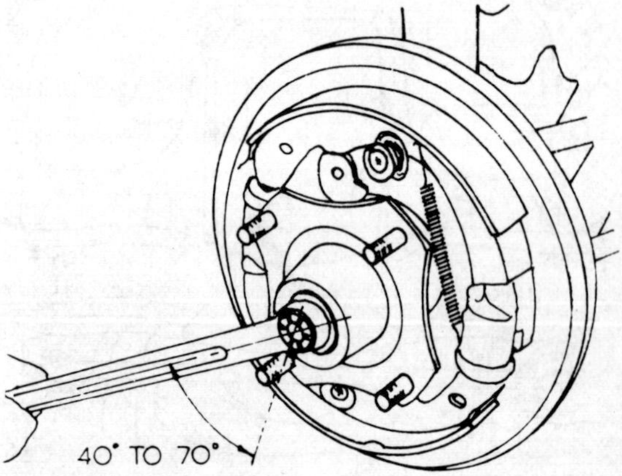

FIG 9:12 Loosening the wheel bearing locknut by the correct amount

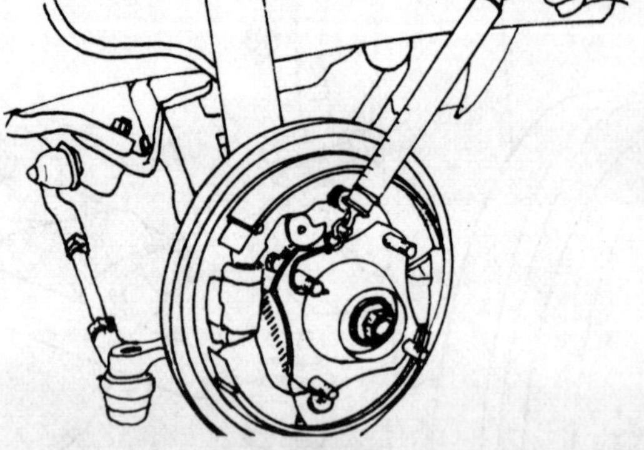

FIG 9:13 Measuring the force needed to turn the wheel hub

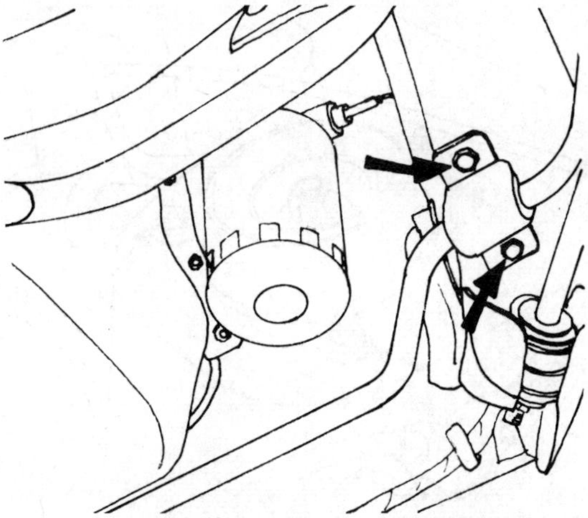

FIG 9:14 **Detaching the stabilizer bar from the body**

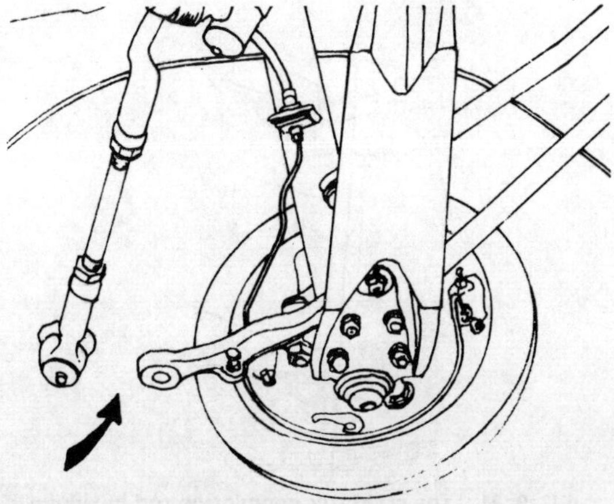

FIG 9:15 **Removing the steering tie rod from the knuckle arm**

bearing locknut as shown in **FIG 9:11** to a torque figure between 16 and 17 lb ft. Turn the hub a few times in each direction to settle the bearings, then retighten the nut to the stated figure. At this stage, make sure that the brake friction pads on disc brake units are not touching the disc and preventing free rotation. If so, the pads must be removed as described in **Chapter 11**. Loosen the nut from the position in which it has been tightened, through a range of 40 to 60 degrees, as shown in **FIG 9:12** and align the cotterpin holes.

Leave the nut in this position just achieved and measure the force needed to turn the hub as shown in **FIG 9:13**, using a spring balance hooked onto a wheel stud. The hub should start to turn at a force of 1.5 lb or less for worn parts or 2.5 lb or less for new parts, and no axial play should be felt at the hub bearing. Adjust the tightness of the nut a little if necessary, to achieve these conditions. When the adjustment is correct, fit the cotterpin to lock the nut. On completion, refit the hub grease cap and the road wheel, and lower the car. Refit the disc brake pads if they were removed, as instructed in **Chapter 11**.

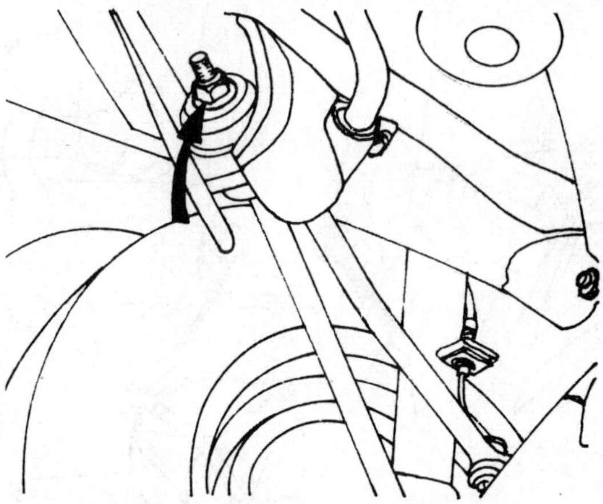

FIG 9:16 **Removing the tension rod nuts and bolts**

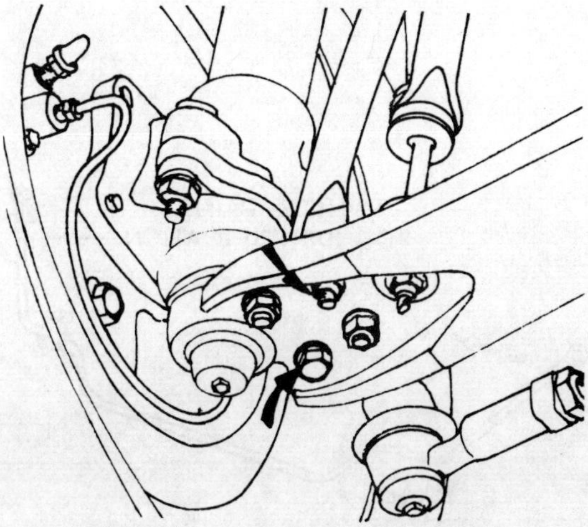

FIG 9:17 **Removing the engine mounting bolts**

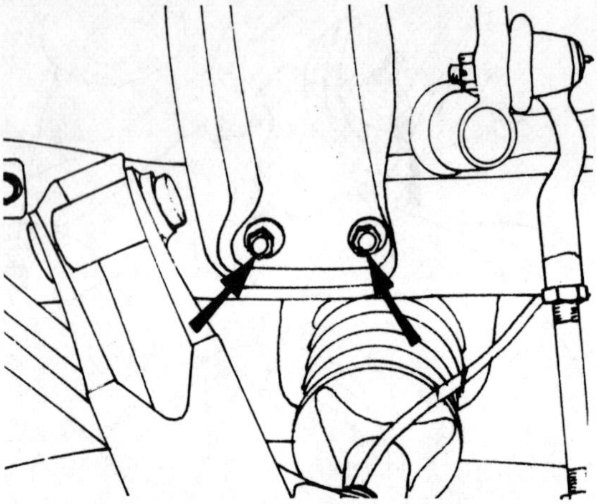

FIG 9:18 Removing the crossmember from the body

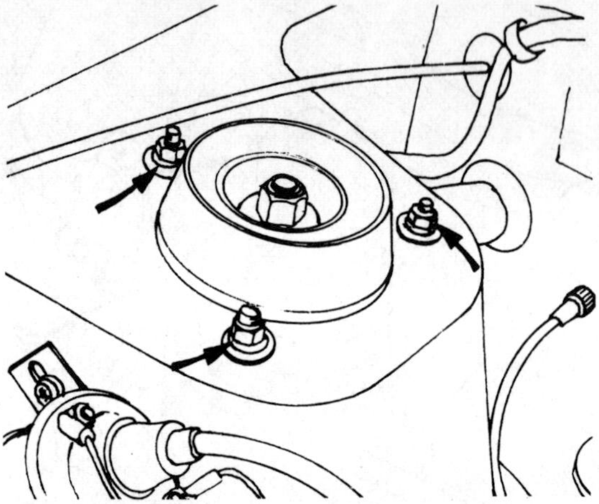

FIG 9:19 Detaching the suspension struts from the body

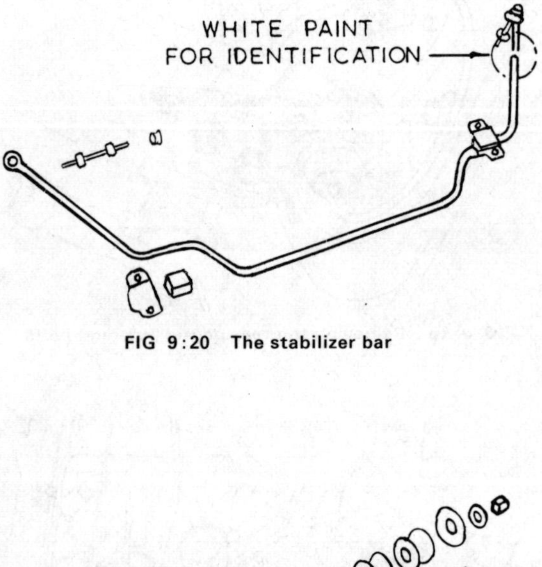

FIG 9:20 The stabilizer bar

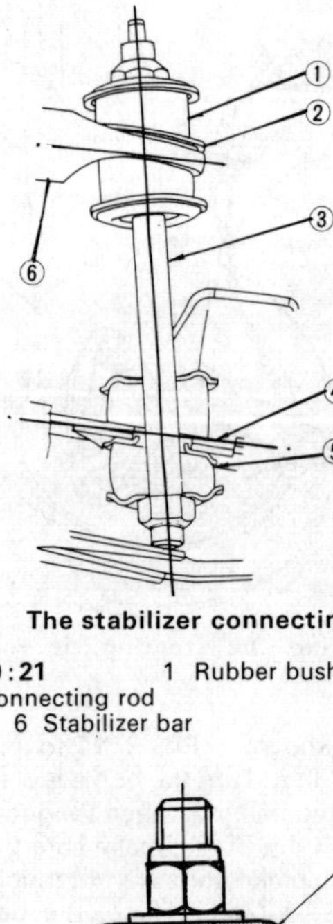

FIG 9:21 The stabilizer connecting rod bushings

Key to Fig 9:21 1 Rubber bush 2 Washer 3 Stabilizer connecting rod 4 Transverse link 5 Washer 6 Stabilizer bar

FIG 9:22 The tension rod markings

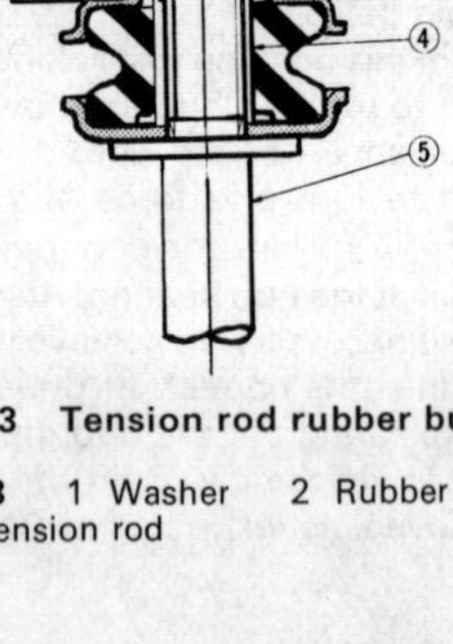

Key to Fig 9:23 Tension rod rubber bush installation

Key to Fig 9:23 1 Washer 2 Rubber bush 3 Frame 4 Collar 5 Tension rod

9:4 Suspension removal and refitting

Removal:

Apply the handbrake, raise the front of the car and support it on floor stands placed beneath the front sides of the body frame. Remove the front wheels and detach the splash board. Disconnect the front brake hoses on both sides, as described in **Section 9:3**.

Remove the bolts shown in **FIG 9:14** on both sides of the car, to detach the stabilizer bar from the body. Remove the cotterpin from the steering tie rod ball joint, remove the castle nut and separate the rod from the knuckle arm as shown in **FIG 9:15**. Remove the nuts from the tension rods on both sides as shown in **FIG 9:16**, remove the tension rod bolts and detach the rods from the car.

Attach suitable lifting equipment to the engine unit and raise the engine slightly to relieve the weight from the engine mountings. The engine must be supported in this manner while the suspension unit is removed, and until it is refitted. Separate the suspension crossmember from the engine by detaching the engine attachment points arrowed in **FIG 9:17**. Raise a jack under the point shown in **FIG 9:3** to support the front crossmember, and separate the crossmember from the car body by removing the bolts shown in **FIG 9:18** from both sides.

Loosen and remove the three self-locking nuts arrowed in **FIG 9:19** on both sides of the car, to detach the upper ends of the suspension struts from the car body. Carefully lower the suspension unit, steadying the assembly by holding the struts, and remove it from beneath the car.

Servicing:

Check all rubber parts, such as the tension rod, transverse link and stabilizer bushings for wear, damage or deterioration. Check the suspension components for damage or distortion. Repair or renew any defective components.

Refitting:

Reinstall the front suspension assembly in the reverse order of removal, noting the following points. Tighten the transverse link mounting bolts to a torque of 28 to 36 lb ft and the stabilizer to body mounting bolts to 7 to 8 lb ft, B210 12 to 15 lb ft, with the vehicle unladen. Fit the stabilizer bar so that the white paint identification mark is to the left side of the car, as shown in **FIG 9:20**. The layout of the stabilizer connecting rod bushings are shown in **FIG 9:21**.

Install the tension rods on the correct side of the car, according to the marks LH for left side and RH for right side, the position of these markings and the layout of the tension rod bushings being shown in **FIG 9:22**. Make sure that the tension rod rubber bushings and washers are correctly installed on each side of the car frame, as shown in **FIG 9:23**. Tightening torque for tension rod mountings is between 40 and 47 lb ft.

On completion, bleed the brakes as described in **Chapter 11** and check the front wheel alignment as described in **Chapter 10**.

9:5 Suspension units

Removal:

Apply the handbrake, jack up the front of the car and support it as described previously. Disconnect the brake lines from the strut assemblies as described in **Section**

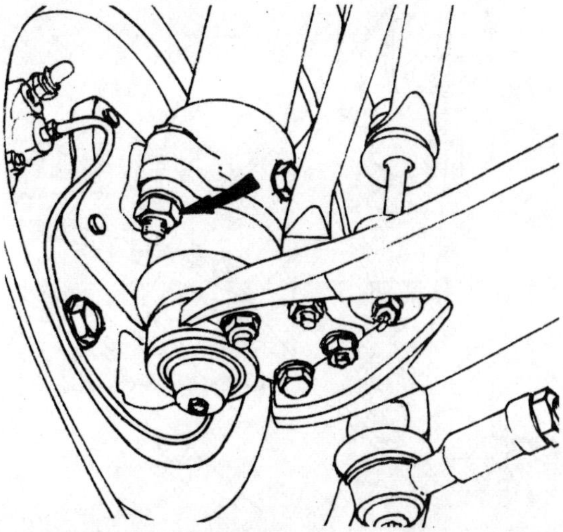

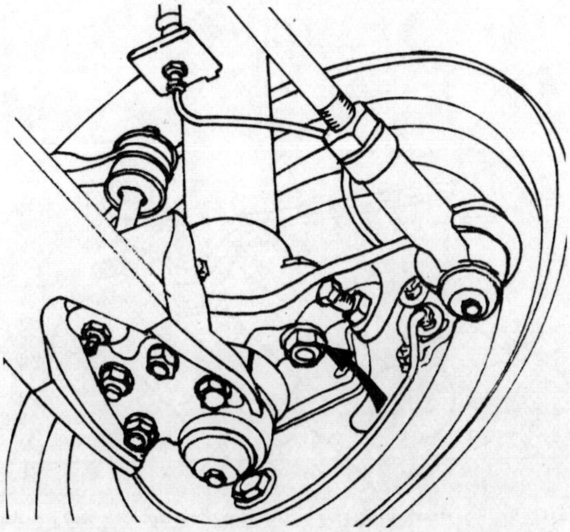

FIG 9:24 Removing the knuckle arm fixing bolts

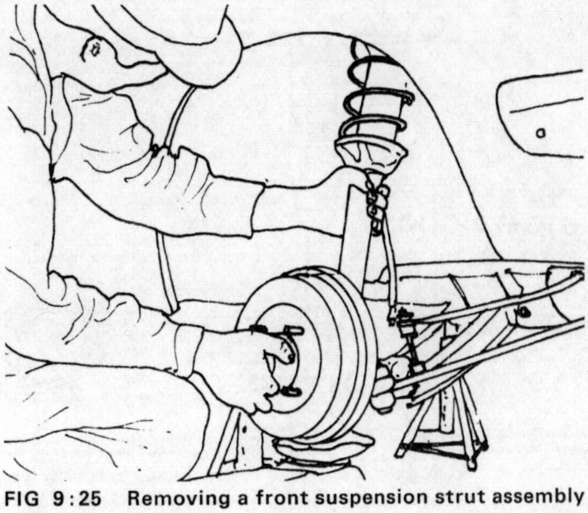

FIG 9:25 Removing a front suspension strut assembly

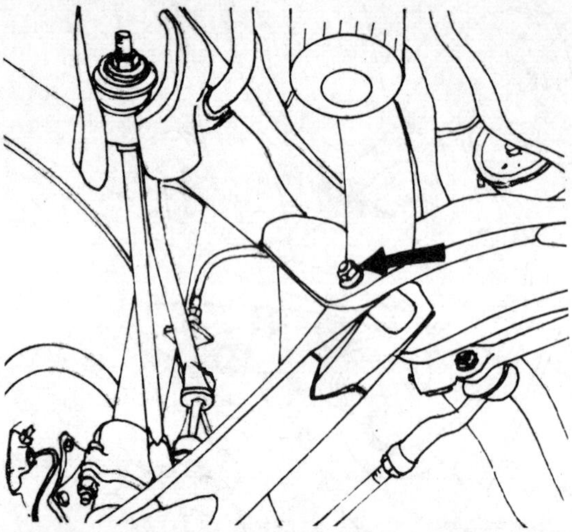

FIG 9:26 Removing the transverse link mounting bolt

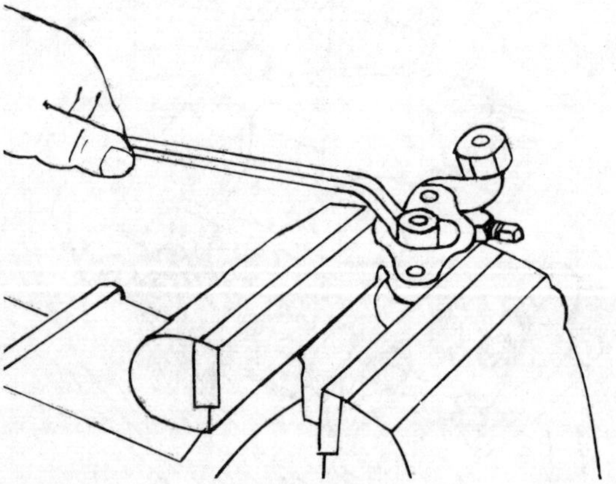

FIG 9:27 Removing the knuckle arm from the ball joint

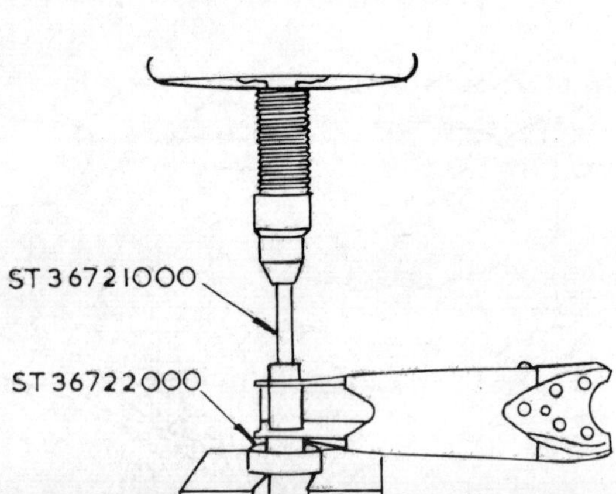

FIG 9:28 Removing the transverse link bushing

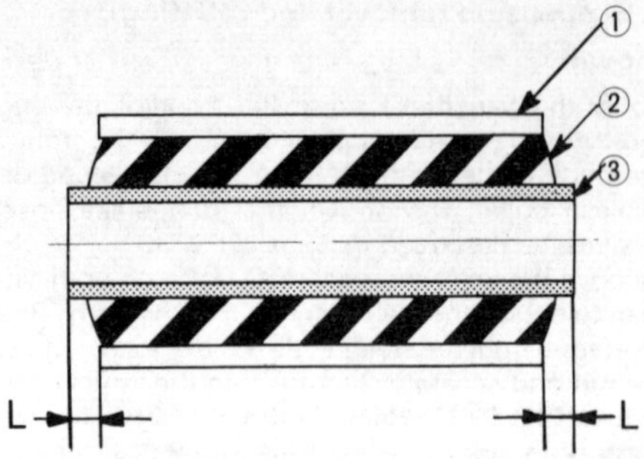

FIG 9:29 Section through the transverse link bushing

Key to Fig 9:29 1 Transverse link 2 Transverse link bushing 3 Inner tube

9:3 and remove the stabilizer bar and tension rods from the transverse links, as described in **Section 9:4**.

Remove the knuckle arm fixing bolts shown in **FIG 9:24** and separate the strut assemblies from the ball joints. Loosen and remove the strut upper self-locking nuts shown in **FIG 9:19**, then remove the strut assembly from the car as shown in **FIG 9:25**.

Due to the need for special tools and equipment, spring removal and refitting and servicing of the suspension strut internal components must be carried out by a fully equipped Datsun agent.

Refitting:

This is the reverse of the removal instructions. Tighten the suspension strut upper self-locking nuts to a torque of 12 to 15 lb ft, 18 to 25 lb ft on B210, the strut to knuckle arm attaching bolts to 34 to 44 lb ft and the tension rod to transverse link bolts to 16 to 21 lb ft. On completion, bleed the brakes as described in **Chapter 11**.

9:6 Transverse link and ball joint

Removal:

Raise the front of the car and support it as described in **Section 9:4**. Remove the road wheel and disconnect the stabilizer bar and tension rod from the transverse link, all as described previously. Remove the knuckle arm fixing bolts shown in **FIG 9:24** and separate the ball joint from the strut assembly. Remove the transverse link mounting bolt shown in **FIG 9:26** and remove the transverse link from the suspension.

Remove the cotterpin from the ball joint castle nut, then remove the castle nut as shown in **FIG 9:27** and remove the knuckle arm from the ball joint. Undo the ball joint mounting nut and remove the ball joint from the transverse link. Use special tool ST.36722000 and a press to remove the bushing from the transverse link, as shown in **FIG 9:28**.

Servicing:

FIG 9:29 shows a section through the transverse link bushing. If the rubber and the bonded inner or outer tube joints are sticky, melted or cracked, renew the transverse link assembly complete.

If the rubber dust cover on the ball joint is cracked or split, renew the ball joint assembly, as dirt or grit which will have entered cannot be removed. Measure the axial play of the ball joint, which should not exceed .06 inch (1.5 mm). Use a spring balance as shown in **FIG 9 : 30** to measure the force needed to pivot the ball joint, making the test in several directions. The force needed at the cotterpin position should be between 15 and 24 lb. Renew the ball joint if it is defective in any way. Lubricate the ball joint as described in **Section 9 : 2**.

Refitting:

This is a reversal of the removal procedure, noting the following points. Remove any rust from the inside of the transverse link bushing bore, using emerycloth. Wet the bushing and bore with a soapy water solution to ease fitting, then press the bushing into the bore, using the special tool shown in **FIG 9 : 31**. Finely adjust the distances (**L** in **FIG 9 : 29**) between both side transverse link collar end surfaces and bushing inner tubes, so that they are evenly aligned.

Install the ball joint on the transverse link and tighten the lower installation bolt to 16 to 21 lb ft. Fit the knuckle arm onto the ball joint and tighten the castle nut to 40 to 53 lb ft. Fit and bend the cotterpin to lock the nut. Make sure that all parts are clean and apply sealing agent over the castle nut to prevent rust from forming. Fit the knuckle arm beneath the strut assembly and tighten the installation bolts to 34 to 44 lb ft. Be sure to use the shorter bolt for the front side and the longer bolt for the rear side. All parts must be completely clean. The bolt fitting configuration is shown in **FIG 9 : 32**.

Install the transverse link on the suspension crossmember and temporarily tighten the mounting bolts, making sure that the nut side of the bolt faces to the front of the car. Install the tension rod and stabilizer bar to the transverse link. Lower the car and remove the jack so that the car is resting under its own weight, then tighten the transverse link mounting bolt to 30 to 36 lb ft.

9 : 7 Adjustments

The castor and camber angles, given in **Technical Data** in the **Appendix**, are preset and cannot be adjusted. If either of these angles are incorrect, a check must be made for worn, damaged or deformed suspension components. Front wheel alignment (toe-in) must be checked and adjusted as described in **Chapter 10**. Some types of uneven front tyre wear can indicate incorrect castor or camber angles. A tyre and wheel specialist service station can advise on this, and also make quick checks on the accuracy of suspension geometry with special equipment.

9 : 8 Front suspension system, 1000 models

The components of the early type suspension are shown in the exploded diagram of **FIG 9 : 33** and a sectional view of one side of the assembly in **FIG 9 : 34**. From these it will be seen how the steering knuckle is mounted between the two outer ends of the pivoting suspension arms of which the lower arm is directly influenced by the transverse leaf spring. Control of the vertical movements

FIG 9 : 30 Measuring the ball joint pivoting torque

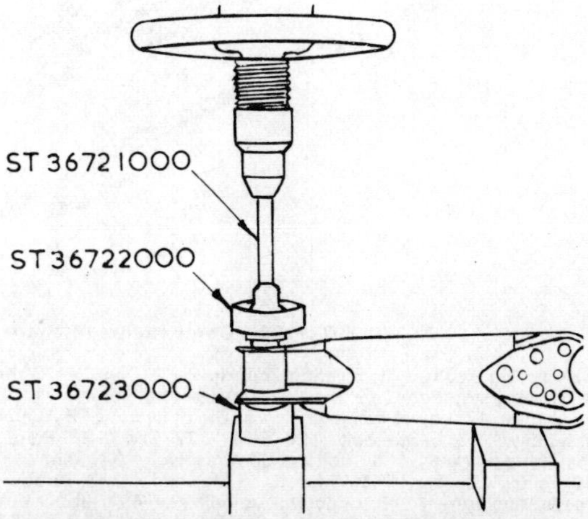

FIG 9 : 31 Fitting the transverse link bushing

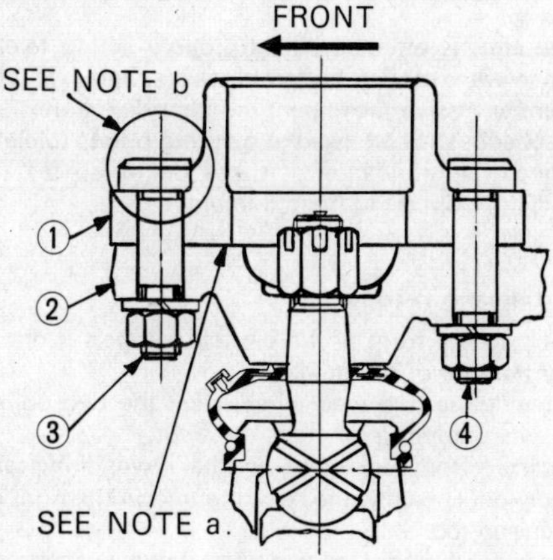

FIG 9 : 32 Installing the knuckle arm to the strut assembly

Key to Fig 9 : 32 1 Strut assembly 2 Knuckle arm 3 Installation bolt (short) 4 Installation bolt (long)

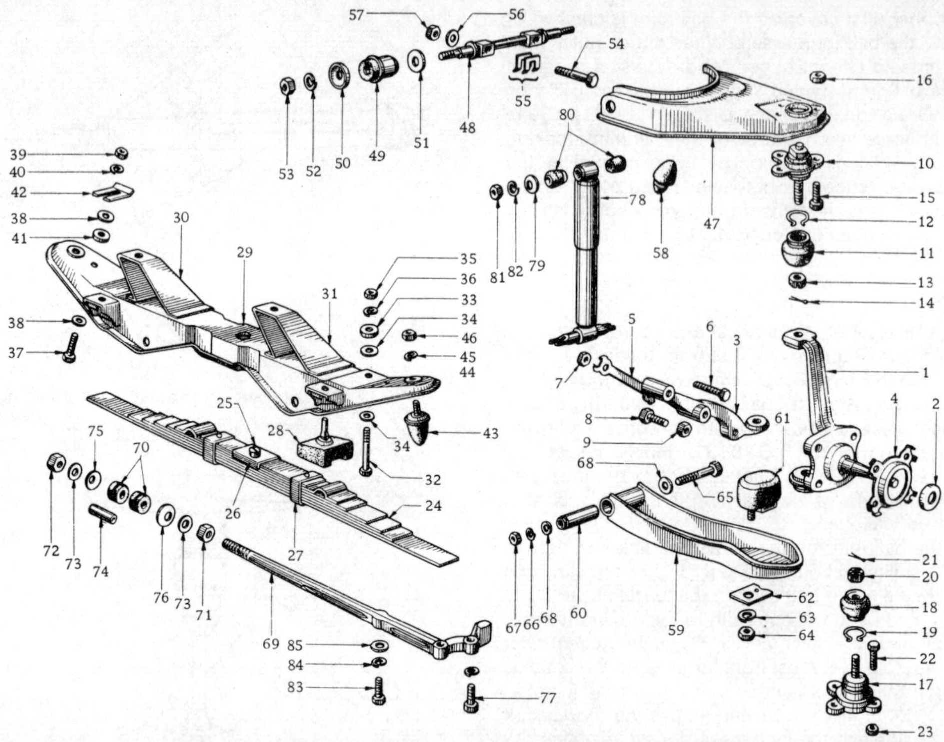

FIG 9:33 Components of the front suspension used on 1000 model cars

Key to Fig 9:33 1 Steering knuckle 2 Collar 3 Knuckle arm 4 Grease catcher 5 Lockplate 6 Bolt 7 Nut 8 Steering stop bolt 9 Nut 10 Upper ball joint 11 Dust cover 12 Spring clamp 13 Nut 14 Splitpin 15 Bolt 16 Nut 17 Lower ball joint 18 Dust cover 19 Clamp 20 Nut 21 Splitpin 22 Bolt 23 Nut 24 Leaf spring assembly 25 Centre bolt 26 Seat 27 Clip 28 Pivot seat 29 Crossmember 30 Engine mounting bracket 31 Engine mounting bracket 32 Bolt 33 Washer 34 Shim 35 Nut 36 Spring washer 37 Bolt 38 Washer 39 Nut 40 Spring washer 41 Washer 42 Shim 43 Rubber buffer 44 Washer 45 Spring washer 46 Nut 47 Upper suspension arm 48 Upper link spindle 49 Rubber bush 50 Washer 51 Washer 52 Spring washer 53 Nut 54 Upper link spindle bolt 55 Camber shims 56 Lockwasher 57 Nut 58 Rubber buffer 59 Lower suspension arm 60 Rubber bush 61 Rubber support 62 Support plate 63 Washer 64 Nut 65 Lower link pin 66 Washer 67 Nut 68 Washer 69 Tension rod 70 Bushing 71 Self-locking nut 72 Nut 73 Washer 74 Collar 75 Special washer 76 Special washer 77 Bolt 78 Damper 79 Washer 70 Rubber bush 81 Nut 82 Lockwasher 83 Bolt 84 Lockwasher 85 Washer

of the arms is effected by the double-acting telescopic damper with rubber buffer blocks suitably located to prevent excessive movement in either direction.

Rubber bushes are used at pivoting points to eliminate the need for lubrication at these points so that maintenance is reduced to the minimum.

Front spring removal:

Jack up the front of the car and support it on stands under the side of the frame.

Remove the two road wheels and the two bolts from the lower damper mountings.

Unscrew the two bolts on the lower link from the tension rod. Unscrew the securing nut on the front end of the tension rod.

Place a jack under the end of the lower suspension arm where the tension rod was attached, take the weight on the jack and then extract the splitpin and remove the securing nut from the lower link pin. Support the spring while removing the other link pin and remove the spring.

Refitting:

Carefully inspect the spring after cleaning it thoroughly and replace any leaves which show signs of damage.

Refit the spring to the lower link on that side which was removed last and secure it temporarily.

Adjust the position of the spring so that its centre bolt, the pivot seat and the hole in the front suspension crossmember all coincide, then jack-up the free end of the spring and hold it temporarily with the clamp ST-4369 or any suitable tool while inserting the lower link pin.

Refit the lower ball joint to the steering knuckle, tighten the nut to 40-53 lb ft (5.5-7.6 kg m) and insert the splitpin.

The bolts on the tension rod and the lower link pins are now tightened to a torque of 30-35 lb ft (4.2-5.0 kg m).

The remaining parts are replaced in the reverse order of removal.

Upper arm:

To remove an upper suspension arm, first jack-up the car and support it on stands.

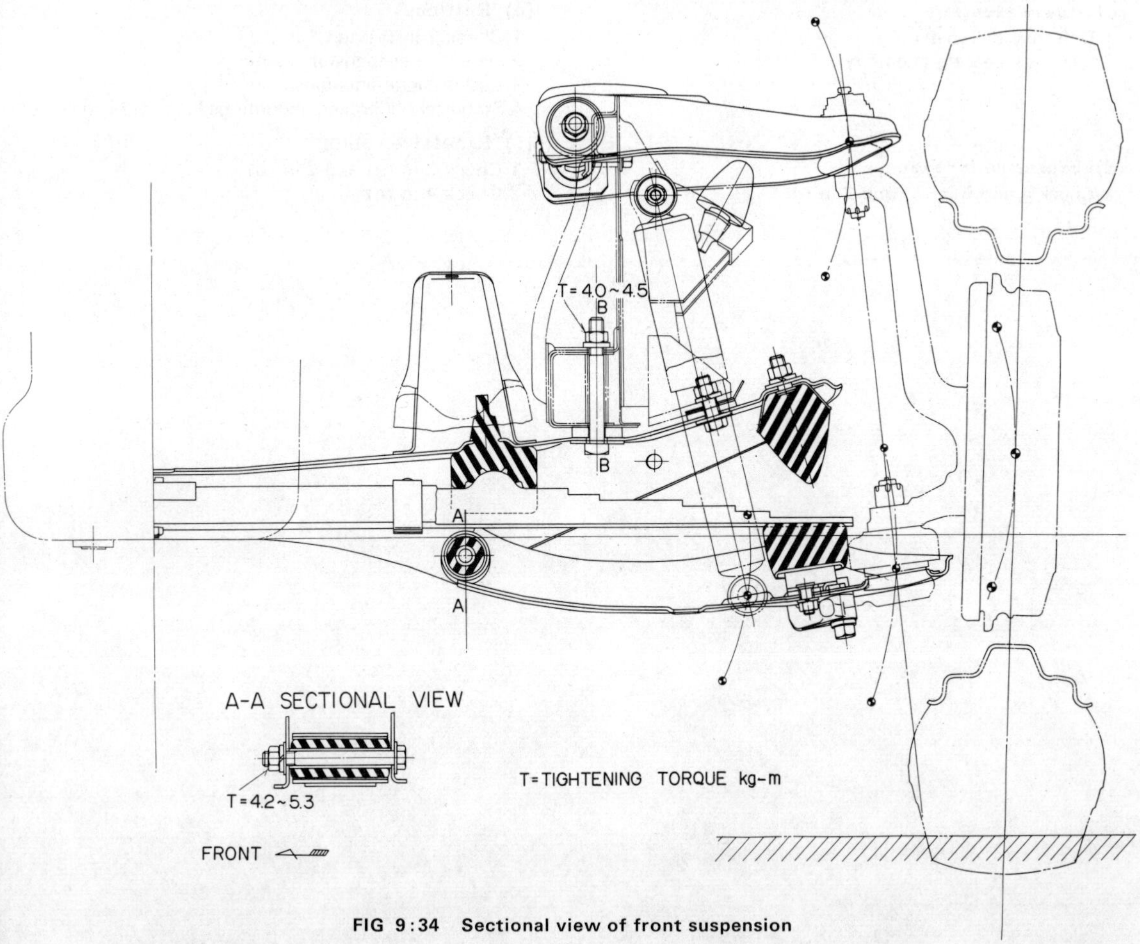

FIG 9:34 Sectional view of front suspension

Take out the splitpin and remove the nut securing the upper ball joint. Remove the ball joint from the swivel axle.

From inside the engine compartment remove the cover at the top of the valance and unscrew the two upper link spindle bolts.

Lift away the upper link.

Refitting is a reversal of the removal procedure.

Lower arm:

With the car firmly supported on stands remove the two nuts from the lower damper mounting.

Undo the tension rod retaining bolts.

Take out the splitpin and unscrew the nut securing the lower ball joint, undo the lower link pivot pin and remove the lower suspension arm.

Refit in the reverse order.

The correct tightening torques for the nuts and bolts removed in these last operations are as follows:

Upper ball joint	25 to 35 lb ft (3.5 to 4.9 kg m)
Upper link spindle	30 to 38 lb ft (4.2 to 5.3 kg m)
Lower ball joint	39 to 53 lb ft (5.5 to 7.6 kg m)
Lower link pin	30 to 38 lb ft (4.2 to 5.3 kg m)

Geometry:

The values of the angles included in the geometry of the front suspension are given in **Technical Data** and the remarks in **Section 9:7** apply equally to this type of system.

9:9 Fault diagnosis

(a) Wheel wobble

1 Worn or loose hub bearings
2 Broken or weak front springs
3 Uneven tyre wear
4 Worn suspension linkage
5 Loose wheel fixings
6 Incorrect tracking (toe-in)

(b) 'Bottoming' of suspension

1 Check 2 in (a)
2 Suspension struts internally defective

(c) Heavy steering

1 Defective ball joints
2 Incorrect steering geometry

(d) Excessive tyre wear

1 Check 4 and 6 in (a) and 2 in (c)

(e) Rattles

1 Check 2 in (a) and 1 in (c)
2 Defective suspension bushings
3 Strut attachments loose
4 Stabilizer bar broken, mountings loose or bushes worn

(f) Excessive rolling

1 Check 2 in (a) and 2 in (b)
2 Check 4 in (e)

CHAPTER 10
THE STEERING GEAR

10:1 Description

Worm and recirculating ball steering gear is fitted to models covered by this manual, the layout of the steering box and column assembly being shown in **FIG 10:1**.

Steering motion is transmitted to the ballrace mounted inner column worm, the ball nut moving up or down the worm according to the amount and direction of the steering wheel movement. The teeth on the ball nut are engaged with the teeth on the sector shaft, steering motion being transmitted through the sector shaft by this means and passed to the drop arm which is mounted on the sector shaft lower end. The drop arm operates the steering linkage, one tie rod being directly connected to the drop arm, the other tie rod being connected through a centre tie rod and idler arm linkage.

A collapsible steering column assembly may be fitted, these units being described in detail in **Section 10:6**.

10:2 Maintenance

Every 6000 miles, the oil level in the steering box should be checked and, if necessary, topped up to the level of the combined filler and level plug located in the steering box case. Use only the correct lubricant as supplied by a Datsun agent.

Every 30,000 miles the steering linkage ball joints should be greased. **FIG 10:2** shows an outer tie rod ball stud, **FIG 10:3** a centre tie rod ball stud. To lubricate the ball joint assemblies, use multi-purpose grease and proceed in the following manner.

Clean the area around the plug on the ball joint assembly to prevent the entry of dirt. The plug is located at the top or bottom of outer tie rod ball joints, at the side of centre tie rod ball joints. Fit a grease nipple in the place of the plug. Use a grease gun to inject grease into the joint until all of the old grease is ejected and the joint is filled with new grease. If a pressure grease gun is used, keep the pressure low to prevent grease from being forced out under the dust cover clamp.

10:3 Removing the steering wheel

Disconnect the battery and remove the horn pad, either by unscrewing the two bolts behind the steering wheel bar or, on the three-spoke wheel, by pulling it out. Remove the steering wheel nut as shown in **FIG 10:4**, mark the position of the wheel on the shaft, then pull off the steering wheel using the puller ST.27180000 or ST.27180001 or similar. **FIG 10:5** shows the steering wheel and horn ring.

Refitting:

This is a reversal of the removal procedure. Make sure that the steering wheel is centred with the front wheels pointing straight-ahead and tighten the steering wheel nut to between 21 and 25 lb ft torque.

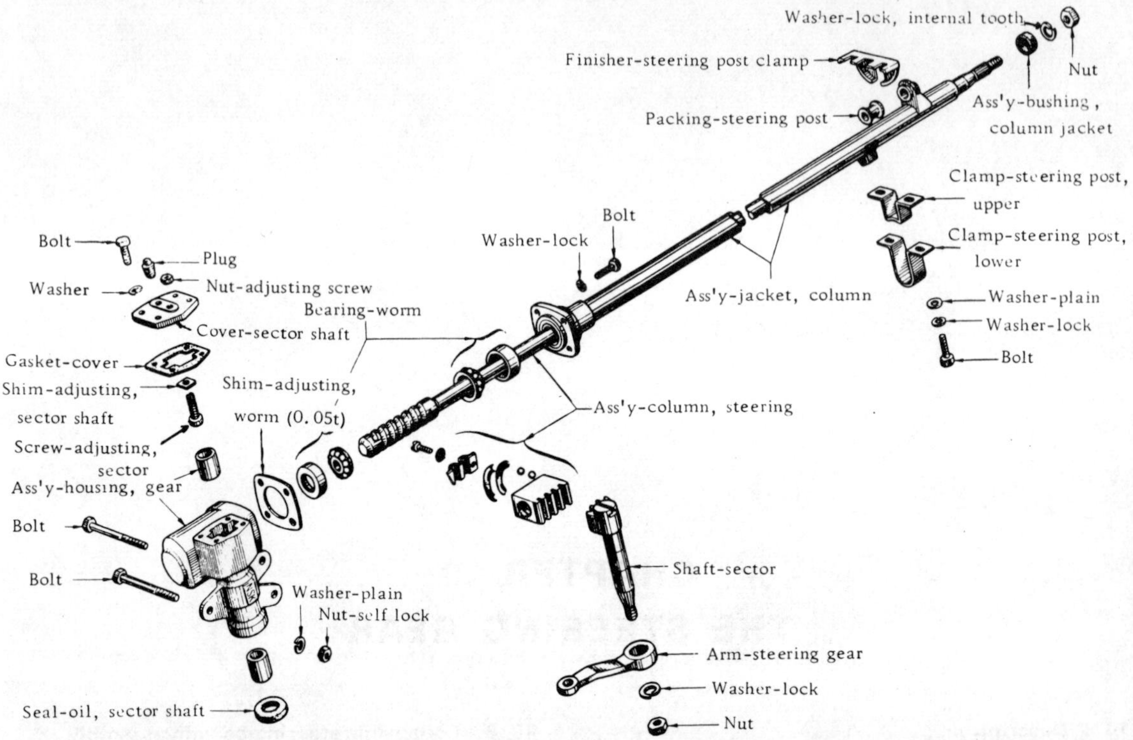

FIG 10:1 Components of the steering gear and column assembly 1000 model illustrated

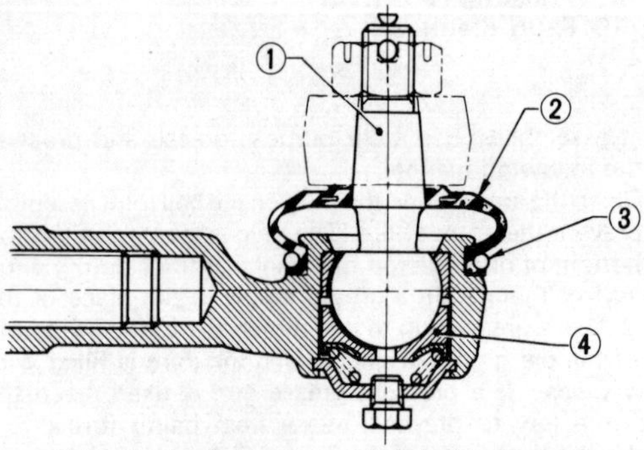

FIG 10:2 Outer tie rod ball joint assembly

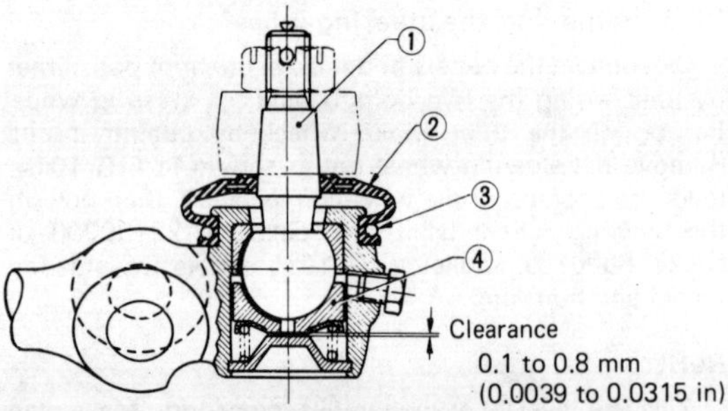

FIG 10:3 Centre tie rod ball joint assembly

Key to Figs 10:2 and 10:3 1 Ball stud 2 Dust cover 3 Clamp 4 Spring seat

10:4 Removing and refitting steering gear

Removal:

Disconnect the battery. Remove the steering wheel from the column as described in **Section 10:3**. Remove the steering column shell covers as shown in **FIG 10:6**, then remove the turn signal and lighting switch complete as shown in **FIG 10:7**.

On cars fitted with column mounted gearchange assemblies, disconnect the gearlever from the control rod assembly by unscrewing the fixing bolts.

On the B210 disconnect the flexible coupling from the steering box.

Remove the two fixing bolts shown in **FIG 10:8** which secure the column upper clamp to the instrument panel. Remove the six bolts arrowed in **FIG 10:9**, four bolts on B210 models, which secure the column lower coverplate to the body.

On B210 models pull the steering column into the driver's compartment.

On cars fitted with column mounted gearchange assemblies, remove the cotterpin from the trunnion and remove the gearchange rod from the lever and the selector rod from the selector lever.

Disconnect the steering drop arm from the centre tie rod.

Remove the three bolts shown in **FIG 10:10** which secure the steering gear housing in the car body. Pull the steering gear and column assembly on early cars out towards the engine compartment. Remove the gearchange control from the column, if fitted, referring to **Chapter 6, Section 6:7**.

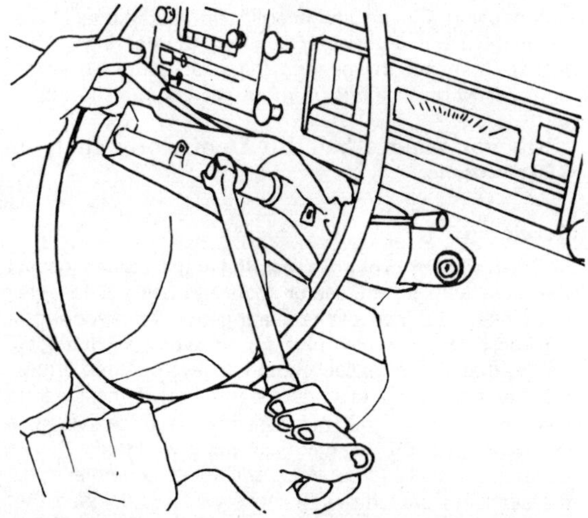

FIG 10:4 Removing the steering wheel locknut

Refitting:

This is a reversal of the removal procedure. Make sure that the steering wheel turns smoothly from lock to lock and that it is correctly aligned. Steering wheel free travel should be between .8 and 1.0 inch at the rim. Check the steering gear lubricant as described in **Section 10:2**. Tightening torques are 14 to 18 lb ft for steering gear fixing bolts, 6 to 7 lb ft for steering column clamp bolts.

On B210 models set the wheels in the straightahead position. Ensure that the steering box rocker shaft is in the middle of the worm and the cut-out for the flexible clamp bolt is facing upwards. The punch mark at the top of the column shaft must also face upwards. Tighten the flexible clamp bolt, on the worm shaft serrations, to a torque of 29 to 36 lb ft. The upper clamp bolts to 11 to 13 lb ft and the dash panel bolts 2.5 to 3.3 lb ft (see **FIG 10:32**).

10:5 Dismantling and reassembling steering gear

Dismantling:

Remove the drop arm fixing nut and use a puller to remove the drop arm from the sector shaft, tool ST.27140000 or ST.27140001 for B210, being available for this purpose. Remove the plug and drain the oil from the steering gear housing. Loosen the adjusting screw nut and turn the sector shaft adjusting screw a few turns anticlockwise. Remove the four sector shaft cover fixing bolts as shown in **FIG 10:11**, then pull the cover complete with sector shaft from the housing.

Removing the four fixing bolts which secure the wormshaft cover to the steering gear housing and pull out the wormshaft assembly as shown for early models in **FIG 10:12**. **Take care not to allow the ball nut to run up or down the end of the worm during this operation, otherwise the ends of the ball guides will be damaged.**

Pull the inner column assembly on early models from the column jacket. Remove the sector shaft oil seal, noting that the sector shaft bearings are press-fitted on the

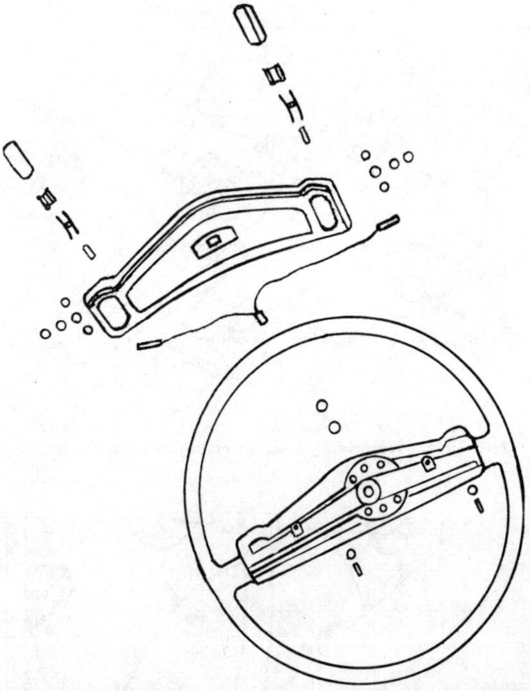

FIG 10:5 The steering wheel and horn ring components

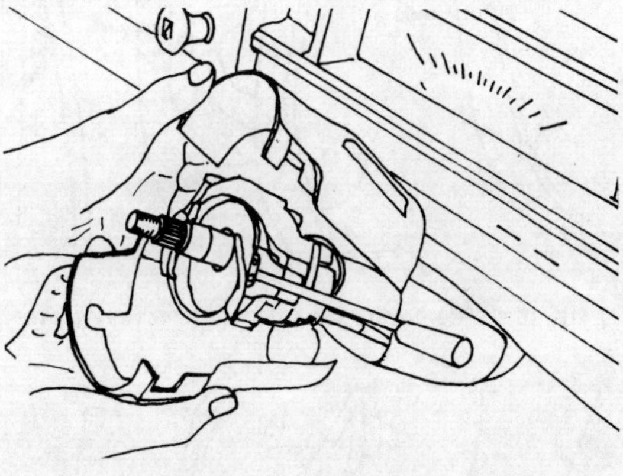

FIG 10:6 Removing the steering column shell covers

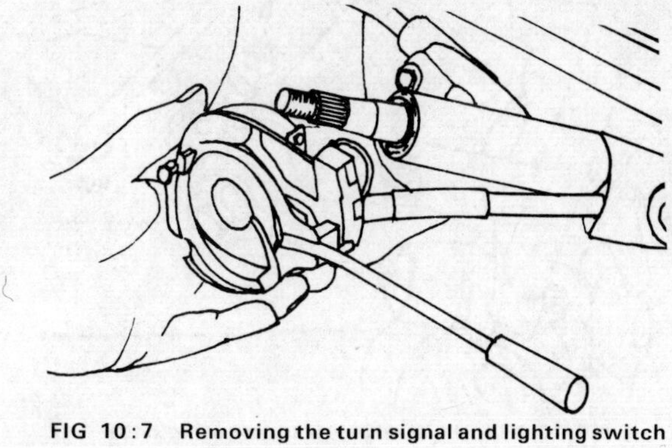

FIG 10:7 Removing the turn signal and lighting switch

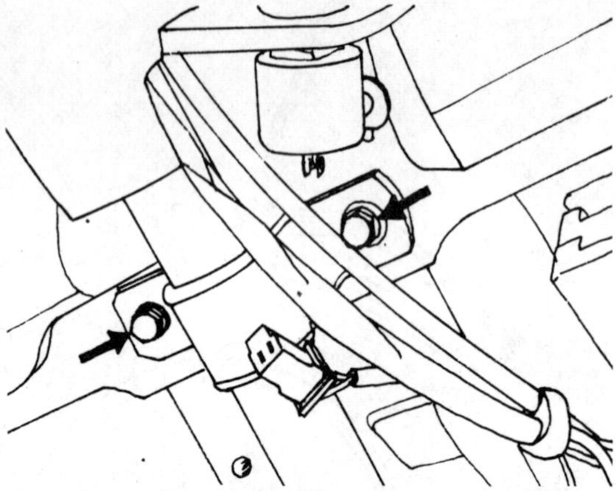

FIG 10:8 Removing the upper column clamp bolts

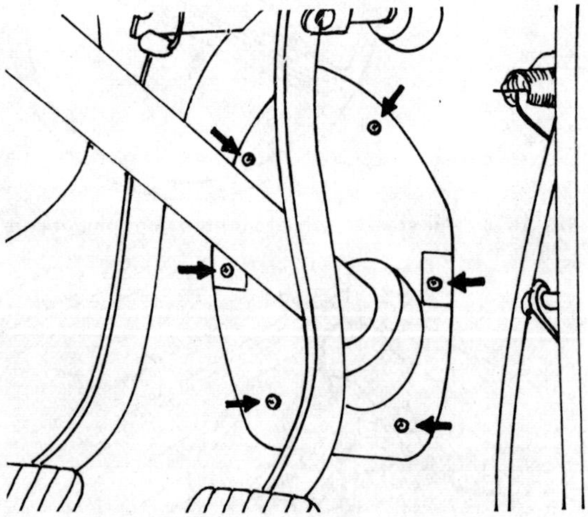

FIG 10:9 Removing the column lower coverplate

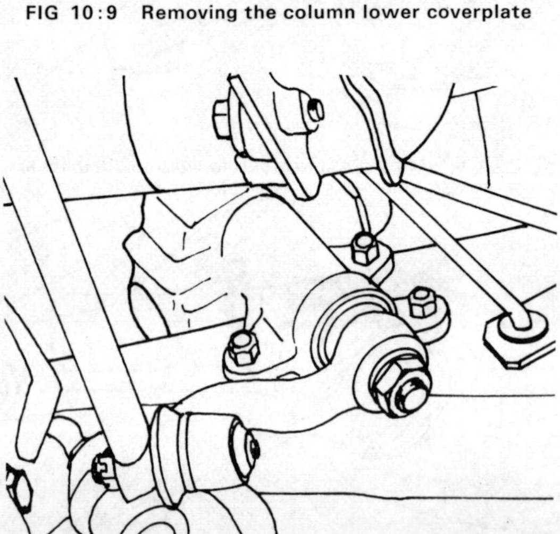

FIG 10:10 The steering gear mounting bolts

gearhousing. Use a suitable puller on 1200 models to remove the rear bearing outer race from the steering column jacket. Take out the bearing inner races from the front and rear worm bearings. Remove the column shaft bearing.

Do not remove ball nut from worm shaft on 120Y models.

Servicing:

Clean all parts in petrol or paraffin and dry them. Inspect the gear teeth on the sector shaft and ball nut for wear or damage and inspect the bearings for wear, scoring or slackness. Renew any part found worn or damaged, noting that a new oil seal should always be fitted, unless the original seal is in perfect condition. If the steering column, worm or ball nut assembly is defective, it is recommended that a new assembly is fitted, this is mandatory on 120Y models, due to the complexity of the servicing procedures. If, however, it is decided that servicing will be carried out, the procedure is as follows. If sector shaft bushes on 120Y models, are worn, the casing must be renewed.

Ball nut assembly, 1000, 1200 models:

Remove the clamp on the ball nut tubes and detach the guide tubes from the ball nut, collecting 11 steel balls from each guide tube. Turn the ball nut upside down and rotate the steering column back and forth until all 38 steel balls have dropped from the ball nut. Take care not to lose any of the steel balls, and check that a total of 60 has been obtained. The ball nut can then be removed.

Clean all parts in petrol or paraffin and dry them. Check the ball guide tubes for damage at the ends where they pick up the steel balls from the helical path, renewing the guides if not perfect in appearance. If the steel balls or ball nut unit are worn or damaged, a new assembly should be fitted.

Slide the ball nut onto the column worm with the holes upwards. Drop 19 balls into each of the ball nut holes, on the same side of the ball nut. Turn the column gradually away from the hole being filled and continue until all 38 balls are installed. In cases where the balls are stopped by the end of the column worm, hold down the balls already installed with a suitable blunt instrument and turn the column a few turns in the reverse direction. The filling of the circuit can then be continued as before. It may be necessary to work the column back and forth, holding the balls down first in one hole then the other, in order to close the spaces between the balls and fill the circuits completely. **The full complement of steel balls must be fitted into the ball nut.**

Place the remaining 22 steel balls in the halves of the ball guides, 11 balls to each half. Close each filled half of the guides with the mating half. Close the ends of each guide with a plug of vaseline so that the steel balls will not drop out during installation. Push the ball guide tubes into the guide holes of the ball nut and retain them in position by fitting the guide tube clamp.

Reassembly and adjustment, 1000, 1200 models

Press the oil seal into the housing, after applying a coat of multi-purpose grease to the oil seal lips. Insert the column assembly into the column jacket and install them,

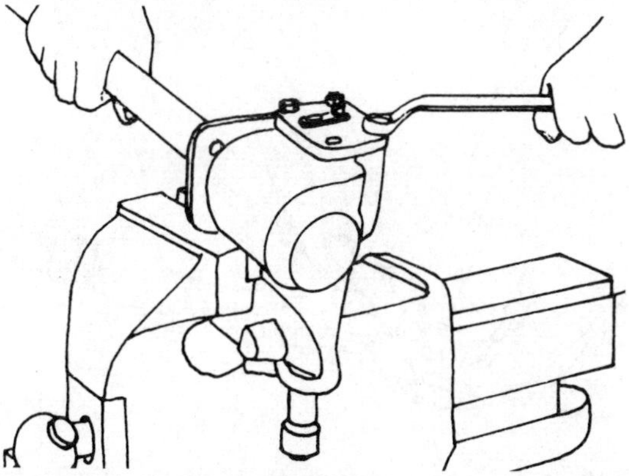

FIG 10:11 Removing the sector shaft cover bolts

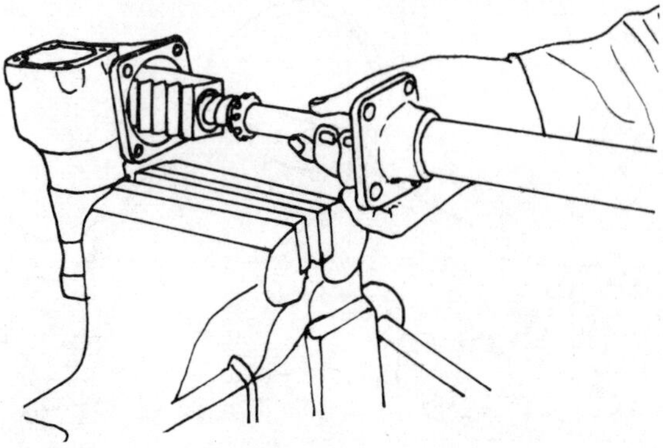

FIG 10:12 Removing the column assembly from the steering gear housing

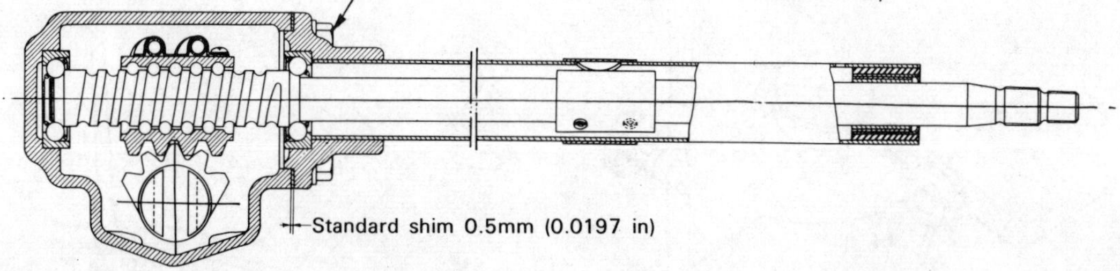

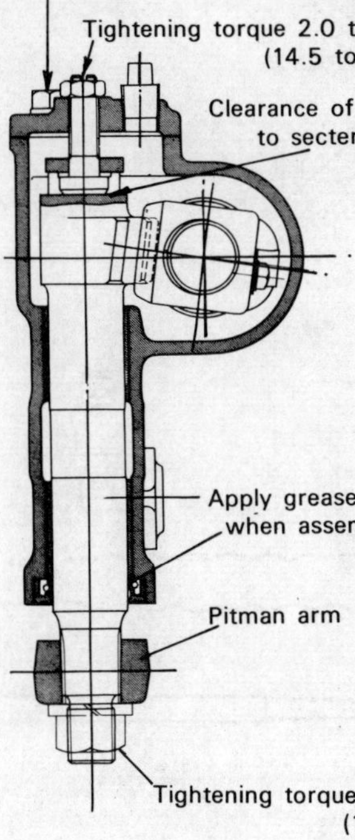

FIG 10:13 Section through the steering gear

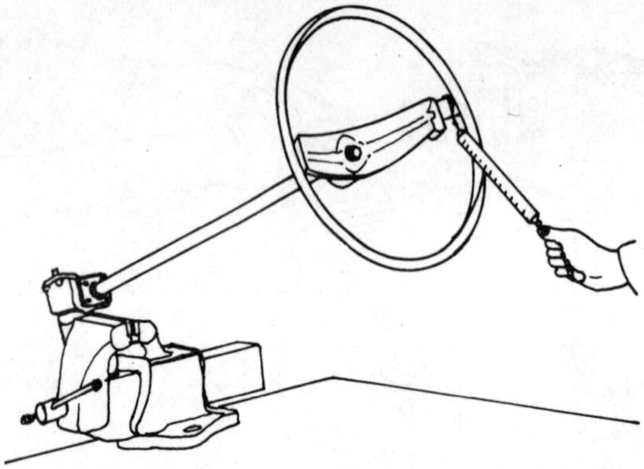

FIG 10:14 Measuring the initial turning torque of the steering shaft

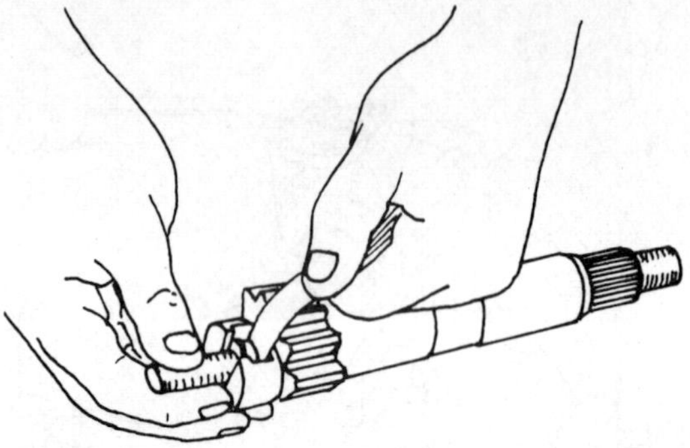

FIG 10:15 Checking the sector shaft adjuster clearance

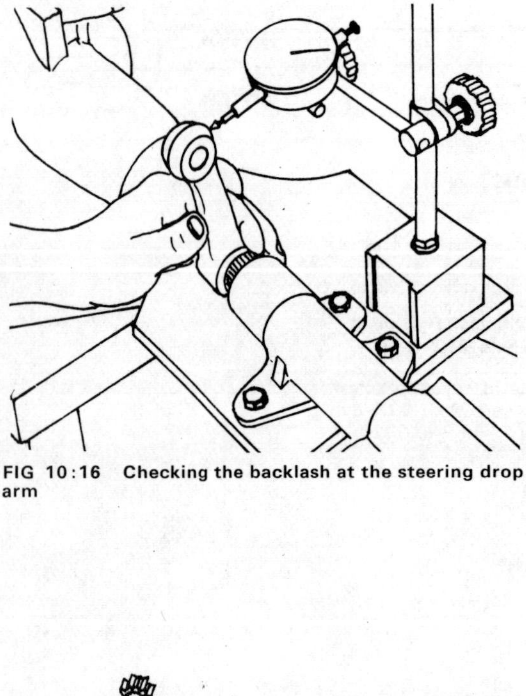

FIG 10:16 Checking the backlash at the steering drop arm

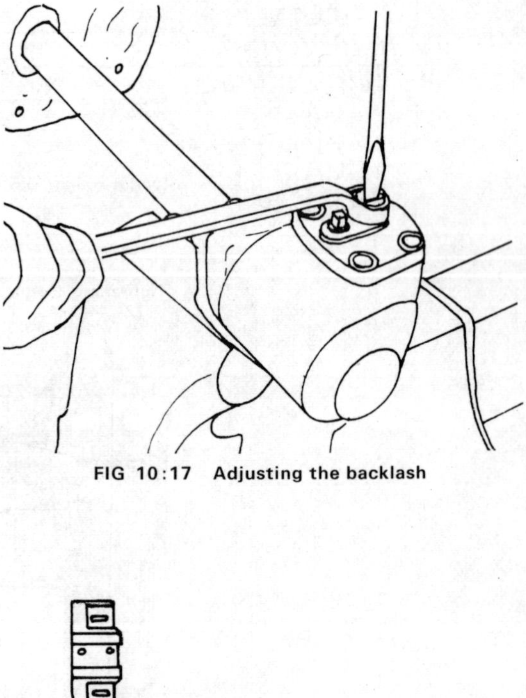

FIG 10:17 Adjusting the backlash

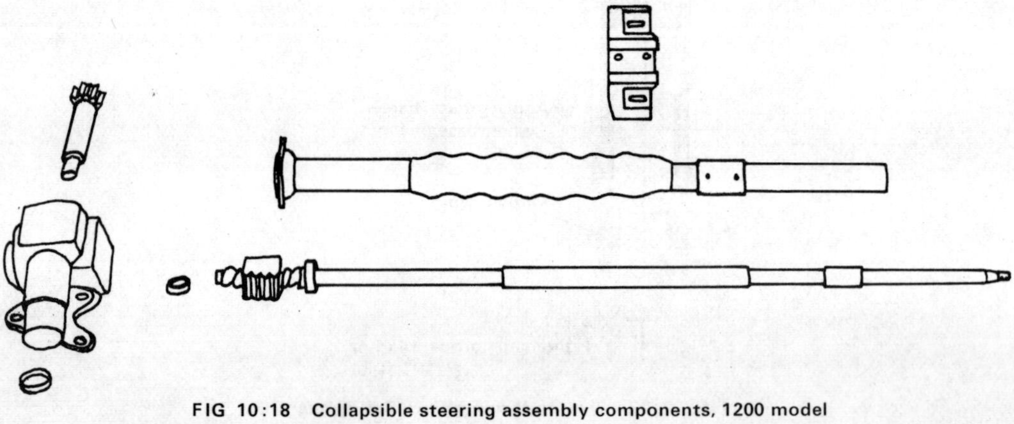

FIG 10:18 Collapsible steering assembly components, 1200 model

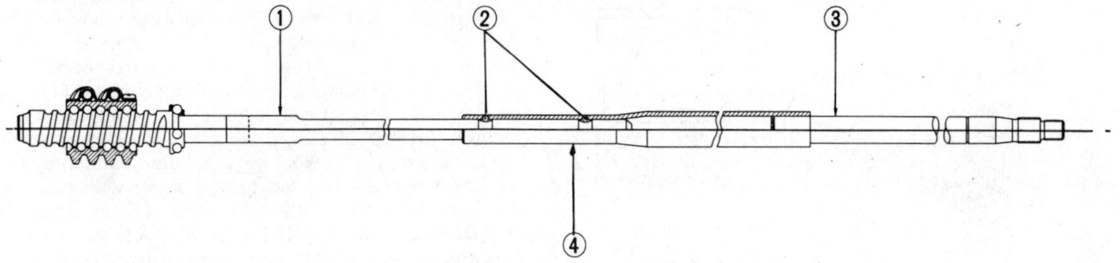

FIG 10:19 Inner column assembly, 1200 models

Key to Fig 10:19 1 Lower column shaft 2 Plastic pin 3 Upper column shaft 4 Lower column tube

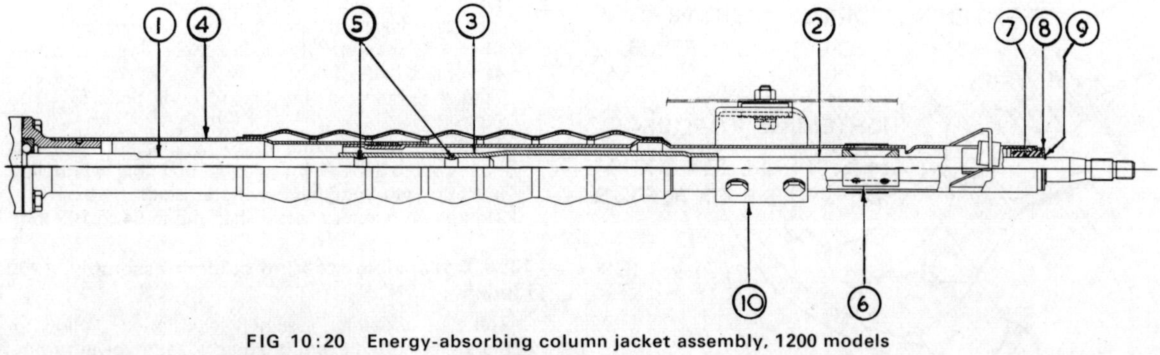

FIG 10:20 Energy-absorbing column jacket assembly, 1200 models

Key to Fig 10:20 1 Lower column shaft 2 Upper column shaft 3 Lower column tube 4 Jacket tube 5 Plastic pin 6 Column collar 7 Bush 8 Washer 9 Snap ring 10 Steering column clamp bracket

with bearing shims and 'O' ring to the housing, using the four flange fixing bolts. **FIG 10:13** shows a section through the steering gear housing and indicates the shim position. If a replacement column bearing assembly is to be fitted, fill the new housing assembly with multi-purpose grease and cement it to the column.

Fit the steering wheel temporarily in position as shown in **FIG 10:14** and check the effort needed to turn the steering wheel. Use a spring balance positioned at the steering wheel outer circumference and take the reading while the wheel is turning. Note that, for this test, the sector shaft must not be installed and the bearings must be lubricated with the correct gear oil. Turning torque of the steering wheel under these conditions must be between 30 and 65 oz/inch. If necessary, select and fit suitable shims between the cover and casing from the thicknesses which are available.

Fit the sector shaft adjuster and a shim into the sector shaft and measure the clearance between the adjuster and shaft as shown in **FIG 10:15**, using a feeler gauge. Modify the shim thickness until the correct clearance of .002 inch (.05mm) is obtained, five shim thicknesses being available for this purpose. Oil the sector shaft and teeth, rotate the steering column until the ball nut is at the centre of the worm, then enter the sector shaft into position so that the centre tooth on the sector shaft enters the centre tooth space on the ball nut. With a new gasket in position, push the sector shaft cover, complete with sector shaft, into place. After making sure that there is some degree of play between the ball nut and sector teeth, tighten the sector cover bolts to between 13 and 20 lb ft.

Lock the adjuster screw temporarily with its locknut. Move the sector shaft several times from the drop arm side to ensure that it turns smoothly. Connect the drop arm to the sector shaft as shown in **FIG 10:16**, matching the alignment marks on the arm and shaft correctly. Arrange the steering gear in the central (straight-ahead) position and fit a dial gauge assembly as shown. Adjust the backlash in this neutral position by tightening the

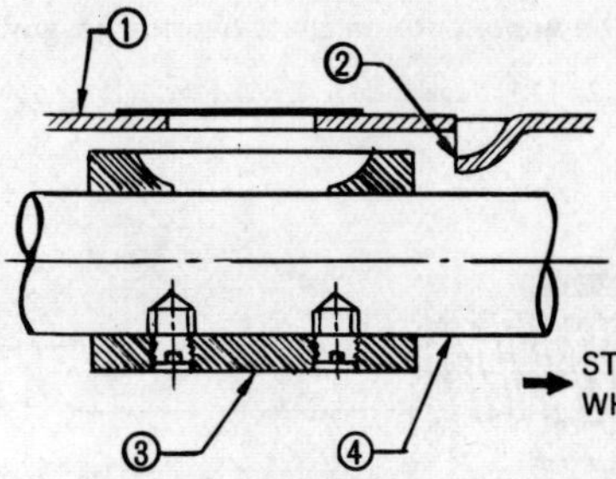

FIG 10:21 Steering shaft stopper action

Key to Fig 10:21 1 Jacket tube 2 Shaft stopper 3 Column collar 4 Column shaft

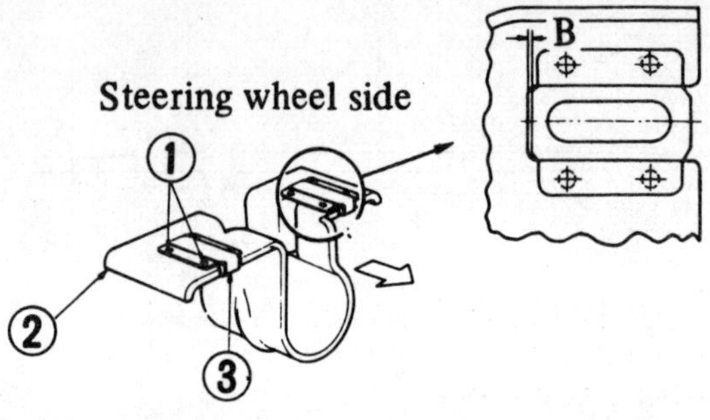

FIG 10:22 The steering column sliding clamp assembly

Key to Fig 10:22 1 Plastic pin 2 Clamp 3 Sliding block B=0

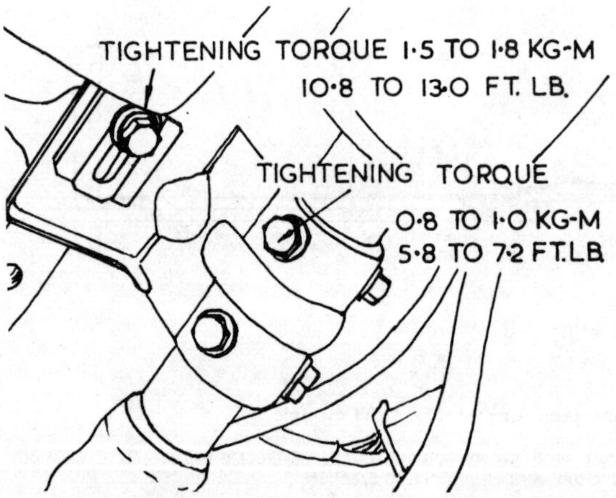

FIG 10:23 Mounting bracket bolt torque values

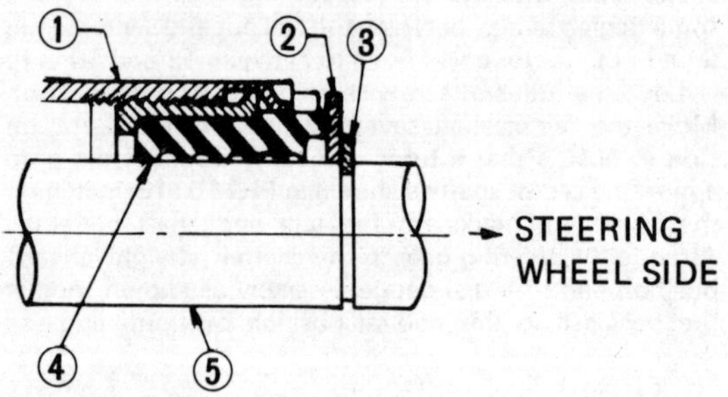

FIG 10:24 The upper column shaft bearing assembly

Key to Fig 10:24 1 Jack tube 2 Washer 3 Snap ring 4 Column bush 5 Column shaft

adjuster screw until the free movement at the top of the drop arm is limited to within .004 inch (.1 mm) at a radius of 5 inches (127 mm). The steering gear must not be tight, this small play being essential. When the backlash is correctly adjusted, lock the adjuster with the locknut and recheck. **FIG 10:17** shows the adjuster and locknut.

Fit the drop arm locking nut and tighten to a torque of 101 lb ft. Fill the steering gear housing with gear oil, noting that approximately .4 Imp pints (.5 US pints, .23 litre) will be required. Refit the steering gear to the car as described in **Section 10:4** and recheck the oil level. Make sure that the steering operates smoothly and without binding from lock to lock.

Assemble B210 generally as for 1000, 1200 models, noting the following exceptions:

1 The worm bearing preload without sector shaft fitted is 28 to 69 inch oz (see **FIG 11:33**).
2 Final turning torque at centre position is 56 to 125 inch oz, maximum turning torque over range is less than 153 inch oz. If outside these limits re-adjust sector shaft adjustment screw.
3 Torque tighten steering box to body bolts to 43 to 58 lb ft.
4 Tighten flexible coupling to wormshaft serrations bolt to 29 to 36 lb ft. Be sure that bolt hole in coupling lines up with undercut in serrated shaft.
5 Tighten drop arm to sector shaft nut to 94 to 108 lb ft.

10:6 Collapsible steering column assembly, 1200 models

This type of column assembly is designed to allow for compression in the event of an accident involving front-end impact, and to prevent injury resulting from the driver being thrown against the column assembly in such a situation.

In a front-end collision, the column resists the primary force of impact and does not tend to be pushed into the passenger compartment. When the secondary force occurs as the driver is thrown forward, the column shaft shears and telescopes downwards, the specially designed column jacket collapsing progressively to absorb a considerable amount of the force which is applied. **FIG 10:18** shows the components of the collapsible steering assembly.

When the collapsible steering column is installed in the car, it is no more susceptible to damage than a standard column assembly. However, when a collapsible column is removed, special care is required in handling to avoid damage. When the column has been removed, actions such as a sharp blow on the shaft or gearchange levers or dropping the assembly to the ground or bench could bend the column jacket, especially the bellows portion which absorbs collision shocks. For this reason, great care must

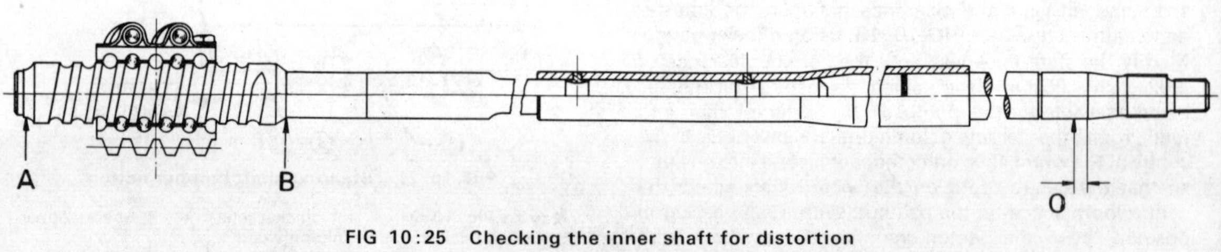

FIG 10:25 Checking the inner shaft for distortion

be taken to avoid any shocks or blows, as, if the column assembly is damaged a new assembly will be required.

The construction of the column is shown in **FIG 10:19** and the energy absorbing column jacket is shown in **FIG 10:20**. Steering motion is transmitted by the lower shaft and upper tube. The lower shaft is of special shape and the upper tube interior fits tightly against the lower shaft exterior, four plastic pins completely eliminating any gap between the two parts. When a collision force is applied to the end of the column assembly, the plastic pins mentioned are sheared off and the lower shaft is fitted into the upper tube. When this happens, the shaft end

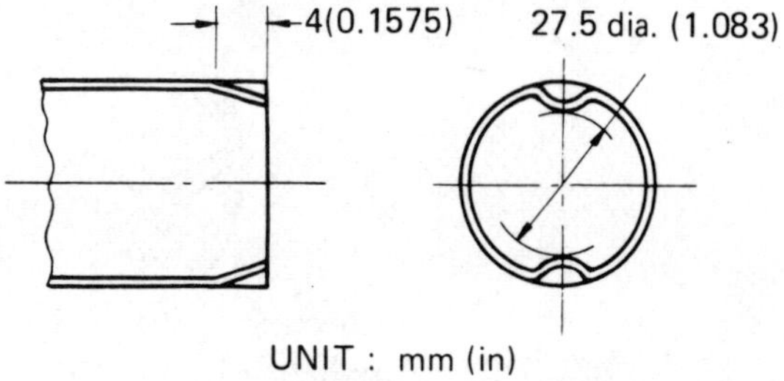

FIG 10:26 Indent the jacket tube upper end

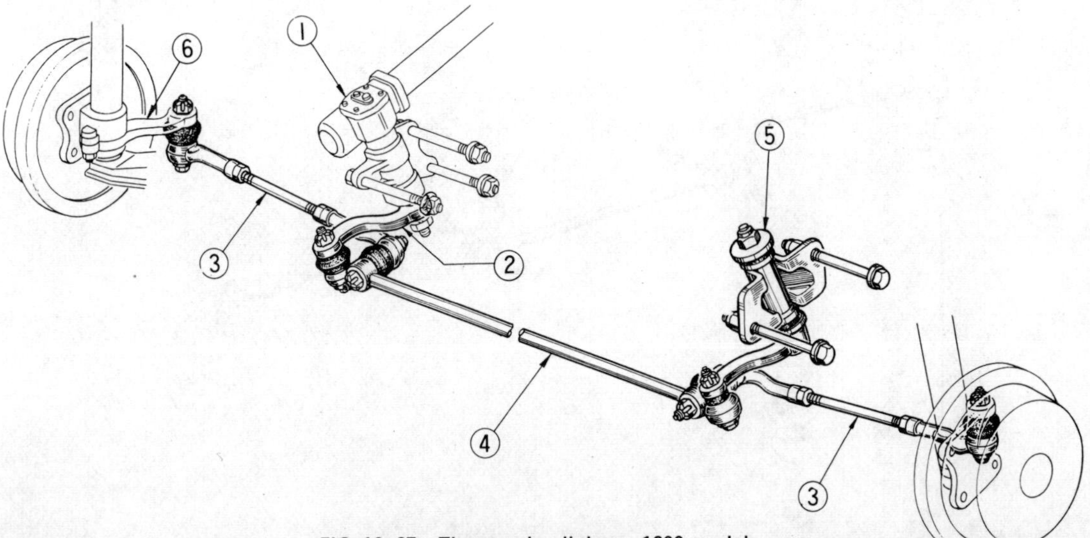

FIG 10:27 The steering linkage. 1200 models

Key to Fig 10:27 1 Steering gear 2 Drop arm 3 Outer tie rods 4 Centre tie rod 5 Idler arm assembly 6 Steering knuckle arm

spreads and the lower shaft cannot then be withdrawn unless an exceptionally high load is applied. The shaft is prevented from moving into the passenger compartment due to the collar for steering lock mounting, which is fitted to the shaft, contacting three stoppers which project from the outer jacket tube, this being shown in **FIG 10:21**.

The jacket tube is of mesh construction, part of which is specially punched to form an energy-absorbing medium. Upper and lower guide tubes, joined with polyacetal resin are inserted in the mesh tube, so that energy generated in a collision can be absorbed as smoothly as possible, these guide tubes also serving to improve the rigidity of the entire tube assembly.

The steering column clamp shown in **FIG 10:22** is of special design, being secured to the jacket tube and instrument panel with bolts. Additionally, two aluminium sliding blocks are incorporated, being held onto the main body with plastic pins. When a large impact occurs from the driving side of the column, the plastic pins shear off and, leaving the sliding block in the column bracket side, the clamp proper is disengaged and slides downwards with the column jacket as the latter collapses. By the design of the slotted bracket mountings, it can be seen that the bracket assembly will not allow the column assembly to move rearwards, so that the possibility of the assembly being forced into the passenger compartment is eliminated.

It must be noted that the bolts which secure the mounting bracket in position on the instrument panel and column assembly should be tightened according to the information in **FIG 10:23** if the mounting is disturbed or removed. Additionally, the bolts used to attach the mounting to the column assembly are of a certain exact length and must never be replaced by alternative length bolts. Always use the correct bolts in this location, together with a washer under the head. If a bolt is lost or damaged during servicing procedures, obtain a new correct bolt, part number 81.10812.1 to replace it. A bolt of incorrect length may interfere with the inner column shaft and cause a highly dangerous condition to arise.

Collapsible steering column assembly, 120Y and B210 models:

The column fitted to these models is of a modified type which reacts in the same manner to shocks but is of a steel ball, sliding tube construction. It cannot be dismantled. The following checks must be carried out if damage is suspected.

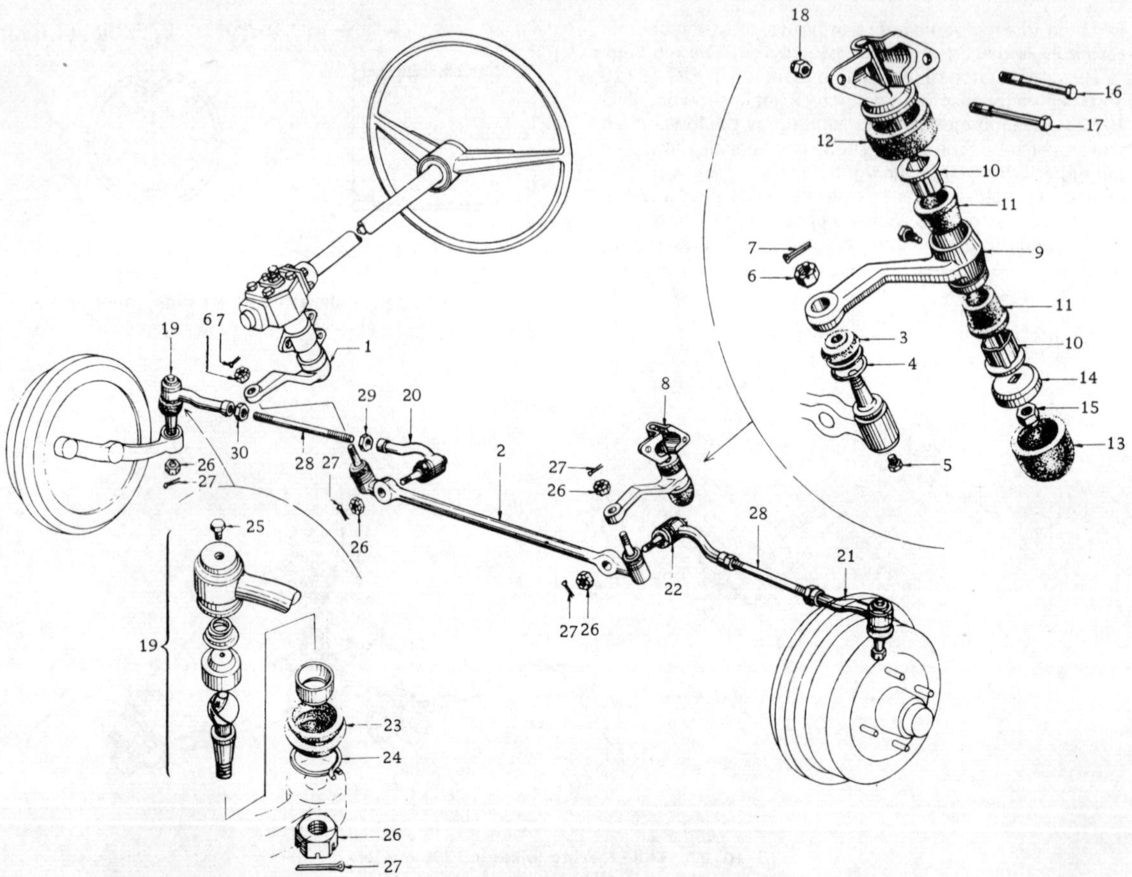

FIG 10:28 The steering linkage. 1000 models

Key to Fig 10:28 1 Drop arm 2 Centre tie rod 3 Dust cover 4 Dust cover clip 5 Plug 6 Nut 7 Splitpin 8 Idler assembly 9 Idler arm 10 Bush 11 Rubber bush 12 Dust cover 13 Dust cover 14 Washer 15 Self-locking nut 16 Bolt 17 Bolt 18 Nut 19 Side rod end assembly 20 Side rod end assembly 21 Side rod outer end 22 Side rod inner end 23 Dust cover 24 Cover clip 25 Filter plug 26 Nut 27 Splitpin 28 Side rod 29 Locknut 30 Locknut

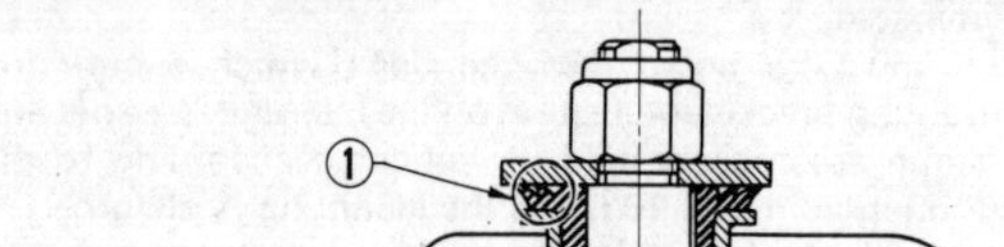

FIG 10:29 Section through the idler arm assembly 1200 models

Key to Fig 10:29 1 Sealing lip assembly 2 Rubber bushing

1 Measure dimension **D** (see **FIG 10:32**), if less than 7.035 inch a new column must be fitted.
2 Measure dimension **B** (see **FIG 10:22**), if any clearance is present the column must be renewed.
3 Check at **E** (see **FIG 10:32**) for axial play of steering shaft, if play is present renew the column.

Steering lock:

A steering lock is fitted to the column of the B210 models secured to the column by self-shear screws. Remove by drilling out the screws. Replace with the lock aligned with the steering tube aperture, and screw in new self-shear screws until the heads shear off.

10:7 Removing and refitting collapsible steering, 1200 models

Removal:

First remove the snap ring from the upper surface of the steering column bushing, then remove the steering gear in the manner described for standard assemblies in **Section 10:4**. The upper column bushing and the location of the snap ring are shown in **FIG 10:24**.

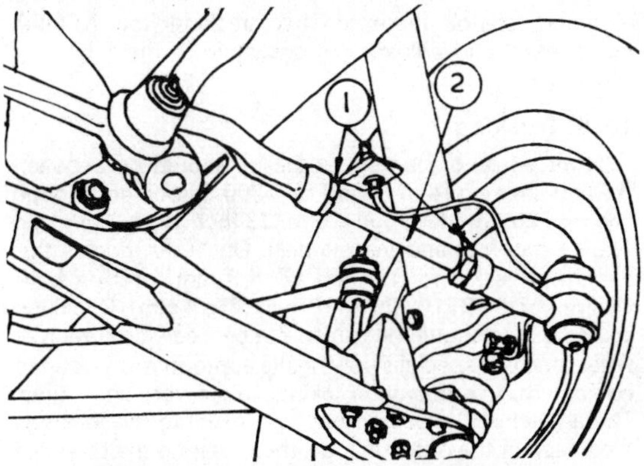

FIG 10:30 Toe-in adjustment points

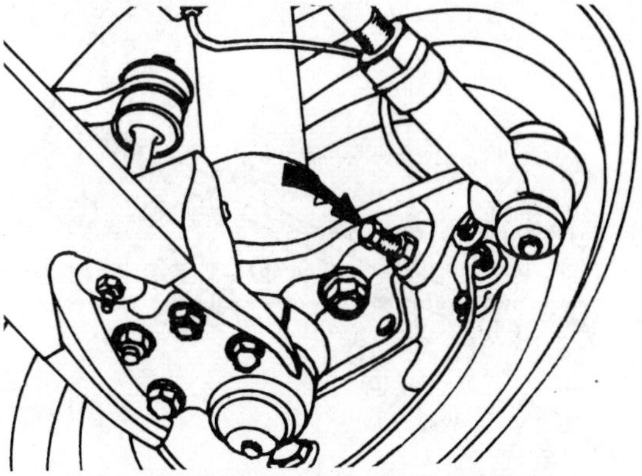

FIG 10:31 Steering angle adjusting bolt

Servicing:

Dismantle, clean and inspect the steering gear and column assembly in the manner described in **Section 10:5** for standard units. Carry out the following further inspections on the energy-absorbing and collapsible parts.

Check the column shaft plastic pin for cracks and the column steering lock collar for warping or breakdown of its screw. Check the jacket tube for damage, or any signs of its length being reduced. Check the inner shaft for bending and the column clamp sliding block for tightness. To check the shaft for bending, support it at the points **A** and **B** as shown in **FIG 10:25**. Bending must not exceed .04 inch (1.0mm) at point **C** when tested under these conditions. If in any doubt about the condition of the collapsible column components, take the assembly to a Datsun agent for an expert opinion. Renew any components found worn or damaged.

Refitting:

This is carried out in a manner similar to that described in **Section 10:4** for standard column units, noting the following extra points.

Adjust the alignment and install the worm shaft and jacket tube on the steering gear housing. Apply sufficient multi-purpose grease to the interior of the column bush and screw the bush in above the rated position. Fit the washer and apply the snap ring firmly and correctly into the groove. Return the bush, allowing its top surface to contact the lower surface of the washer, then adjust the clearance to less than .04 inch (1.0mm). Finely adjust the position of the bush until the turning torque is at the rated value, as checking in the manner described in **Section 10:5** and shown in **FIG 10:14**. Note that, if the bushing is set up too tightly, the steering will be heavy to turn.

Line up the jacket tube upper end to the groove on the outer circumference of the column bushing, and securely depress two opposite positions on the circumference as shown in **FIG 10:26**. When this is done, make sure that the inner diameter of the jacket tube is 1.09 inch (27.5 mm) and that the length of the indentation is .16 inch (4 mm). Take care not to crack the tube or deform the bush during the operation. Make certain that the outer diameter of the jacket tube is now less than 1.25 inch (31.8 mm). If the column bush is found to be incorrect after the operation, re-work or adjust the bush position with shims. Shims are available in two thicknesses for this purpose.

Install the sector shaft, adjusting screw and cover and complete the reassembly and refitting as described for standard units.

10:8 Steering linkage

The steering linkage consists of the centre tie rod which connects the steering drop arm and idler arm, the idler arm assembly, and the outer tie rods which are connected to the steering knuckle arms. **FIG 10:27** shows the steering linkage for 1200 model cars, the B210 being similar, and **FIG 10:28** shows the earlier layout in the 1000 models. This latter is slightly different on account of the variation in front suspension arrangements, most noticeable is the changed idler arm and the ball joint assemblies. Ball joints are used at the rod connections, lubrication of these joints being described in **Section 10:2**.

Removing the linkage:

Apply the handbrake, raise the front of the car and safely support it on floor stands. Remove the cotterpins and castle nuts which secure the track rod ball studs to the steering knuckle arms. Free the ball studs from the knuckle arms by supporting the boss with a large hammer and striking the opposite side with a second hammer. Remove the centre tie rod ball studs in the manner just described. The centre and outer tie rods can now be removed as an assembly. Remove the idler assembly from the sidemember by taking out the two fixing bolts.

Dismantling:

Disconnect the outer tie rods from the centre tie rod in the manner described previously. Loosen the clamp bolts, unscrew the socket assembly and remove the socket from the outer tie rod. Remove the idler arm nut and dismantle the idler assembly, a sectioned view being shown in **FIG 10:29**.

Servicing:

Check the idler arm rubber bushing for damage, wear or play and the centre and outer tie rods for damage, cracks or bending. Check the ball joints assemblies for

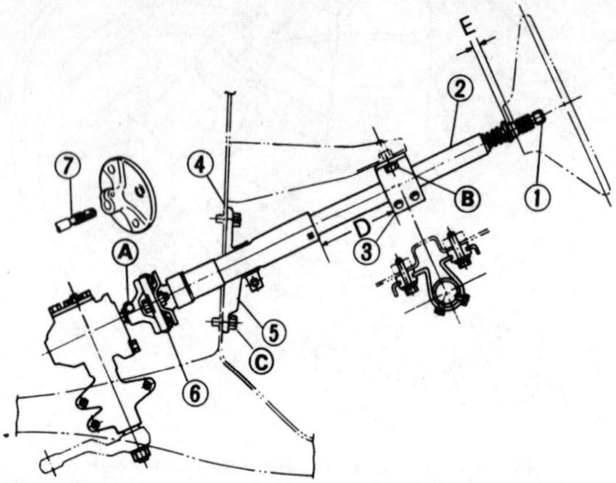

FIG 10:32 Steering column assembly on B210 models

Key to Fig 10:32 1 Column shaft 2 Upper column tube 3 Upper clamp 4 Front panel 5 Lower column tube flange 6 Flexible coupling 7 Worm shaft A Torque tighten clamp bolt to 29 to 36 lb ft B 11 to 13 lb ft C 2.5 to 3.3 lb ft D 7.035 inch (187.7 mm) E Axial play

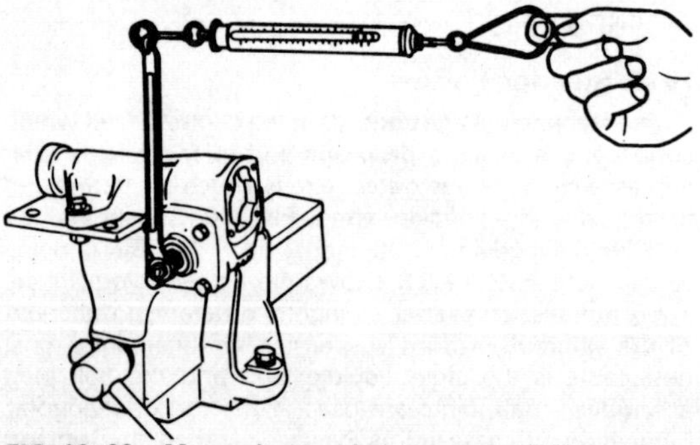

FIG 10:33 Measuring turning torque on B210 models

play due to lack of internal spring effort and for damage. Renew any faulty components. Ball joints are of the sealed type and cannot be dismantled, so faulty ball joint assemblies must be renewed complete. A ball joint should also be renewed if the rubber dust cover is torn or split, as dirt or grit which will have entered the joint cannot be removed. Lubricate the ball joints as described in **Section 10:2**.

Reassembly and refitting:

This is carried out in the reverse order of the removal and dismantling instructions, noting the following points. Apply soapy water to the outer circumference of the idler arm bush and press the bush carefully into position so that it protrudes equally at both sides. Fit the idler arm body in the rubber bushing. Keep the idler arm centre line parallel to the car chassis centre line.

Reassemble the outer tie rods so that their lengths are 11.7 inch (297 mm) on 1200 models, 11.752 inch (298.5 mm) on 120Y or 12.05 inch (306 mm) on USA B210 models when measured between the ball stud centres, screwing each half equally into the centre socket and tightening the locknuts. Tighten the ball stud nuts to between 22 and 36 lb ft or 40 to 55 lb ft on USA models and the idler arm nut to between 42 and 45 lb ft.

On completion, the front wheel tracking (toe-in) must be checked and adjusted as described in the following section.

10:9 Tracking

Front wheel alignment, or toe-in, should be between .16 and .24 inch (4 to 6 mm) on 1200 Saloon and Coupé and all 120Y models, and .20 to .28 inch (5 to 7 mm) on 1200 Estate car and van models. On 1000 models this dimension is .08 to .12 inch (2 to 3 mm) and on USA versions of the B210, .08 to .16 inch (2 to 4 mm). Checking and adjusting should be carried out by a service station or wheel and tyre specialist having the appropriate measuring equipment, this operation taking only a very short time. The adjustment is carried out by loosening the locknuts 1 on each of the outer tie rods, then rotating the threaded socket assemblies 2 equally until the correct toe-in is obtained. The locknuts must be firmly tightened on completion (see **FIG 10:30**).

Steering angle adjustment:

This is the angle that the front wheels are turned on full lock in each direction, the figures being inner wheel 42 deg. to 44 deg., outer wheel 34 deg. to 36 deg. The checking and adjusting of the steering angles should be carried out with the front wheels resting on turntables. Adjustment is effected by altering the length of projection of the bolts shown in **FIG 10:31**. Make sure that the clearance between the tyre and the front suspension tension rod is 1.2 inch (30 mm) or more. When the clearance is less than the stated figure, increase it by extending the bolt. On completion, the bolt length must not exceed 1.09 inch (27.5 mm).

10:10 Fault diagnosis

(a) Wheel wobble

1 Unbalanced wheels and tyres
2 Slack steering connections
3 Incorrect steering geometry
4 Excessive play in steering gear
5 Faulty suspension
6 Worn hub bearings

(b) Wander

1 Check 2, 3 and 4 in (a)
2 Uneven tyre pressures
3 Uneven tyre wear
4 Ineffective dampers

(c) Heavy steering

1 Check 3 in (a)
2 Very low tyre pressures
3 Neglected lubrication
4 Wheels out of track
5 Steering gear adjustment too tight
6 Collapsible column bush too tight
7 Inner steering shaft bent.

(d) Lost motion

1 Loose steering wheel, worn splines
2 Worn steering gear components
3 Worn steering linkage ball joints
4 Worn steering knuckle ball joints
5 Slack steering shaft bearings

CHAPTER 11

THE BRAKING SYSTEM

11 :1 Description

The braking system fitted may be either of the all-drum arrangement, or of the disc front and drum rear layout. When drum brakes are fitted to all four wheels, the front brakes are of the two leading shoe type, in which two wheel cylinders are used with each brake unit so that the leading edges of both shoes are forced towards the drum, giving a self-wrapping servo effect which increases the effective retardation available for a given pedal effort. This self-servo effect does not occur in reverse, or when the car is stationary facing up a hill. In all cases, drum rear brakes are of the single leading shoe type, so that equal braking effort is available in forward and reverse directions. All drum brakes are provided with shoe adjustment points, one adjuster being provided at each rear drum unit, two adjusters at each front drum unit.

Disc brakes have a floating caliper with two self-adjusting friction pads between which the brake disc rotates. The friction pads are applied by two pistons operated by hydraulic pressure from the master cylinder, both pistons operating simultaneously to exert equal pressure on the pads.

The brakes on all four wheels are operated hydraulically from the brake pedal, the handbrake operating the rear brakes only through a mechanical linkage. Some early models use a single master cylinder which connects to both front and rear brake circuits. All later models use a dual master cylinder which provides separate circuits to the front and rear brakes. The dual circuit system is an additional safety feature, as if the brakes on one circuit should fail, the remaining circuit will continue to provide braking effect, albeit of reduced efficiency. **FIG 11 :1** shows a typical hydraulic brake system, using a tandem master cylinder and dual circuits.

11 :2 Maintenance

Regularly check the level of the fluid in the master cylinder supply tank and replenish if necessary up to the full mark on the tank. Make sure that both tanks are checked when dealing with dual master cylinder installations. Wipe dirt from around the filler cap before removing it and check that the vent hole in the cap is unobstructed. If frequent topping up is required the system should be examined for leaks, but it should be noted that disc brake systems will need topping up more frequently than all-drum systems, due to disc brake wheel cylinder movement compensating for friction pad wear. Use only the correct grade of hydraulic fluid for topping up, as recommended and supplied by a Datsun agent.

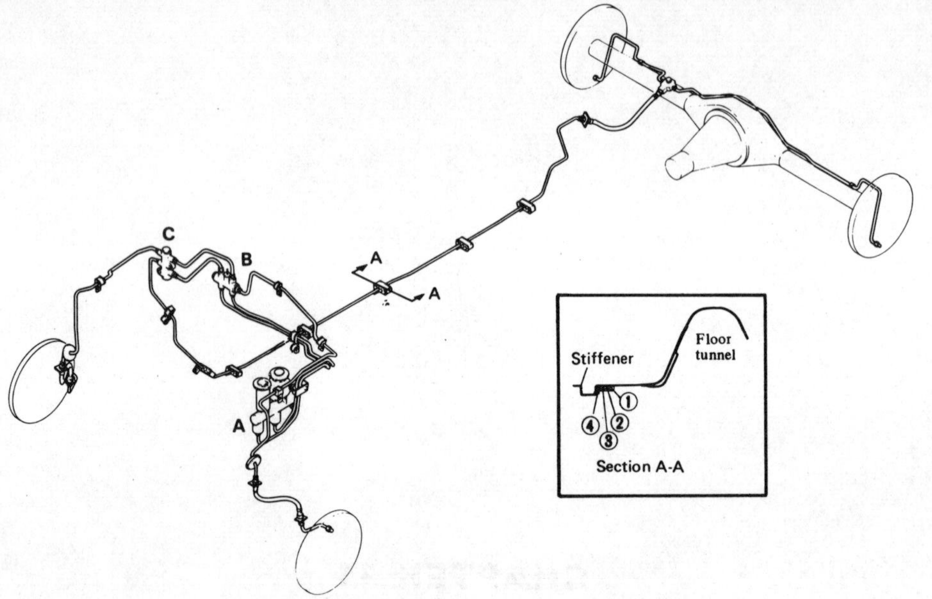

FIG 11 : 1 A typical tandem braking system layout

Key to Fig 11 : 1 A Master cylinder B Warning light switch C NP valve

Inset, arrangement of pipes on USA models: 1 Evaporative pipe 2 Fuel feed pipe 3 Brake pipe 4 Fuel return pipe

When brake pedal travel becomes excessive, adjust all the brakes on drum systems or the rear drums when disc brakes are fitted. Adjustment is carried out as follows. Note that adjustment of the handbrake is covered in **Section 11 : 8**.

Front drum brake adjustment:

Raise the car and remove the front wheel. The brake adjusting cams are shown in **FIG 11 : 2** with the brake drum removed for clarity; the drum must not be removed to adjust the brakes. Working from the rear of the brake plate, turn one of the adjusting cams until the shoe can be felt to contact the drum when the drum is turned by hand, then slacken off a fraction until the drum is just free to turn. Repeat the procedure on the second adjusting cam on the same brake assembly. Press the brake pedal several times and check that the brakes operate correctly and that the drum does not bind when turned by hand. If the drum binds, slacken the adjusters a little to prevent this. Repeat the entire adjustment procedure on the other front brake assembly.

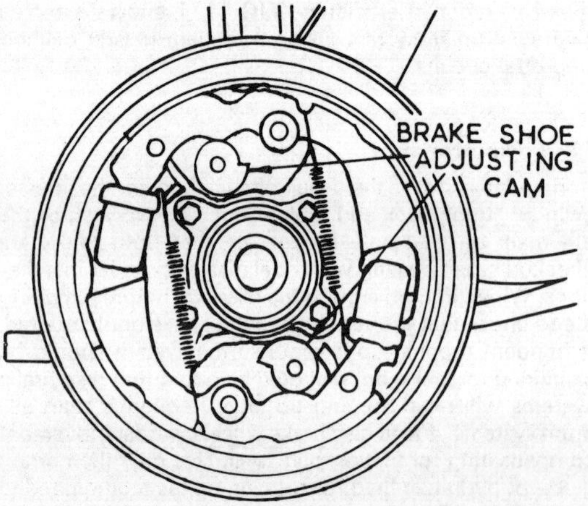

FIG 11 : 2 Front drum brake adjusters

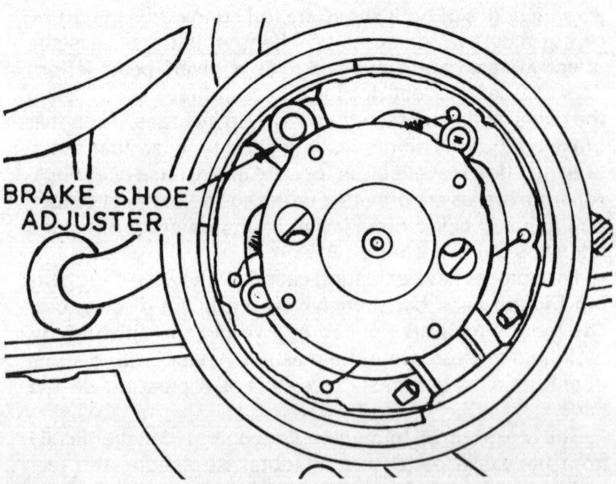

FIG 11 : 3 Rear drum brake adjuster, early models

Rear drum brake adjustment:

Chock the front wheels, raise the rear of the car, remove the rear wheel and release the handbrake fully. **FIG 11 : 3** shows the rear drum brake adjusting cam, with the brake drum removed for clarity. Do not remove the drum. Working from the rear of the brake plate, turn the adjusting cam until the shoes can be felt to contact the drum when the drum is turned by hand, then slacken off a fraction until the drum is just free to turn. Press the brake pedal a few times and check that the brakes operate correctly and that the drum does not bind when turned by hand. If the drum binds, slacken the adjuster a little to prevent this.

Brake adjustment is automatic on the rear wheels of the 120Y models, and is reset whenever the handbrake is operated, by an extension on the handbrake lever acting on the adjusting wheel 3 (see **FIG 11 : 3 (a)**). When removing the brake drum the adjusting wheel can be unlocked with a screwdriver as shown in **FIG 11 : 3 (b)** and the adjusting wheel turned to increase clearance between drum and shoes.

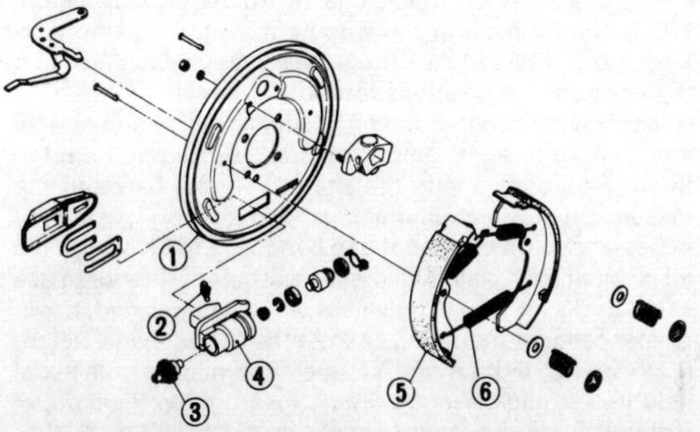

FIG 11 : 3(a) Components of rear brakes on B210 models

Key to Fig 11 : 3(a) 1 Brake backplate 2 Bleed valve 3 Adjusting wheel 4 Wheel cylinder 5 Brake shoes 6 Return springs

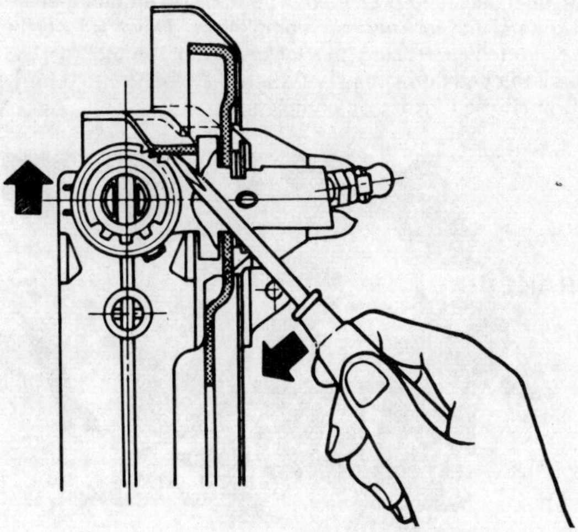

FIG 11 : 3(b) Unlocking adjusting wheel

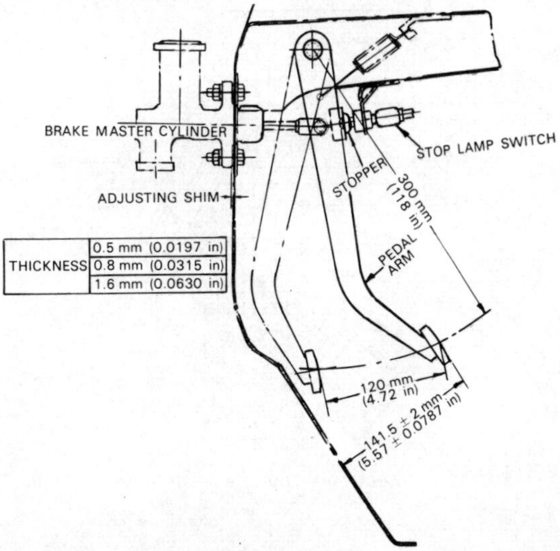

FIG 11 : 4 Adjusting the brake pedal travel (early cars)

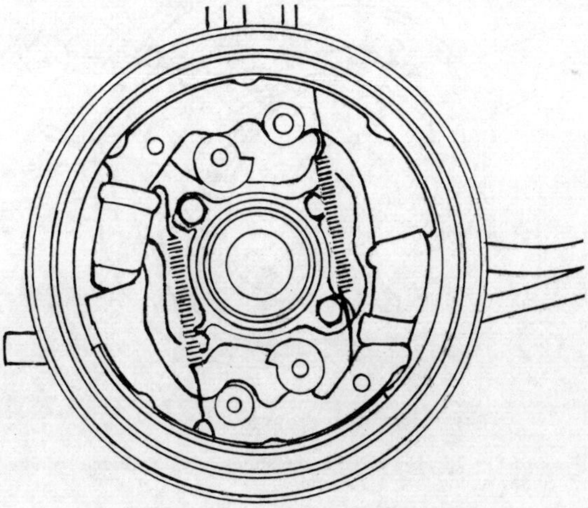

FIG 11 : 5 The front drum brake assembly

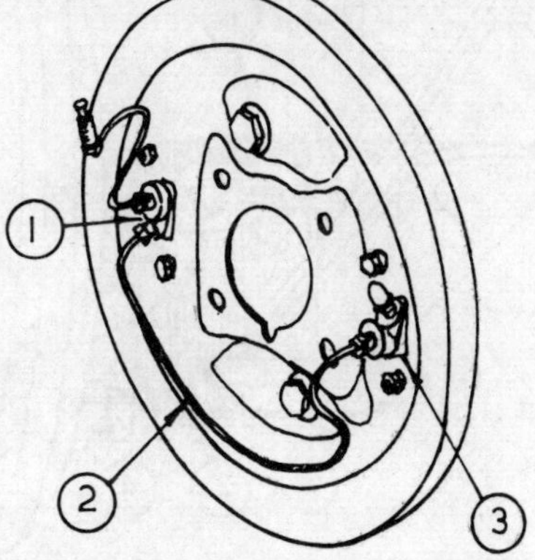

FIG 11 : 6 The front brake wheel cylinders and bridge pipes

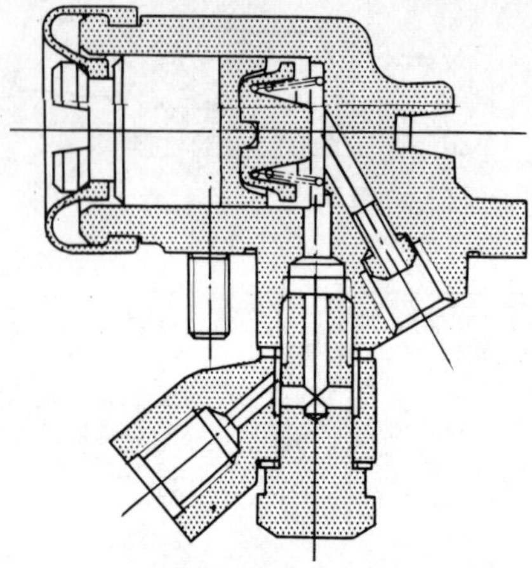

FIG 11:7 Section through a front wheel cylinder

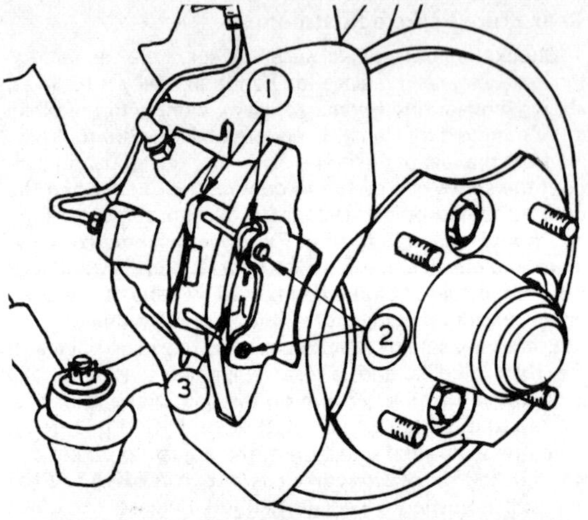

FIG 11:10 Removing the brake pad retaining pins

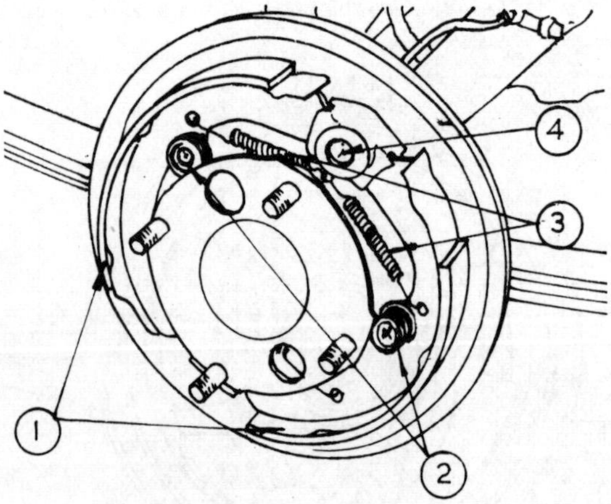

FIG 11:8 Rear drum brake assembly

Key to Fig 11:8 1 Brake shoes 2 Shoe retainers 3 Return spring 4 Adjuster

Brake pedal adjustment:

The brake pedal is adjusted by shims on cars before 1973, and by moving the stop light switch assembly on later cars. **FIG 11:4** shows the measurements, shim thicknesses and positions for the earlier cars.

Loosen the stopper until it is separated from the pedal arm. Measure the height of the brake pedal pad from the floor panel and modify the shim thickness between the master cylinder mounting lugs and the body panel if necessary, to give a height of 5.6 inches (143 mm). Shims are available in three thicknesses as shown. Be sure to use shim packs of equal thickness at the upper and lower master cylinder mountings. When the correct pedal height is achieved, tighten the stopper down until the pedal height is as shown in the figure, then tighten the stopper locknut. Pedal free travel should be .24 to .60 inch (6 to 15 mm) and the pedal working stroke should be 4.8 inches (120 mm).

To adjust the brake pedal height on later cars, release the locknut on the stop light switch until the measurement from the floor to the pedal pad is 6.14 inch (156 mm) on manual cars, and 6.22 inch (158 mm) on automatic cars. Tighten the locknut on completion. Now adjust the pushrod by releasing the locknut and turning the rod until the pedal free play is .039 to .117 inch (1 to 3 mm). Tighten the locknut on completion.

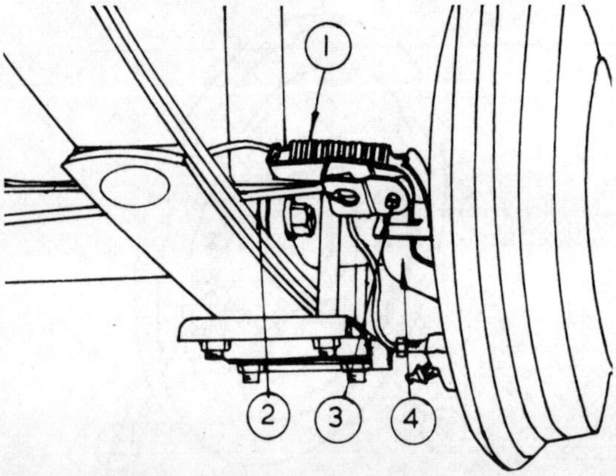

FIG 11:9 Disconnecting the handbrake cable from a rear wheel cylinder lever

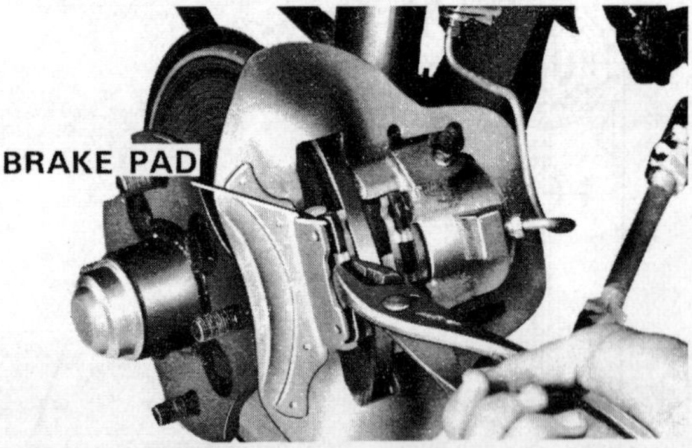

FIG 11:11 Withdrawing the brake pads and shims

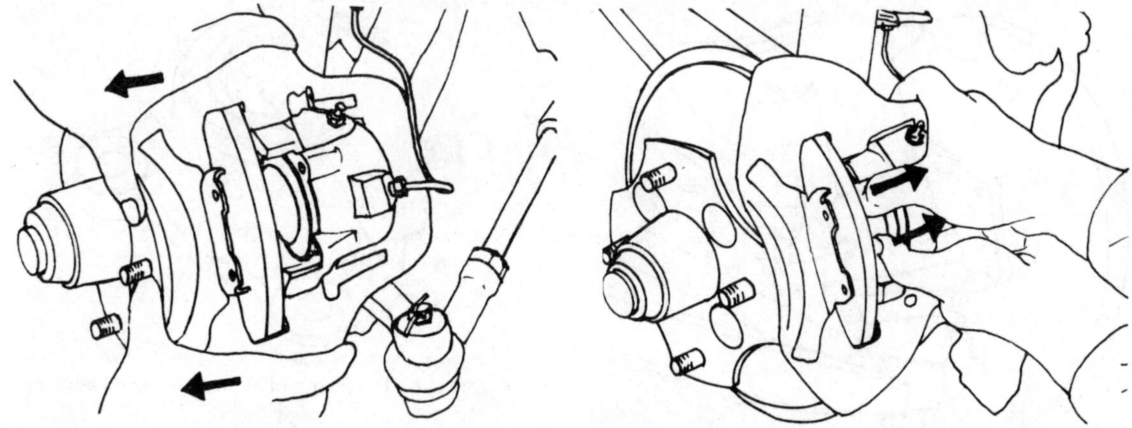

FIG 11:12 Pressing the caliper pistons down in their bores

11:3 Drum brakes

Front brake shoe removal:

Apply the handbrake, raise the front of the car and safely support on floor stands. Remove the road wheel and the brake drum. Unhook the two shoe return springs shown in **FIG 11:5** and remove the brake shoes.

Refitting:

Clean the brake drum and backing plate thoroughly, taking care to avoid dirt entering the wheel bearings. Apply a thin smear of multi-purpose grease to all pivots and sliding surfaces. Make sure that the shoes are correctly fitted at the wheel cylinders and pivots, then refit the return springs to the shoe webs. Slacken off the brake adjusters as described in **Section 11:2**, refit the brake drum and adjust the brake shoes.

Relining brake shoes:

If the linings are worn down to a thickness of .06 inch (1.5 mm) or less, they must be renewed. It is not recommended that owners attempt to reline brake shoes themselves. It is important that the linings be properly bonded to the shoes and ground for concentricity. For this reason, sets of replacement shoes should be obtained or the relining carried out by a service station. **Do not allow grease, oil or brake fluid to contact the linings.** If the linings are contaminated in any way they must be renewed, as they cannot be successfully cleaned. Always renew brake linings on all four front brake shoes at the same time. If new linings are fitted singly, uneven braking will result.

Servicing front wheel cylinders:

Remove the road wheel, brake drum and brake shoes as described previously. Disconnect the brake line from the front suspension strut unit as described in **Chapter 9, Section 9:3**. Refer to **FIG 11:6** and disconnect the bridge pipe 2, then remove the two wheel cylinders 1 and 3. Remove the boots, pistons and springs from the cylinders, taking care not to mix the parts between the cylinders. **FIG 11:7** shows a section through a front wheel cylinder.

Discard the rubber boots and cups and thoroughly clean the remaining parts in the correct grade of brake fluid. Inspect the pistons and cylinder bores for scoring or corrosion. Light corrosion may be removed with very fine steel wool, but if the corrosion is deep or there is scoring present, the part should be renewed. Renew both piston and cylinder if the clearance between the two parts exceeds .006 inch (.15 mm).

Dip the internal parts in brake fluid and assemble them wet. Use the fingers to insert the new rubber cups to avoid damage to their edges. Fit the new rubber boots. Install the wheel cylinders onto the brake backplate and reconnect the hydraulic fluid pipes. Refit the shoes, drum and road wheel, then bleed the brakes as described in **Section 11:5**.

Rear brake shoe removal:

Chock the front wheels, raise the rear of the car and support it on floor stands, then remove the rear wheel and brake drum. Refer to **FIG 11:8**. Remove the shoe retainers 2, the return spring 3 and lift out the shoes 1.

Refitting:

Clean the brake drum and backing plate thoroughly, taking care to avoid dirt entering the wheel bearings. Apply a thin smear of multi-purpose grease to the shoe web supports, these being similar to those shown for the front brake in **FIG 11:6**. Fit the shoes correctly to the wheel cylinder and pivot and fit the return springs and retainers, noting that the longer return spring is fitted to the wheel

FIG 11:13 Fitting the shims to the friction pads

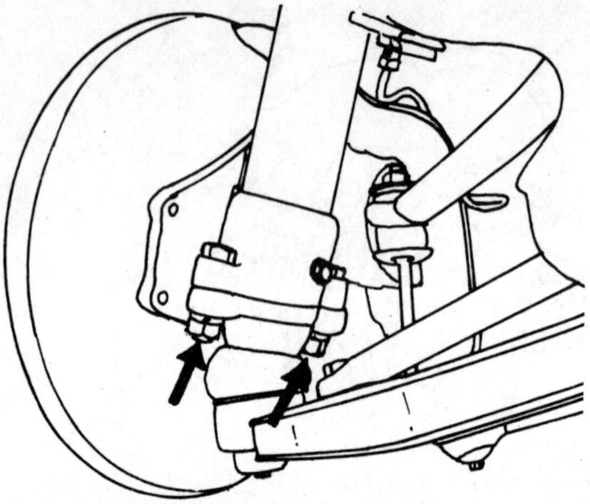

FIG 11:14 Removing the strut and steering knuckle fixing bolts

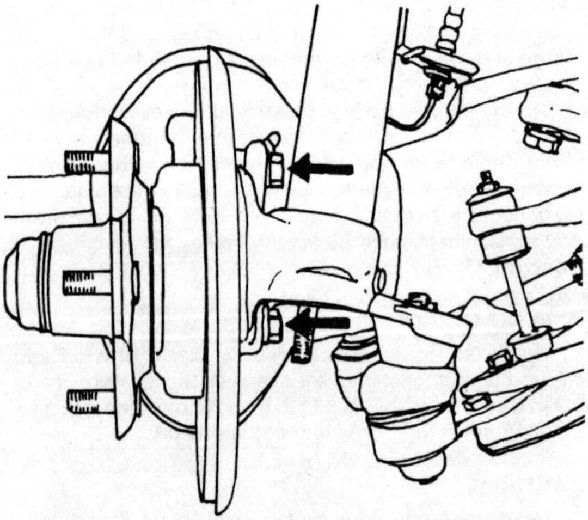

FIG 11:15 Removing the caliper fixing bolts

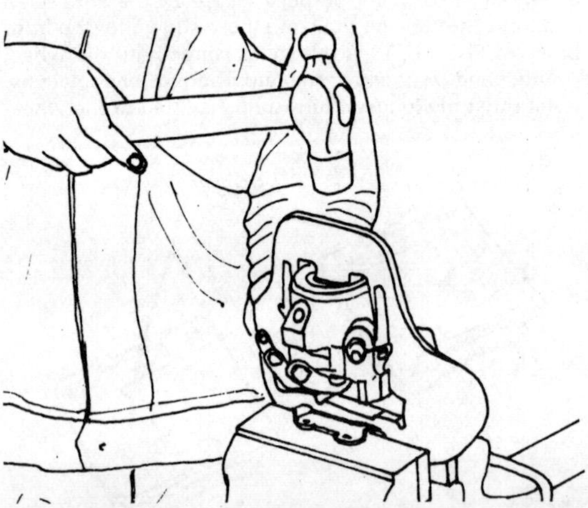

FIG 11:16 Tapping the caliper yoke head to remove the cylinder body

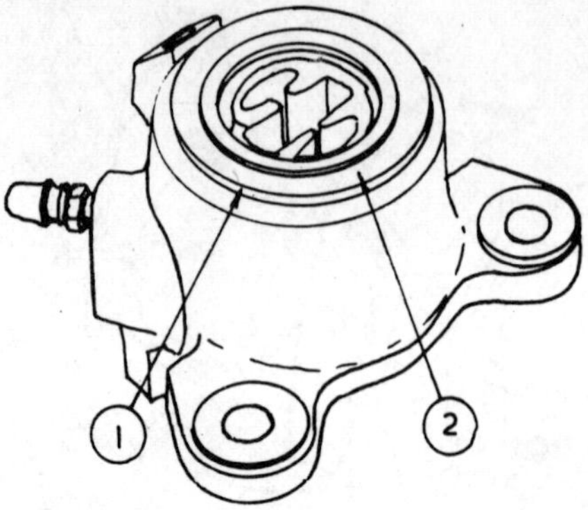

FIG 11:17 The piston retaining ring 1 and boot 2

cylinder side, the shorter spring to the adjuster side where fitted. Slacken off the adjuster as described in **Section 11:2**, refit the brake drum and adjust the brake shoes.

Relining:

This is carried out in the manner described previously.

Servicing a rear wheel cylinder:

Remove the road wheel, brake drum and brake shoes as described previously. Disconnect the brake fluid line from the wheel cylinder and use a plug to prevent fluid loss. With the handbrake released, remove the clevis pin 3 from the lever 4 and disconnect the handbrake cable 2, as shown in **FIG 11:9**. Remove the return spring 1. Remove the dust cover, adjusting shims and plates, then remove the wheel cylinder from the brake backplate.

Dismantle, clean and service the rear wheel cylinder in the manner previously described for front wheel cylinders.

11:4 Disc brakes

Disc brake friction pads should be checked for wear every 5000 miles, or more frequently if the car is operated in mountainous country or under other conditions where the brakes are subjected to harder than normal usage. When the thickness of the friction lining on any pad is less than .07 inch (1.6 mm), this being a total pad and lining thickness of .25 inch (6 mm), renew all four friction pads. Do not renew the pads singly or on one side only as uneven braking will result.

Renewing friction pads:

Raise the front of the car safely onto floor stands and remove the front wheels. Refer to **FIG 11:10** and remove the clip 3 from the retaining pins. Supporting the brake pads, remove the retaining pins and coil spring. Unhook the hanger spring and withdraw the brake pads and shims as shown in **FIG 11:11**, using a pair of pliers.

Before fitting new friction pads, clean the recesses in the caliper and the pad installing parts. Push both pistons down to the bottom of their bores in the caliper, to provide clearance for installation of the pads. Note that, as the pistons are pushed down, the level of fluid in the master cylinder supply tank will rise and that it may be necessary to syphon off some of the fluid to prevent overflowing. The method of pressing each piston into its

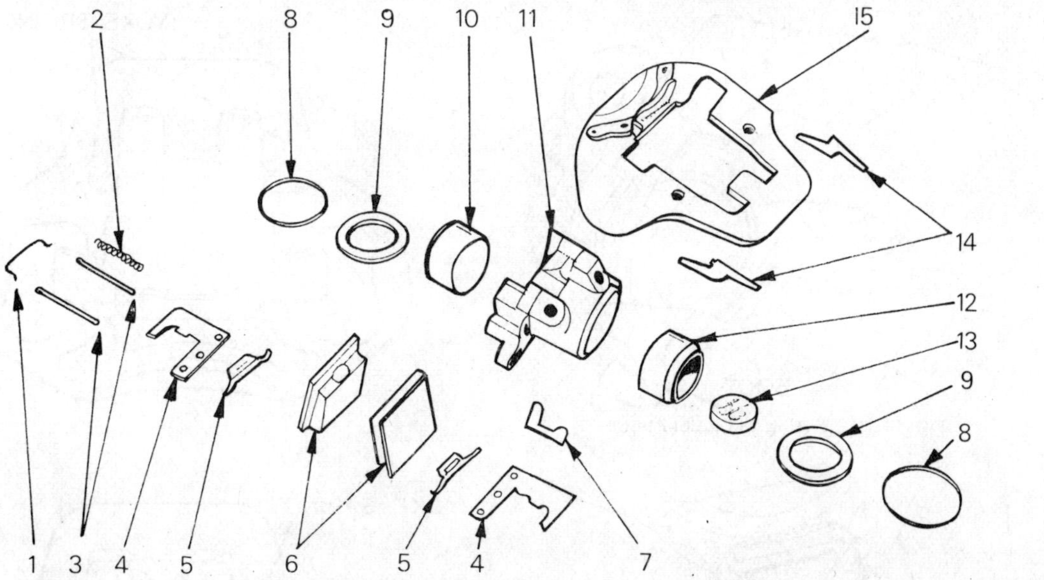

FIG 11:18 Brake caliper components

Key to Fig 11:18 1 Clip 2 Spring 3 Clevis pin 4 Shim 5 Hanger spring 6 Friction pad 7 Bleed screw 8 Retaining ring 9 Boot 10 Piston **B** 11 Cylinder body 12 Piston **A** 13 Bias ring 14 Yoke spring 15 Yoke

bore is shown in **FIG 11:12**. Take care not to push the pistons too far into their bores or the seals will be damaged. If the pistons are pushed down too far and the grooves in the pistons go inside the seals, the caliper will have to be dismantled as described later in order to return the pistons.

Install the shims to the friction pads as shown in **FIG 11:13**, with the arrow marks on the shims pointing in the direction of forward brake disc rotation. Refit the pads and retaining pins in the reverse order of removal, fitting the coil spring to the retaining pin which is furthest from the bleed screw. On completion, depress the brake pedal several times to bring the pads up to the brake disc and to allow the brakes to self-adjust. If this is not done, the brakes may fail to operate the first time they are used. Finally, check the fluid level in the master cylinder supply tank and top up if necessary.

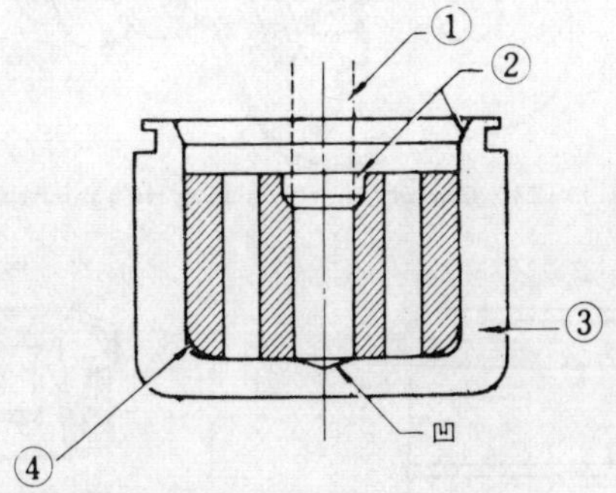

FIG 11:19 Installing the bias ring to piston A

Key to Fig 11:19 1 Yoke 2 Chamfer 3 Piston **A** 4 Roundish portion

Removing and dismantling a caliper:

Jack up the car and remove the road wheel. Remove the friction pads as described previously. Disconnect the brake line from the caliper assembly and plug the line to prevent fluid loss. To facilitate caliper removal, remove the strut assembly and steering knuckle bolts as shown arrowed in **FIG 11:14**. Remove the caliper installation bolts arrowed in **FIG 11:15** and separate the caliper from the strut assembly.

Thoroughly clean the outside of the caliper assembly before dismantling, to prevent the entry of dirt. Drain the brake fluid from the caliper. Loosen the caliper bleed screw, then press both pistons into their bores as described in the previous instructions for renewing friction pads. Secure the caliper yoke in a vice and tap the yoke head with a hammer as shown in **FIG 11:16**. The cylinder body can then be removed from the yoke, taking care

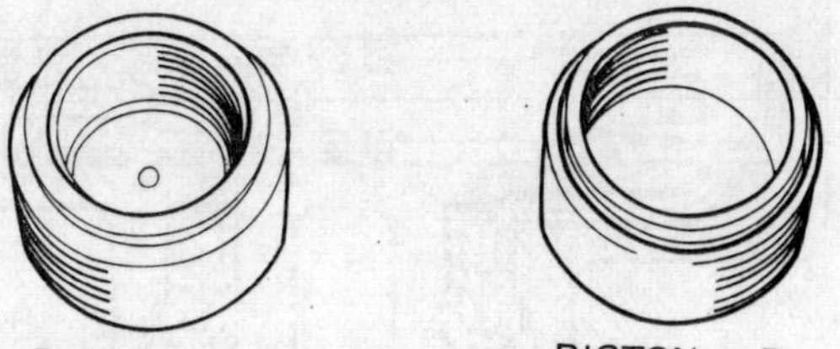

FIG 11:20 The brake caliper pistons

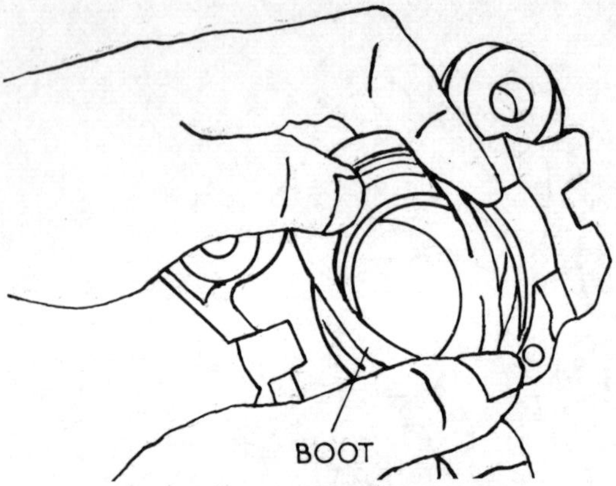

FIG 11:21 Fitting the rubber boot

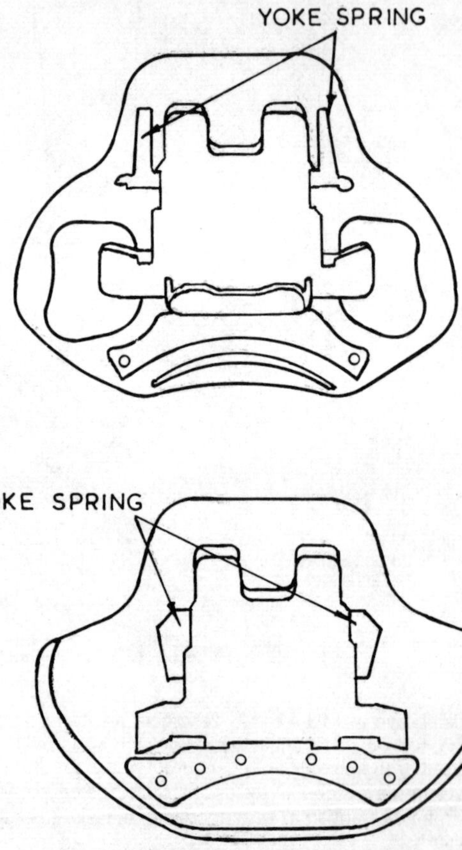

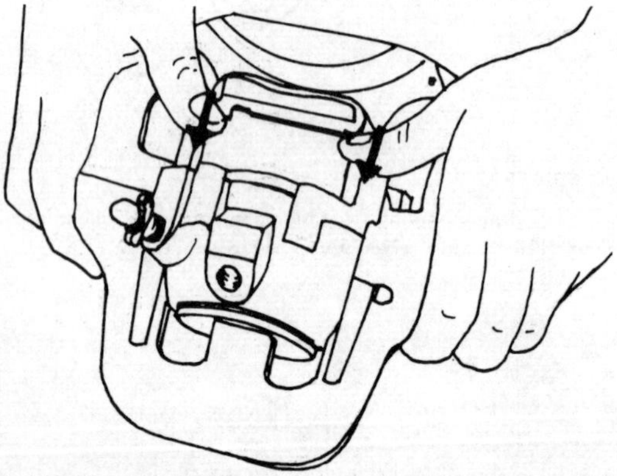

FIG 11:23 Correcting the bias spring position

FIG 11:22 Installing the yoke spring

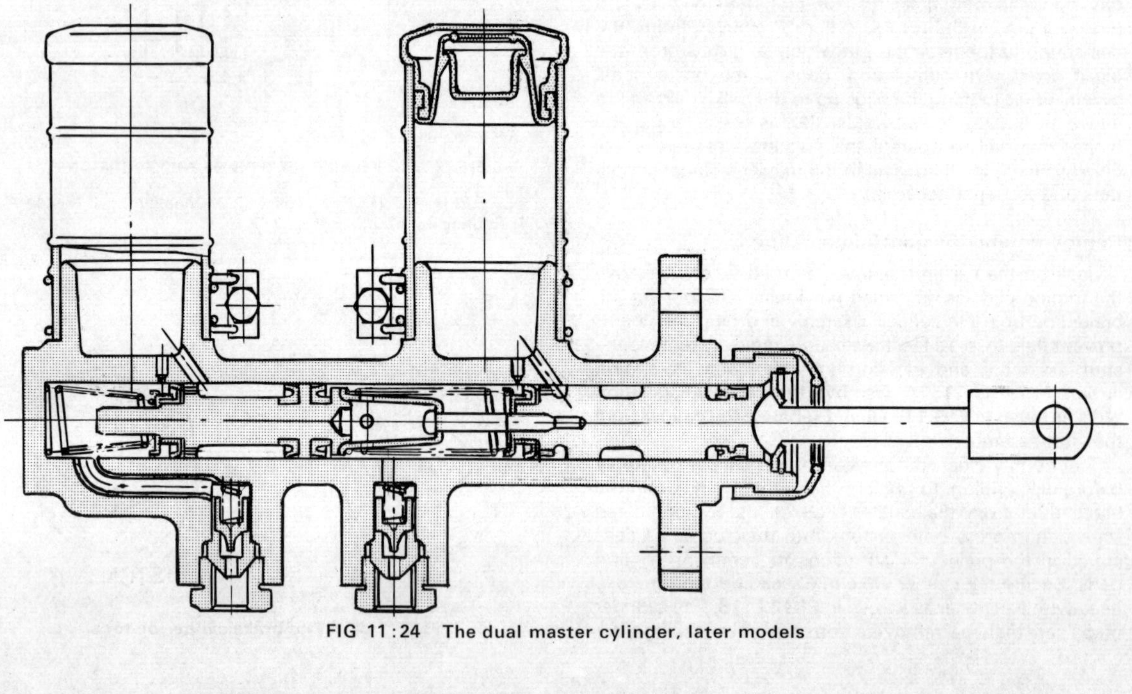

FIG 11:24 The dual master cylinder, later models

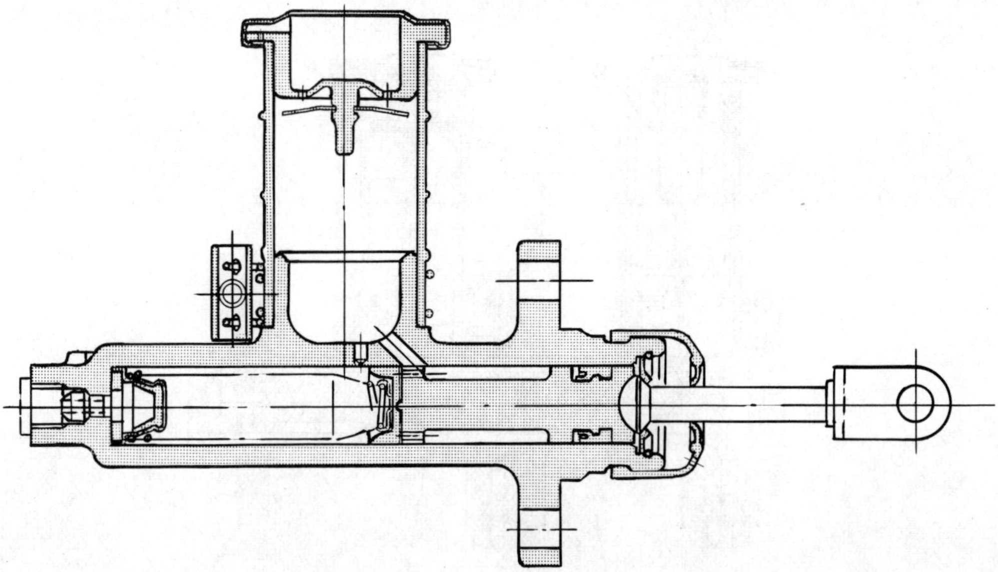

FIG 11:25 The single master cylinder

when doing so to avoid the piston coming out of the cylinder. Remove the piston bias ring and remove the retaining rings and boots from both pistons. Depress and remove the pistons from the cylinders. Use the fingers only to remove the seals from the cylinders to avoid damage to the cylinder walls. Remove the yoke spring and bias spring from the yoke. **FIG 11:18** shows the components of the caliper assembly.

Servicing:

Thoroughly clean all parts in the correct grade of brake fluid. Inspect the cylinder bores for wear or damage, which would dictate renewal of the parts. If the cylinder walls are rusted or contaminated, lightly polish with very fine steel wool or emerycloth, taking care not to damage the walls. If the walls are badly scored or corroded the parts must be renewed. Examine the pistons for signs of uneven wear, damage or rusted surfaces. The sliding surface of the piston is plated, so not attempt must be made to clean it with any sort of abrasive. A faulty piston must be renewed. Always fit new rubber seals and dust covers.

Check the brake disc for deep scoring or distortion. If disc runout exceeds .0012 inch (.03 mm) at the outer diameter, or if the disc is deeply scored, it should be reground true at a service station. Note, however, that the disc must not be reduced below .34 inch (8.4 mm) in thickness when reconditioning. If regrinding would reduce disc thickness to less than this figure, the disc must be renewed. Renew the disc if it is cracked or damaged. To remove the disc, first remove the hub and disc assembly as described in **Chapter 9, Section 9:3**, then unbolt the disc from the hub.

Reassembling the caliper:

Observe absolute cleanliness at all stages of reassembly, to prevent particles of dirt or grit remaining on the surfaces or seals. Dip all internal parts in brake fluid and assemble them wet. Insert the bias ring into piston **A** so that the roundish part of the bias ring is at the bottom of the piston, as shown in **FIG 11:19**. Take care not to confuse piston **A** with piston **B**, the differences being shown in **FIG 11:20**. Install the piston seals into the cylinder bore grooves with the fingers only, to avoid damage to the seals. Fit the pistons into the bores, taking care not to press them too far down into the cylinders. Install the boots as shown in **FIG 11:21** and fit the retaining rings. Make sure that the yoke groove in the bias ring of piston **A** coincides with the yoke groove in the cylinder.

Install the yoke spring so that the projecting part faces towards the disc as shown in **FIG 11:22**. Install the bias spring to the yoke so that the bias spring is on the brake bleed screw side of the cylinder. With the yoke spring inserted into the cylinder groove lightly, correct the

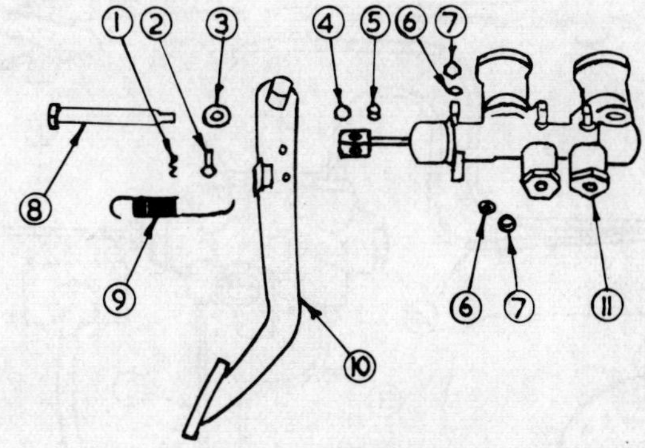

FIG 11:26 The master cylinder and brake pedal connections

Key to Fig 11:26 1 Spring pin 2 Clevis pin 3 Washer 4 Spring washer 5 Nut 6 Spring washer 7 Nut 8 Pivot shaft 9 Return spring 10 Pedal arm 11 Master cylinder

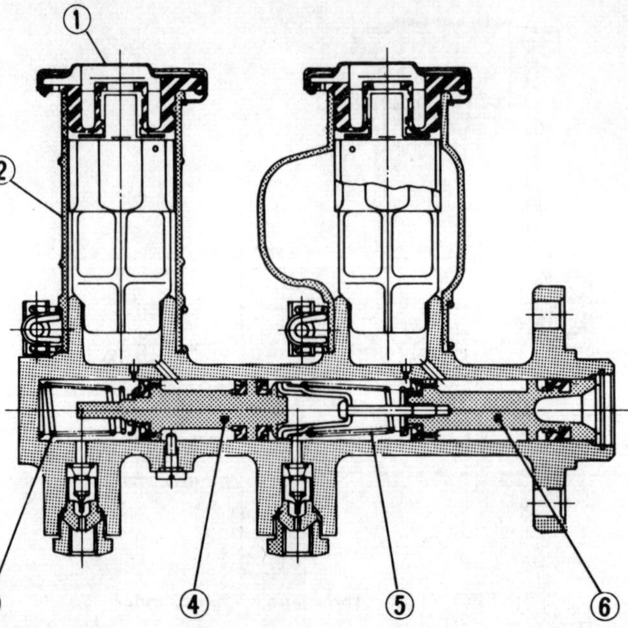

FIG 11:27 The tandem master cylinder fitted to B210 models

Key to Fig 11:27 1 Reservoir cap 2 Reservoir 3 Secondary return spring 4 Secondary piston 5 Primary return spring 6 Primary piston

position of the bias spring so that the bias spring groove coincides with the yoke, as shown in **FIG 11:23**. Assemble the cylinder body and yoke by tapping the yoke lightly. Apply brake grease to the yoke sliding groove of the cylinder. Install the bleed screw.

Refit the caliper to the suspension strut in the reverse order of removal, tightening the caliper mounting bolts to a torque of 34 to 44 lb ft. On completion, bleed the brakes as described in **Section 11:5**.

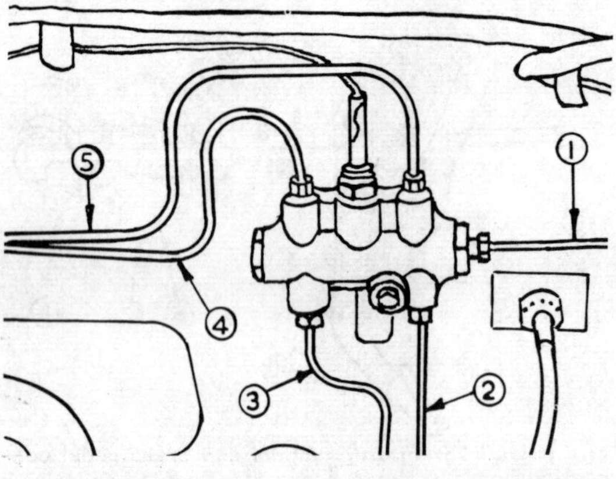

FIG 11:28 The brake warning light switch

Key to Fig 11:28 1 To left front brake 2 From master cylinder front 3 From master cylinder rear 4 To rear brakes left and right 5 To right front brake

11:5 Bleeding the system

This is not routine maintenance and is only necessary if air has entered the system due to parts being dismantled, or because the fluid level in the master cylinder supply tank has dropped too low. The need for bleeding is indicated by a spongy feeling of the brake pedal, accompanied by poor braking performance. **Do not bleed the system with any drum or caliper removed.** Always bleed the master cylinder first, followed by the brake furthest from the master cylinder, and finishing with the brake nearest the master cylinder.

Check the fluid level in the supply tank and refill if necessary up to the full mark. Clean all dirt from around the appropriate bleed screw and remove the dust cap.

Attach a length of rubber or plastic hose to the bleed screw and lead the free end of the tube into a clean glass jar containing a little brake fluid. Get an assistant to apply firm pressure to the brake pedal, then open the bleed screw to allow fluid to flow from the system. When the pedal reaches the floor, tighten the bleed screw. With the bleed screw tightened, allow the brake pedal to return slowly. Repeat the operation until the fluid flowing into the jar is free of air bubbles. Check and top up the brake fluid in the supply tank several times during this operation to ensure that the level does not drop too low.

On completion, top up the fluid to the correct level. **It is not advisable to re-use brake fluid that has been bled from the system. Always store brake fluid in clean, airtight containers.**

11:6 The master cylinder

The master cylinder fitted to cars covered by this manual may be of either single or dual type, as described in

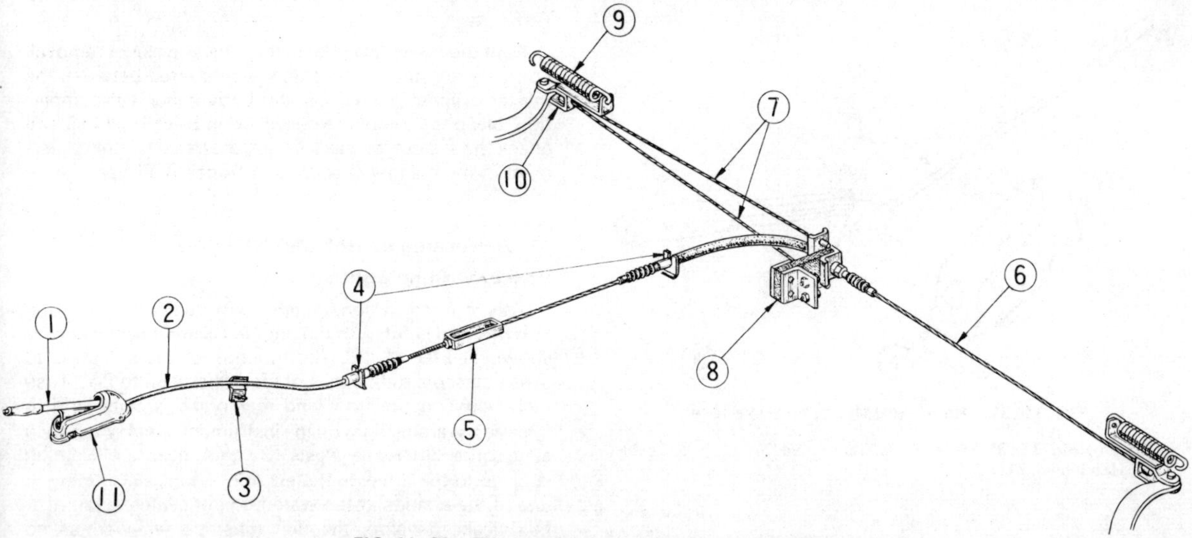

FIG 11 : 29 The handbrake mechanism and cables

Key to Fig 11 : 29 1 Handbrake lever 2 Cable 3 Clip 4 Lockplate 5 Turnbuckle 6 and 7 Cables 8 Hanger strap 9 Return spring 10 Cable shank 11 Lever cover

Section 11 : 1. FIG 11 : 24 shows a section through the 1200 dual master cylinder, **FIG 11 : 25** a section through the single master cylinder. **FIG 11 : 27** shows the B210 type. Removal and servicing instructions are the same for both types, the dual system being described.

Removal:

Disconnect the brake lines from the master cylinder. On B210 models, fitted with a servo unit, unscrew the two nuts securing the master cylinder and detach the cylinder. On models without servo, refer to **FIG 11 : 26** which shows the master cylinder and brake pedal connections. Remove the clevis pin 2 and separate the brake pedal arm 10 from the master cylinder pushrod. Working inside the engine compartment, unscrew the mounting nuts and remove the master cylinder.

Dismantling:

Drain the brake fluid from the unit and remove the stopper bolt. Remove the dust cover, snap ring and stopper ring, then withdraw the pushrod assembly. Remove the primary piston, secondary piston and piston spring. The secondary piston, shown in **FIG 11 : 27**, can be removed after unscrewing the stop screw fitted at the bottom of the cylinder. The single master cylinder unit has no secondary piston. Remove the valve cap and withdraw the valve assembly. Do not remove the fluid supply tanks unless it is necessary to renew parts, and do not remove the seals from the pistons.

Servicing:

Thoroughly clean all internal parts with brake fluid. Renew the piston cups, packing and valves as a matter of course. Check the piston and cylinder bore for scoring, damage and uneven wear, renewing any defective part. Renew parts as necessary if the piston to cylinder clearance exceeds .006 inch (.15 mm). Check the return springs for wear, damage or weakening and fit new parts as necessary. Make sure that the ports and passages in the master cylinder body are unobstructed.

Reassembly:

This is a reversal of the dismantling procedure. Observe absolute cleanliness at all stages of reassembly, to prevent particles of dirt or grit remaining on the surfaces or seals. Dip all internal parts in brake fluid and assemble them wet. Use only the fingers to insert the rubber cups and seals to avoid damage to their edges.

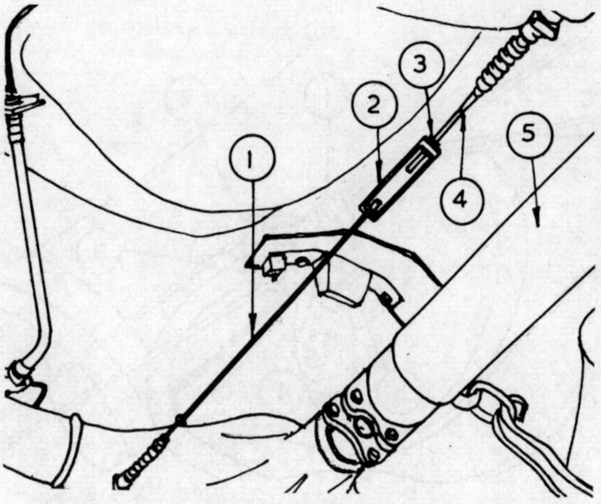

FIG 11 : 30 The handbrake cable connector

Key to Fig 11 : 30 1 Rear cable 2 Turnbuckle adjuster 3 Locknut 4 Front cable 5 Propeller shaft

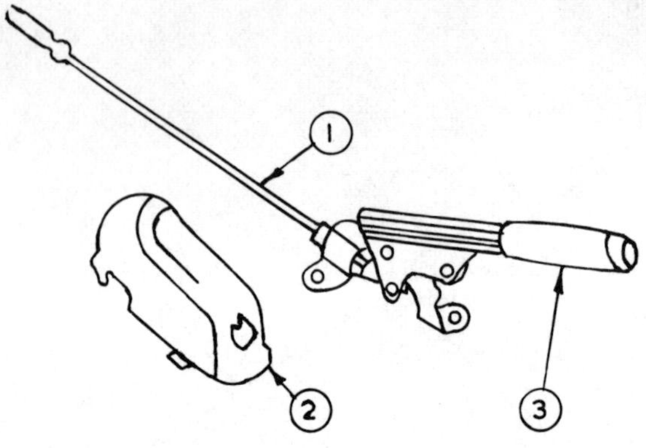

FIG 11 : 31 **Removing the handbrake lever**

Key to Fig 11 : 31 1 Front cable 2 Cover 3 Handbrake lever

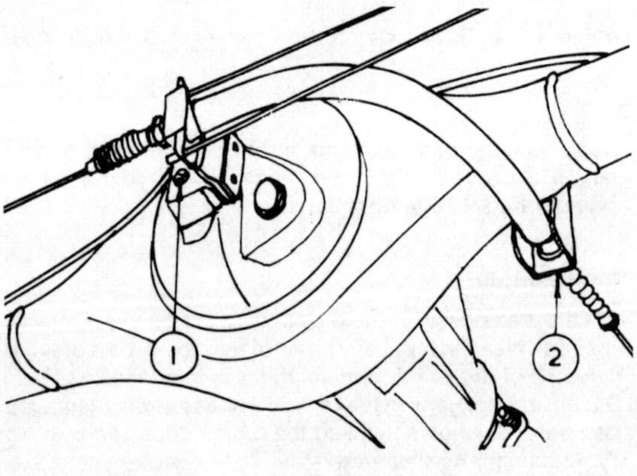

FIG 11 : 32 **Disconnecting the rear cable**

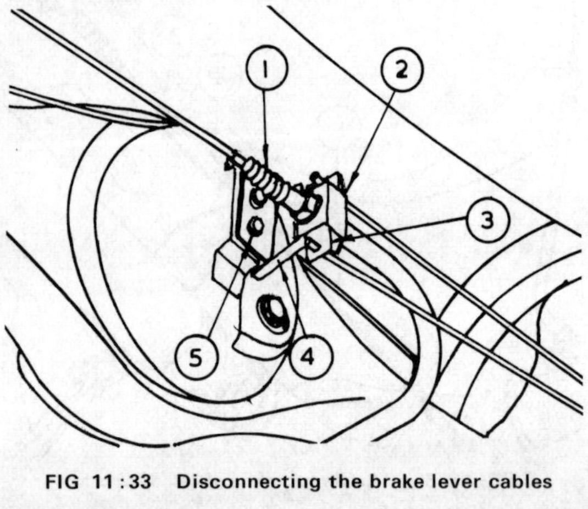

FIG 11 : 33 **Disconnecting the brake lever cables**

Key to Fig 11 : 33 1 Dust cover 2 Hanger strap washer 3 Bracket 4 Hanger strap 5 Hanger strap fixing nut

Refitting:

Refit the master cylinder in the reverse order of removal, correctly reinstalling the shims where fitted between the master cylinder mountings and body panel. On completion, bleed the system as described in **Section 11 : 5** and check the system for leaks. Check the pedal height adjustment in the manner described in **Section 11 : 2**.

11 : 7 Warning switch and NP valve

Brake warning light switch:

This is fitted in conjunction with dual-circuit braking systems and is fitted to the engine compartment panel as shown in **FIG 11 : 28**. The function of the switch is to sense pressure differences of more than 185 to 242 lb/sq inch between the front and rear brake circuits, and to operate a warning light on the instrument panel when such a pressure difference exists. By this means, a warning is given to the driver in the event of a fault developing in one of the circuits. If the warning light switch is faulty or fluid leaks develop, the unit must be renewed as no repairs are possible.

NP valve:

On B210 models the front and rear brake circuits are separated by the NP Valve. This valve controls pressure to the rear brake circuit to prevent rear wheels locking before front wheels.

To test, drive the car at 30 mile/hr and brake hard, the front and rear wheels should lock together, or the front before the rear. If the rear locks before the front, renew the NP valve.

11 : 8 The handbrake

The layout of the handbrake cables and operating mechanisms is shown in **FIG 11 : 29**.

Removal:

Loosen the locknut (3 in **FIG 11 : 30**) and unscrew the turnbuckle 2 to separate the front and rear cables. Remove the lockplate immediately in front of the turnbuckle, remove the clip from the passenger compartment side and disconnect the front cable.

Remove the handbrake lever cover and detach the lever assembly complete with front cable, as shown in **FIG 11 : 31**.

Remove the hanger strap fixing bolt 1 shown in **FIG 11 : 32**, withdraw the lockplate 2 and disconnect the rear cable. Refer to **FIG 11 : 33** and remove the hanger strap nut 5, then detach the component parts. **Do not remove the dust cover 1.**

Refitting:

This is a reversal of the removal instructions. Lubricate the moving and sliding parts of the linkage and cables with multi-purpose grease. On completion, check the handbrake adjustment as described next.

Handbrake adjustment:

Normally, adjustment of the rear brake shoes as described in **Section 11 : 2** will automatically correct any

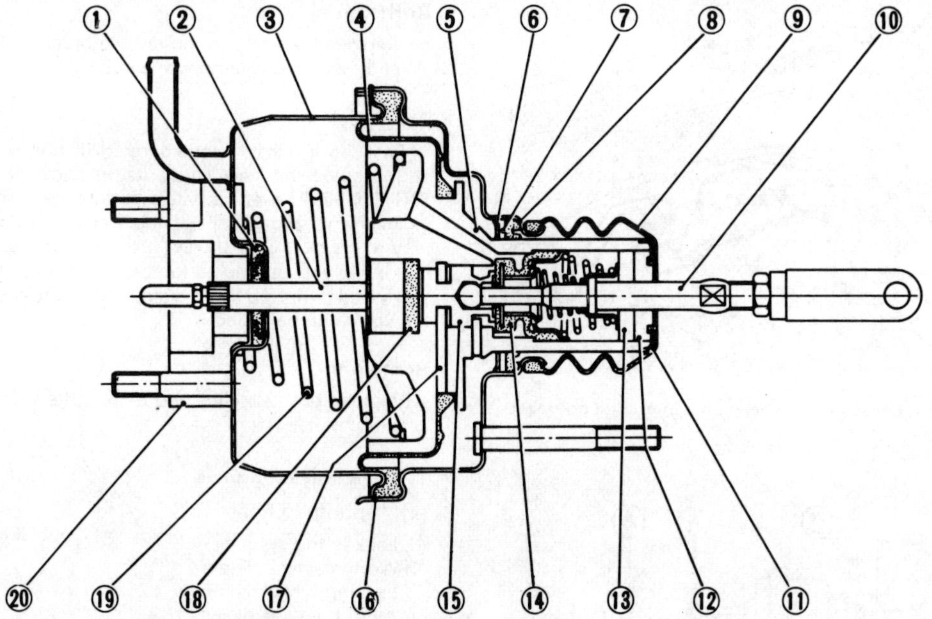

FIG 11:34 Section through vacuum servo

Key to Fig 11:34 1 Plate and seal assembly 2 Pushrod 3 Front shell 4 Diaphragm 5 Diaphragm plate and valve body 6 Retainer 7 Bearing 8 Valve body seal 9 Valve body guard 10 Valve operating rod 11 Silencer retainer 12 Silencer filter (felt) 13 Silencer (rubber) 14 Poppet assembly 15 Plunger assembly (valve operating rod, poppet assembly) 16 Rear shell 17 Valve plunger stop key 18 Reaction disc 19 Diaphragm return spring 20 Flange

slackness in the handbrake linkage. However, if the handbrake cables have been disconnected for servicing operations, or if the cables are slack due to stretching, adjust as follows:

Check the adjustment of the rear brake shoes as described in **Section 11:2**. After doing so, adjust the handbrake cable by acting on the turnbuckle 2 in **FIG 11:30** so that the handbrake can be applied by six clicks on the ratchet under a 25 to 33 lb pull. When this is achieved, fully release the handbrake and check that the rear wheels do not bind, releasing the adjuster a little if necessary.

11:9 The Master-Vac vacuum servo

A vacuum servo is installed in later models between the brake master cylinder and the brake pedal, the pedal and master cylinder are interconnected through the servo by a control rod fixed to the brake arm and a pushrod operating directly onto the master cylinder piston. A sectional drawing of the vacuum servo is shown in **FIG 11:34**. A partial vacuum is created in the front shell chamber by induction from the inlet manifold, between which a connecting pipe is fitted. Embodied in the pipe is a detachable check valve (see **FIG 11:35**) which controls the negative pressure in the chamber to a predesigned limit. The front chamber is sealed from the rear chamber by a diaphragm 4. The rear chamber is opened to atmosphere by valves, influenced initially by the movement of the control rod under pressure from the footbrake pedal arm. Air enters the rear chamber and assists the foot pressure by exerting energy on the diaphragm and plate in an effort to expand into the vacuum chamber, the combination of effort forces the pushrod 2 forward directly onto the master cylinder piston.

The design of the valves and seals enables the driver to maintain control at all times, to either reduce or increase negative or atmospheric pressure by the control rod, depending on the amount of foot pedal pressure applied. As soon as the pedal is released the diaphragm and plate are returned to their normal position by the action of the return spring and back pressure exerted on the pushrod from the hydraulic fluid.

A reduction in the efficiency or a complete breakdown of the vacuum servo will not render the brakes ineffective, as pressure from the pedal is in direct contact with the master cylinder piston. The effort required to retard or stop the car will be greater, but not dangerously so if the car is driven at sensible speeds in relation to the existing pressure required to stop the car.

Servicing the Master-Vac:

No individual part in the vacuum servo is supplied as a service item, the failure of a component will entail the renewal of the complete unit.

To check whether the vacuum servo unit is working, switch off the engine and pump the brake pedal several times so that all vacuum in the system is dispelled. Now hold a steady light pressure on the brake pedal and start the engine. If the servo is working properly, the pedal will move further down without extra foot pressure as the system is evacuated.

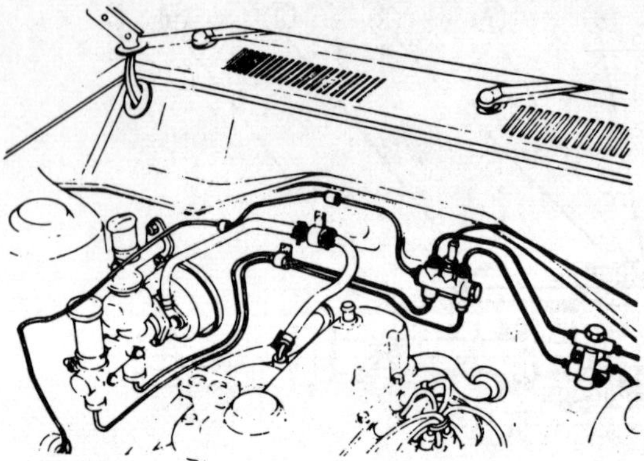

FIG 11 :35 Location of check valve in engine compartment

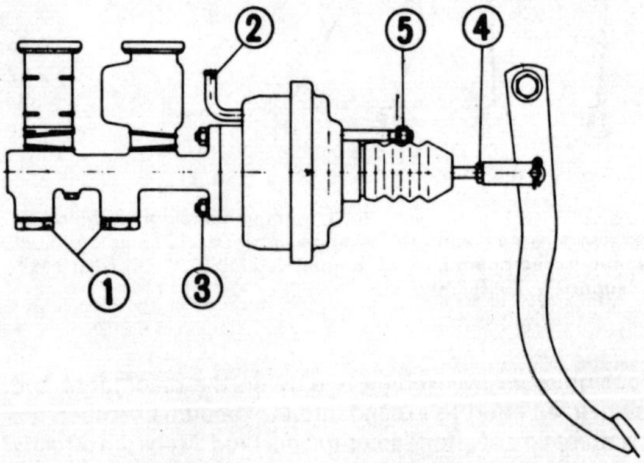

FIG 11 :36 Removing vacuum servo

Removing the servo:

1 Refer to **FIG 11 :36** and take off the master cylinder (see **Section 11 :6**).
2 Disconnect the induction hose from the pipe 2, uncouple control rod 4 from the pedal arm.
3 Remove the securing bolts 5 and detach the servo.

Refitting:

4 Replace the servo in the reverse order of dismantling and test for satisfactory operation.

The check valve:

The check valve is incorporated in the vacuum pipe and secured by two clips; its location is shown in **FIG 11 :35**. The check valve cannot be dismantled to examine the spring, ball valve or valve seat and the only way to check it is to subject it to vacuum tests on a test rig or by substituting it for one that is known to be serviceable. Many service agents have test rigs on which the valve can be tested.

Removing

Remove the two clips and extract the valve from the vacuum tubes.

11 :10 Fault diagnosis

(a) 'Spongy' pedal

1 Leak in the system
2 Worn master cylinder
3 Leaking wheel cylinders
4 Air in the fluid system
5 Gaps between drum brake linings and shoes

(b) Excessive pedal movement

1 Check 1 and 4 in (a)
2 Pedal height adjustment incorrect
3 Very low fluid level in supply tank
4 Excessive lining or pad wear

(c) Brakes grab or pull to one side

1 Distorted disc or drums
2 Wet or oily pads or linings
3 Loose backplate or caliper
4 Disc loose on hub
5 Worn suspension or steering connections
6 Mixed linings of different grades
7 Uneven tyre pressures
8 Broken shoe return springs
9 Seized piston in wheel or caliper cylinder
10 Seized handbrake cable
11 Blocked flexible or rigid fluid pipe

CHAPTER 12

THE ELECTRICAL EQUIPMENT

12:1 Description

All models covered by this manual have 12-volt electrical systems in which the negative battery terminal is earthed to the car bodywork.

There are wiring diagrams in **Technical Data** at the end of this manual which will enable those with electrical experience to trace and correct faults.

Instructions for servicing the electrical equipment are given in this chapter, but it must be pointed out that it is not sensible to repair units which are seriously defective, electrically or mechanically. Such equipment should be replaced by new or reconditioned units, which can be obtained on an exchange basis.

12:2 The battery

To maintain the performance of the battery it is essential to carry out the following operations, particularly in winter when heavy current demands must be met.

Keep the top and surrounding parts of the battery dry and clean, as dampness can cause current leakage. Clean off corrosion from the metal parts of the battery mounting with diluted ammonia and coat them with anti-sulphuric paint. Clean the terminal posts and smear them with petroleum jelly before remaking the connections and tightening the terminal clamps securely. High electrical resistance due to corrosion at the terminals can be responsible for a lack of sufficient current to operate the starter motor.

Top up the electrolyte in the battery cells to the line marked on the battery case, using distilled water. Test the condition of the cells with an hydrometer. Never add neat acid to the battery. If it is necessary to prepare new electrolyte due to loss or spillage, add sulphuric acid to distilled water. It is highly dangerous to add water to acid. It is safest to have the battery refilled with electrolyte, if necessary, by a service station.

The indications from the hydrometer readings of the specific gravity are as follows:

For climates below 27°C or 80°F:	*Specific gravity*
Cell fully charged	1.270 to 1.290
Cell half discharged	1.190 to 1.210
Cell discharged	1.110 to 1.130
For climates above 27°C or 80°F:	
Cell fully charged	1.210 to 1.230
Cell half discharged	1.130 to 1.150
Cell discharged	1.050 to 1.070

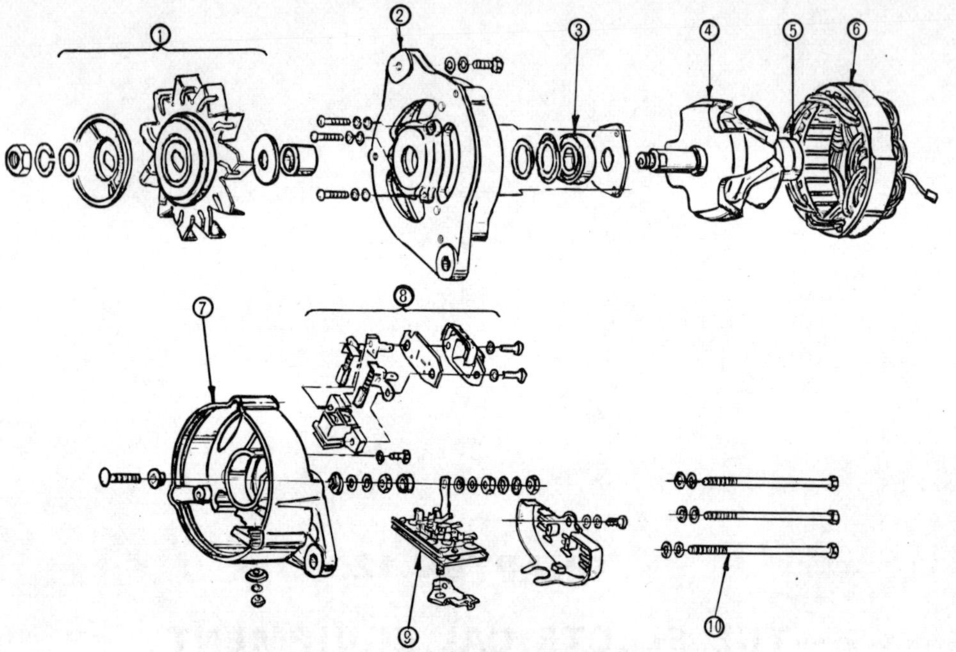

FIG 12:1 The alternator components

Key to Fig 12:1 1 Pulley assembly 2 Front cover 3 Front bearing 4 Rotor 5 Rear bearing 6 Stator 7 Rear cover 8 Brush assembly 9 Diode plate assembly 10 Through-bolt

These figures assume an electrolyte temperature of 60°F or 16°C. If the temperature of the electrolyte exceeds this, add .002 to the readings for each 5°F or 3°C rise. Subtract .002 for any corresponding drop below 60°F or 16°C.

All cells should read approximately the same. If one differs radically from the others, it may be due to an internal fault or to spillage or leakage of the electrolyte.

If the battery is in a low state of charge, take the car for a long daylight run or put the battery on a charger at 5 amps with the vents removed, until it gasses freely. Do not use a naked light near the battery as the gas is inflammable. If the battery is to stand unused for long periods, give a refreshing charge every month. It will be ruined if it is left uncharged.

12:3 The alternator

The alternator provides current for the various items of electrical equipment and to charge the battery, the unit operating at all engine speeds. An alternating current is produced, this being rectified to a direct current supply by diodes mounted in the alternator casing. Alternator drive is taken from the fan belt. Very little maintenance is needed, apart from the occasional check on belt tension as described in **Chapter 4, Section 4:4**. The alternator must never be run with the battery disconnected, nor must the battery cables be reversed at any time. Test connections must be carefully made, and the battery and alternator wiring must be completely disconnected before any electric welding is carried out on any part of the car. These warnings must be observed, otherwise extensive damage to the alternator components, particularly the diodes, will result.

Testing when the alternator is not charging:

Check the drive belt tension to ensure that a loose belt is not the cause of the trouble. Switch off all the lights and accessories and connect an ammeter in series with the battery and control box. Start the engine and check the ammeter reading as engine speed is raised. The output should be 18 amps minimum at an alternator speed of 2500 rev/min. If the alternator is in order, check the continuity of the cables to the control box. If the fault persists, remove the ammeter, reconnect the wires and have the control box tested at an auto-electrical service station.

Removing the alternator:

Disconnect the negative lead from the battery and the two lead wires and connector from the alternator. Loosen the alternator mounting bolts and remove the fan belt. Remove the mounting bolts and lift the alternator from the car.

Refit in the reverse order, adjusting the belt tension as described in **Chapter 4**.

Dismantling the alternator:

FIG 12:1 shows the components of the alternator. Remove the pulley nut, pulley rim, fan and spacer, as shown in **FIG 12:2**. Remove the brush holder fixing screws and cover. Remove the holder complete with brushes in a forward direction, as shown in **FIG 12:3**.

Loosen and remove the three through-bolts and separate the two parts of the housing as shown in **FIG 12:4**, by tapping the front bracket lightly with a wooden mallet.

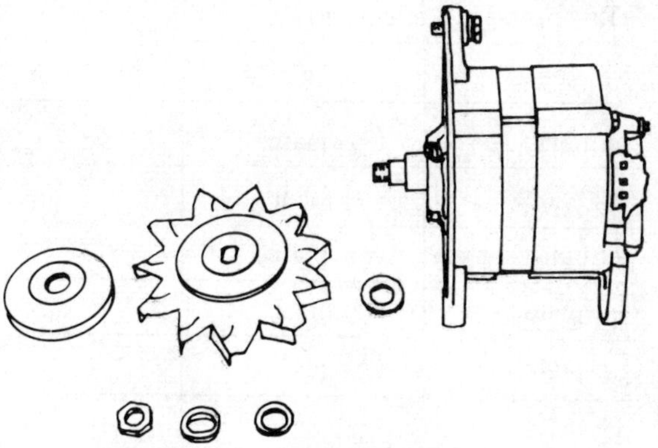

FIG 12:2 Removing the pulley and fan

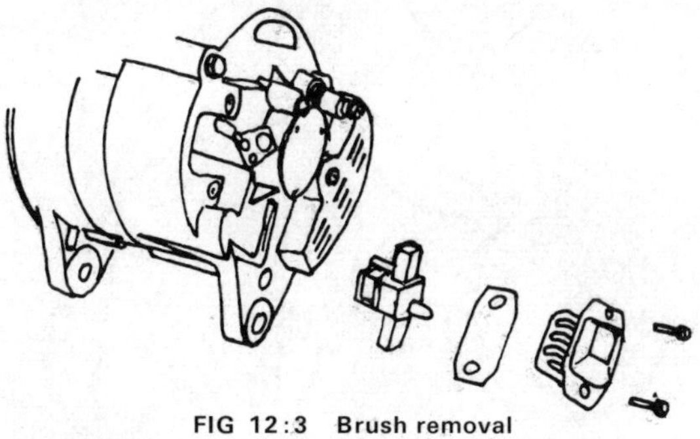

FIG 12:3 Brush removal

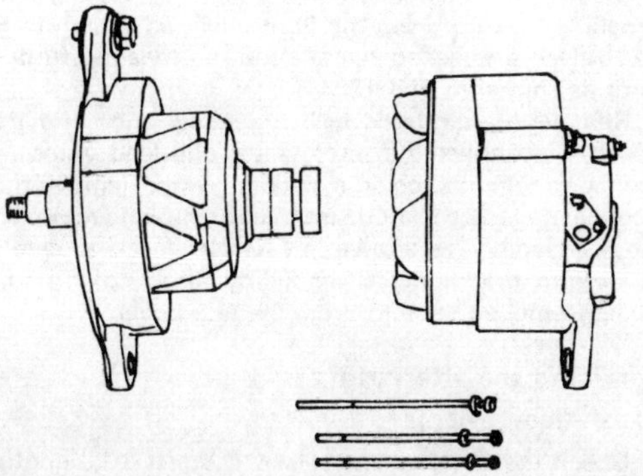

FIG 12:4 Separating the two parts of the housing

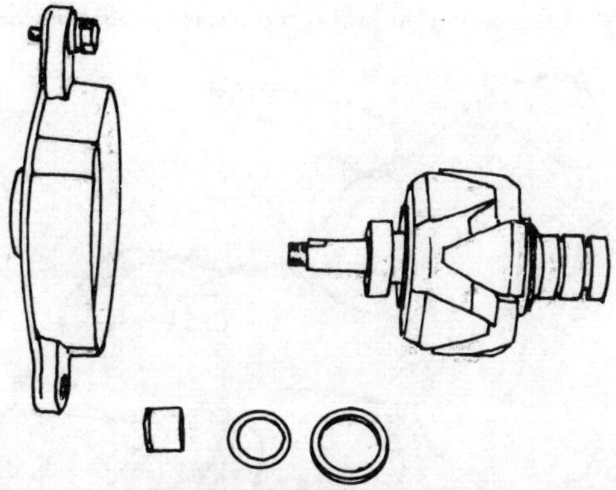

FIG 12:5 Removing the rotor from the front cover

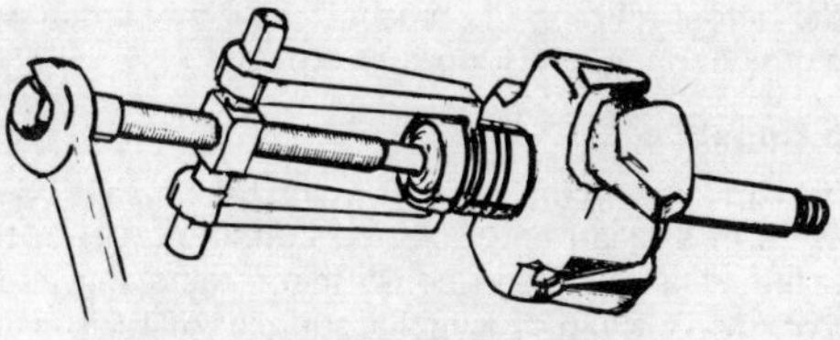

FIG 12:6 Pulling off the rear bearing

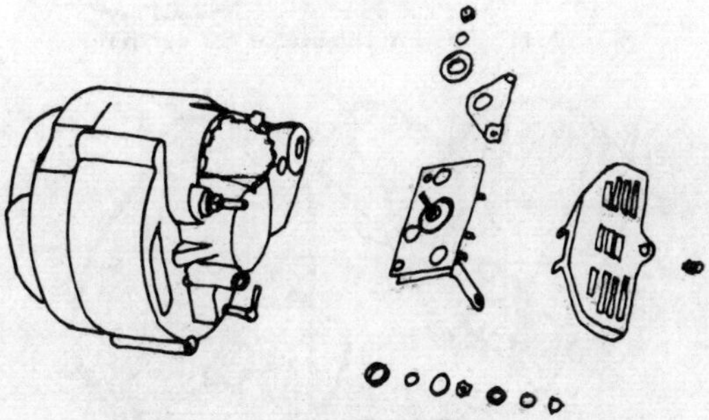

FIG 12:7 Removing the diode assembly

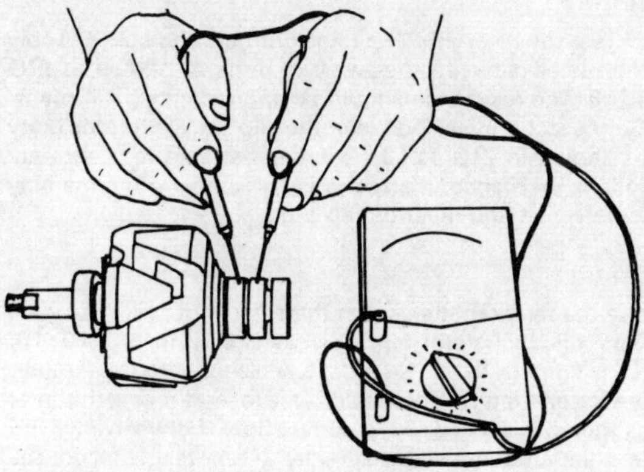

FIG 12:8 Testing the rotor field coil for conduction

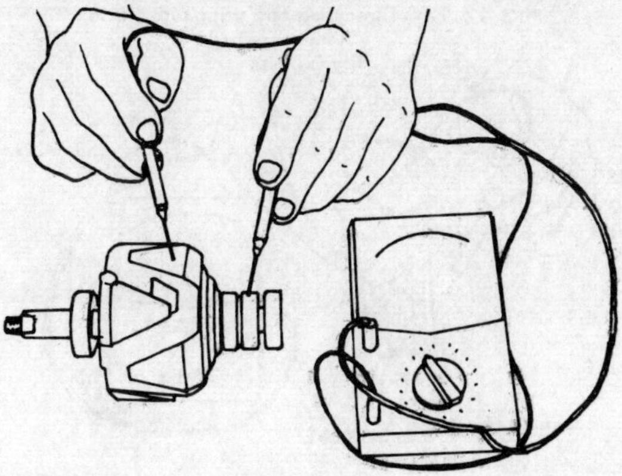

FIG 12:9 Testing the rotor field coil for earthing

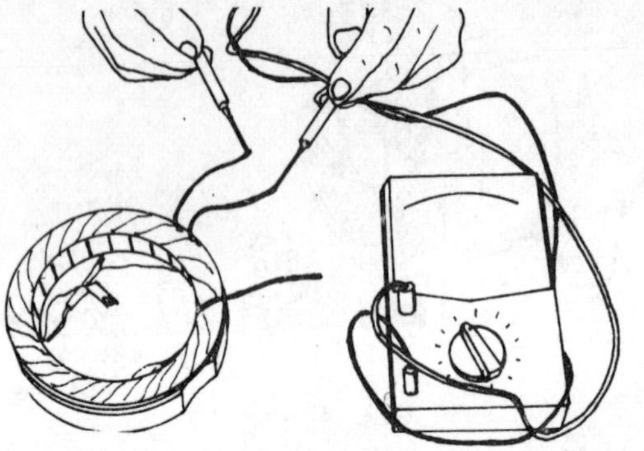

FIG 12:10 Testing the stator terminals for conduction

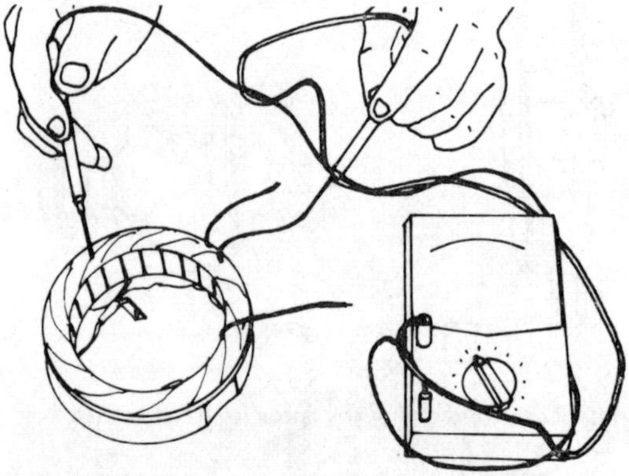

FIG 12:11 Testing the stator for earthing

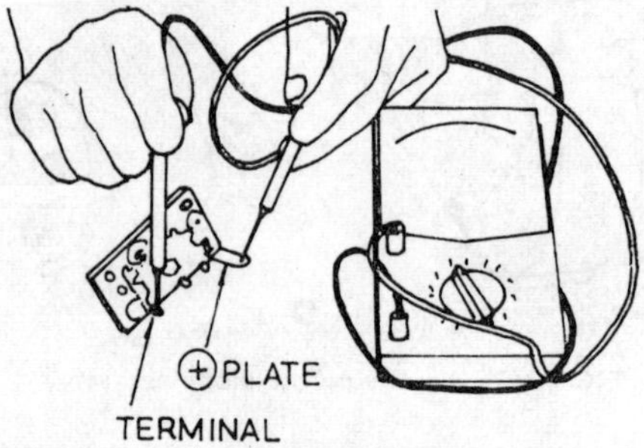

FIG 12:12 Checking the positive diodes

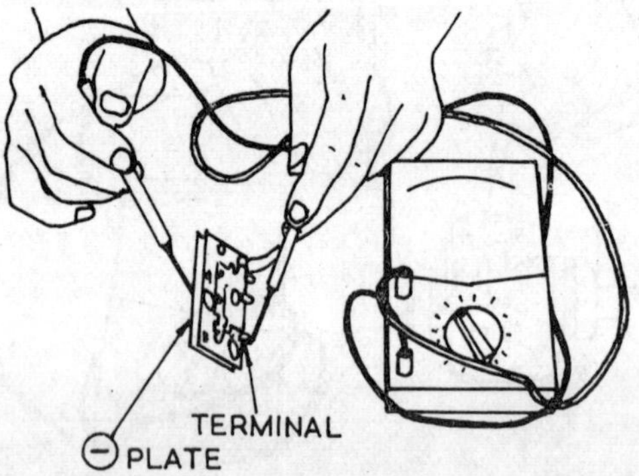

FIG 12:13 Checking the negative diodes

Test probe of a circuit tester		Conduction
⊖	⊕	
terminal	⊕ plate	X
⊕ plate	terminal	–
terminal	⊖ plate	–
⊖ plate	terminal	X
⊖ plate	⊕ plate	X
⊕ plate	⊖ plate	–

FIG 12:14 Test connections for diode testing

Remove three screws from the bearing retainer, then separate the rotor from the front cover as shown in **FIG 12:5**. Use a puller to remove the rear bearing from the rotor as shown in **FIG 12:6**.

Remove the diode cover fixing screw and remove the cover. Disconnect the three stator coil lead wires from the diode terminal, using a soldering iron. Remove the **A** terminal nut and the diode installation nut and remove the diode assembly, as shown in **FIG 12:7**, taking care not to deform the diode assembly by applying too much force. Remove the stator from the rear cover.

Servicing the alternator:

Brush gear:

Check the brushes and renew if worn to a length of .28 inch (7 mm) or less. Check that the brushes move freely in their holders. If a brush binds, remove it and ease the sides against a smooth file. Clean the inside of the holder before refitting the brush. Renew any brush when its pigtail connection is loose or broken.

Slip rings:

The slip rings on the rotor on which the brushes operate must be in a clean and polished condition. Clean them with fine sandpaper and polish them, removing all dust afterwards. To avoid causing flat surfaces on the slip rings, this operation is best carried out while spinning the rotor in a lathe.

Rotor:

Test the rotor and slip rings with an ohmmeter. Apply the meter between the two slip rings as shown in **FIG 12:8**. The resistance should be approximately 4.4 ohms. Connect the meter between the slip ring and rotor body as shown in **FIG 12:9**. The meter should indicate near infinite resistance. If any test is failed, the rotor assembly is defective and must be renewed.

Stator:

Use the meter to check that there is conduction between the individual stator terminals, as shown in **FIG 12:10**. If any terminal fails to conduct when connected to another, the stator is faulty. Check each wire for earthing to the core, as shown in **FIG 12:11**. If current flows between any wire and the core, the stator is faulty. If any test is failed, the stator must be renewed.

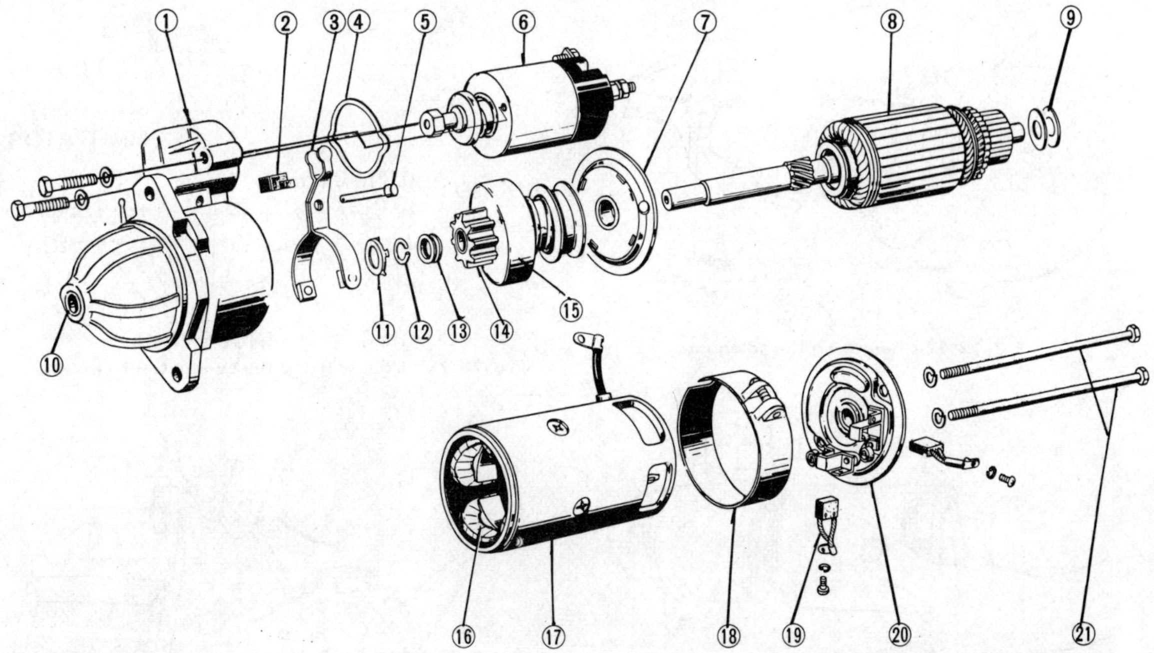

FIG 12:15 The starter components

Key to Fig 12:15 1 Gear case 2 Dust cover 3 Engagement lever 4 Dust cover 5 Engagement lever pin 6 Solenoid 7 Centre housing 8 Armature 9 Thrust washer 10 Bush 11 Stopper washer 12 Stopper clip 13 Pinion stopper 14 Pinion 15 Overrunning clutch 16 Field coil 17 Yoke 18 Brush cover 19 Brush 20 Rear cover 21 Through-bolt

Diodes:

If the alternator output is low, one or more of the diodes may be defective. To check the diodes, use a circuit tester as shown in **FIGS 12:12** and **12:13**, or a 12-volt current supply and test lamp bulb. Diodes pass current in one direction only. Those mounted on the positive (+) plate are positive diodes and must pass current from the terminal to the plate, but not from the plate to the terminal; those mounted on the negative(—) plate are negative diodes and must pass current from the plate to the terminal, but not from the terminal to the plate. Any diode that passes current in both directions or that does not pass current at all is defective. Connect the tester or test lamp between the points listed in **FIG 12:14**. If any connection made does not give the correct passing or blocking of current, one or more of the diodes is defective and the six diodes must be renewed as an assembly.

Reassembling the alternator:

Proceed in the reverse order of dismantling, renewing the ballbearings if they are worn or damaged. Lubricate the bearings with high-melting point grease. Reconnect any wires that were unsoldered, working quickly with a hot iron to avoid damage to the diodes which are very sensitive to heat. Refit the alternator and adjust the drive tension as described previously.

12:4 The starter

The starter is a brush type series wound motor equipped with an overrunning clutch and operated by a solenoid. The armature shaft is supported in sintered metal bushes which are factory packed with lubricant and require no servicing between overhauls. **FIG 12:15** shows the starter components.

When the starter is operated from the ignition switch, the engagement lever moves the pinion into mesh with the flywheel ring gear. When the pinion meshes with the ring gear teeth, the solenoid contact disc closes the circuit and the starter motor operates to turn the engine over. When the engine starts, the speed of the rotating flywheel causes the pinion to overrun the clutch and armature. The pinion continues in engagement until the lever is released, when it returns under spring action.

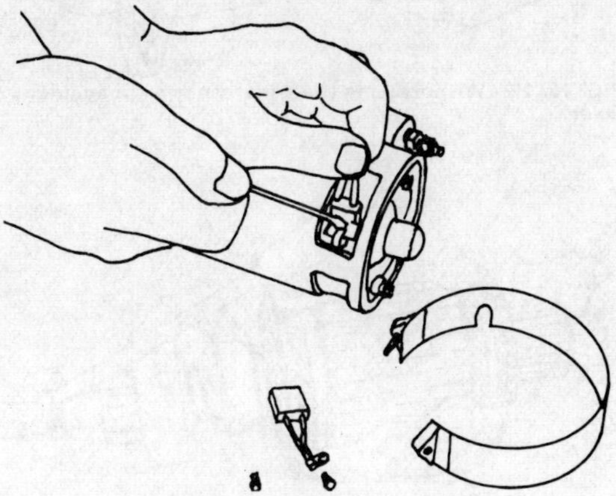

FIG 12:16 Removing the brushes

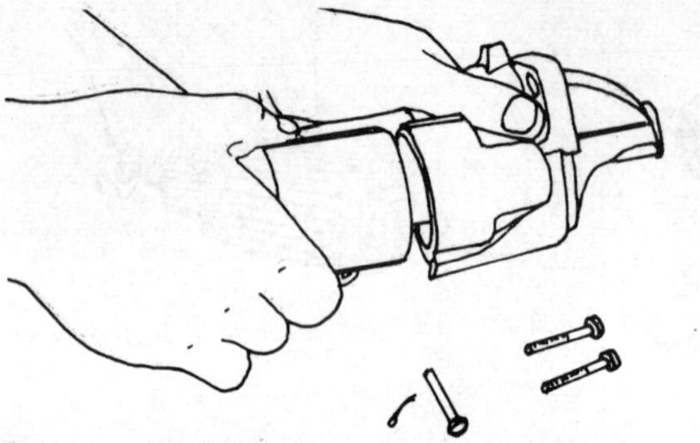

FIG 12:17 Removing the solenoid

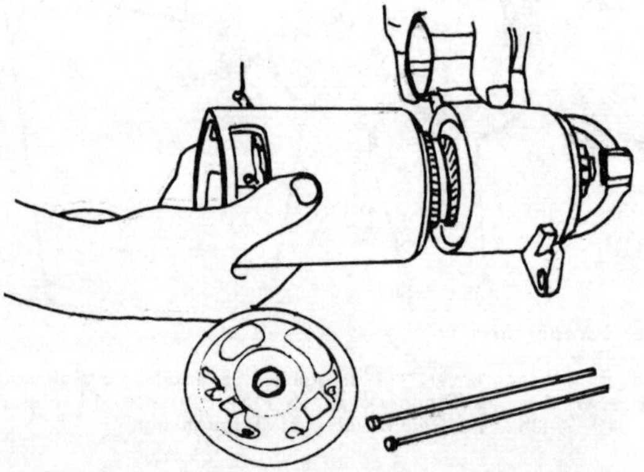

FIG 12:18 Removing the brush cover and yoke assembly

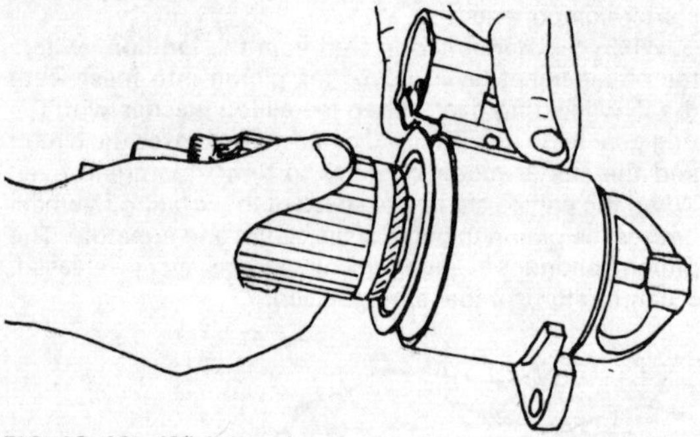

FIG 12:19 Withdrawing the armature and engagement lever

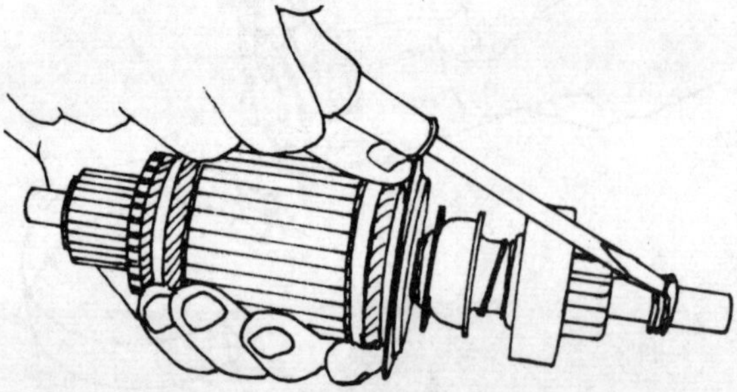

FIG 12:20 Removing the overrunning clutch assembly

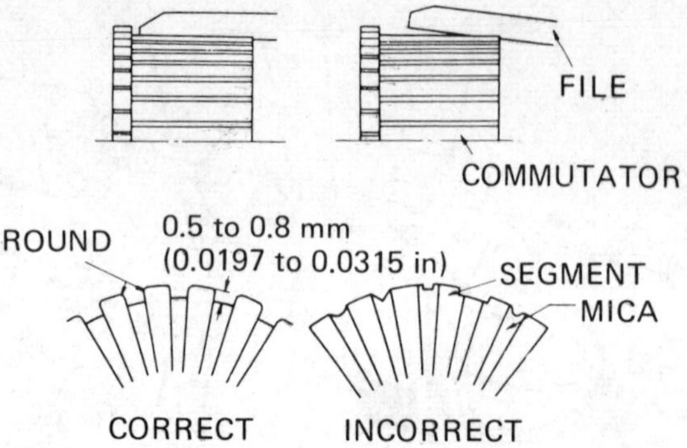

FIG 12:21 Undercutting the commutator insulation

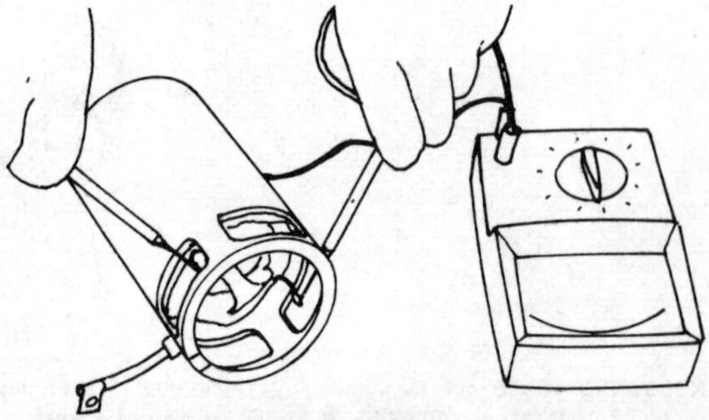

FIG 12:22 Testing the field coils for continuity

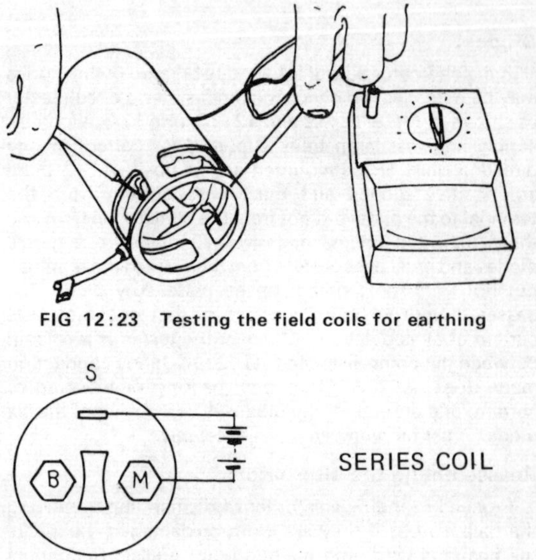

FIG 12:23 Testing the field coils for earthing

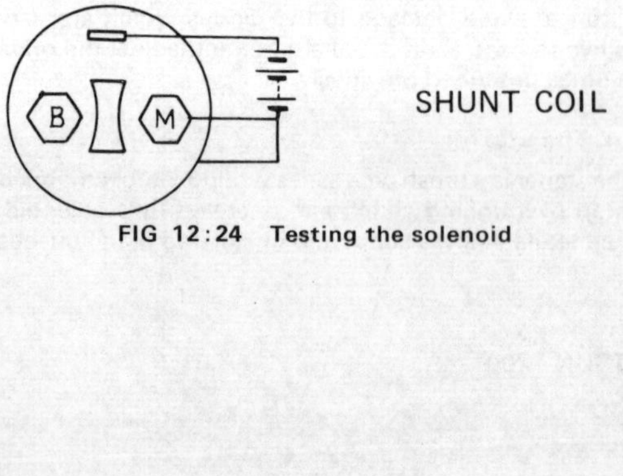

FIG 12:24 Testing the solenoid

Tests for a starter which does not operate:

Check that the battery is in good condition and fully charged and that its connections are clean and tight. Switch on the headlamps and operate the starter switch. Current is reaching the starter if the lights dim when the starter is operated, in which case it will be necessary to remove the starter for servicing. If the lights do not dim significantly, switch them off and operate the starter switch while listening for a clicking sound at the starter motor, which will indicate that the solenoid is operating.

If no sound can be heard at the starter when the switch is operated, check the wiring and connections between the battery and starter switch and between the switch and solenoid. If the solenoid can be heard operating when the starter switch is operated, check the wiring and connections between the battery and the main starter terminals, taking care not to accidentally earth the battery to starter motor lead. If the wiring is not the cause of the trouble, the fault is internal and the starter motor must be removed and serviced.

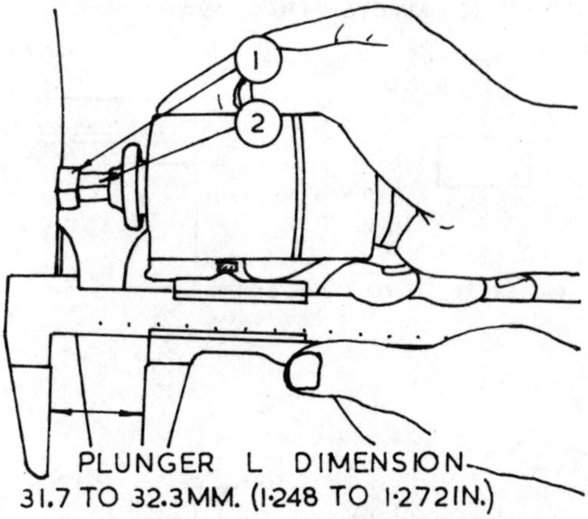

FIG 12:25 Adjusting the solenoid plunger

Removing the starter:

Disconnect the battery earth cable. Disconnect the black and yellow wire from the starter solenoid terminal and the black battery cable from the battery terminal. Remove the two bolts which secure the starter motor to the clutch bellhousing, then pull the starter motor assembly forwards and lift it from the car.

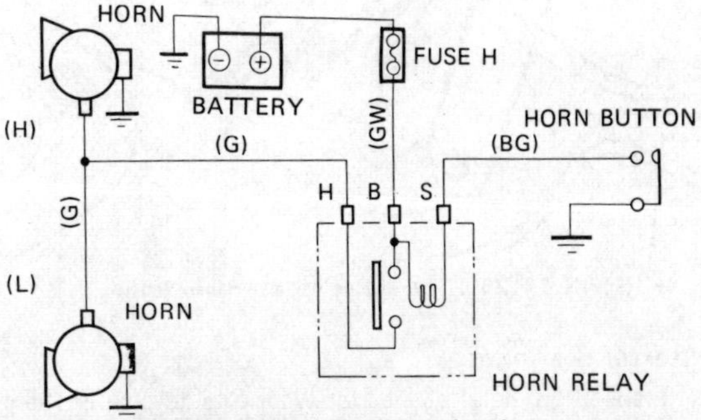

FIG 12:26 The horn circuit

Dismantling the starter:

Remove the brush cover and take out the brushes as shown in **FIG 12:16**. Loosen the nut securing the connecting plate to the solenoid M terminal and remove the two screws which secure the solenoid. Remove the cotter-pin and withdraw the engagement lever pivot pin, then withdraw the solenoid as shown in **FIG 12:17**. Remove the two through bolts and rear cover assembly, then remove the yoke assembly as shown in **FIG 12:18**, tapping lightly on the yoke with a wooden mallet. Withdraw the armature and engagement lever as shown in **FIG 12:19**.

Remove the pinion stopper from the armature shaft end. To do this, remove the stopper washer, push the stopper to the overrunning clutch side and, after removing the stopper clip, remove the stopper together with the over-running clutch as shown in **FIG 12:20**.

Servicing the starter:

Brush gear:

Check the brushes and renew them if worn to a length of .3 inch (7 mm) or less. If the brush contact is loose, fit a new brush. If a brush binds or moves sluggishly in its housing, remove it and ease the sides against a smooth file. Clean the inside of the holder before refitting the brush.

The commutator:

A commutator in good condition will be smooth and free from pitting and burned segments. Clean with a cloth and, if necessary, polish with fine glasspaper. Do not use emerycloth. Skim a badly worn commutator in a lathe, using a high speed and taking a light cut with a sharp tool. Remove the minimum amount necessary to clean up, then polish with fine glasspaper. Note that the wear limit for the commutator diameter is .08 inch (2 mm). If this figure is exceeded, the armature assembly must be renewed. Undercut the insulation between the commutator segments as shown in **FIG 12:21**, using a special file or a hacksaw blade ground to the thickness of the insulation.

The armature:

A damaged armature should always be renewed. No attempt should be made to straighten a bent shaft or to machine the core. An electrically suspect armature should be checked by a service station equipped with the necessary armature testing facilities.

Testing field coils:

Use a test lamp or circuit tester to check the field coils. Connect the tester between the field coil positive terminal and the positive brush holder as shown in **FIG 12:22**, to test for continuity. If current does not flow, the field circuit or coil is open. Connect the tester between the yoke and the field coil positive terminal as shown in **FIG 12:23**. If resistance is shown, the field coils are earthed. Unsolder the connected part of each coil and check each circuit for earthing as before. If the field coil circuit is open, earthed or shorted, the field coils are defective and must be renewed.

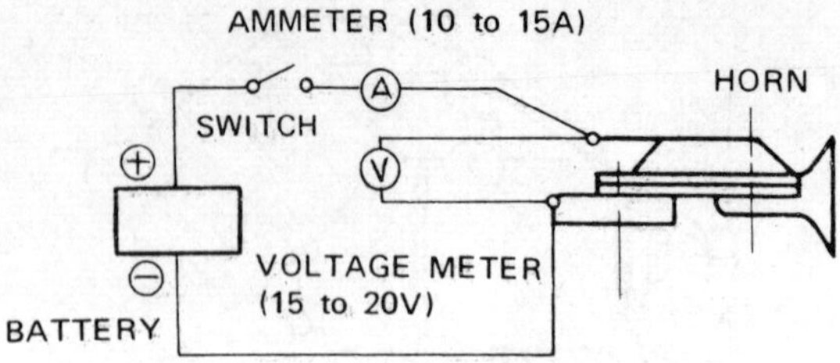

FIG 12:27 Horn testing and adjusting circuit

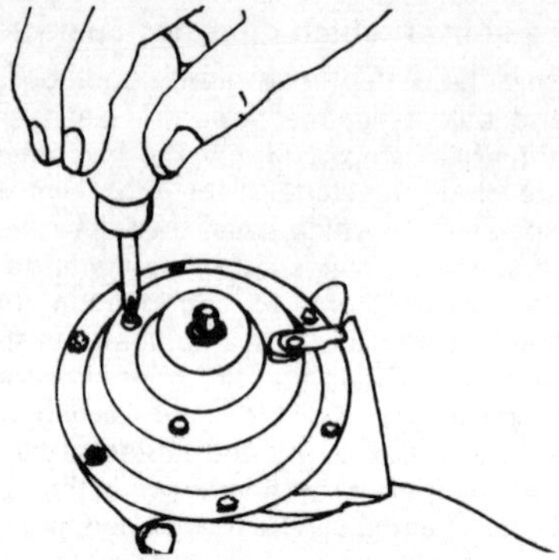

FIG 12:28 Adjusting the horn volume, 1200 model

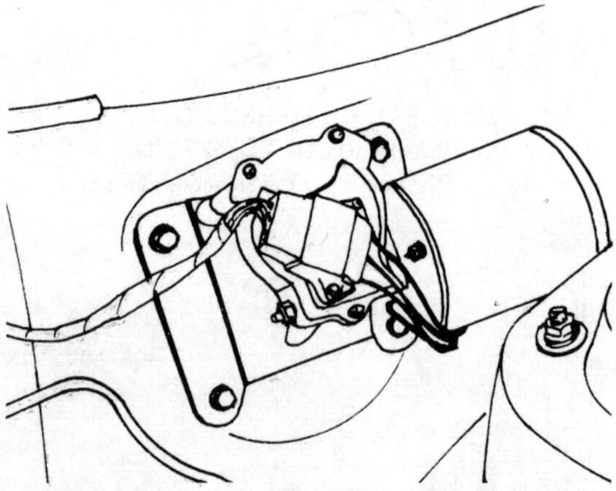

FIG 12:29 The wiper motor mountings

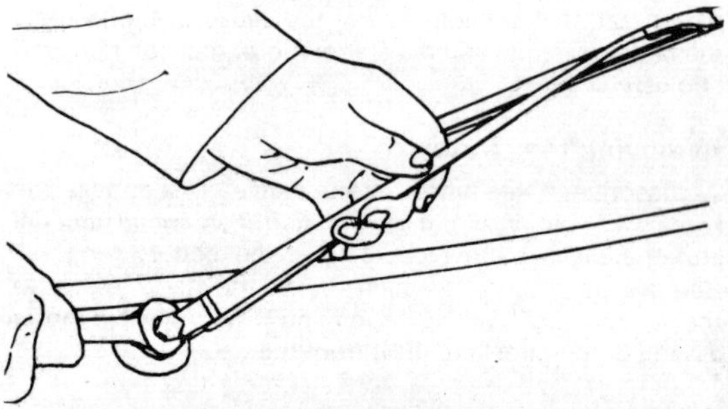

FIG 12:30 Removing a wiper arm

Starter bearings:

Inspect the metal bushes for wear or side play. If the clearance between the bush and the armature shaft is more than .008 inch (.2mm), renew the bush. Press out the old bearing bushes and press the new ones in until they are flush with the case. New bearings must be reamed to give a clearance of .0012 to .004 inch (.03 to .10mm).

Pinion and clutch assembly:

Do not clean the overrunning clutch with solvents as this would wash the grease from inside the clutch. Check for smooth operation and good condition of the teeth on the pinion. Renew if worn or damaged.

Solenoid:

Check the solenoid contacts for wear or roughness and renew them if they are defective in any way. The plunger should operate when a 12-volt current supply is connected between the **S** and **M** terminals, as shown in **FIG 12:24**. If so, the series coil is in order. Connect the **S** and **M** terminals and the solenoid body as shown in the same figure. With the plunger operated in this manner, open the **M** terminal. If the plunger remains in the operated position, the shunt coil is in order. If any test is failed, renew the solenoid assembly.

Check the **L** dimension of the solenoid plunger as shown in **FIG 12:25**. Press the plunger against a wall and measure the length **L** between the adjusting nut and the solenoid cover. Adjust if necessary to bring the dimension within the stated limits. The adjusting nut is shown at 1 and the plunger at 2.

Reassembling the starter:

This is the reverse of the dismantling procedure. Grease the armature shaft splines and the sliding parts of the engagement lever mechanism. Lightly oil the bearing bushes.

12:5 The horns

A pair of horns is fitted, one high-tone and one low-tone. The horn circuit incorporates a fuse and a relay as shown in **FIG 12:26**.

Adjusting horn volume:

To adjust the horn volume on 1200 models, connect a voltmeter and ammeter into the horn circuit as shown in **FIG 12:27**. Turn on the switch, check that the voltmeter indicates 12 to 12.5 volts, then adjust as follows to obtain a reading on the ammeter of 2.5 amp for flat-type horns, 5.0 amp for spiral-type horns. Turn the adjusting screw shown in **FIG 12:28** until a proper sound is obtained at the stated amperage. On completion, run the engine so that full alternator voltage is obtained and check that the sound is still correct at this higher voltage. If not make further minor adjustments.

Horns on 120Y models cannot be adjusted.

12:6 Windscreen wipers

The wiper motor unit consists of a two-speed electric motor and auto-stop mechanism. The motor drives the wiper blades through a mechanical linkage located behind the instrument panel. If the wiper motor is inoperative, check the fuse, wiring and connections. If the

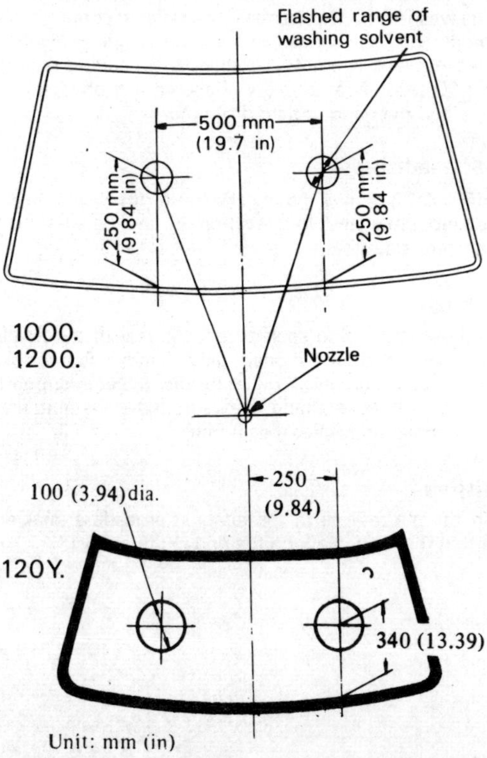

FIG 12:31 Adjusting windscreen washer nozzles

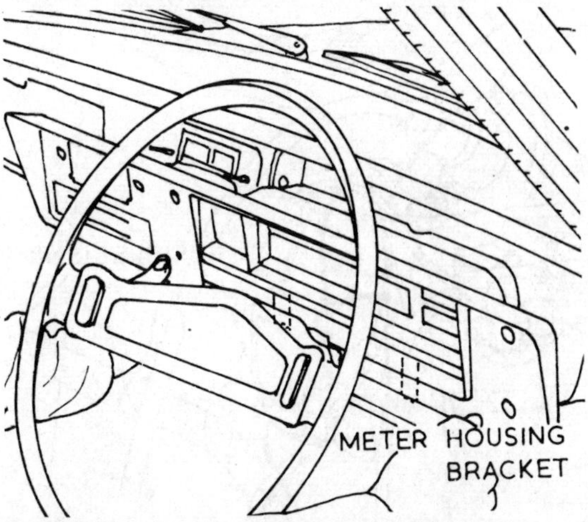

FIG 12:32 Removing the instrument panel

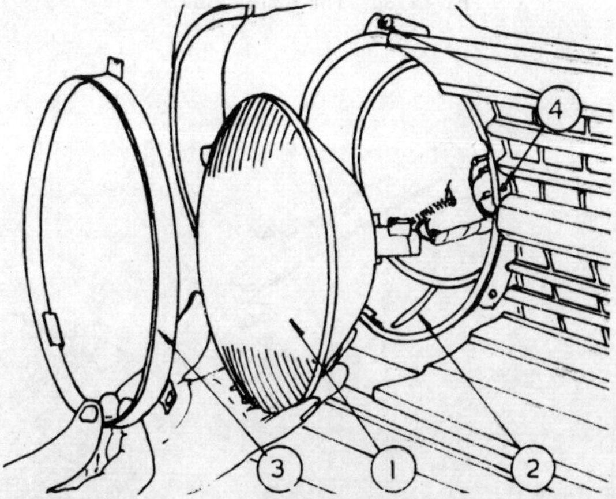

FIG 12:33 The headlamp sealed-beam unit

Key to Fig 12:33 1 Sealed-beam unit 2 Mounting ring 3 Retaining ring screws 4 Headlamp beam-setting adjustment

motor runs but wiper operation is slow, noisy or laborious, check the linkage for binding or damage. If the wiper motor becomes defective after a long period of use, it is recommended that a service exchange reconditioned unit be obtained and fitted.

Wiper motor removal:

Remove the connector plug from the wiper motor, then remove the nut which connects the motor worm wheel shaft to the connecting rod, this being located at the passenger compartment side of the dash panel. Remove the three bolts attaching the wiper motor to the dash panel, shown in **FIG 12:29**, then lift off the wiper motor.

Refitting is a reversal of the removal instructions.

Removing wiper arms:

Remove the wiper arm attaching bolt as shown in **FIG 12:30**, then pull the wiper arm from the pivot shaft. When refitting the wiper arm, make sure that the wiper blade is approximately 1 inch (27 mm) from the lower edge of the windscreen when the arms are in the parked position.

12:7 Windscreen washers

The windscreen washer unit is electrically operated from the wiper switch, by turning this switch sideways. If the sprays from the washer nozzles are wrongly aimed, adjust them by moving them with a pair of pliers until the jets of water are directed onto the windscreen as shown in **FIG 12:31**.

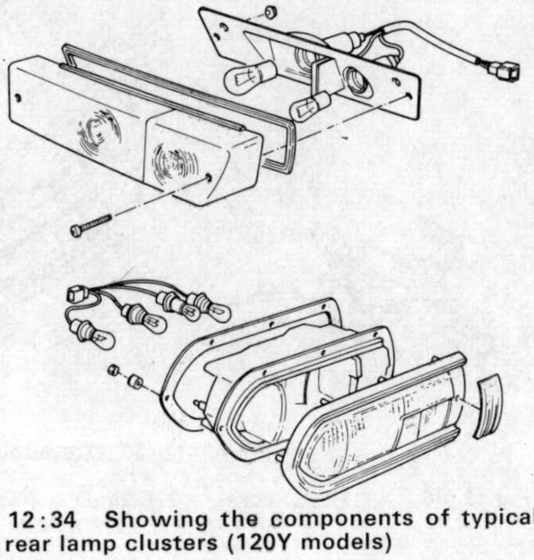

FIG 12:34 Showing the components of typical front and rear lamp clusters (120Y models)

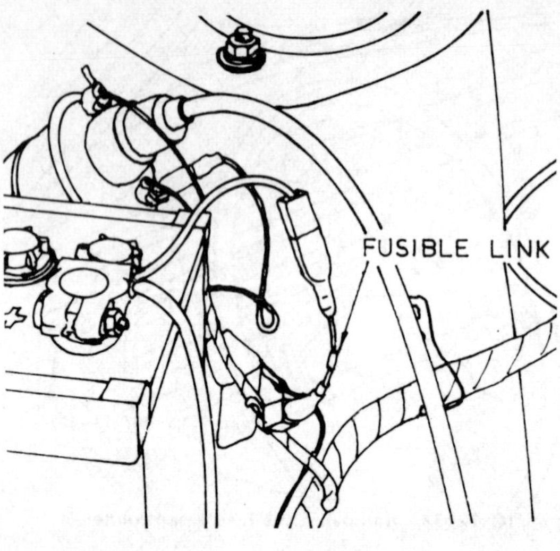

FIG 12:35 The fusible link

The washer unit should never be operated continuously for more than 30 seconds, nor should it be operated when the washer tank is empty. Limiting the operating time to about 10 seconds at a time will ensure that efficiency is maintained over a long period of time.

12:8 Headlamps

FIG 12:33 shows the installation of the sealed beam headlamp units and the location of the beam-setting adjustment screws.

Removal:

Remove the wiring socket from the rear of the headlamp unit. On Coupé models only, remove the screws which secure the front grille to the radiator support. Remove the three retaining screws from the retaining ring 3 and remove the sealed-beam unit.

Refitting:

This is the reverse of the removal procedure, making sure that the 'Top' mark on the ring is uppermost.

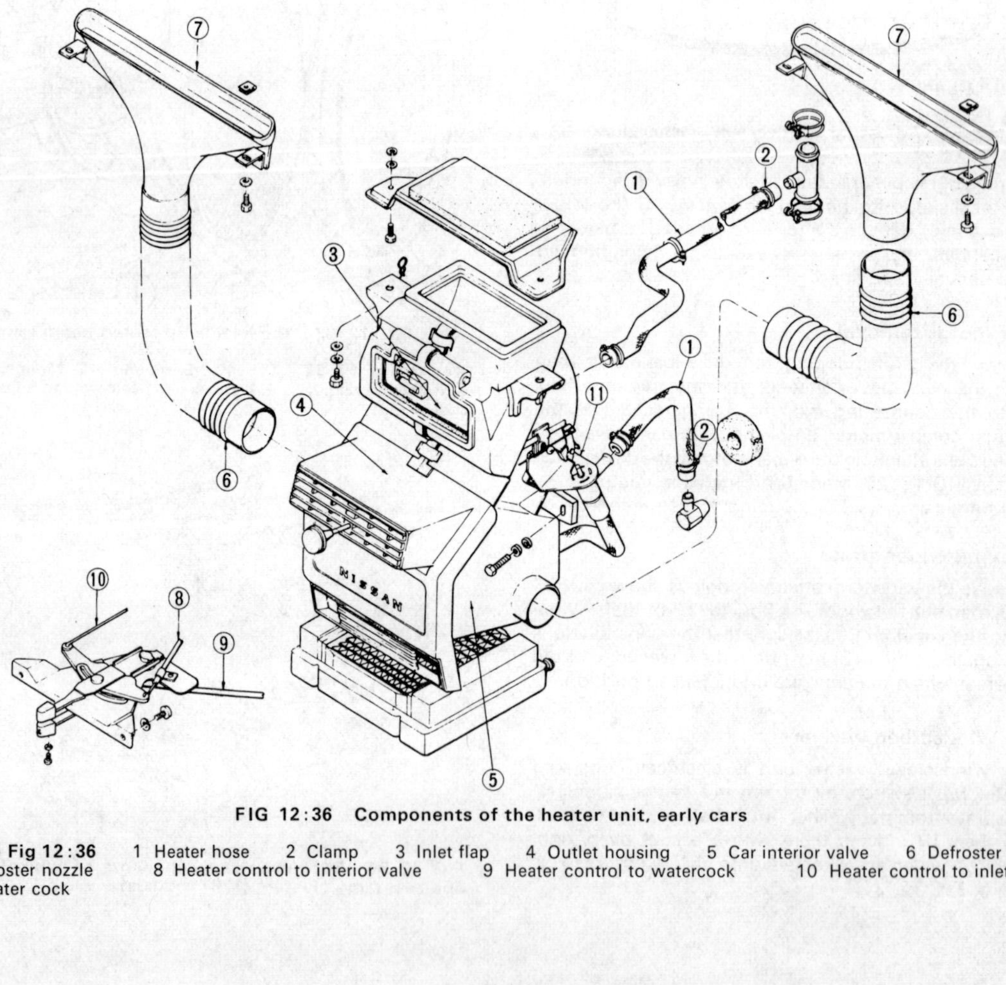

FIG 12:36 Components of the heater unit, early cars

Key to Fig 12:36 1 Heater hose 2 Clamp 3 Inlet flap 4 Outlet housing 5 Car interior valve 6 Defroster hose 7 Defroster nozzle 8 Heater control to interior valve 9 Heater control to watercock 10 Heater control to inlet flap 11 Heater cock

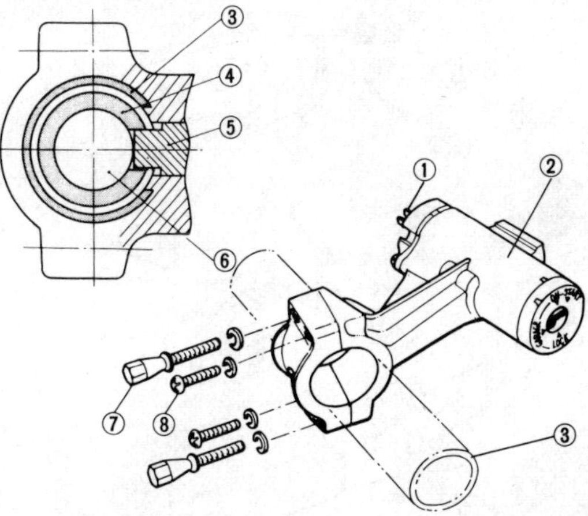

FIG 12:37 Components of ignition switch and steering lock

Key to Fig 12:37 1 Ignition switch connections 2 Cylinder 3 Steering jacket tube 4 Lock collar 5 Lock tongue 6 Steering shaft 7 Shear type screw 8 Attaching screw

Beam setting:

Headlamps should be set so that, when the car is normally loaded, the main beams are parallel to each other and to the road. Accurate beam-setting is best left to a service station having special optical beam-setting equipment.

Side and tail lamp clusters:

A variety of fittings for these lamps may be used, but typical assemblies are shown in **FIG 12:34**, these are fitted to 120Y models. As will be seen from the illustrations, renewal of a bulb in the front cluster is effected by removing two screws and lifting off the lens, while bulbs in the rear units are withdrawn from inside the luggage compartment.

12:9 Fuses

According to model there may be six or eight fuses mounted in a fuse box located behind the instrument panel to protect the main electrical circuits. The fuse block carries a plate giving the rated capacity of each fuse and the circuits it protects. A fusible link, shown in **FIG 12:35** protects the charging circuit.

If a break in any circuit is suspected, check the fuse and its contacts first. If a fuse blows, it may be due to a temporary overload, in which case renewal of the fuse is all that is required. However, the circuits protected by that fuse should always be checked for faults and the wiring and units checked for shortcircuits which could be the cause of the trouble. It is wise to carry spare fuses in the car. The fusible link can be checked visually, by feeling for a break with the fingertips, or by the use of a circuit tester. If the fusible link blows, make sure that the correct replacement is obtained, as this section of wire carries a higher current than the standard fuses.

12:10 Lighting circuits

Lamps give insufficient light:

Refer to **Section 12:2** and check the condition of the battery, recharging it if necessary. Check the setting of the headlamps as described in **Section 12:9** and renew any lamp units which have darkened with age.

Bulbs burn out frequently:

Have the control box settings checked by an auto-electrical service station.

Lamps light when switched on but gradually fade:

Refer to **Section 12:2** and check the battery, as it is not capable of supplying current for any length of time.

Lamp brilliance varies with the speed of the car:

Check the condition of the battery and its connections. Make sure that the connections are clean and tight and renew any faulty cables.

12:11 The heater

The components of the heater unit for early cars are clearly shown in **FIG 12:36** and the procedure for its removal is as follows:

First disconnect the battery then remove the ashtray and parcel shelf.

Loosen the hose clamps and disconnect the two heater hoses at the engine.

Disconnect the cables from the heater unit, the heater control and the main harness.

Remove the wire clamp and disconnect the two control wires between the water cock and heater control and the car interior valve and the heater control at the heater unit. Disconnect the control rod from the inlet flap. Note that for this operation the upper lever on the heater control should be set to DEF and the lower lever to OFF.

Detach the two defroster hoses. Unscrew the four screws holding the heater unit to the facia panel and withdraw it carefully.

When removing the heater control from the instrument panel, first take out the screw holding the control knob then undo the two screws securing the control assembly to the panel.

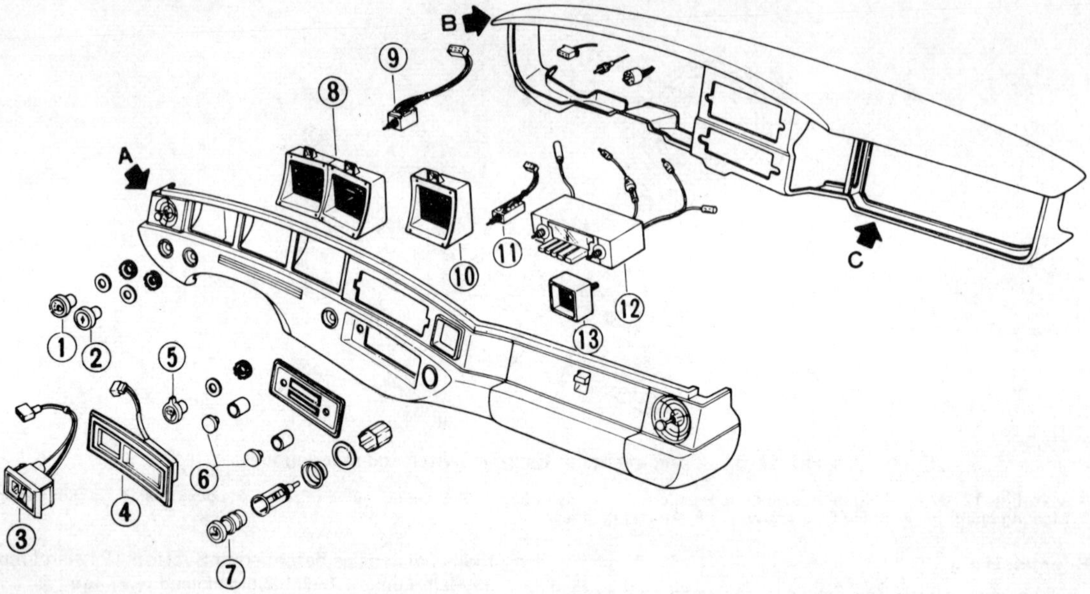

FIG 12:38 A typical instrument panel assembly

Key to Fig 12:38 A Instrument panel B Facia pad C Facia 1 Lighting switch 2 Choke control 3 Heated rear window switch 4 Escutcheon 5 Wiper switch 6 Radio controls 7 Lighter 8 Combination meter 9 Lighting switch 10 Tachometer (if fitted) 11 Wiper switch 12 Radio 13 Clock

The defroster nozzles are removed by taking out the two self-tapping screws from the back of the panel.

Installation is a reversal of the removal procedure.

On 120Y disconnect the negative terminal of the battery, drain the coolant, remove defroster pipes from sides of unit, disconnect the wires from harness to unit (one black, the other blue with white tracer). Remove water hose from right side of heater at water cock. Remove the securing bolt on each side of unit and one on top. Pull unit back and out. Replace in the reverse order.

12:12 Ignition switch and steering lock

This components, which is shown in **FIG 12:37** is secured by two shear type screws and these must be drilled out and the two attaching screws undone to remove the lock from the steering jacket tube.

When fitting a new lock it is necessary to tighten the two shear screws until their heads break off.

12:13 Instrument panel

There are some differences in the layout used on the various cars in the range, but a typical example is shown in **FIG 12:38**. Removal and dismantling are carried out as follows:

Instrument panel:

Disconnect the battery. Remove the steering column shell covers. It will assist if the steering wheel and direction indicator switch are removed, but this may not be necessary.

Pull out the ash tray and remove the knobs of the wiper and lighting switches and retaining nuts. The knobs are removed by pressing and turning anticlockwise. Remove choke control if applicable.

Remove the radio knobs and then the retaining nuts. These knobs are simply pulled off.

Nine screws are commonly used to retain the instrument panel to the facia; four on the upper part of the panel, three underneath, one on the outer case of the ash tray and one in the glove box. Note that only the centre screw in the ash tray needs to be removed.

Pull the panel out slightly and disconnect the lead to the cigarette lighter and withdraw the panel.

Combination meter (see FIG 12:39):

This is retained by four screws. Pull the meter out sufficiently to disconnect the speedometer drive and the multi-point connector, also the leads from the tachometer and clock if applicable. Withdraw the combination meter.

Speedometer:

Remove the combination meter as described and then the glass cover (four screws). Remove the six screws securing the lower housing to the upper housing and two screws securing the speedometer in the lower part and remove it.

Fuel and water temperatures gauges:

Each of these is retained by three screws at the back of the combination meter assembly. Remove these screws and lift the gauge away from the panel.

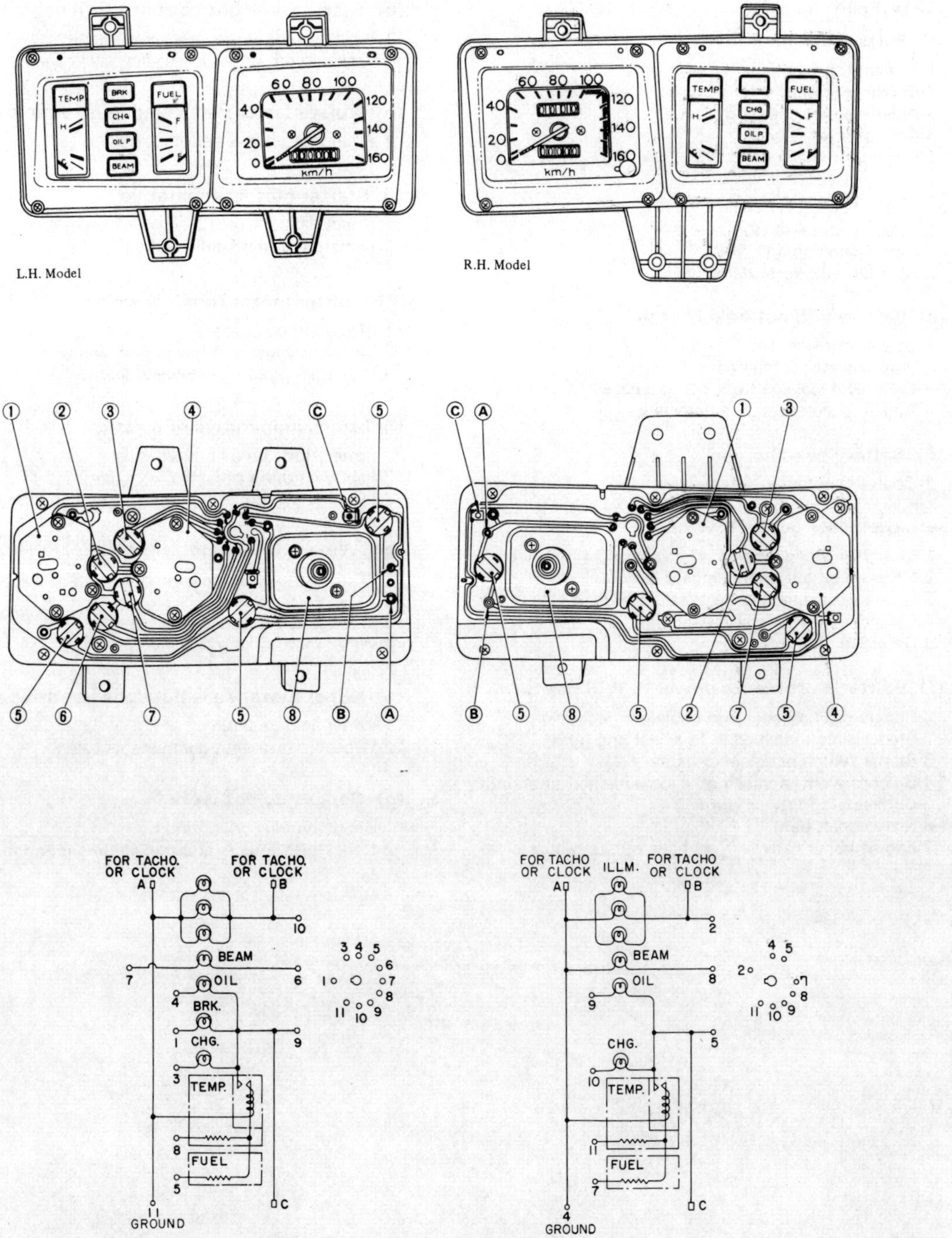

FIG 12:39 The combination meter, righthand and lefthand drive models

Key to Fig 12:39 1 Water temperature gauge 2 Oil pressure warning 3 Headlamp main beam 4 Fuel gauge 5 Panel illumination 6 Brake warning lamp 7 Charge indicator 8 Speedometer

12:14 Fault diagnosis

(a) Battery discharged

1 Terminal connections loose or dirty
2 Shorts in lighting circuits
3 Alternator not charging
4 Control box faulty
5 Battery internally defective

(b) Insufficient charge rate

1 Check 1 and 4 in (a)
2 Drive belt slipping
3 Alternator diode(s) defective

(c) Battery will not hold charge

1 Low electrolyte level
2 Battery plates sulphated
3 Electrolyte leakage from cracked case
4 Battery plate separators defective

(d) Battery overcharged

1 Control box faulty

(e) Alternator output low or nil

1 Belt broken or slipping
2 Control box out of adjustment
3 Brushes sticking, springs weak or broken
4 Defective rotor or stator windings
5 Defective diode(s)

(f) Starter motor lacks power or will not turn

1 Battery discharged, loose cable connections
2 Starter pinion jammed in flywheel ring gear
3 Starter switch or solenoid faulty
4 Brushes worn or sticking, leads detached or shorting
5 Commutator dirty or worn
6 Starter shaft bent
7 Engine abnormally stiff, perhaps due to rebore

(g) Starter runs but does not turn engine

1 Pinion engagement mechanism faulty
2 Broken teeth on pinion or flywheel gears

(h) Noisy starter when engine is running

1 Pinion return mechanism faulty

(j) Starter motor inoperative

1 Check 1 and 4 in (f)
2 Armature or field coils faulty

(k) Starter motor rough or noisy

1 Mounting bolts loose
2 Pinion engagement mechanism faulty
3 Damaged pinion or flywheel teeth

(l) Lamps inoperative or erratic

1 Battery low, bulbs burned out
2 Faulty earthing of lamps or battery
3 Lighting switch faulty, loose or broken connections

(m) Wiper motor sluggish, taking high current

1 Wiper motor defective internally
2 Lack of lubrication
3 Linkage worn or binding
4 Wiper motor fixing bolts loose

(n) Wiper motor runs but does not drive arms

1 Wiper linkage faulty
2 Wiper transmission components worn

(o) Gauges do not work

1 Check wiring for continuity
2 Check instruments and transmitters for continuity

CHAPTER 13

THE BODYWORK

13:1 Bodywork finish

Large scale repairs to body panels are best left to expert panel beaters. Even small dents can be tricky, as too much hammering will stretch the metal and make things worse instead of better. If panel beating is to be attempted, use a dolly on the opposite side of the panel. The head of a large hammer will suffice for small dents, but for large dents a block of metal will be necessary. Use light hammer blows to reshape the panel, pressing the dolly against the opposite side of the panel to absorb the blows. If this method is used to reduce the depth of dents, final smoothing with a suitable filler will be easier, although it may be better to avoid hammering minor dents and just use the filler.

Clean the area to be filled, making sure it is free of paint, rust and grease, then roughen the area with emerycloth to ensure a good bond. Use a proprietary fibreglass filler paste mixed according to the instructions and press it into the dent with a putty knife. Allow the filler to stand proud of the surrounding area to allow for rubbing down after hardening. Use a file and emerycloth or a disc sander to blend the repaired area to the surrounding bodywork, using finer grade abrasives as the work nears completion. Apply a coat of primer surfacer and, when it is dry, rub down with 'Wet or dry' paper lubricated with soapy water, finishing with 400 grade. Apply more primer and repeat the operation until the surface is perfectly smooth. Take time on achieving the best finish possible at this stage as it will control the final effect.

The touching up of paintwork can be carried out with self-spraying cans of paint, these being available in a wide range of colours. Use a piece of newspaper or board as a test panel to practice on first, so that the action of the spray will be familiar when it is used on the panel. Before spraying the panel, remove all traces of wax polish. Mask off large areas such as windows with newspaper and masking tape. Small areas such as trim strips or door handles can be wrapped with masking tape or carefully coated with vaseline or grease. Apply the touching up paint, spraying with short bursts and keeping the spray moving. Do not attempt to cover the area in one coat, applying several coats with a few minutes drying time between each. If too much paint is applied at one time, runs may develop. If so, do not try to remove the run by wiping, but wait until it has dried and rub down as before.

After the final coat is applied, allow a few hours of drying time before blending the new finish to the old with a fine cutting compound and a cloth, buffing with a light, circular motion. Finish with the application of a good quality polish.

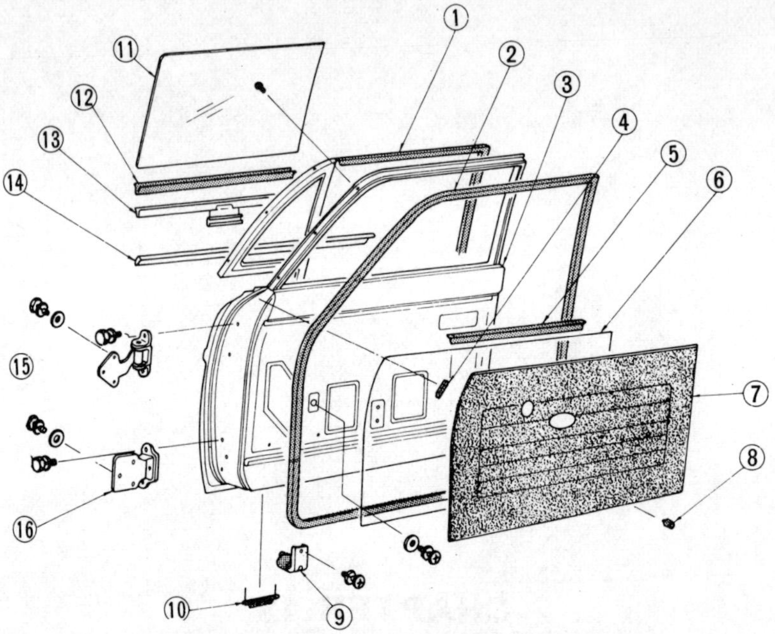

FIG 13:1 Front door components, 1200 model

Key to Fig 13:1 1 Rubber channel 2 Weatherstrip 3 Door panel 4 Weatherstrip spacer 5 Weatherstrip 6 Seal panel 7 Door trim 8 Bumper rubber 9 Glass stopper 10 Drain hole cover 11 Door glass 12 Glazing rubber 13 Bottom channel 14 Outer moulding 15 Upper hinge 16 Lower hinge

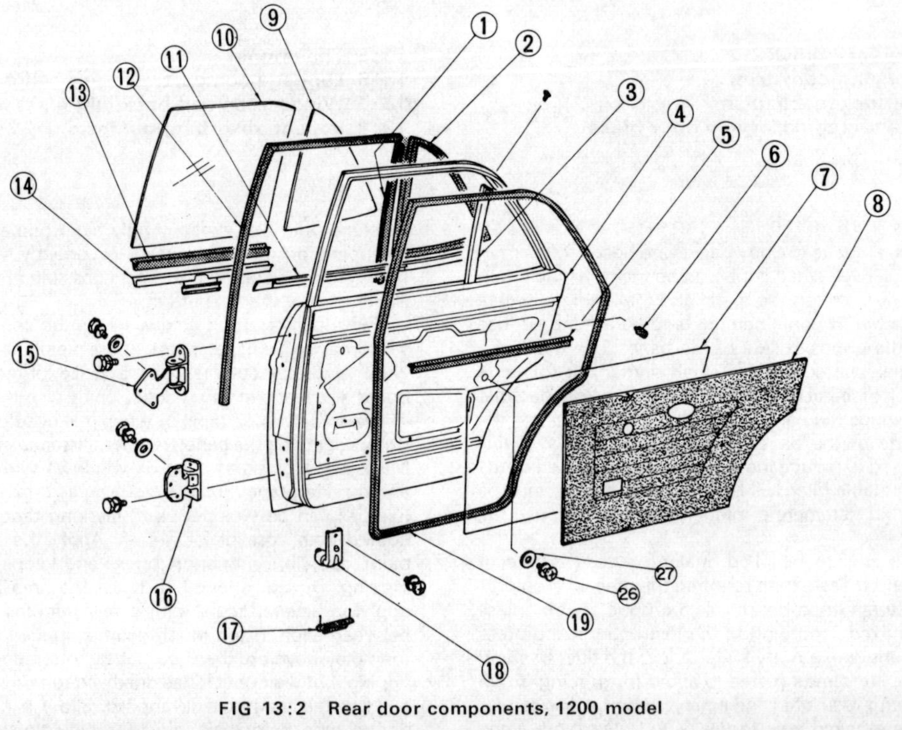

FIG 13:2 Rear door components, 1200 model

Key to Fig 13:2 1 Rubber channel 2 Partition weatherstrip 3 Partition sash 4 Door panel 5 Weatherstrip 6 Bumper rubber 7 Seal panel 8 Door trim 9 Door corner glass 10 Door glass 11 Outer moulding 12 Rubber channel 13 Glazing rubber 14 Bottom channel 15 Upper hinge 16 Lower hinge 17 Drain hole cover 18 Door glass stopper 19 Weatherstrip 26 Screws 27 Washer

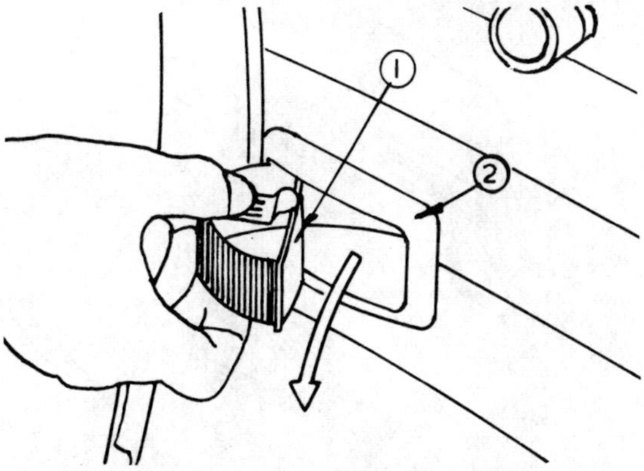

FIG 13:3 Removing the ashtray assembly

13:2 Removing door trim

FIGS 13:1 and **13:2** show the components of typical front and rear doors. Door trim removal is similar for either. The door must be kept open during these operations.

Removal:

Take out the retaining screws for the inside door lock escutcheon, window regulator handle and armrest, and remove these components. Remove the ashtray where fitted as shown in **FIG 13:3**, removing the tray 1 firstly, then removing the outer case 2. Pull the door trim away from the door panel, releasing the spring clips which hold it in position.

Refit in the reverse order, ensuring that the damp screen, if fitted, is in perfect condition.

13:3 Door lock mechanism

Front door lock removal:

Remove the door trim as described in **Section 13:2**, then remove the door seal panel. Refer to **FIG 13:4**. Remove the door lock knob 1, then remove the remote control rod which connects the lock to the lock cylinder from the cylinder. Remove the fixing screw from the inside handle 2 and the screws attaching the lock assembly 3. Remove the lock assembly from the service hole in the door panel, withdrawing the outside handle rod from the opening on the lock assembly. Detach the leaf clip and remove the lock cylinder.

Refitting:

Refer to **FIG 13:5**. Install the remote control and adjust so that the stopper 6 of the inside handle 3 lightly contacts the baseplate of the lock 1. If the remote control is installed with the inside handle 3 pulled, the locking plate 4 does not mesh with the ratchet completely at full stroke and the lock knob will not lower. On 120Y move the inside handle to the rear in the elongated slots, with the lock knob in the closed position, as far as possible and secured in this position.

Set the locking plate 4 to the full ratchet position, insert the nylon nut 9 on the handle rod 8 into the locking plate hole 4, then adjust the nylon nut and secure it with adhesive, in a position where the outside handle rod 8 is provided with .08 to .12 inch (2 to 3mm) play in its

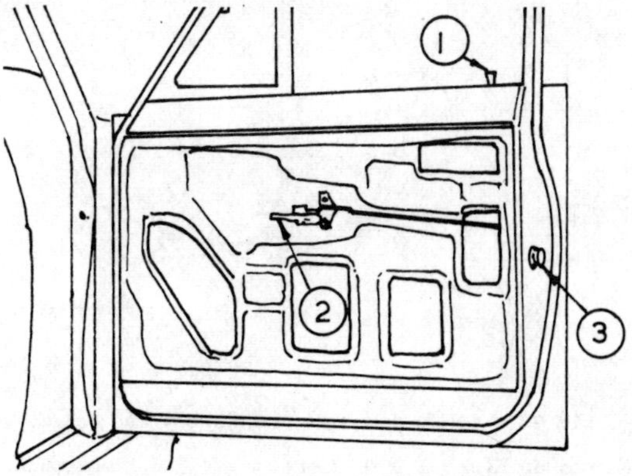

FIG 13:4 Removing the door lock mechanism

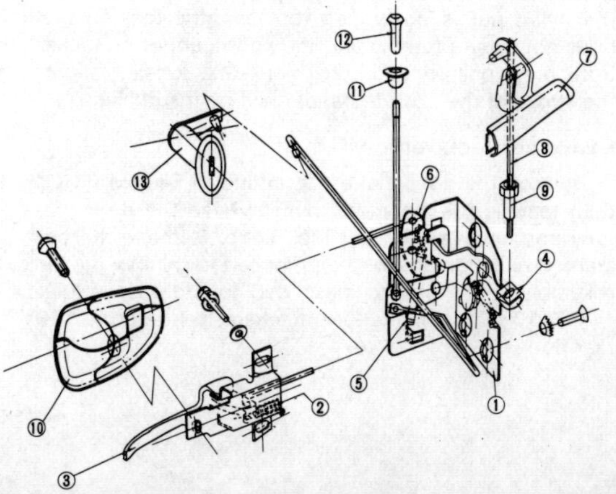

FIG 13:5 Front door lock mechanism, 1200 model

Key to Fig 13:5 1 Door lock 2 Spring 3 Inside handle 4 Locking plate 5 Spring 6 Stopper 7 Outside handle 8 Outside handle rod 9 Nylon nut 10 Escutcheon 11 Knob grommet 12 Door lock knob 13 Lock cylinder

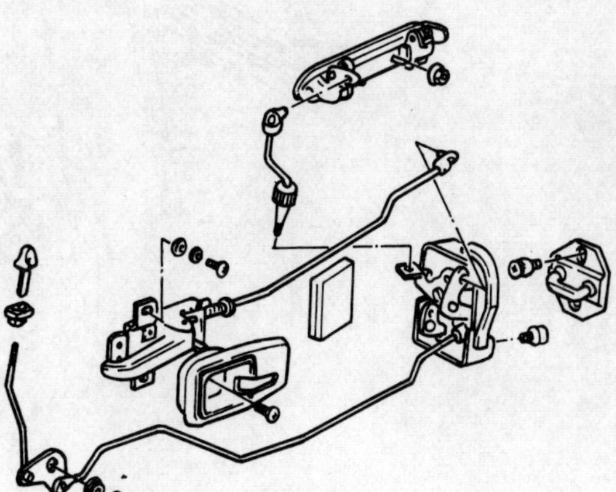

FIG 13:6 The components of a 120Y rear door lock mechanism

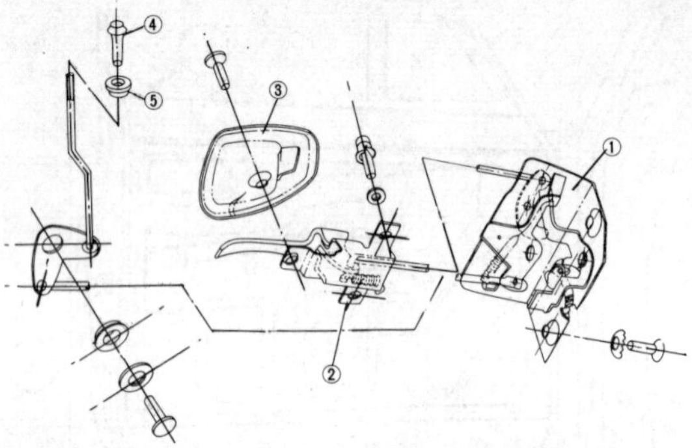

FIG 13:7 Rear door lock mechanism, early cars

Key to Fig 13:7 1 Door lock 2 Inside handle 3 Escutcheon 4 Door lock knob 5 Knob grommet

stroke, .004 to .118 inch (.1 to 3 mm) on 120Y models. If the nylon nut is positioned too low, the locking plate does not mesh properly and the knob cannot be locked: If the nut is positioned too high or works loose in service, the stroke of the outside handle will be insufficient.

Rear door lock removal:

Remove the door trim as described in **Section 13:2**, then remove the door seal panel. Raise the door glass fully and remove the door lock knob. Remove the bell-crank installation screw, then proceed to remove the lock assembly in the manner described for front door locks.

FIG 13:6 shows the lock mechanism fitted to a 120Y rear door.

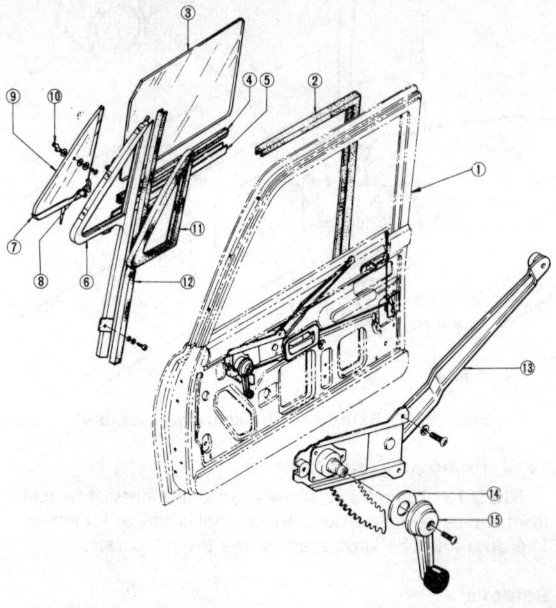

FIG 13:8 Front door glass and regulator components, Typical

Key to Fig 13:8 1 Door panel 2 Rubber channel 3 Window glass 4 Glazing rubber 5 Bottom channel 6 Ventilator frame 7 Ventilator rubber channel 8 Catch handle 9 Ventilator glass 10 Pivot bracket 11 Weatherstrip 12 Rubber channel 13 Window regulator 14 Washer 15 Regulator handle

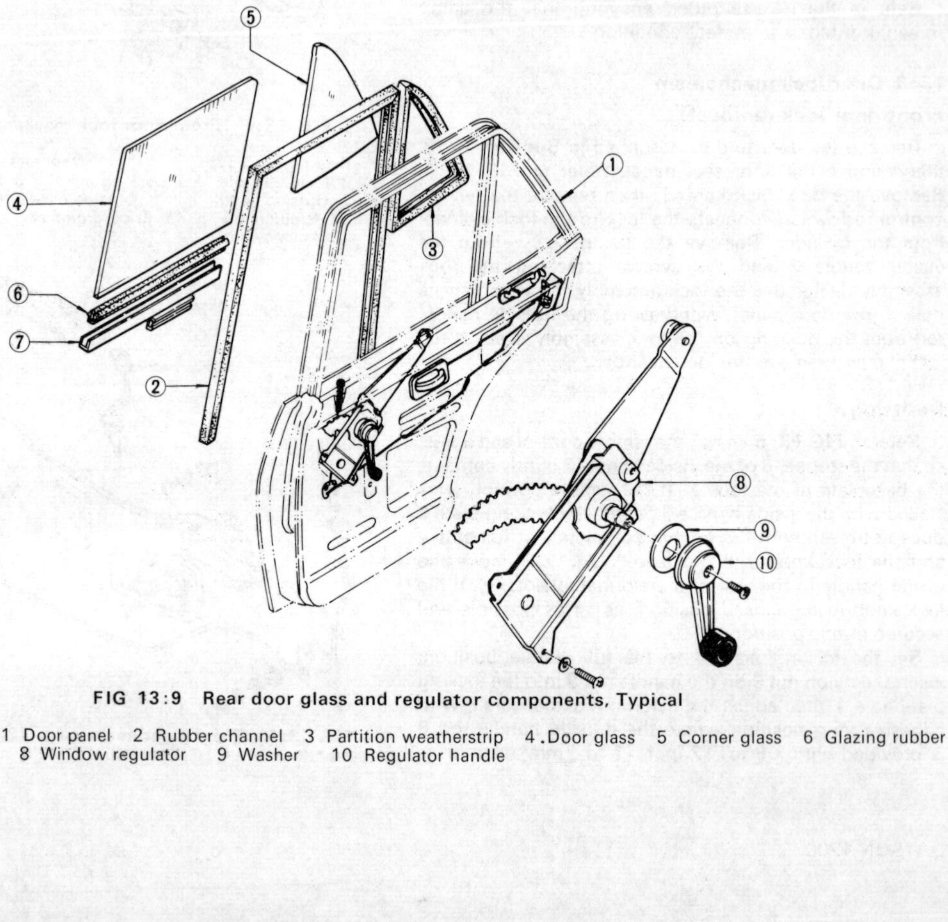

FIG 13:9 Rear door glass and regulator components, Typical

Key to Fig 13:9 1 Door panel 2 Rubber channel 3 Partition weatherstrip 4 Door glass 5 Corner glass 6 Glazing rubber 7 Bottom channel 8 Window regulator 9 Washer 10 Regulator handle

FIG 13:10 Removing front door ventilator, 1200 model

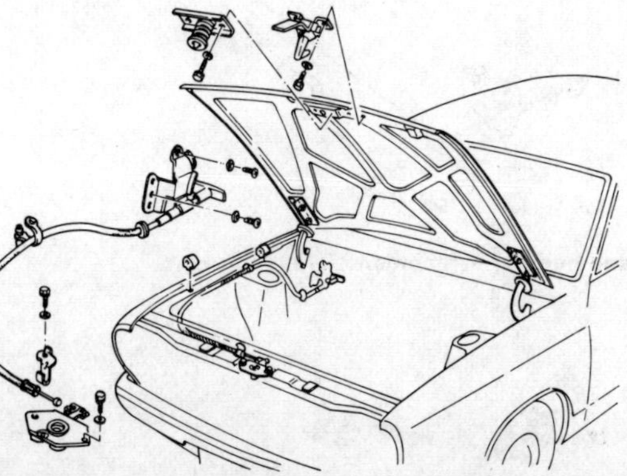

FIG 13:12 Showing the bonnet attachments on 120Y models

Refitting:

This is a reversal of the removal procedure. Note that all installation notes for front door locks apply. **FIG 13:7** shows the components of the 1000, 1200 rear door lock.

13:4 Window regulator and door glass

FIG 13:8 shows the components for front door assemblies on early cars, **FIG 13:9** those for rear door assemblies. Remove the door trim and seal panel as described previously, on 120Y remove outside moulding and inside weatherstrip. Remove the door glass stopper and lower the glass completely. Remove the front door ventilator on early cars after taking out the four fixing screws, as shown in **FIG 13:10**.

On 120Y models detach the front lower sash from the glass panel after removing the two retaining screws, leave it in position, support the glass and remove the three retaining screws of the bottom channel. Pull the door glass upward and remove it. Remove the three regulator assembly installation screws and on 120Y the two guide channel screws and remove the regulator assembly and guide channel on 120Y through the bottom opening in the door panel. **FIG 13:11** gives an exploded view of the front door lock and window regulating mechanisms.

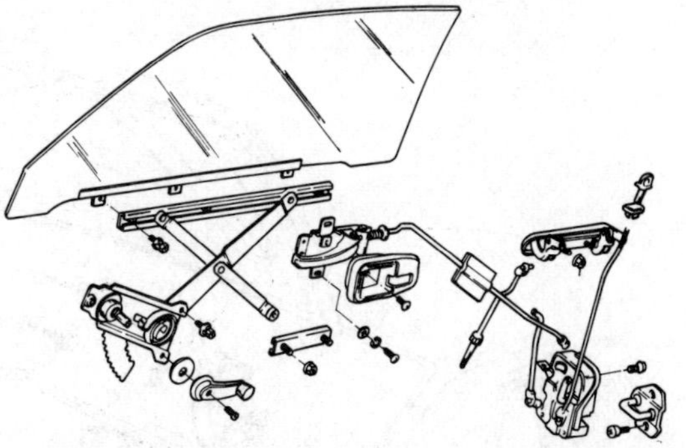

FIG 13:11 120Y front door lock and window regulating mechanisms

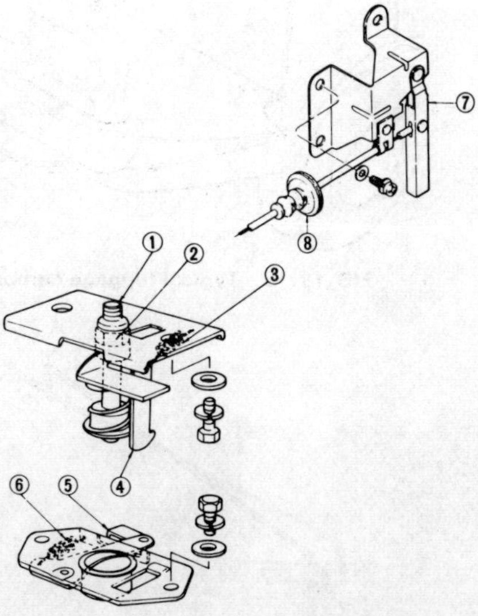

FIG 13:13 Bonnet lock components, early cars

Key to Fig 13:13 1 Dovetail bolt 2 Dovetail nut 3 Spring 4 Safety catch lever 5 Locking lever 6 Spring 7 Lock control lever 8 Rubber grommet

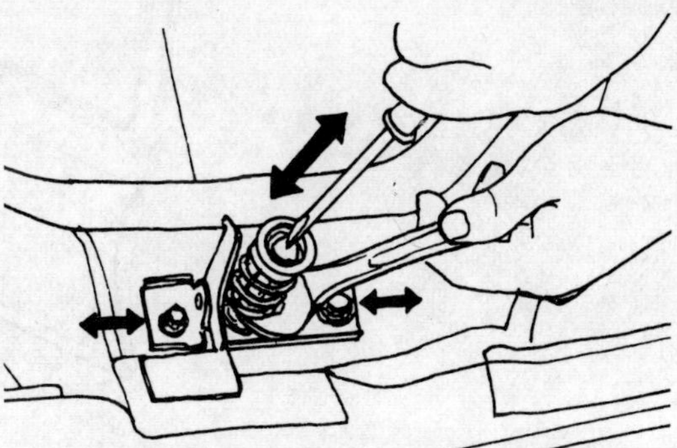

FIG 13:14 Adjusting the bonnet dovetail bolt

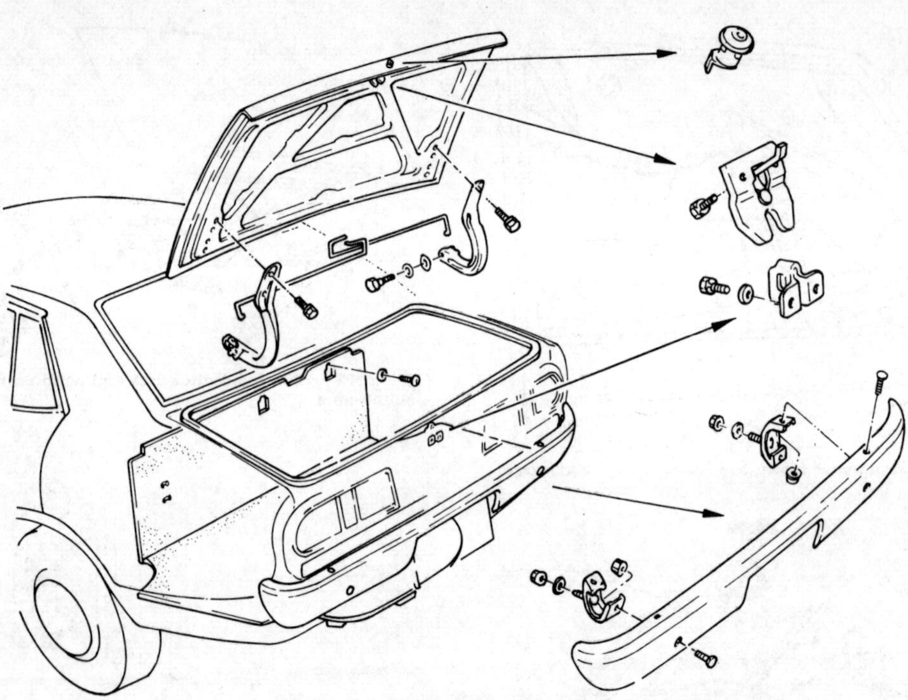

FIG 13:15 Typical luggage compartment lid and bumper attachments (120Y shown)

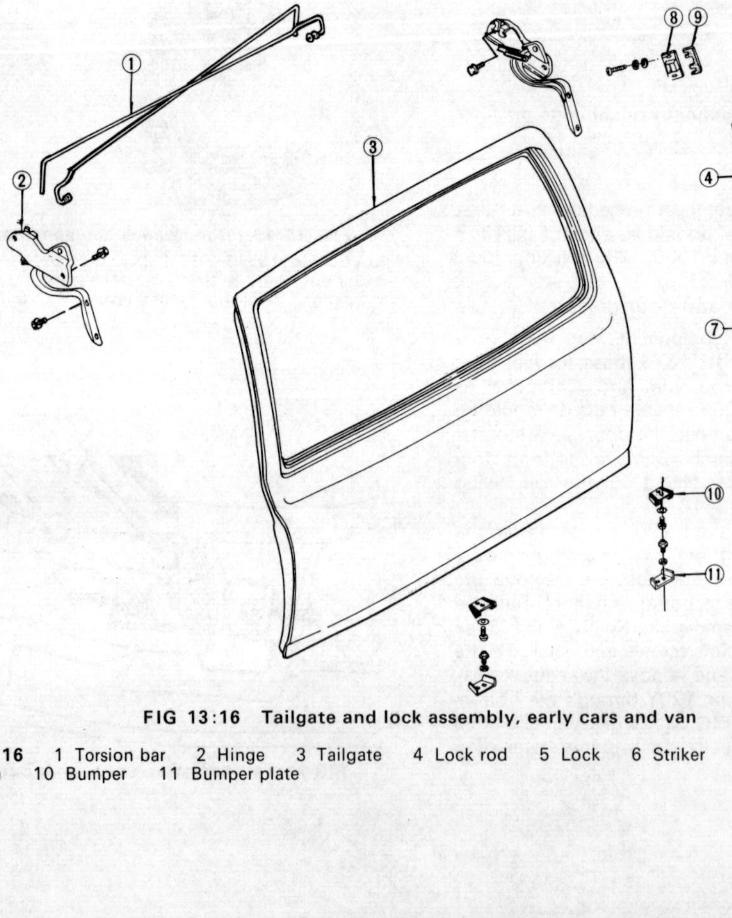

FIG 13:16 Tailgate and lock assembly, early cars and van

Key to Fig 13:16 1 Torsion bar 2 Hinge 3 Tailgate 4 Lock rod 5 Lock 6 Striker 7 Striker shim 8 Dovetail 9 Dovetail shim 10 Bumper 11 Bumper plate

Refitting:

This is a reversal of the removal procedure.

On 120Y the glass is aligned by partially tightening the front and rear lower sashes. With the glass in the up position align the rear lower sash with the glass and the front lower sash. Raise and lower glass to gain a good fit. Move the guide channel up and down to align the glass with the door aperture. Move front lower sash to obtain free play.

13:5 The bonnet

Removal:

FIG 13:12 shows the complete bonnet and fastening installation on 120Y models for guidance in removing, refitting and adjusting the bonnet on these cars. Earlier cars are very similar.

Where applicable, disconnect the windscreen washer hose at the bonnet nozzle and then position some sheets to prevent the bonnet from scratching the surrounding paintwork. Mark the hinge locations to ensure correct refitting and remove the four hinge bolts, not forgetting to have an assistant at hand to support the bonnet as it is released.

Refitting:

This is a reversal of the removal instructions, making sure of correct alignment.

Bonnet lock removal:

FIG 13:13 shows the early bonnet lock components. Remove the radiator grille. Disconnect the operating cable from the lower bonnet lock plate. Remove both upper and lower lock plate assemblies after removing the two fixing screws from each. If necessary, the lock control can be removed from the inside of the car.

Refitting:

This is the reverse of the removal instructions.

Bonnet lock adjustment:

The bonnet lock upper plate on early models is provided with slotted mountings to allow adjustment from side to side, the lower plate with slotted mountings to allow adjustment from front to rear. Using these combinations, adjust so that the two parts of the lock are correctly centralized. The male hood lock and secondary latch on 120Y models are adjustable from side to side and from front to rear, and are used to align with female lock.

If excessive force is needed to operate the bonnet release mechanism, release the dovetail bolt retaining nut and increase the length of the bolt as shown in **FIG 13:14**. This will reduce the force of the spring and allow lighter operation of the release lever.

13:6 Luggage compartment and tailgate locks

The luggage compartment lid and lock components fitted to Sedan models are shown in **FIG 13:15**, the torsion bar tailgate fitted to Station Wagon and Van models being shown in **FIG 13:16**.

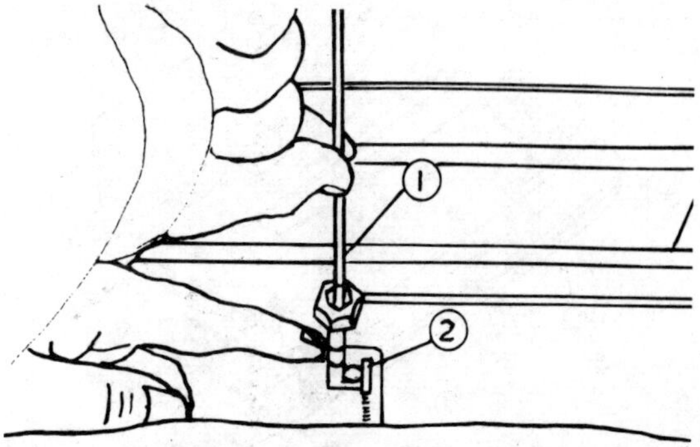

FIG 13:17 Removing the tailgate lock rod, 1200 model

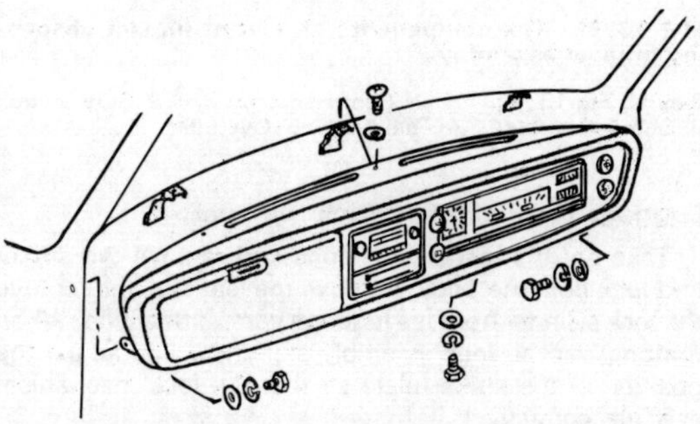

FIG 13:18 Removing the facia, 1200 model

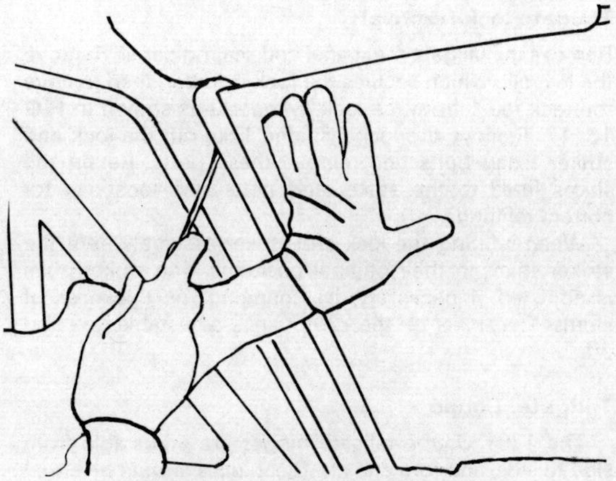

FIG 13:19 Removing the windscreen

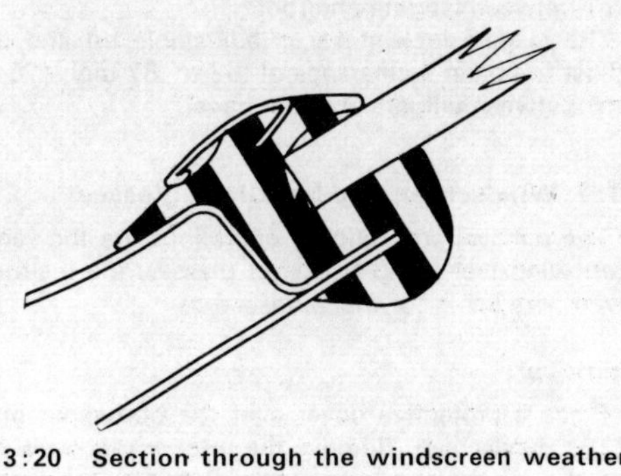

FIG 13:20 Section through the windscreen weatherstrip

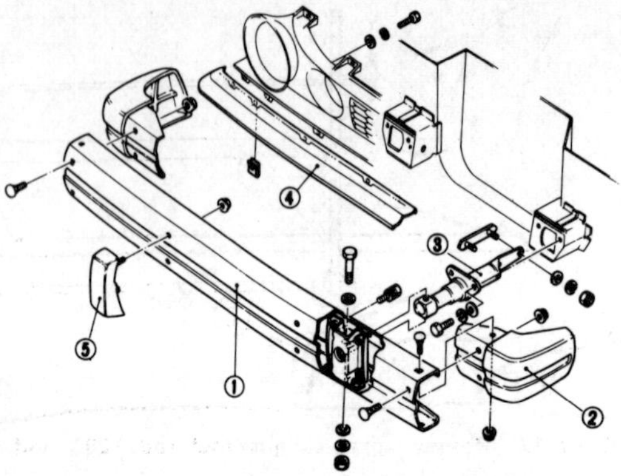

FIG 13:21 The components of a front impact absorbing bumper assembly

Key to Fig 13:21 1 Centre section 2 Side section 3 Shock absorber 4 Trim bar 5 Overrider

Luggage compartment lock removal:

Take out the installation bolts and remove the striker and lock from the body. Remove the leaf clip and remove the lock cylinder from the luggage compartment lid. When refitting, set the lock assembly stationary and adjust the position of the striker plate so that the lock mechanism engages correctly.

Tailgate lock removal:

Remove the tailgate trim panel and sealing panel. Remove the leaf clip which secures the lock cylinder, then remove the lock rod 1 from the lock cylinder 2 as shown in **FIG 13:17**. Remove the lock cylinder. Take out the lock and striker fixing bolts and remove these parts. Retain the shims fitted to the striker and note their locations for correct refitting.

When refitting the lock and striker assembly, refit the striker shims in their original positions. The striker plate is adjusted, if necessary, by changing the thickness of shims. The striker on the 120Y van is adjustable fore and aft.

Tailgate, Coupé

The 120Y Coupé tailgate hinges are adjustable from side to side, and fore and aft. Clearances should be equal on each side, and a clearance of .16 to .24 inch (4 to 6 mm) between tailgate and roof.

The tailgate lock striker is adjustable up and down. Adjust to obtain a clearance of .63 to .87 inch (16 to 22 mm) between tailgate and rear panel.

13:7 Windscreen and backlight glasses

The removal and refitting operations are the same for both windscreen and backlight glasses, the instructions given here being for the windscreen.

Removal:

Place a protective cover over the bodywork in front of the windscreen. Remove the interior rear-view mirror and the windscreen wiper arms. Run a suitable pointed instrument around the inside of the screen to loosen the rubber moulding from the body flange. Apply firm hand pressure to the glass to push the windscreen out of the aperture, lipping the rubber surround over the flange as shown in **FIG 13:19**. Have an assistant ready to steady the glass from the outside. Remove the chrome mouldings from the rubber before removing the rubber from the glass.

Refitting:

Before fitting the glass, clean the aperture flange of all old sealer and make sure that there are no particles of glass in the weatherstrip channels. Renew the rubber if it is cracked or perished, otherwise leaks may occur. Fit the weatherstrip to the glass. Thread a length of strong blind cord around the body flange slot in the rubber weatherstrip so that the ends of the cord come out at the lower centre of the windscreen. Cross the ends of the cord at this point, then place the windscreen assembly into position, centring it in the bottom of the aperture. Apply steady hand pressure to the outside of the glass while an assistant pulls out the cord to lip the rubber over the body flange. Work equally on each side of the windscreen. Do not fit one side then try to fit the other, as stress may be induced. Use a pressure gun to inject sealing adhesive to the entire periphery of all the flanges, removing excess compound with a suitable solvent which will not harm the paintwork. Refit the chrome moulding. **FIG 13:20** shows a section through the windscreen weatherstrip. Refit the interior mirror and wiper arms.

13:8 Impact absorbing bumpers

At both front and rear these consist of a central bumper bar, mounted on two gas-filled, strut-type, shock absorbers and two side pieces. The central portion is designed to withstand or reduce the effect of direct impact while the side pieces, consisting of a steel panel and porous urethane or rubber, reduce incidental damage to the car bodywork.

The components of a typical front bumper assembly are shown in **FIG 13:21**, the rear bumper is very similar.

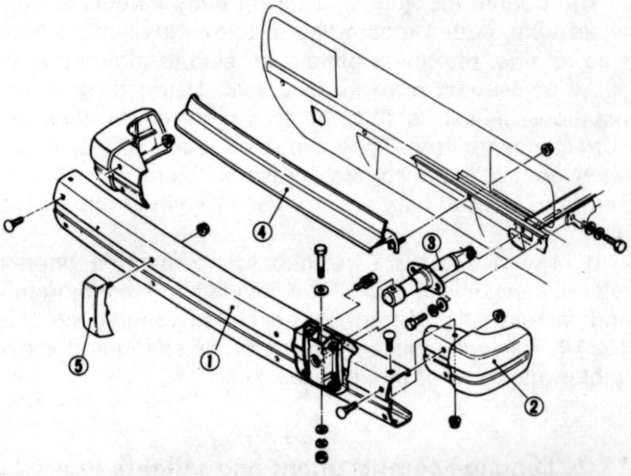

FIG 13:22 The components of a rear impact absorbing bumper assembly

Key to Fig 13:22 1 Centre section 2 Side section 3 Shock absorber 4 Trim bar 5 Overrider

Instructions for checking the bumper installed height and shock absorber operation are given, but it is stressed that on no account should any attempt be made to adjust or dismantle a shock absorber unit.

Front:

This is shown in **FIG 13:21** and removal is effected as follows:

Remove the bolts attaching the centre bar to the shock absorbers and remove the bumper, then remove the bolts securing the shock absorbers to the chassis members and lift off.

After refitting the bumper assembly in the reverse order, it must be checked for height with the car standing on level ground at kerb weight and with the tyres correctly inflated. The distance between the top surface of the bumper and the ground must be between 19.57 and 22.56 inch (497 to 573 mm) when measured at the two mounting locations. If adjustment is required, loosen the shock absorber mounting bolts and adjust as necessary.

The length of the shock absorber inner member projecting from the outer body tube must be between 2.8 and 3.0 inch (70 to 77 mm).

When suitably applying pressure, a jack used sideways for instance, to the bumper bar, the shock absorber should retract by 2 inch (50 mm) and return to its original position when pressure is released. Any shock absorber failing these checks should be renewed, making sure that both units are by the same maker and of the same rating.

Rear:

Refer to **FIG 13:22**. From inside the luggage compartment undo the five bolts securing the trim bar 4 and remove it.

Unscrew the nuts retaining the bumper to the shock absorbers and remove the bumper. Finally, unscrew the bolts securing the shock absorbers to the chassis members and lift off.

Refit the bumper assembly in the reverse order and check its installed position, dimensions are the same as for the front bumper.

NOTES

APPENDIX

Inches	Decimals	Millimetres	Inches to Millimetres		Millimetres to Inches	
			Inches	mm	mm	Inches
$\frac{1}{64}$	.015625	.3969	001	.0254	.01	.00039
$\frac{1}{32}$	.03125	.7937	.002	.0508	.02	.00079
$\frac{3}{64}$	.046875	1.1906	.003	.0762	.03	.00118
$\frac{1}{16}$	.0625	1.5875	.004	.1016	.04	.00157
$\frac{5}{64}$	.078125	1.9844	.005	.1270	.05	.00197
$\frac{3}{32}$	.09375	2.3812	.006	.1524	.06	.00236
$\frac{7}{64}$	.109375	2.7781	.007	.1778	.07	.00276
$\frac{1}{8}$	.125	3.1750	.008	.2032	.08	.00315
$\frac{9}{64}$	.140625	3.5719	.009	.2286	.09	.00354
$\frac{5}{32}$	.15625	3.9687	.01	.254	.1	.00394
$\frac{11}{64}$	.171875	4.3656	.02	.508	.2	.00787
$\frac{3}{16}$	.1875	4.7625	.03	.762	.3	.01181
$\frac{13}{64}$	.203125	5·1594	.04	1.016	.4	.01575
$\frac{7}{32}$	.21875	5.5562	.05	1.270	.5	.01969
$\frac{15}{64}$	.234375	5.9531	.06	1.524	.6	.02362
$\frac{1}{4}$	.25	6.3500	.07	1.778	.7	.02756
$\frac{17}{64}$	.265625	6.7469	.08	2.032	.8	.03150
$\frac{9}{32}$	.28125	7.1437	.09	2.286	.9	.03543
$\frac{19}{64}$	.296875	7.5406	.1	2.54	1	.03937
$\frac{5}{16}$	.3125	7.9375	.2	5.08	2	.07874
$\frac{21}{64}$	.328125	8.3344	.3	7.62	3	.11811
$\frac{11}{32}$	.34375	8.7312	.4	10.16	4	.15748
$\frac{23}{64}$	.359375	9.1281	.5	12.70	5	.19685
$\frac{3}{8}$	.375	9.5250	.6	15.24	6	.23622
$\frac{25}{64}$	.390625	9.9219	.7	17.78	7	.27559
$\frac{13}{32}$	.40625	10.3187	.8	20.32	8	.31496
$\frac{27}{64}$	.421875	10.7156	.9	22.86	9	.35433
$\frac{7}{16}$	.4375	11.1125	1	25.4	10	.39370
$\frac{29}{64}$	.453125	11.5094	2	50.8	11	.43307
$\frac{15}{32}$	.46875	11.9062	3	76.2	12	.47244
$\frac{31}{64}$	.484375	12.3031	4	101.6	13	.51181
$\frac{1}{2}$	.5	12.7000	5	127.0	14	.55118
$\frac{33}{64}$	.515625	13.0969	6	152.4	15	.59055
$\frac{17}{32}$	.53125	13.4937	7	177.8	16	.62992
$\frac{35}{64}$	.546875	13.8906	8	203.2	17	.66929
$\frac{9}{16}$	.5625	14.2875	9	228.6	18	.70866
$\frac{37}{64}$	.578125	14.6844	10	254.0	19	.74803
$\frac{19}{32}$	.59375	15.0812	11	279.4	20	.78740
$\frac{39}{64}$	.609375	15.4781	12	304.8	21	.82677
$\frac{5}{8}$	.625	15.8750	13	330.2	22	.86614
$\frac{41}{64}$	.640625	16.2719	14	355.6	23	.90551
$\frac{21}{32}$	.65625	16.6687	15	381.0	24	.94488
$\frac{43}{64}$	.671875	17.0656	16	406.4	25	.98425
$\frac{11}{16}$	.6875	17.4625	17	431.8	26	1.02362
$\frac{45}{64}$	.703125	17.8594	18	457.2	27	1.06299
$\frac{23}{32}$	.71875	18.2562	19	482.6	28	1.10236
$\frac{47}{64}$	.734375	18.6531	20	508.0	29	1.14173
$\frac{3}{4}$	.75	19.0500	21	533.4	30	1.18110
$\frac{49}{64}$	.765625	19.4469	22	558.8	31	1.22047
$\frac{25}{32}$	.78125	19.8437	23	584.2	32	1.25984
$\frac{51}{64}$	.796875	20.2406	24	609.6	33	1.29921
$\frac{13}{16}$	.8125	20.6375	25	635.0	34	1.33858
$\frac{53}{64}$	.828125	21.0344	26	660.4	35	1.37795
$\frac{27}{32}$	.84375	21.4312	27	685.8	36	1.41732
$\frac{55}{64}$	.859375	21.8281	28	711.2	37	1.4567
$\frac{7}{8}$	.875	22.2250	29	736.6	38	1.4961
$\frac{57}{64}$	.890625	22.6219	30	762.0	39	1.5354
$\frac{29}{32}$	.90625	23.0187	31	787.4	40	1.5748
$\frac{59}{64}$	.921875	23.4156	32	812.8	41	1.6142
$\frac{15}{16}$	.9375	23.8125	33	838.2	42	1.6535
$\frac{61}{64}$	.953125	24.2094	34	863.6	43	1.6929
$\frac{31}{32}$	.96875	24.6062	35	889.0	44	1.7323
$\frac{63}{64}$	.984375	25.0031	36	914.4	45	1.7717

UNITS	Pints to Litres	Gallons to Litres	Litres to Pints	Litres to Gallons	Miles to Kilometres	Kilometres to Miles	Lbs. per sq. In. to Kg. per sq. Cm.	Kg. per sq. Cm. to Lbs. per sq. In.
1	.57	4.55	1.76	.22	1.61	.62	.07	14.22
2	1.14	9.09	3.52	.44	3.22	1.24	.14	28.50
3	1.70	13.64	5.28	.66	4.83	1.86	.21	42.67
4	2.27	18.18	7.04	.88	6.44	2.49	.28	56.89
5	2.84	22.73	8.80	1.10	8.05	3.11	.35	71.12
6	3.41	27.28	10.56	1.32	9.66	3.73	.42	85.34
7	3.98	31.82	12.32	1.54	11.27	4.35	.49	99.56
8	4.55	36.37	14.08	1.76	12.88	4.97	.56	113.79
9		40.91	15.84	1.98	14.48	5.59	.63	128.00
10		45.46	17.60	2.20	16.09	6.21	.70	142.23
20				4.40	32.19	12.43	1.41	284.47
30				6.60	48.28	18.64	2.11	426.70
40				8.80	64.37	24.85		
50					80.47	31.07		
60					96.56	37.28		
70					112.65	43.50		
80					128.75	49.71		
90					144.84	55.92		
100					160.93	62.14		

UNITS	Lb ft to kgm	Kgm to lb ft	UNITS	Lb ft to kgm	Kgm to lb ft
1	.138	7.233	7	.967	50.631
2	.276	14.466	8	1.106	57.864
3	.414	21.699	9	1.244	65.097
4	.553	28.932	10	1.382	72.330
5	.691	36.165	20	2.765	144.660
6	.829	43.398	30	4.147	216.990

TECHNICAL DATA

Dimensions are in millimetres with inches in brackets

ENGINE

Capacity, bore and stroke:		
A10: 988 cc (60.3 cu. inch)	73 × 59 mm (2.87 × 2.32 inch)	
A12: 1171 cc (71.5 cu. inch)	73 × 70 mm (2.87 × 2.76 inch)	
A13: 1288 cc (78.59 cu. inch)	73 × 77 mm (2.87 × 3.03 inch)	
A14: 1397 cc (85.24 cu. inch)	76 × 77 mm (2.99 × 3.03 inch)	
Compression ratio	8.5 or 9.0:1	
Crankshaft:		
Journal diameter	49.951 to 49.964 (1.9666 to 1.9671)	
Clearance	.020 to .062 (.0008 to .0024)	
End float	.05 to .15 (.002 to .006)	
Crankpin diameter	44.961 to 44.974 (1.7701 to 1.7706)	
Clearance	.020 to .050 (.0008 to .0020)	
Runout limit	.05 (.002)	
Connecting rods:		
Side clearance	.2 to .3 (.008 to .012)	
Weight difference	5 gr. max.	
Gudgeon pins:		
Diameter, 1397 cc	18.995 to 19.000 (.7478 to .7480)	
others	17.447 to 17.452 (.6869 to .6871)	
Clearance in piston, 1397 cc	.008 to .012 (.0003 to .0005)	
others	.006 to .008 (.0002 to .0003)	
Fit in connecting rod (interference)	.017 to .034 (.0007 to .0013)	
Pistons:		
Diameter, 1397 cc	75.967 to 76.017 (2.9908 to 2.9927)	
others	72.967 to 73.017 (2.8727 to 2.8747)	
Oversizes	.5, 1.0, 1.5 (.019, .039, .058)	
Piston rings:		
Clearance in groove:		
Top	.04 to .07 (.0016 to .0028)	
Middle	.03 to .06 (.0012 to .0024)	
Bottom	.04 to .08 (.0016 to .0031)	
Fitted gap:		
Top	.20 to .35 (.0079 to .0138)	
Middle	.15 to .30 (.0059 to .0118)	
Bottom	.30 to .90 (.0118 to .0354)	
Camshaft:		
End float	.01 to .05 (.0004 to .002)	
Valves:		
Head diameter:	*988/1171 cc*	*1288/1397 cc*
Inlet	35 (1.378)	37 (1.46)
Exhaust	29 (1.142)	30 (1.18)
Stem diameter:	*1288 cc*	*Others*
Inlet	7.95 to 7.96	7.97 to 7.99
Exhaust	7.95 to 7.96	7.95 to 7.96
Clearance in guide:		
Inlet	.015 to .045 (.0006 to .0018)	
Exhaust	.040 to .070 (.0016 to .0028)	
Valve springs:	*988 cc*	*Others*
Free length	45.7 (1.799)	46.5 (1.831)
Rocker clearances:		
Cold	.25 (.010)	
Hot	.35 (.014)	

FUEL SYSTEM

Carburetter:		
988 cc engines	Hitachi DCG 286	
1171 cc engines	Hitachi DCG 306	
1288 cc engines	Hitachi DCH 306-6 or -7	
1397 cc engines	Hitachi DCH 306-10 to -15	
988 cc engines:	*Primary*	*Secondary*
Choke	26	28
Venturi	20	24
Main jet	98	140
Idle jet	40	—
Power jet	60	
Float level	19 ± 1	
1171 cc engines:		
Choke	26	30
Venturi	20	26
Main jet	98	135
Idle jet	43	50
Power jet	60	
Float level	19 ± 1	
1288 cc engines:		
Choke	26	30
Venturi	22	27
Main jet	104	145
Idle jet	43	50
Power jet	55	
1397 cc engines (1975):		
Choke	26	30
Venturi	23	27
Main jet	102 (104 Calif.)	150
Idle jet	45	50
Power jet	45 (43 Calif.)	
1397 cc engines (1976):		
Choke	26	30
Venturi	23	27
Main jet	102 (104 Calif.)	145
Idle jet	45	50
Power jet	45 (43 Calif.)	
Fuel pump:		
Type	Mechanical	
Drive	Eccentric on camshaft	
Pressures:		
988 and 1171 cc engines	2.6 lb/sq. inch	
1288 and 1397 cc engines	3.0 to 3.8 lb/sq. inch	

IGNITION SYSTEM

Sparking plugs:	
Type, 988 cc engines	Hitachi L45 or NGK B-6E
1171 cc engines	Hitachi L46-P or NGK BP-6E
other engines	Hitachi L46-PW or NGK BP-5ES
Gap, 1397 cc engines	1.0 to 1.1 (.039 to .043)
other engines	.8 to .9 (.031 to .035)

Distributor:	
Make	Hitachi or Mitsubishi
Direction of rotation	Anticlockwise
Firing order	1–3–4–2
Points gap	.45 to .55 (.017 to .021)
Dwell angle	49 to 59 deg.
Electronic distributor:	
Make and type, manual	Hitachi D4F5–01
automatic	Hitachi D4F4–02
Air gap	0.2 to 0.4 (.008 to .016)
Timing	See **Chapter 3, Section 3:5**

COOLING SYSTEM

Type	Pressurised with fan and pump
Thermostat opening temperatures:	
Standard	82°C
Cold	88°C
Tropical	76.5°C
Valve lift (all types)	8 (.31)
Radiator pressure	13 lb/sq. inch

CLUTCH

Type	Single dry plate, diaphragm spring
Operation	Cable or hydraulic
Pedal adjustment	See **Chapter 5**

TRANSMISSION

Manual:		
Type	3- or 4-forward speed and reverse	
Synchromesh	All forward ratios	
Ratios, 988 and 1171 cc engines:	*3-speed*	*4-speed*
First	3.380:1	3.757:1
Second	1.734:1	2.169:1
Third	1:1	1.404:1
Fourth	—	1:1
Reverse	3.640:1	3.640:1
Ratios, 1288 cc engines	As 4-speed above	
Ratios, 1397 cc engines:	*4-speed*	*5-speed*
First	3.513:1	3.382:1
Second	2.170:1	2.013:1
Third	1.378:1	1.312:1
Fourth	1:1	1:1
Fifth	—	0.854:1
Reverse	3.764:1	3.570:1
Automatic:		
Type	3N71B	
Ratios:		
First	2.458:1	
Second	1.458:1	
Third	1:1	
Reverse	2.182:1	
Final gear ratio	3.7:1, 3.889:1 or 3.9:1	

FRONT SUSPENSION

Type:			
Early cars	Transverse leaf		
Later cars	McPherson strut		
Dampers	Telescopic hydraulic		
Suspension geometry:	*Castor*	*Camber*	*KPI*
988 cc	2° 15′	1° 45′	6° 30′
1171 cc	1° 15′	1° 5′	7° 55′
120Y models	1° 65′ ± 50′	1° 60′ ± 50′	8° ± 50′
1288 cc	1° 65′ ± 50′	90′ ± 50′	8° ± 50′
1397 cc	1° 45′ ± 45′	70′ ± 45′	8° 17′ ± 45′

REAR SUSPENSION

Type	Semi-elliptic leaf spring
Dampers	Telescopic hydraulic

STEERING

Type	Recirculating ball			
Ratio	15:1			
Toe-in (unladen):	*988 cc*	*1171 cc*	*1288 cc*	*1397 cc*
	2 to 3	4 to 6	2 to 4	2 to 4
	(.08 to .12)	(.16 to .24)	(.08 to .16)	(.08 to .16)

BRAKING SYSTEM

Type	Footbrake, hydraulic on four wheels Handbrake, mechanical on rear wheels Front, disc or drum. Rear, drum
Pedal free play	See **Chapter 11, Section 11:2**
Hydraulic fluid	Girling Green or to specification DOT 3

ELECTRICAL EQUIPMENT

System type	12-volt, negative earth
Alternator	According to model and year
Minimum brush length	7 (.28)
Starter type	Hitachi, pre-engaged S114–87
Minimum brush length	7 (.28)
Fuses	Six or eight. Circuits and ratings shown on fuse board

CAPACITIES

Fuel tank:	
988 cc models:	
Saloon	35 litres (7.7 gallons)
Estate	30 litres (6.6 gallons)
1171 cc models:	
Saloon	40 litres (8.8 gallons)
Estate	38 litres (8.4 gallons)
120Y models:	
Saloon	47 litres ($10\frac{3}{8}$ gallons)
Coupé	43 litres ($9\frac{1}{2}$ gallons)
Van	40 litres ($8\frac{3}{4}$ gallons)
B210 models:	
Saloon	44 litres ($9\frac{5}{8}$ gallons)
Coupé	43 litres ($9\frac{1}{2}$ gallons)

Engine oil:	
988 and 1171 engines	2.7 litres ($4\frac{3}{4}$ pints)
120Y models	3.2 litres ($5\frac{1}{2}$ pints)
B210 models	3.6 litres ($6\frac{1}{4}$ pints)
Cooling system:	
988 and 1171 engines	4.5 litres (8 pints)
120Y models	5.1 litres ($8\frac{3}{4}$ pints)
B210 models	5.8 litres ($10\frac{1}{4}$ pints)
Gearbox:	
4-speed	1.3 litres ($2\frac{1}{4}$ pints)
5-speed	1.7 litres (3 pints)
Automatic transmission	5.3 litres ($9\frac{1}{4}$ pints)

TORQUE WRENCH SETTINGS

Settings are given in kgm (lb ft)

988 and 1171 cc engines:	
Cylinder head bolts	5.5 to 6 (40 to 43)
Connecting rod nuts	3.2 to 3.6 (23 to 26)
Flywheel bolts, 988 cc	4.5 to 5.5 (33 to 40)
1171 cc	5.5 to 7.5 (47 to 54)
Main bearing cap bolts	5.0 to 6.0 (36 to 43)
Camshaft sprocket bolts	4.0 to 4.8 (29 to 35)
Crankshaft pulley bolt	15.0 to 16.0 (108 to 116)
Oil pump bolts	1.1 to 1.7 (8 to 12)
1288 and 1397 cc engines:	
Cylinder head bolts	7.0 to 7.5 (51 to 54)
Rocker shaft bolts	2.0 to 2.5 (14 to 18)
Flywheel bolts	7.5 to 8.5 (54 to 61)
Main bearing cap bolts	5.0 to 6.0 (36 to 43)
Engine mounting bolts	1.9 to 2.5 (14 to 18)
Water pump bolts	0.9 to 1.4 (6 to 10)
Timing chain cover bolts	0.5 to 0.7 (4 to 5)
Transmission to engine bolts	1.6 to 2.2 (12 to 16)
Crossmember bolts	3.2 to 4.0 (23 to 29)
Propeller shaft flange bolts	2.4 to 3.3 (17 to 24)
Starter motor bolts	3.0 to 4.0 (22 to 29)
Drive plate to crankshaft	6.5 to 7.5 (47 to 54)
Drive plate to converter	4.0 to 5.0 (29 to 36)
Converter housing bolts	4.0 to 5.0 (29 to 36)
Transmission to extension	2.0 to 2.5 (14 to 18)
Inhibitor switch	0.5 to 0.7 (4 to 5)
Oil cooler pipes	3.0 to 5.0 (22 to 36)
Drive pinion nut	14 to 30 (101 to 217)
Ring gear bolt	6.0 to 7.0 (43 to 51)
Side bearing cap	5.0 to 6.0 (36 to 43)
Damper upper nut	1.9 to 2.4 (14 to 17)
Damper lower bolt	3.6 to 4.5 (26 to 33)
U-bolt nuts	4.0 to 5.0 (29 to 36)
Shackle nuts	1.6 to 2.0 (12 to 14)
Differential carrier bolts	1.7 to 2.5 (12 to 18)
Wheel nuts	8.0 to 9.0 (58 to 65)
Anti-roll bar to frame	1.6 to 2.1 (12 to 15)
Anti-roll bar connecting rod	1.2 to 1.7 (9 to 12)
Tension rod	4.5 to 5.5 (33 to 40)
Tension rod bracket bolt	3.2 to 4.3 (23 to 31)
Transverse link	9.0 to 10.0 (65 to 72)
Ball joint	5.5 to 6.3 (40 to 46)
Knuckle arm to strut	7.3 to 9.9 (53 to 72)
Caliper mounting bolts	4.6 to 6.1 (33 to 42)
Disc to hub	3.9 to 5.3 (28 to 38)
Master cylinder mounting nuts	0.8 to 1.2 (6 to 9)
Brake pipe connections	1.5 to 1.8 (11 to 13)
Steering wheel nut	3.0 to 3.5 (22 to 25)
Flexible coupling to worm shaft	1.5 to 2.2 (11 to 16)
Flexible coupling securing bolts	4.0 to 5.0 (29 to 36)
Jacket tube to panel	0.35 to 0.45 (2.5 to 3.3)
Steering gear to body	6.0 to 8.0 (43 to 58)
Rear cover bolts	1.7 to 2.8 (12 to 20)
Idler arm to frame	6.0 to 8.0 (43 to 58)
Idler shaft nut	4.0 to 5.0 (29 to 36)
Side rod locknuts	8.0 to 10.0 (58 to 72)

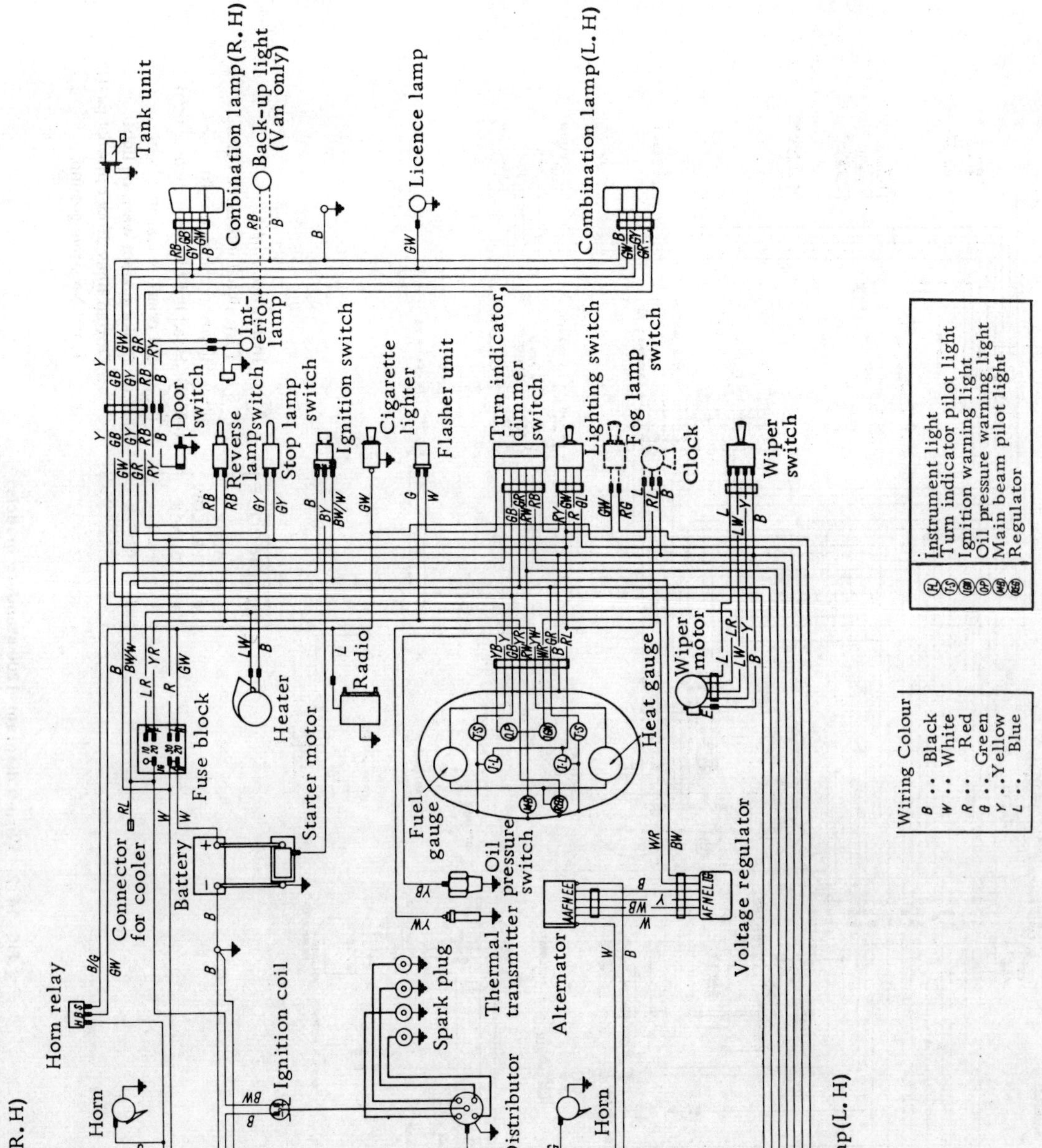

FIG 14:1 Wiring diagram, 1000 models

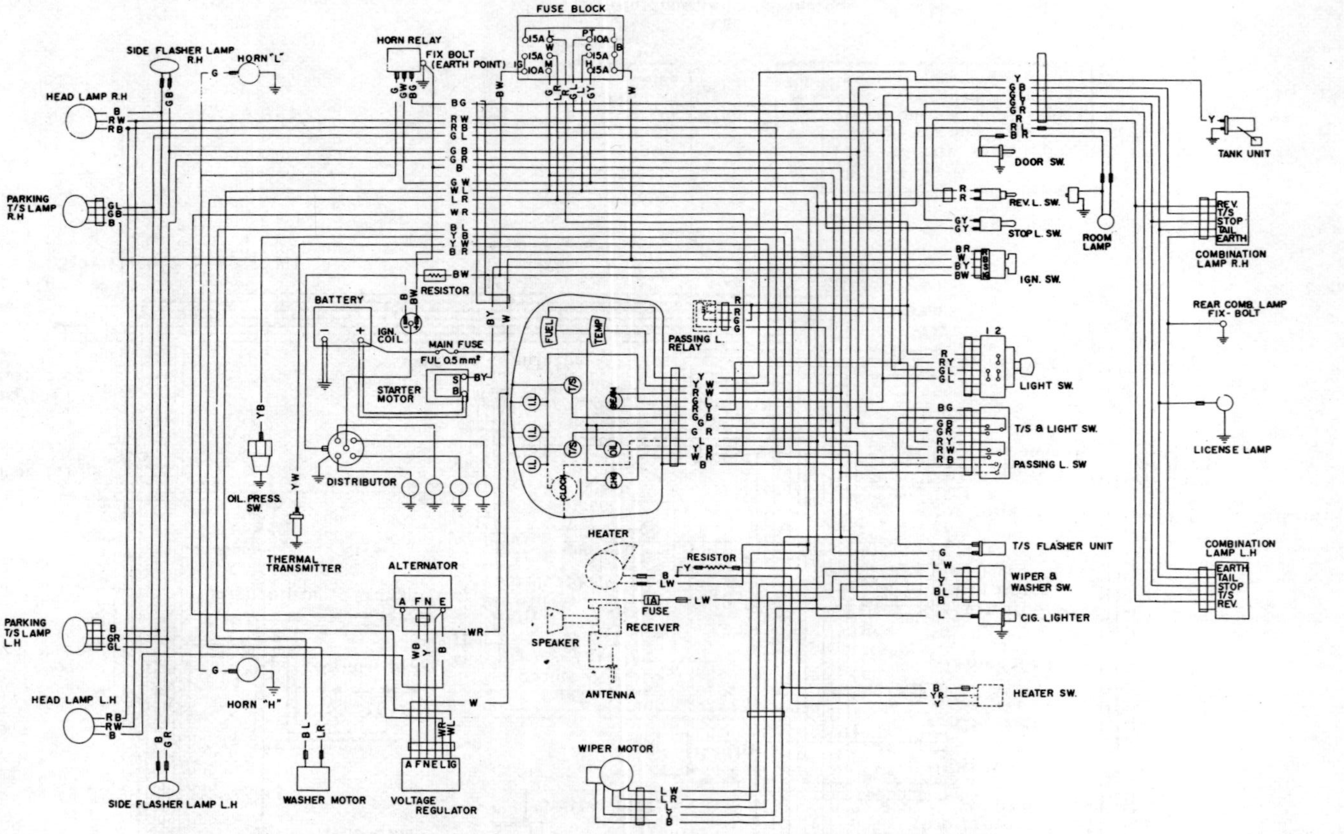

COLOR CODE		
L	:	BLUE
Y	:	YELLOW
B	:	BLACK
R	:	RED
W	:	WHITE
G	:	GREEN

- (I.L) Instrument light
- (T.S) Turn signal indicator light
- (CHG) Ignition warning light
- (BEAM) Head light beam indicator light
- (OIL) Oil pressure warning light
- (BRAKE) Brake system warning light
- ※ Dotted lines show optional parts
- ※ 12V: Negative ground

FIG 14:2 Wiring diagram, 1200 standard models

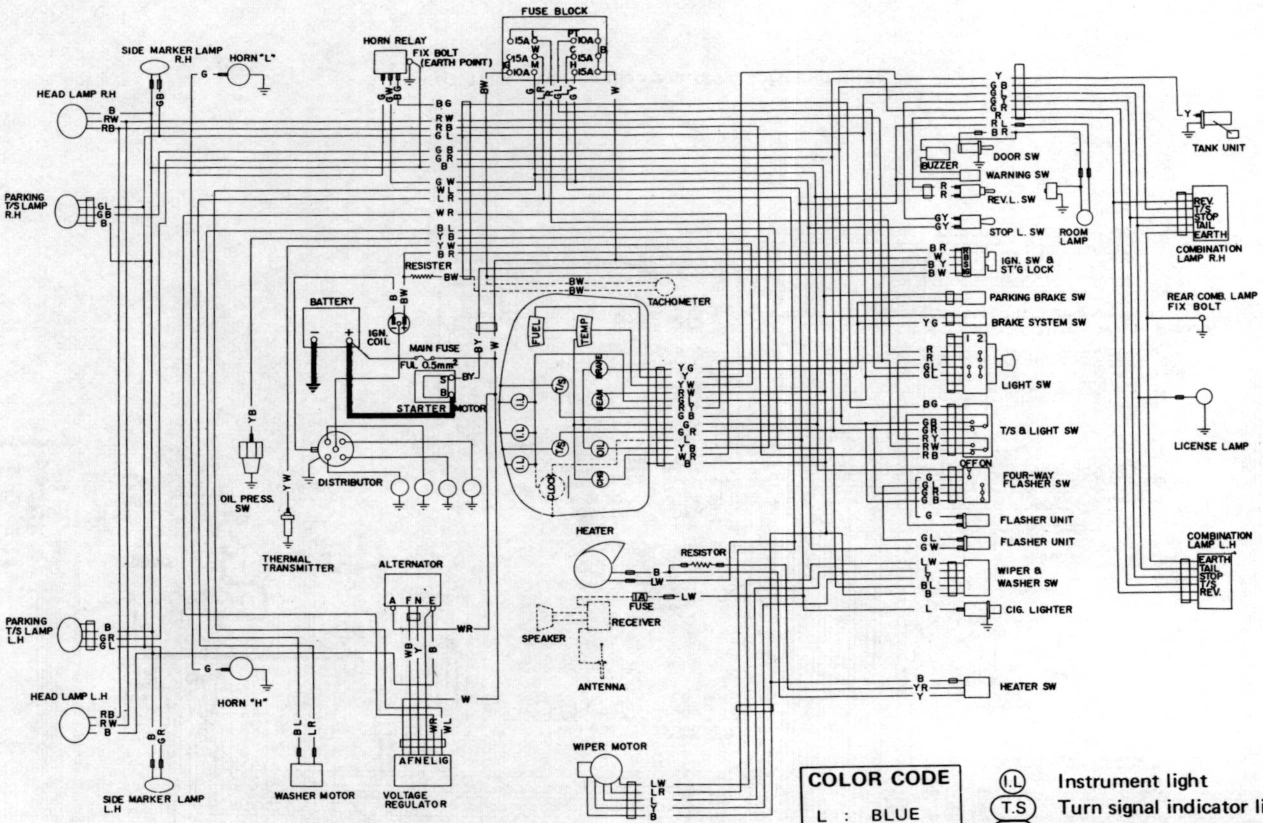

COLOR CODE

L : BLUE
Y : YELLOW
B : BLACK
R : RED
W : WHITE
G : GREEN

(I.L) Instrument light
(T.S) Turn signal indicator light
(CHG) Ignition warning light
(BEAM) Head light beam indicator light
(OIL) Oil pressure warning light
(BRAKE) Brake system warning light
※ Dotted lines show optional parts
※ 12V: Negative ground

FIG 14:3 Wiring diagram, 1200 USA and Canada models

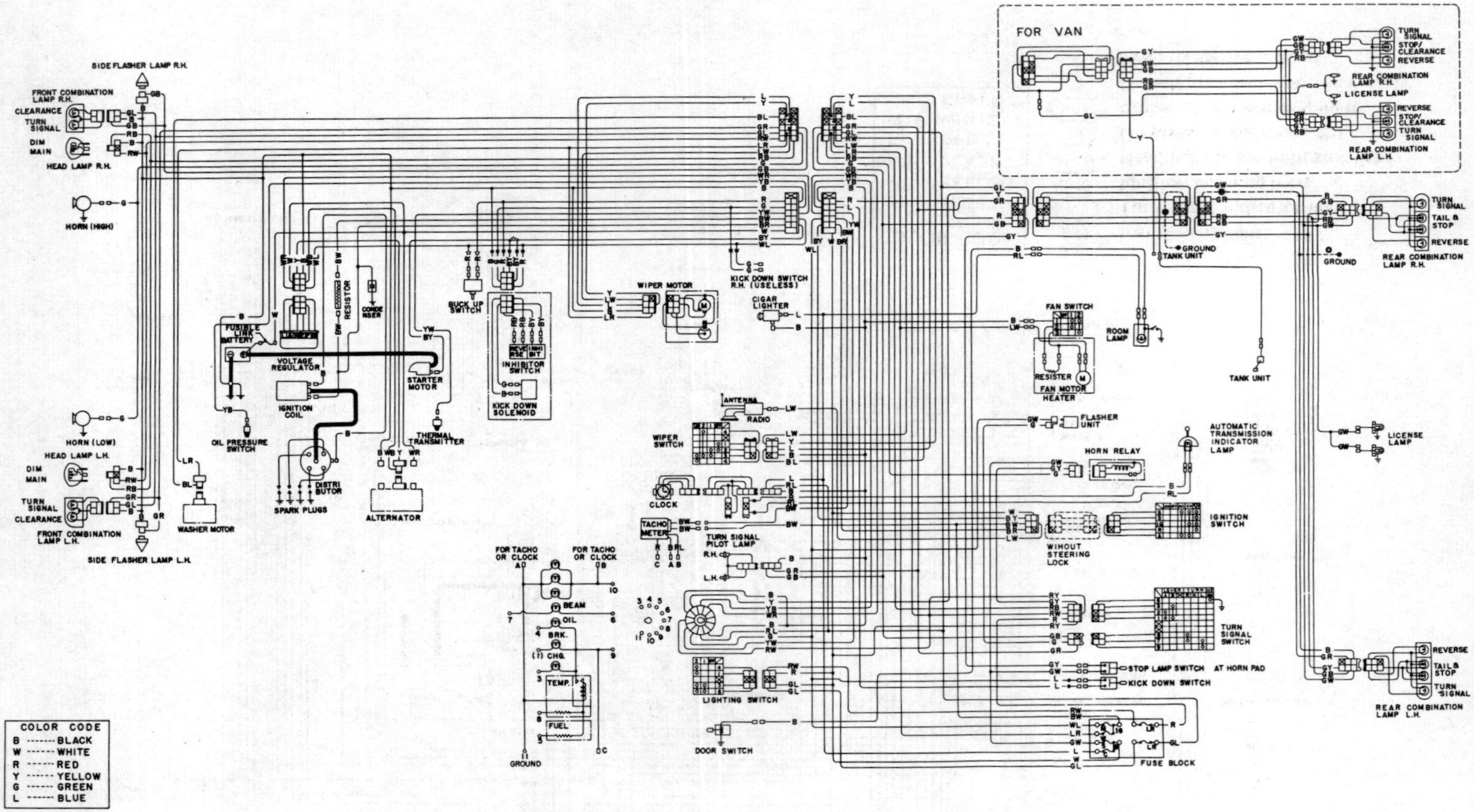

FIG 14:4 Wiring diagram 120Y, lefthand drive

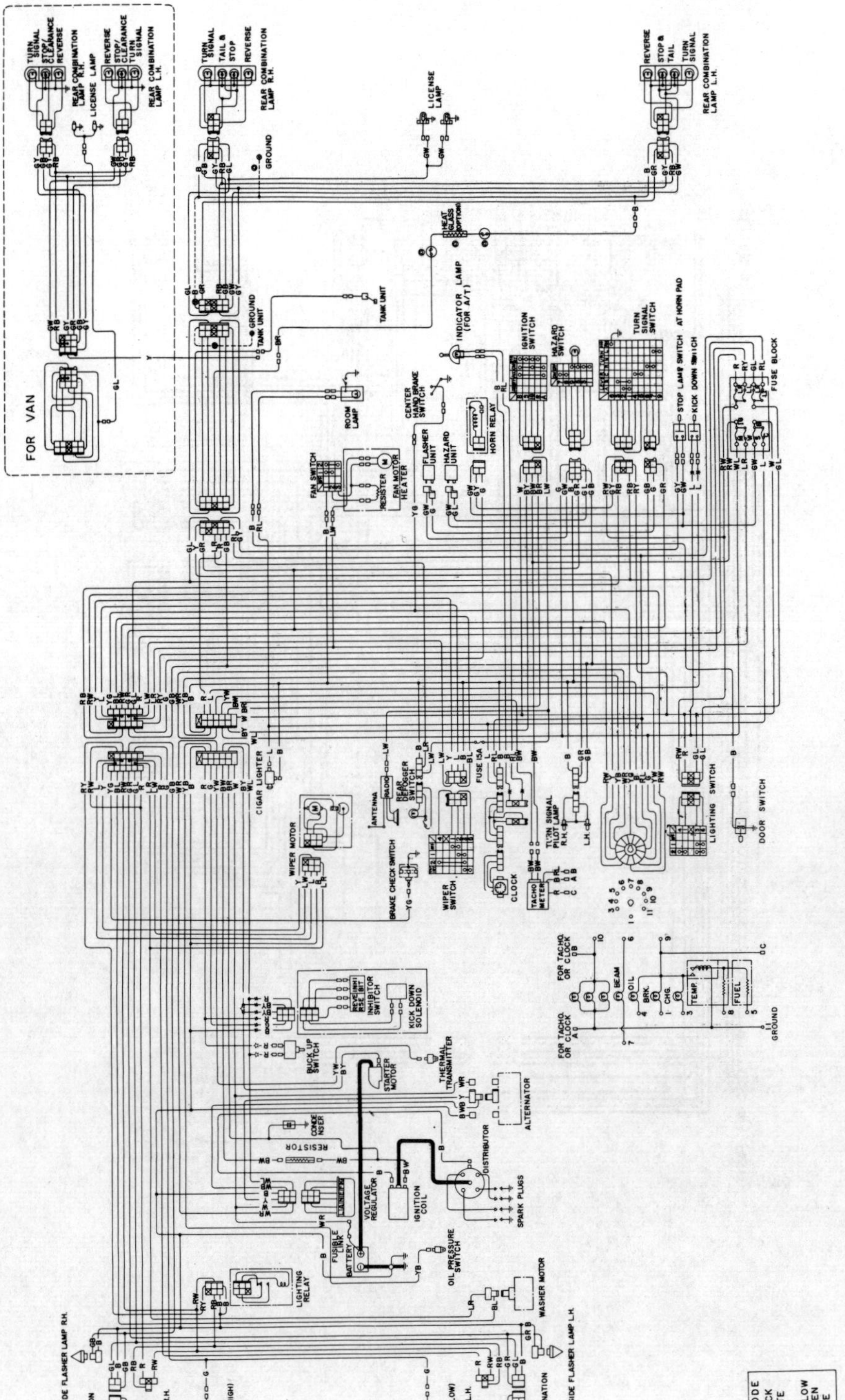

FIG 14:5 Wiring diagram 120Y, righthand drive

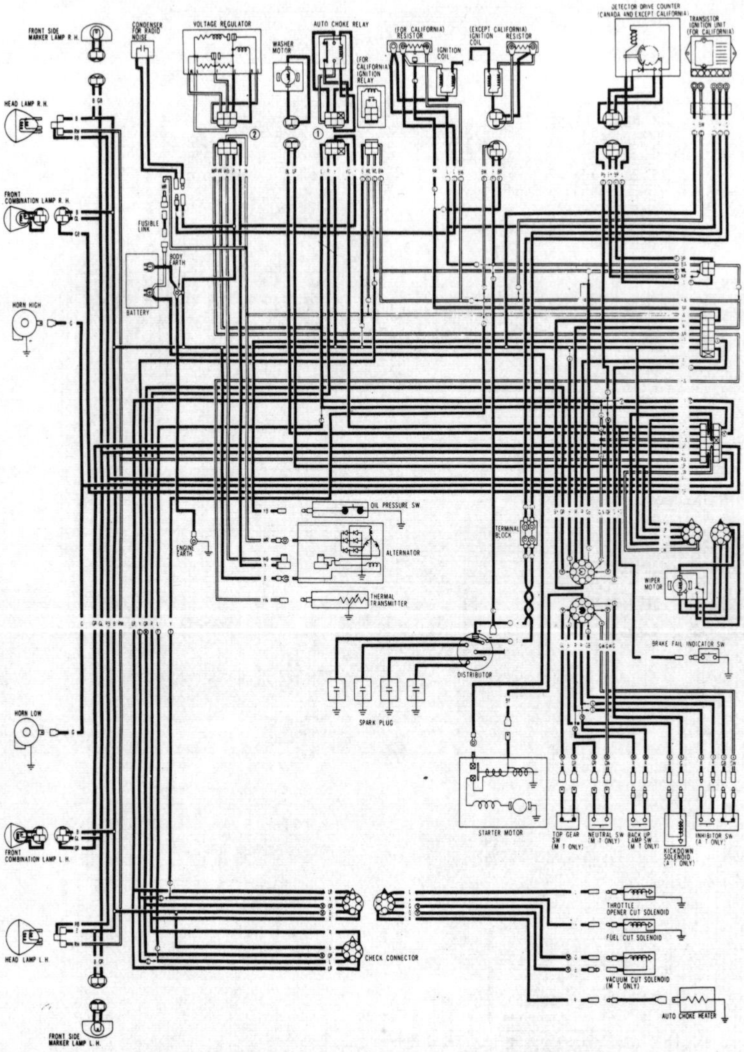

FIG 14:6 Wiring diagram, B210 series, USA and Canada—part 1

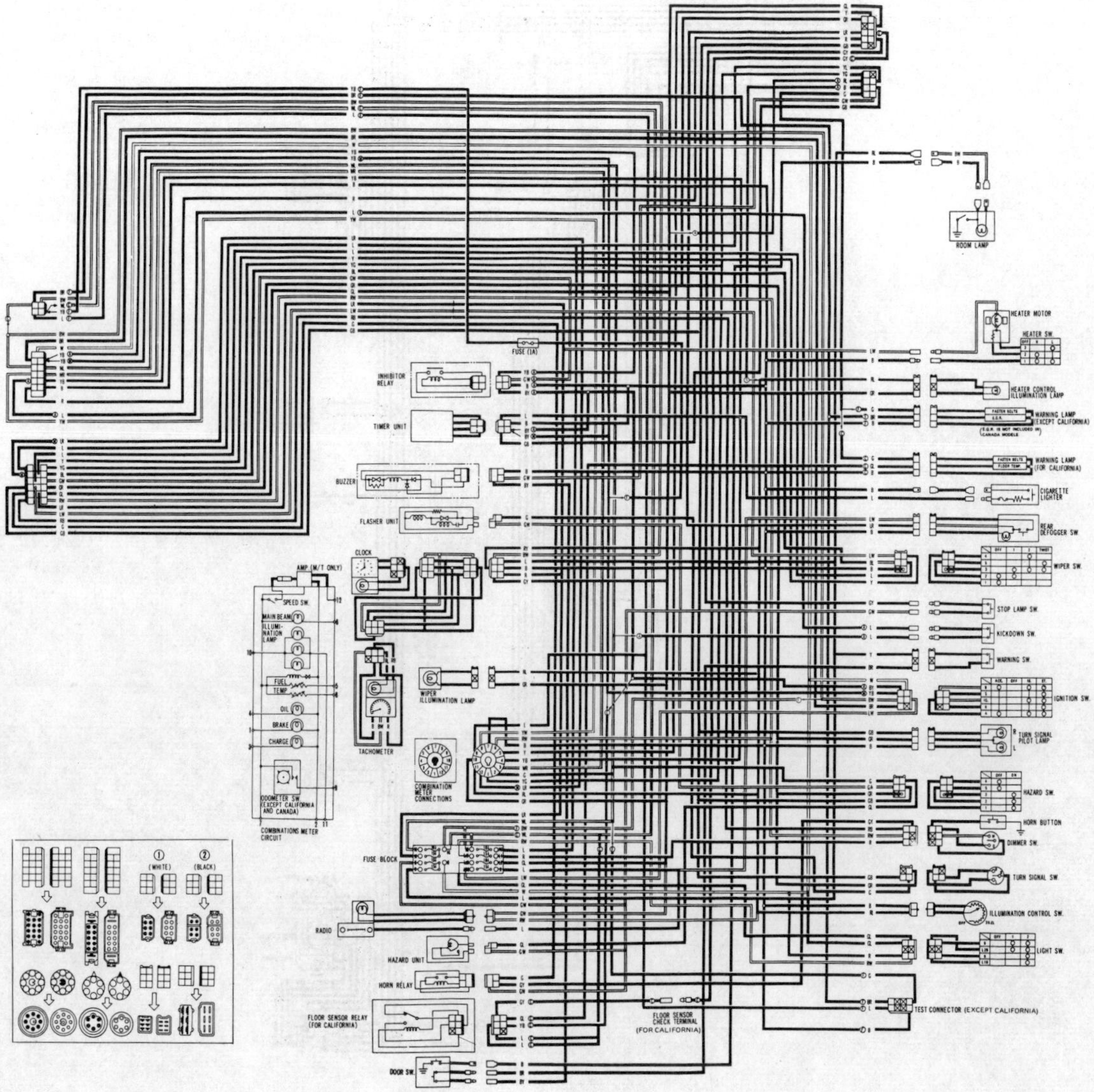

FIG 14:6 Wiring diagram, B210 series, USA and Canada—part 2

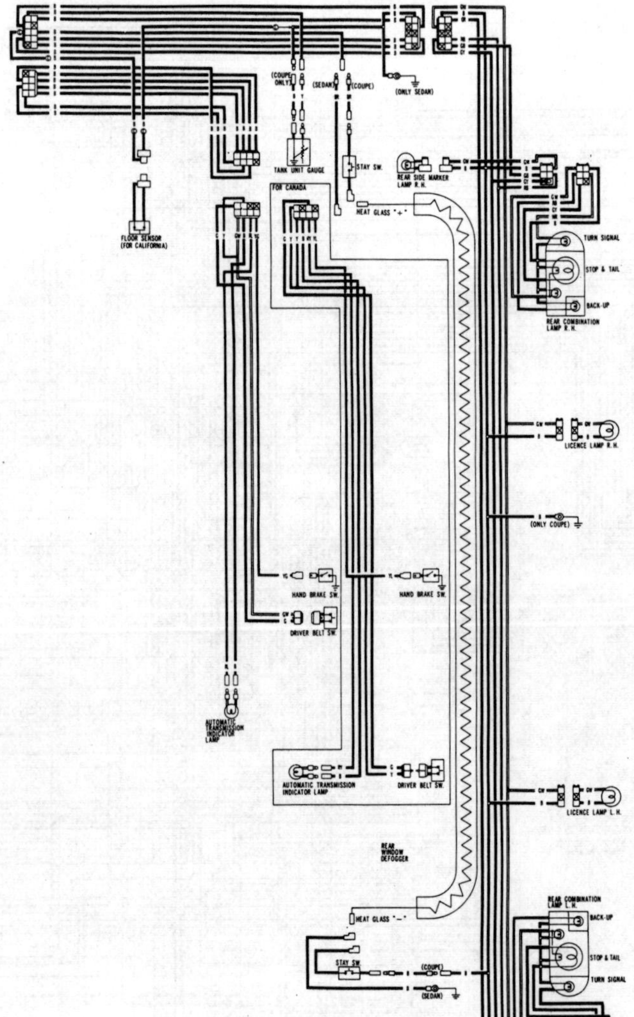

FIG 14:6 Wiring diagram, B210 series, USA and Canada—part 3

Key to Fig 14:6:
Lettered connectors: A Automatic transmission M Manual transmission C For California F Except California
Switch and relay positions: 1 Ignition switch locked, key removed 2 Lighting or wiper switch off 3 Seats unoccupied 4 Doors closed 5 Transmission in neutral 6 Handbrake released

Key to wiring colours: **B** Black **R** Red **Y** Yellow **W** White **G** Green **L** Blue

HINTS ON MAINTENANCE AND OVERHAUL

There are few things more rewarding than the restoration of a vehicle's original peak of efficiency and smooth performance.

The following notes are intended to help the owner to reach that state of perfection. Providing that he possesses the basic manual skills he should have no difficulty in performing most of the operations detailed in this manual. It must be stressed, however, that where recommended in the manual, highly-skilled operations ought to be entrusted to experts, who have the necessary equipment, to carry out the work satisfactorily.

Quality of workmanship:

The hazardous driving conditions on the roads to-day demand that vehicles should be as nearly perfect, mechanically, as possible. It is therefore most important that amateur work be carried out with care, bearing in mind the often inadequate working conditions, and also the inferior tools which may have to be used. It is easy to counsel perfection in all things, and we recognise that it may be setting an impossibly high standard. We do, however, suggest that every care should be taken to ensure that a vehicle is as safe to take on the road as it is humanly possible to make it.

Safe working conditions:

Even though a vehicle may be stationary, it is still potentially dangerous if certain sensible precautions are not taken when working on it while it is supported on jacks or blocks. It is indeed preferable not to use jacks alone, but to supplement them with carefully placed blocks, so that there will be plenty of support if the car rolls off the jacks during a strenuous manoeuvre. Axle stands are an excellent way of providing a rigid base which is not readily disturbed. Piles of bricks are a dangerous substitute. Be careful not to get under heavy loads on lifting tackle, the load could fall. It is preferable not to work alone when lifting an engine, or when working underneath a vehicle which is supported well off the ground. To be trapped, particularly under the vehicle, may have unpleasant results if help is not quickly forthcoming. Make some provision, however humble, to deal with fires. Always disconnect a battery if there is a likelihood of electrical shorts. These may start a fire if there is leaking fuel about. This applies particularly to leads which can carry a heavy current, like those in the starter circuit. While on the subject of electricity, we must also stress the danger of using equipment which is run off the mains and which has no earth or has faulty wiring or connections. So many workshops have damp floors, and electrical shocks are of such a nature that it is sometimes impossible to let go of a live lead or piece of equipment due to the muscular spasms which take place.

Work demanding special care:

This involves the servicing of braking, steering and suspension systems. On the road, failure of the braking system may be disastrous. Make quite sure that there can be no possibility of failure through the bursting of rusty brake pipes or rotten hoses, nor to a sudden loss of pressure due to defective seals or valves.

Problems:

The chief problems which may face an operator are:

1 External dirt.
2 Difficulty in undoing tight fixings.
3 Dismantling unfamiliar mechanisms.
4 Deciding in what respect parts are defective.
5 Confusion about the correct order for reassembly.
6 Adjusting running clearance.
7 Road testing.
8 Final tuning.

Practical suggestions to solve the problems:

1 Preliminary cleaning of large parts—engines, transmissions, steering, suspensions, etc,—should be carried out before removal from the car. Where road dirt and mud alone are present, wash clean with a high-pressure water jet, brushing to remove stubborn adhesions, and allow to drain and dry. Where oil or grease is also present, wash down with a proprietary compound (Gunk, Teepol etc,) applying with a stiff brush—an old paint brush is suitable—into all crevices. Cover the distributor and ignition coils with a polythene bag and then apply a strong water jet to clear the loosened deposits. Allow to drain and dry. The assemblies will then be sufficiently clean to remove and transfer to the bench for the next stage.

On the bench, further cleaning can be carried out, first wiping the parts as free as possible from grease with old newspaper. Avoid using rag or cotton waste which can leave clogging fibres behind. Any remaining grease can be removed with a brush dipped in paraffin. If necessary, traces of paraffin can be removed by carbon tetrachloride. Avoid using paraffin or petrol in large quantities for cleaning in enclosed areas, such as garages, on account of the high fire risk.

When all exteriors have been cleaned, and not before, dismantling can be commenced. This ensures that dirt will not enter into interiors and orifices revealed by dismantling. In the next phases, where components have to be cleaned, use carbon tetrachloride in preference to petrol and keep the containers covered except when in use. After the components have been cleaned, plug small holes with tapered hard wood plugs cut to size and blank off larger orifices with grease-proof paper and masking tape. Do not use soft wood plugs or matchsticks as they may break.

2 It is not advisable to hammer on the end of a screw thread, but if it must be done, first screw on a nut to protect the thread, and use a lead hammer. This applies particularly to the removal of tapered cotters. Nuts and bolts seem to 'grow' together, especially in exhaust systems. If penetrating oil does not work, try the judicious application of heat, but be careful of starting a fire. Asbestos sheet or cloth is useful to isolate heat.

Tight bushes or pieces of tail-pipe rusted into a silencer can be removed by splitting them with an open-ended hacksaw. Tight screws can sometimes be started by a tap from a hammer on the end of a suitable screwdriver. Many tight fittings will yield to the judicious use of a hammer, but it must be a soft-faced hammer if damage is to be avoided, use a heavy block on the opposite side to absorb shock. Any parts of the steering system which have been damaged should be renewed, as attempts to repair them may lead to cracking and subsequent failure, and steering ball joints should be disconnected using a recommended tool to prevent damage.

3 If often happens that an owner is baffled when trying to dismantle an unfamiliar piece of equipment. So many modern devices are pressed together or assembled by spinning-over flanges, that they must be sawn apart. The intention is that the whole assembly must be renewed. However, parts which appear to be in one piece to the naked eye, may reveal close-fitting joint lines when inspected with a magnifying glass, and, this may provide the necessary clue to dismantling. Left-handed screw threads are used where rotational forces would tend to unscrew a right-handed screw thread.

Be very careful when dismantling mechanisms which may come apart suddenly. Work in an enclosed space where the parts will be contained, and drape a piece of cloth over the device if springs are likely to fly in all directions. Mark everything which might be reassembled in the wrong position, scratched symbols may be used on unstressed parts, or a sequence of tiny dots from a centre punch can be useful. Stressed parts should never be scratched or centre-popped as this may lead to cracking under working conditions. Store parts which look alike in the correct order for reassembly. Never rely upon memory to assist in the assembly of complicated mechanisms, especially when they will be dismantled for a long time, but make notes, and drawings to supplement the diagrams in the manual, and put labels on detached wires. Rust stains may indicate unlubricated wear. This can sometimes be seen round the outside edge of a bearing cup in a universal joint. Look for bright rubbing marks on parts which normally should not make heavy contact. These might prove that something is bent or running out of true. For example, there might be bright marks on one side of a piston, at the top near the ring grooves, and others at the bottom of the skirt on the other side. This could well be the clue to a bent connecting rod. Suspected cracks can be proved by heating the component in a light oil to approximately 100°C, removing, drying off, and dusting with french chalk, if a crack is present the oil retained in the crack will stain the french chalk.

4 In determining wear, and the degree, against the permissible limits set in the manual, accurate measurement can only be achieved by the use of a micrometer. In many cases, the wear is given to the fourth place of decimals; that is in ten-thousandths of an inch. This can be read by the vernier scale on the barrel of a good micrometer. Bore diameters are more difficult to determine. If, however, the matching shaft is accurately measured, the degree of play in the bore can be felt as a guide to its suitability. In other cases, the shank of a twist drill of known diameter is a handy check.

Many methods have been devised for determining the clearance between bearing surfaces. To-day the best and simplest is by the use of Plastigage, obtainable from most garages. A thin plastic thread is laid between the two surfaces and the bearing is tightened, flattening the thread. On removal, the width of the thread is compared with a scale supplied with the thread and the clearance is read off directly. Sometimes joint faces leak persistently, even after gasket renewal. The fault will then be traceable to distortion, dirt or burrs. Studs which are screwed into soft metal frequently raise burrs at the point of entry. A quick cure for this is to chamfer the edge of the hole in the part which fits over the stud.

5 **Always check a replacement part with the original one before it is fitted.**

If parts are not marked, and the order for reassembly is not known, a little detective work will help. Look for marks which are due to wear to see if they can be mated. Joint faces may not be identical due to manufacturing errors, and parts which overlap may be stained, giving a clue to the correct position. Most fixings leave identifying marks especially if they were painted over on assembly. It is then easier to decide whether a nut, for instance, has a plain, a spring, or a shakeproof washer under it. All running surfaces become 'bedded' together after long spells of work and tiny imperfections on one part will be found to have left corresponding marks on the other. This is particularly true of shafts and bearings and even a score on a cylinder wall will show on the piston.

6 Checking end float or rocker clearances by feeler gauge may not always give accurate results because of wear. For instance, the rocker tip which bears on a valve stem may be deeply pitted, in which case the feeler will simply be bridging a depression. Thrust washers may also wear depressions in opposing faces to make accurate measurement difficult. End float is then easier to check by using a dial gauge. It is common practice to adjust end play in bearing assemblies, like front hubs with taper rollers, by doing up the axle nut until the hub becomes stiff to turn and then backing it off a little. Do not use this method with ballbearing hubs as the assembly is often preloaded by tightening the axle nut to its fullest extent. If the splitpin hole will not line up, file the base of the nut a little.

Steering assemblies often wear in the straight-ahead position. If any part is adjusted, make sure that it remains free when moved from lock to lock. Do not be surprised if an assembly like a steering gearbox, which is known to be carefully adjusted outside the car, becomes stiff when it is bolted in place. This will be due to distortion of the case by the pull of the mounting bolts, particularly if the mounting points are not all touching together. This problem may be met in other equipment and is cured by careful attention to the alignment of mounting points.

When a spanner is stamped with a size and A/F it means that the dimension is the width between the jaws and has no connection with ANF, which is the designation for the American National Fine thread. Coarse threads like Whitworth are rarely used on cars to-day except for studs which screw into soft aluminium or cast iron. For this reason it might be found that the top end of a cylinder head stud has a fine thread and the lower end a coarse thread to screw into the cylinder block. If the car has mainly UNF threads then it is likely that any coarse threads will be UNC, which are not the same as Whitworth. Small sizes have the same number of threads in Whitworth and UNC, but in the $\frac{1}{2}$ inch size for example, there are twelve threads to the inch in the former and thirteen in the latter.

7 After a major overhaul, particularly if a great deal of work has been done on the braking, steering and suspension systems, it is advisable to approach the problem of testing with care. If the braking system has been overhauled, apply heavy pressure to the brake pedal and get a second operator to check every possible source of leakage. The brakes may work extremely well, but a leak could cause complete failure after a few miles.

Do not fit the hub caps until every wheel nut has been checked for tightness, and make sure the tyre pressures are correct. Check the levels of coolant, lubricants and hydraulic fluids. Being satisfied that all is well, take the car on the road and test the brakes at once. Check the steering and the action of the handbrake. Do all this at moderate speeds on quiet roads, and make sure there is no other vehicle behind you when you try a rapid stop.

Finally, remember that many parts settle down after a time, so check for tightness of all fixings after the car has been on the road for a hundred miles or so.

8 It is useless to tune an engine which has not reached its normal running temperature. In the same way, the tune of an engine which is stiff after a rebore will be different when the engine is again running free. Remember too, that rocker clearances on pushrod operated valve gear will change when the cylinder head nuts are tightened after an initial period of running with a new head gasket.

Trouble may not always be due to what seems the obvious cause. Ignition, carburation and mechanical condition are interdependent and spitting back through the carburetter, which might be attributed to a weak mixture, can be caused by a sticking inlet valve.

For one final hint on tuning, never adjust more than one thing at a time or it will be impossible to tell which adjustment produced the desired result.

NOTES

GLOSSARY OF TERMS

Allen key Cranked wrench of hexagonal section for use with socket head screws.

Alternator Electrical generator producing alternating current. Rectified to direct current for battery charging.

Ambient temperature Surrounding atmospheric temperature.

Annulus Used in engineering to indicate the outer ring gear of an epicyclic gear train.

Armature The shaft carrying the windings, which rotates in the magnetic field of a generator or starter motor. That part of a solenoid or relay which is activated by the magnetic field.

Axial In line with, or pertaining to, an axis.

Backlash Play in meshing gears.

Balance lever A bar where force applied at the centre is equally divided between connections at the ends.

Banjo axle Axle casing with large diameter housing for the crownwheel and differential.

Bendix pinion A self-engaging and self-disengaging drive on a starter motor shaft.

Bevel pinion A conical shaped gearwheel, designed to mesh with a similar gear with an axis usually at 90 deg. to its own.

bhp Brake horse power, measured on a dynamometer.

bmep Brake mean effective pressure. Average pressure on a piston during the working stroke.

Brake cylinder Cylinder with hydraulically operated piston(s) acting on brake shoes or pad(s).

Brake regulator Control valve fitted in hydraulic braking system which limits brake pressure to rear brakes during heavy braking to prevent rear wheel locking.

Camber Angle at which a wheel is tilted from the vertical.

Capacitor Modern term for an electrical condenser. Part of distributor assembly, connected across contact breaker points, acts as an interference suppressor.

Castellated Top face of a nut, slotted across the flats, to take a locking splitpin.

Castor Angle at which the kingpin or swivel pin is tilted when viewed from the side.

cc Cubic centimetres. Engine capacity is arrived at by multiplying the area of the bore in sq cm by the stroke in cm by the number of cylinders.

Clevis U-shaped forked connector used with a clevis pin, usually at handbrake connections.

Collet A type of collar, usually split and located in a groove in a shaft, and held in place by a retainer. The arrangement used to retain the spring(s) on a valve stem in most cases.

Commutator Rotating segmented current distributor between armature windings and brushes in generator or motor.

Compression ratio The ratio, or quantitative relation, of the total volume (piston at bottom of stroke) to the unswept volume (piston at top of stroke) in an engine cylinder.

Condenser See capacitor.

Core plug Plug for blanking off a manufacturing hole in a casting.

Crownwheel Large bevel gear in rear axle, driven by a bevel pinion attached to the propeller shaft. Sometimes called a 'ring gear'.

'C'-spanner Like a 'C' with a handle. For use on screwed collars without flats, but with slots or holes.

Damper Modern term for shock-absorber, used in vehicle suspension systems to damp out spring oscillations.

Depression The lowering of atmospheric pressure as in the inlet manifold and carburetter.

Dowel Close tolerance pin, peg, tube, or bolt, which accurately locates mating parts.

Drag link Rod connecting steering box drop arm (pitman arm) to nearest front wheel steering arm in certain types of steering systems.

Dry liner Thinwall tube pressed into cylinder bore

Dry sump Lubrication system where all oil is scavenged from the sump, and returned to a separate tank.

Dynamo See Generator.

Electrode Terminal, part of an electrical component, such as the points or 'Electrodes' of a sparking plug.

Electrolyte In lead-acid car batteries a solution of sulphuric acid and distilled water.

End float The axial movement between associated parts, end play.

EP Extreme pressure. In lubricants, special grades for heavily loaded bearing surfaces, such as gear teeth in a gearbox, or crownwheel and pinion in a rear axle.

Fade Of brakes. Reduced efficiency due to overheating.

Field coils Windings on the polepieces of motors and generators.

Fillets Narrow finishing strips usually applied to interior bodywork.

First motion shaft Input shaft from clutch to gearbox.

Fullflow filter Filters in which all the oil is pumped to the engine. If the element becomes clogged, a bypass valve operates to pass unfiltered oil to the engine.

FWD Front wheel drive.

Gear pump Two meshing gears in a close fitting casing. Oil is carried from the inlet round the outside of both gears in the spaces between the gear teeth and casing to the outlet, the meshing gear teeth prevent oil passing back to the inlet, and the oil is forced through the outlet port.

Generator Modern term for 'Dynamo'. When rotated produces electrical current.

Grommet A ring of protective or sealing material. Can be used to protect pipes or leads passing through bulkheads.

Grubscrew Fully threaded headless screw with screwdriver slot. Used for locking, or alignment purposes.

Gudgeon pin Shaft which connects a piston to its connecting rod. Sometimes called 'wrist pin', or 'piston pin'.

Halfshaft One of a pair transmitting drive from the differential.

Helical In spiral form. The teeth of helical gears are cut at a spiral angle to the side faces of the gearwheel.

Hot spot Hot area that assists vapourisation of fuel on its way to cylinders. Often provided by close contact between inlet and exhaust manifolds.

HT High Tension. Applied to electrical current produced by the ignition coil for the sparking plugs.

Hydrometer A device for checking specific gravity of liquids. Used to check specific gravity of electrolyte.

Hypoid bevel gears A form of bevel gear used in the rear axle drive gears. The bevel pinion meshes below the centre line of the crownwheel, giving a lower propeller shaft line.

Idler A device for passing on movement. A free running gear between driving and driven gears. A lever transmitting track rod movement to a side rod in steering gear.

Impeller A centrifugal pumping element. Used in water pumps to stimulate flow.

Journals Those parts of a shaft that are in contact with the bearings.

Kingpin The main vertical pin which carries the front wheel spindle, and permits steering movement. May be called 'steering pin' or 'swivel pin'.

Layshaft The shaft which carries the laygear in the gearbox. The laygear is driven by the first motion shaft and drives the third motion shaft according to the gear selected. Sometimes called the 'countershaft' or 'second motion shaft.'

lb ft A measure of twist or torque. A pull of 10 lb at a radius of 1 ft is a torque of 10 lb ft.

lb/sq in Pounds per square inch.

Little-end The small, or piston end of a connecting rod. Sometimes called the 'small-end'.

LT Low Tension. The current output from the battery.

Mandrel Accurately manufactured bar or rod used for test or centring purposes.

Manifold A pipe, duct, or chamber, with several branches.

Needle rollers Bearing rollers with a length many times their diameter.

Oil bath Reservoir which lubricates parts by immersion. In air filters, a separate oil supply for wetting a wire mesh element to hold the dust.

Oil wetted In air filters, a wire mesh element lightly oiled to trap and hold airborne dust.

Overlap Period during which inlet and exhaust valves are open together.

Panhard rod Bar connected between fixed point on chassis and another on axle to control sideways movement.

Pawl Pivoted catch which engages in the teeth of a ratchet to permit movement in one direction only.

Peg spanner Tool with pegs, or pins, to engage in holes or slots in the part to be turned.

Pendant pedals Pedals with levers that are pivoted at the top end.

Phillips screwdriver A cross-point screwdriver for use with the cross-slotted heads of Phillips screws.

Pinion A small gear, usually in relation to another gear.

Piston-type damper Shock absorber in which damping is controlled by a piston working in a closed oil-filled cylinder.

Preloading Preset static pressure on ball or roller bearings not due to working loads.

Radial Radiating from a centre, like the spokes of a wheel.

Radius rod	Pivoted arm confining movement of a part to an arc of fixed radius.
Ratchet	Toothed wheel or rack which can move in one direction only, movement in the other being prevented by a pawl.
Ring gear	A gear tooth ring attached to outer periphery of flywheel. Starter pinion engages with it during starting.
Runout	Amount by which rotating part is out of true.
Semi-floating axle	Outer end of rear axle halfshaft is carried on bearing inside axle casing. Wheel hub is secured to end of shaft.
Servo	A hydraulic or pneumatic system for assisting, or, augmenting a physical effort. See 'Vacuum Servo'.
Setscrew	One which is threaded for the full length of the shank.
Shackle	A coupling link, used in the form of two parallel pins connected by side plates to secure the end of the master suspension spring and absorb the effects of deflection.
Shell bearing	Thinwalled steel shell lined with antifriction metal. Usually semi-circular and used in pairs for main and big-end bearings.
Shock absorber	See 'Damper'.
Silentbloc	Rubber bush bonded to inner and outer metal sleeves.
Socket-head screw	Screw with hexagonal socket for an Allen key.
Solenoid	A coil of wire creating a magnetic field when electric current passes through it. Used with a soft iron core to operate contacts or a mechanical device.
Spur gear	A gear with teeth cut axially across the periphery.
Stub axle	Short axle fixed at one end only.
Tachometer	An instrument for accurate measurement of rotating speed. Usually indicates in revolutions per minute.
TDC	Top Dead Centre. The highest point reached by a piston in a cylinder, with the crank and connecting rod in line.
Thermostat	Automatic device for regulating temperature. Used in vehicle coolant systems to open a valve which restricts circulation at low temperature.
Third motion shaft	Output shaft of gearbox.
Threequarter floating axle	Outer end of rear axle halfshaft flanged and bolted to wheel hub, which runs on bearing mounted on outside of axle casing. Vehicle weight is not carried by the axle shaft.
Thrust bearing or washer	Used to reduce friction in rotating parts subject to axial loads.
Torque	Turning or twisting effort. See 'lb ft'.
Track rod	The bar(s) across the vehicle which connect the steering arms and maintain the front wheels in their correct alignment.
UJ	Universal joint. A coupling between shafts which permits angular movement.
UNF	Unified National Fine screw thread.
Vacuum servo	Device used in brake system, using difference between atmospheric pressure and inlet manifold depression to operate a piston which acts to augment brake pressure as required. See 'Servo'.
Venturi	A restriction or 'choke' in a tube, as in a carburetter, used to increase velocity to obtain a reduction in pressure.
Vernier	A sliding scale for obtaining fractional readings of the graduations of an adjacent scale.
Welch plug	A domed thin metal disc which is partially flattened to lock in a recess. Used to plug core holes in castings.
Wet liner	Removable cylinder barrel, sealed against coolant leakage, where the coolant is in direct contact with the outer surface.
Wet sump	A reservoir attached to the crankcase to hold the lubricating oil.

NOTES

INDEX

NOTES

NOTES